p.s. who: leoli/ jane

p.h:

MALE
SUBJECTIVITY
AT THE
MARGINS

MALE SUBJECTIVITY AT THE MARGINS

KAJA SILVERMAN

Routledge • New York & London

Published in 1992 by

Routledge
An imprint of Routledge, Chapman and Hall, Inc.
29 West 35 Street
New York, NY 10001

Published in Great Britain by

Routledge
11 New Fetter Lane
London EC4P 4EE

Library of Congress Cataloging in Publication Data

Silverman, Kaja.
  Male subjectivity at the margins / Kaja Silverman.
    p. cm.
  Includes bibliographical references.
  ISBN 0-415-90418-8 : $49.95—ISBN 0-415-90419-6 (pbk.) : $15.95
    1. Masculinity (Psychology)—History. 2. Subjectivity—History.
  3. Masculinity (Psychology) in motion pictures. 4. Masculinity
  (Psychology) in literature. 5. Psychoanalysis and feminism.
  I. Title.
  BF175.5.M37S55   1992
  155.3'32—dc20   91-44680
                                                CIP

British Library Cataloguing in Publication Data

Silverman, Kaja.
  Male subjectivity at the margins.
  I. Title
  305.31

  ISBN 0-415-90418-8
  ISBN 0-415-90419-6 pbk

In Memory of Craig Owens: Outlaw in Feminism

•

Table of Contents

Acknowledgments

Most of this book was written during the three stimulating years I spent at the University of Rochester. It was enabled in all kinds of ways by my colleagues and students :n the English Department, the Film Program, the Comparative Arts Program, and the Susan B. Anthony Center. Constance Penley, Tom Di Piero, Rosemary Kegl, Norman Bryson, Sharon Willis, and the students who populated my graduate courses all read parts of the book in manuscript, and offered valuable criticism and advice. Ken Gross, Jim Longenbach, Michael Holly, Joanna Scott, Keith Moxie, and Janet Woolf not only contributed intellectually to the book, but helped to sustain me while I was writing it. Mieke Bal, who was always there when I needed her, did even more; she read every page of the manuscript in its penultimate version, at a speed which left me (but not her) breathless, and offered detailed and insightful suggestions for improving upon it. Finally, I want to thank Craig Owens, to whom this book is dedicated; he did not live till its completion, but he played a vital role in its early stages, and he will always remain in my memory as the very prototype of the male subject on whose behalf it was written.

I also want to thank a number of other people. Carol Ann Tyler and Michael Moon were of enormous assistance to me in the planning stages of Chapters 8 and 4, respectively. Neil Lazarus, Naomi Schor, Elizabeth Weed, and Homi Bhabha contributed in a variety of ways to Chapter 7. Jonathan Dollimore, Peter Wollen, David Miller, Alan Sinfield, Michael Silverman, Janet Bergstrom, Joan Copjec, Richard Meyer, Griselda Pollack, Deborah Linderman, and Richard Dellamora read portions of the book, and provided encouragement and intellectual support. Leo Bersani, who was an untiring reader of chapter after chapter, contributed perhaps more than anyone else to the ideational matrix within which the book was written, both through our on-going conversations, and through his own work. Carol Clover not only read every page of this book at least once, and responded in consistently fresh and challenging ways, but talked through many of its arguments with me at each stage of the writing process. *Male Subjectivity at the Margins* is indebted to her in ways that exceed conventional academic acknowledgement. As with previous projects, Mary Russo remained a constant source of psychic and intellectual sustenance, as well as an astute and constructive critic. Even more importantly, she never permitted me to forget everything that I have learned from, and that I owe to, feminism.

Last, but not least, I would like to thank Bethany Hicok for her diligent and unfailingly intelligent research assistance throughout the writing of this book; Barbara Miller and Carol Lafayette for helping me with the frame enlargements; and Diane Gibbons for her excellent copyediting.

Portions of this book have been previously published in some form. Parts of Chapter 2 appeared in *Framework*, no.14 (1981), and *Psychoanalysis and Cinema*, ed. E. Ann Kaplan (New York: Routledge, 1990), under the titles "Male Subjectivity and the Celestial Suture," and "Historical Trauma and Male Subjectivity," respectively. Slightly different versions of Chapters 3 and 5 appeared under the same titles in *Camera Obscura*, no. 19 (1989), and no. 17 (1988). An earlier draft of Chapter 7 was published in *Differences*, vol. 1, no. 3 (1989). A substantially different version of Chapter 4 was included in *Novel*, vol. 20, nos. 2 & 3 (1988), and subsequently in *Why the Novel Matters: A Postmodern Perplex*, ed. Mark Spilka and Caroline McCracken-Flesher (Bloomington: Indiana University Press, 1990).

Introduction

This book is dedicated to the exploration of some "deviant" masculinities—masculinities whose defining desires and identifications are "perverse" with respect not so much to a moral as to a phallic standard. It will attempt to demonstrate that these masculinities represent a tacit challenge not only to conventional male subjectivity, but to the whole of our "world"—that they call sexual difference into question, and beyond that, "reality" itself.

Foucault has recently questioned whether sexual "deviance" represents a meaningful way of challenging the erotic norm. He argues that those two categories come into existence simultaneously, and are generated by the same discursive imperative. In *The History of Sexuality*, he isolates the female hysteric, the masturbating child, the perverse adult, and the Malthusian couple as the exemplary products of "a great surface network in which the stimulation of bodies, the intensification of pleasures, the incitement to discourse, the formation of special knowledges, the strengthening of controls and resistances, are linked to one another, in accordance with a few major strategies of knowledge and power."[1] Later in the same text, he urges us not to mistake the aberrant sexuality of which each of these figures or couples is illustrative as a negation of power: "We must not think that by saying yes to sex, one says no to power; on the contrary, one tracks along the course laid out by the general deployment of sexuality" (157).[2]

In this book, I will be insisting as fully as Foucault does upon the necessity for reading sexuality in relation to the larger social order; indeed, the pages that follow will be devoted to an interrogation of what might be called the "politics" of desire and identification. *Male Subjectivity at the Margins* will also maintain that there is nothing "natural" or culturally innocent about sexuality. It will, however, attribute a much greater degree of specificity to the psyche than does

The History of Sexuality, and articulate a more complex interaction between it and the social order—an interaction involving a series of "relays." It will argue that we do not directly inhabit either the symbolic order or the mode of production, but are accommodated to their Laws via an ideological facilitation. It will also insist that we accede to this ideological facilitation only through fantasy and imaginary "captation." Finally, *Male Subjectivity at the Margins* will suggest that unconscious desire and identification do not always follow the trajectory delineated for them in advance, and that they sometimes assume forms which are profoundly antipathetic to the existing social formation. It will thus situate not only the perverse adult, but—implicitly— the hysterical woman and the Malthusian couple within a rather different conceptual field than that provided by *The History of Sexuality*.

Male Subjectivity at the Margins will theorize the ideological reality through which we "ideally" live both the symbolic order and the mode of production as the "dominant fiction," and it will posit the positive Oedipus complex as the primary vehicle of insertion into that reality. It will argue, however, that even in the most normative of subjective instances the psyche remains in excess of that complex, and that in other cases desire and identification may actually function as mechanisms for circumventing or even repudiating the dominant fiction, whose most privileged term is the phallus. This book will isolate a historical moment at which the equation of the male sexual organ with the phallus could no longer be sustained, and it will show the disjuncture of those two terms to have led to a collective loss of belief in the whole of the dominant fiction. In so doing, it will foreground masculinity as a crucial site for renegotiating our *vraisemblance*. *Male Subjectivity at the Margins* will then embark upon an extended investigation of some forms of male subjectivity that eschew Oedipal normalization, while nevertheless remaining fully within signification, symbolic castration, and desire. It will at the same time probe the larger political implications of these "deviant" masculinities, some of which do indeed say "no" to power.

The margins with which this book is primarily concerned are thus in the first instance psychic, although I will be at pains to articulate both their social matrices and their social consequences. My project, in other words, is the articulation of what might be called a "libidinal politics." It might seem surprising that I have chosen to pursue this project through male rather than female subjectivity, but I am motivated to do so in significant part because masculinity impinges with such force upon femininity. To effect a large-scale reconfiguration of male identification and desire would, at the very least, permit female subjectivity to be lived differently than it is at present. In my opinion, it would also render null and void virtually everything else that commands general belief. The theoretical articulation of some non-phallic masculinities would consequently seem to be an urgent feminist project.

The kinds of male subjectivity which will be anatomized here are, moreover, precisely those which open in a variety of ways onto the domain of femininity. To state the case slightly differently, the masculinities which this book will interrogate, and even in certain instances work to eroticize or privilege, are those which not only acknowledge but embrace castration, alterity, and specularity. Although these attributes represent the unavoidable tropes of all subjectivity, they generally feature prominently only within the conscious existence of the female subject. Conventional masculinity is largely predicated upon their denial. Saying "no" to power necessarily implies achieving some kind of reconciliation with these structuring terms, and hence with femininity. It means, in other words, the collapse of that system of fortification whereby sexual difference is secured, a system dependent upon projection, disavowal and fetishism. Far from foreclosing upon female subjectivity, then, this book will be at all times centrally concerned with its terms and conditions.

The notion of libidinal politics that I will be elaborating here largely depends upon two psychic categories. The first of these categories— the ego or *moi*—provides the support for "identity" or the "self." The second—the fantasmatic—organizes and regulates unconscious desire. I derive my definition of the ego primarily from Lacan, who purges that category of many of the meanings which it has accreted since the beginning of psychoanalysis, and who locates it emphatically at the level of the imaginary. Lacan often refers to the ego as the *moi*, since for him it is that which is responsible for the production of identity or a "me." He also means thereby to distinguish it as object from the *je* or "I," which is for him the subject proper, i.e. the desiring subject. The *moi* is the psychic "precipitate" of external images, ranging from the subject's mirror image and the parental imagoes to the whole plethora of textually based representations which each of us imbibes daily.[3] What the subject takes to be its "self" is thus both other and fictive. The concept of the fantasmatic comes from Laplanche and Pontalis, who define it as the unconscious prototype for all dreams and fantasies, and as the structuring scenario behind symptoms, transferences and other instances of repetitive behavior. Indeed, for Laplanche and Pontalis, the fantasmatic "shape[s] and order[s]" the subject's life "as a whole."[4] *Male Subjectivity at the Margins* will not only deploy the ego and the fantasmatic as conceptual aids for think-

ing through identification and desire, but it will attempt to demonstrate that they are mutually defining and determining. It will also
situate those two terms within a larger theoretical paradigm, which
I would like briefly to map.

The implicit starting point for virtually every formulation this book
will propose is the assumption that lack of being is the irreducible
condition of subjectivity. In acceding to language, the subject forfeits
all existential reality, and foregoes any future possibility of "wholeness."[5] If we were in possession of an instrument which would permit
us to penetrate deep into the innermost recesses of the human psyche,
we would find not identity, but a void. Lacan says of the subject of
the unconscious that it is "acephalic"—that it is "headless," or, to be
more precise, devoid of "self." He adds that this subject has no ego,
that it is indeed antipathetic to the ego.[6] It speaks, but with "*the voice
of no one*" (170). This subject, which Lacan calls the "*je*," is devoid
both of form and of object; it can perhaps best be defined as pure lack,
and hence as "desire for nothing" (211).

The *je* not only occupies a different psychic register than the *moi*,
but it reveals the latter to be a veritable "mirage" (209) or illusion,
the result of a series of misrecognitions. The irreality of the ego,
however, in no way diminishes its effectivity; Lacan maintains that
"the fundamental, central structure of our experience really belongs
to the imaginary order" (37). He also claims that "at a certain level"
the ego "determines the structuration of the subject" (52), thereby
suggesting that it is at the level of the imaginary that we live what
would otherwise remain inapprehensible—the desire for nothing.

There are two aspects to this "imaginary structuration," as *Seminar
I* calls it.[7] Lacan's formula for fantasy, $\$ < > a$, helps to clarify one
of these aspects, since it encourages us to understand that psychic
formation as a mechanism for plugging the hole of symbolic castration
or lack by positing a particular object as the cause of desire. The "$\$$"
of that formula signifies the subject whose being has been sacrificed
to meaning; "$< >$" designates the phrase "desire for or of"; and "a"
indicates the object which stands in for the mortgaged pound of flesh.[8]
Fantasy thus conjures forth a fictive object for a fundamentally a-
objectal desire. It translates the desire for nothing into the desire for
something. However, we must not forget that the *objet a* exists in a
mirroring relation to the *moi*; it is "one's own ego that one loves in
love, one's own ego made real on the imaginary level."[9] It would thus
seem crucial that we take into account not only how the object figures
within fantasy, but how the ego comes into play. Part of what it means
to pursue the relation of fantasy to the ego is to grasp that the subject's
own bodily image is the first and the most important of all of the

objects through which it attempts to compensate for symbolic castra- √
tion—to understand that the *moi* is most profoundly that through
which it attempts to recover "being." The self, in other words, fills the
void at the center of subjectivity with an illusory plenitude.

The ego or *moi* is consequently the model for all the subsequent
objects that occupy the position of the *a* within the fantasy formula.
Lacan remarks in *Seminar I* that the relation of the subject to its
mirror reflection "provides the fundamental framework for all possible erotism," since "the object relation must always submit to the
narcissistic framework and be inscribed in it" (174). Elsewhere in
the same text, he observes that the subject "originally locates and
recognizes desire through the intermediary" of its own image (147).

But it is not only as the model for the *objet a* but as the subjective
pivot of desire that the *moi* manifests itself within fantasy. At its
deepest level—i.e. at the point at which it falls most fully under the
influence of the primary process[10]—the fantasmatic is "characterized
by the absence of subjectivization," and "all distinction between subject and object [is] lost."[11] The subject has no fixed locus, and can
consequently take up residence anywhere, even at the site of the
fantasy's verb or action.[12] At that level of the fantasmatic which determines how the subject concretely lives its desire, however, the fantasmatic functions as a veritable showcase for the *moi*. Not only is it a
"[script] of organized scenes which are capable of dramatization,"
generally "in a visual form," but "the subject is invariably *present*"
there[13] (my emphasis). Although Laplanche and Pontalis do not say
so, it is only in the guise of the ego that the subject can lay claim to
a "presence" or "being there," whether within fantasy or dreams; the
mise-en-scène of desire can only be staged, in other words, by drawing
upon the images through which the self is constituted. We should
not be surprised to find Lacan insisting, then, that "the notion of
unconscious fantasy . . . is supported only by taking a detour via the
ego,"[14] or that the mirror stage "entirely structures [the subject's]
fantasy life."[15]

There is still more to say about the relation of fantasy and the ego.
We must concern ourselves not only with the bodily images through
which the subject represents itself within the fantasmatic, but with
its symbolic placement there. We must attempt to determine, that is,
"*where* the ego of the subject is" (my emphasis).[16] Although the acephalic *je* is in a sense not only *nothing*, but *nowhere*, every subject lives its
desire from *someplace*, and the fantasmatic is the mechanism through
which that subject-position is articulated. Thus it is that Laplanche
and Pontalis emphasize not only the specularity of that scene within
which desire is staged, but its concern with the *placement* of the

subject. Indeed, they suggest that fantasy is less about the visualization and imaginary appropriation of the other than about the articulation of a subjective locus—that it is "not an *object* that the subject imagines and aims at . . . but rather a *sequence* in which the subject has his own part to play."[17]

Insofar as the ego figures within fantasy—and it would appear that it can never be definitively banished—it works to solidify the distinction between subject and object, and to slow down or even to arrest the identificatory "slide." Laplanche's name is frequently invoked in arguments that seek to stress the mobility of the subject within fantasy.[18] However, he insists in *Life and Death in Psychoanalysis* that a minimum of secondarization or discursive "binding" is necessary for even the deepest unconscious fantasy to "*take form*," and he characterizes binding as "the essence of the ego function."[19] Although Laplanche thereby confers upon the ego attributes which exceed the Lacanian paradigm, he associates its workings with the production of an "imaginary inertia" (126), a phrase which refers us back to that paradigm. He suggests, in effect, that one of the results of that minimal degree of secondarization which is necessary within all fantasy is a certain stabilization of the ego at certain sites.

What I am trying to suggest is that although at the deepest recesses of its psyche the subject has neither identity nor nameable desire, the fantasmatic and the *moi* together work to articulate a mythic but determining version of each. Slavoj Žižek has recently suggested that fantasy not only "provides the co-ordinates of our desire," but "constructs the frame enabling us to desire something." Through fantasy, then, "*we learn 'how to desire'*."[20] Since a crucial part of learning how to desire is the assumption of a desiring position, fantasy would also seem to involve the insertion of the subject into a particular syntax or tableau, and so to play an important part within the formation of identity. The ego similarly intervenes within the articulation of desire. It is only in the guise of the *moi* that the subject takes on a corporeal form, and consequently lays claim to a visual imago, and it is only as a refraction of the *moi* that it is able to desire an object. Identity and desire are so complexly imbricated that neither can be explained without recourse to the other. Furthermore, although those constitutive features of subjectivity are never entirely "fixed," neither are they in a state of absolute flux or "free-play"; on the contrary, they are synonymous with the compulsion to repeat certain images and positionalities, which are relinquished only with difficulty.

As I have already indicated, the images within which the subject "finds" itself always come to it from outside. In *Seminar II*, Lacan describes the ego as "the superimposition of various coats borrowed

from . . . the bric-à-brac of its props department" (155). If the fantasmatic dresses both the subject and the object in these same coats, it
would seem evidently the case that its splendors are also borrowed.
There is also a second sense in which the fantasmatic might be said
to be "second hand." Laplanche and Pontalis maintain in "Fantasy
and the Origins of Sexuality" that fantasy enters from outside—that
it breaks into the infant subject from the earliest moments of its
existence in the guise of the sounds and images of adult sexuality (4–
5). Elsewhere, Laplanche refines upon this formulation in ways which
account not only for the specular and auditory components of the
fantasmatic, but for the *place* which it assigns the subject; he suggests
in *Life and Death in Psychoanalysis* that the child is also penetrated
by the Oedipal *structuration* of parental fantasy:

> We should accustom ourselves to the idea that the meanings im-
> plicit in the slightest parental gesture bear the parents' fantasies;
> for . . . the parents themselves had their own parents; they have
> their "complexes," wishes marked by historicity. . . . In the final
> analysis the complete oedipal structure is *present from the beginning*,
> both "in itself" (in the objectivity of the familial configuration) but
> above all "in the other," outside the child. (45)

We are clearly dealing here with two different kinds of "incorporation"
from outside, one of a specular variety, and the other of which is more
properly characterized as "structural"—that incorporation through
which the *moi* is formed, and upon which the fantasmatic draws for
its images of "self" and other, and that through which the subject
assumes a position within the *mise-en-scène* of desire. The first is
perhaps best understood as "imaginary" identification,[21] and the second as "symbolic" identification. Whereas the mirror stage represents
the model for the former, the Oedipus complex provides the founding
instance of the latter.

   In the pages that follow, I will attempt to show that these two kinds
of identification are mutually coercive, and so to bring the fantasmatic
and the ego into an even closer theoretical alignment. I will argue,
that is, that the fantasmatic helps to determine the images within
which the *moi* is able to "recognize" itself by eroticizing those which
are commensurate with its representational imperatives. Conversely,
a particularly imaginary identification might conform to unconscious
desire at a structural level, but bring with it values capable of shifting
the ideological significance of the fantasmatic, and so of altering its
relation to power. An external representation might, for instance,
pass muster at the level of the fantasmatic through its masochistic
connotations, but at the same time involve an identification with a

masculine corporeal image. Similarly, a subject's structural identification with voyeurism might be ideologically reconfigured through a simultaneous imaginary identification with blackness or femininity. What I am attempting to say is that it not only makes a political difference where the subject "stands" within the *mise-en-scène* of its desire, but what identity it there assumes, or—to state the case somewhat differently—by what values it is marked. It is here that sexual, racial and class difference all come into play in crucial ways, as I will attempt to demonstrate in Chapters 4, 5, 6 and 7.

Male Subjectivity at the Margins will be divided into four sections or theoretical "dossiers," each containing two chapters. The initial section, "Ideology and Masculinity," consisting of Chapters 1 and 2, will explore the issue of ideological belief, which it will locate at a site emphatically exterior to consciousness, and which it will show to be crucial to the maintenance of traditional masculinity. Chapter 1 will argue, with Freud, that belief hinges upon the attribution of reality, and it will attempt to demonstrate that it is ultimately fantasy and the *moi* which are most "real" for the subject. It will also suggest that if ideology is to successfully command the subject's belief, then it must necessarily intervene at the most profound level of the latter's constitution. Chapter 1 will theorize the vehicle through which ideology does this as the "dominant fiction." The dominant fiction will be seen not only as that which mediates between the subject on the one hand, and the symbolic order and the mode of production on the other, but as that which functions to construct and sustain sexual difference.

Chapter 2 will isolate the equation of penis and phallus as a privileged site for the investment of collective belief, and it will emphasize the degree to which our society's entire "reality" depends upon the maintenance of that equation. It will explore a group of films made in Hollywood during the mid-forties which attest to a massive loss of faith in traditional masculinity, and which dramatize the implications of that dissolution not only for gender and the family, but for the larger society. Chapter 2 will attribute this crisis to World War II and the recovery period, which it will theorize as instances of "historical trauma." Finally, it will establish a strong connection between fetishism and ideological belief, and it will argue that Hollywood cinema conventionally calls upon the female subject to disavow the male subject's castration, and—by looking at him with her "imagination" rather than her eyes—to confer upon him a phallic sufficiency.

The second section of *Male Subjectivity at the Margins*, which includes Chapters 3 and 4, will be devoted to an exploration of the gaze and the look. Chapter 3 will pursue that exploration through Lacan's

Seminar XI, and the cinema of Rainer Werner Fassbinder. It will distinguish rigorously between the look and the gaze, situating the former on the side of desire and the disposition of lack, and the latter on the side of Otherness and iridescence. It will attempt to demonstrate that all subjects are necessarily within specularity, even when occupying a viewing position, and that all antitheses of spectator and spectacle are consequently false. Chapter 3 will also theorize the Lacanian "screen" both as a repertoire of ideologically marked images which intervene between the gaze and the subject, and as an important site of cultural contestation.

Chapter 4 will extract a fantasmatic organized around the components of the primal scene from the novels of Henry James, and it will suggest that the subjective locus of this fantasmatic is the position occupied by the excluded child. Since that position is manifestly organized around vision, but is at the same time defined by exclusion and lack, it will facilitate a further differentiation of the look and the gaze. Chapter 4 will also show that the Jamesian fantasmatic situates the subject in a position which is always either too early or too late in relation to genital sexuality, and which is specific neither to the positive nor the negative Oedipus complex.

The third section of this book will explore male masochism. The first of its two chapters will argue that both "moral" and "feminine" masochism hinge upon an intrinsically homosexual beating fantasmatic when they are found at the site of male subjectivity, and it will provide an analysis of each. It will also emphasize the narrow boundary separating moral masochism from an "exemplary" male subjectivity by tracing the evolution of the super-ego back to the negative Oedipus complex. In so doing, it will work once again to expose conventional masculinity as a "fraud." Finally, Chapter 5 will provide a feminist analysis of one of the more extraordinarily ferocious fantasies recounted by Theodor Reik in his study of male masochism, a fantasy hinging upon castration, exhibitionism, and a kind of psychic "shattering." That analysis will lead to the hypothesis that feminine masochism represents a form of phallic divestiture.

Chapter 6, also included in the section on masochism, will direct the reader's attention once again to the cinema of Fassbinder, this time as an instrument for the "ruination" of masculinity, and as an agency for what can only be called, in the strictest sense of the word, masochistic "ecstasy." It will address the various strategies which that cinema devises for returning to the male body all of the violence which it has historically directed elsewhere, strategies ranging from literal castration and dismemberment to homosexual sado-masochism. Chapter 6 will also attempt to show that there are moments within that cinema in which the male psyche is in effect "lifted out" of the male body, and made to feel the pain of other bodies—moments at which identification works according to the logic of "ex-corpora-tion" rather than the logic of incorporation. It will account for this psychic exteriorization through Max Scheler's notion of "hetero-pathic" identification, which it will link to feminine masochism.

The final section of *Male Subjectivity at the Margins*, "Libidinal Poli-tics," will pursue in a more insistent way than any of the other sections the larger political implications of the *moi* and the fantasmatic. The first of its two chapters "White Skin, Brown Masks: The Double Mime-sis, or With Lawrence in Arabia," will explore the shifting relationship between the T.E. Lawrence who emerges from his writings and the racial and class Other. It will also attempt to account for a variety of masochism which is in no way incompatible with virility, and may even represent its complement. Chapter 7 will argue that for the better part of *Seven Pillars of Wisdom: A Triumph*, Lawrence not only identifies with the Arabs with whom he lives and fights, but posits himself as the leader of the Arab Revolt, and hence as its ideal. It will isolate reflexive masochism as the psychic underpinning of this peculiar double mimesis. Chapter 7 will also work to show that Law-rence's reflexive masochism ultimately gives way to feminine masoch-ism, and that it is only through an examination of this shift that we can explain his subsequent retreat from leadership, and his decision to spend most of the remainder of his life serving as a common airman in the R.A.F.

Chapter 8, "A Woman's Soul Enclosed in a Man's Body: Femininity in Male Homosexuality," will begin with a discussion of the place of femininity within traditional accounts of male homosexuality; Schreber's *Memoirs* and Guattari's "Becoming a Woman"; and recent writing by gay men. It will then tease out of assorted Freudian texts three psychoanalytic paradigms for conceptualizing male homosexu-ality. These three paradigms—and most particularly that which I will associate with the name "Leonardo"—will provide the occasion for an extensive rethinking of the category of "the feminine," which will be shown to be capacious enough to include not only specularity, receptivity, masochism, and maternity, but phallic penetration. Chap-ter 8 will conclude with a reading of *A la recherche du temps perdu*, a text which is profoundly structured by the Leonardo model of homo-sexuality. As we will see, the libidinal politics of that text not only function to foreclose upon the Name-of-the-Father, but to route male homosexuality through lesbianism, and to align the male mouth with the female genitals. *Male Subjectivity at the Margins* will thus feature as its final example of a revisionary masculinity one which is able to accommodate not only the psychic, but the physical "stigmata" of femininity.

It should be evident by now that I have organized this book according to theoretical, rather than literary or cinematic principles. However, since those principles will at times be pursued through specific novels and films, it might be useful if I were to indicate briefly at this point the primary bases for my selection, even at the risk of a certain redundancy. First and most importantly, the literary and cinematic texts which will facilitate my exploration of marginal male subjectivity, like that exploration itself, all carve out a privileged space for what has been traditionally assumed to constitute "the feminine." Post-war Hollywood cinema, for instance, stages the male subject's traumatic encounter with castration and specularity. Fassbinder's films push the equation of masculinity and specularity even further, while also giving pride of place to a classically feminine form of identification. James's fiction prioritizes a maternal over a paternal positionality, and strips the male look of its masculine pretensions. Lawrence's writings enact a shift away from leadership to subordination via feminine masochism. Finally, as I suggested a moment ago, Proust's great novel springs into place around a maternal identification, and articulates male homosexuality through lesbianism.

James, Fassbinder, Lawrence, and Proust will also figure prominently in the pages that follow because their work provides such fertile terrain for the exploration of a form of subjectivity which, because it assumes a directly textual guise, is unusually amenable to theoretical analysis, i.e. authorial subjectivity. All four have made autobiographical allusions or metacritical pronouncements which encourage us to look for an authorial imperative in their writings or films, and in each case such scrutiny leads to the discovery of an important textual fantasmatic. Significantly, the authorial subjectivity which is thereby disclosed is antipathetic not only to normative masculinity, but to one of its primary buttresses, traditional notions of authorship. It thus serves a doubly deconstructive purpose.

There are many other determinants behind each of my literary or cinematic choices. For instance, a concern with the historical inducements and ideological ramifications of marginal male subjectivity took me to Hollywood cinema of the mid-forties, as did my desire to conceptualize that subjectivity in group rather than individual terms. My engagement with Lawrence was precipitated by my wish to explore the implications of feminine masochism for race and class. Similarly, Proust's *A la recherche* seemed better calculated than any other twentieth-century text to dramatize the advantages to be derived by the female subject even from those forms of marginal male subjectivity which foreclose upon woman as an erotic object. However, it is perhaps premature at this point to say more about these local determinants, which will become evident as the book progresses. Let us then without further preamble begin our exploration of marginal male subjectivity by attempting to specify the ideological paradigm from which it departs, a paradigm which I will call "the dominant fiction."

Ideology and Masculinity

1

The Dominant Fiction

Twenty-two years since the French publication of Foucault's *The Archaeology of Knowledge*, which can be retrospectively seen to have effected a kind of epistemological "break" with the Althusserian tradition,[1] the word "ideology" may seem to exude the stale aroma of a theoretical anachronism. I would like nevertheless to suggest that, far from having exhausted itself, the great ideology debate of the 1960s and 1970s was broken off prematurely, before a series of crucial issues could be addressed. In exploring some of these issues, this chapter will attempt to demonstrate that the concept of ideology continues to supply an indispensable tool not only for Marxist, but for feminist and gay studies. When a modified Althusserian paradigm is brought into an intimate connection with psychoanalysis and anthropology, it provides the basis for elaborating the relation between a society's mode of production and its symbolic order. This theoretical model also opens the possibility for understanding how the subject is sexually, as well as economically "captated." Finally, Althusser designates the starting point for conceptualizing something which is the precondition for the illusory unity both of the socius and the ego—something which I will call "belief." As we will see, it is through ideological belief that a society's "reality" is constituted and sustained, and that a subject lays claim to a normative identity.

Although these are all manifestly important concerns, they may not seem to impinge directly on masculinity. The aim of this chapter is to demonstrate otherwise—to show that "exemplary" male subjectivity cannot be thought apart from ideology, not only because ideology holds out the mirror within which that subjectivity is constructed, but because the latter depends upon a kind of collective make-believe in the commensurability of penis and phallus. As I will attempt to show, our "dominant fiction" or ideological "reality" solicits our faith above all else in the unity of the family, and the adequacy of the male subject.

If ideology is central to the maintenance of classic masculinity, the affirmation of classic masculinity is equally central to the maintenance of our governing "reality." Because of the pivotal status of the phallus, more than sexual difference is sustained through the alignment of that signifier with the male sexual organ. Within every society, hegemony is keyed to certain privileged terms, around which there is a kind of doubling up of belief. Since everything that successfully passes for "reality" within a given social formation is articulated in relation to these terms, they represent ideological stress points. As both this chapter and the next will attempt to show, within our dominant fiction the phallus/penis equation occupies absolute pride of place. Indeed, that equation is so central to the *vraisemblance* that at those historical moments when the prototypical male subject is unable to recognize "himself" within its conjuration of masculine sufficiency our society suffers from a profound sense of "ideological fatigue."[2] Our entire "world," then, depends upon the alignment of phallus and penis.

Although I will be arguing that ideology is sustained through the maintenance of *collective* belief, I will also be accounting for the operations of belief through recourse to a psychoanalytic paradigm. In other words, I will be theorizing a societal phenomenon through a conceptual model which is attuned to the specificity of the individual psyche. This chapter will maintain that belief is granted not at the level of consciousness, but rather at that of fantasy and the ego or *moi*, and that it consequently comes into play at the most profound sites of the subject's formation. In order for ideology to command belief, then, it must extend itself into the deepest reaches of the subject's identity and unconscious desire. I will propose the positive Oedipus complex as the mechanism through which our dominant fiction seeks to effect this interpellation, and thereby to produce and sustain a normative masculinity. Chapters 3 through 8 will articulate some masculinities which defy the logic of the positive Oedipus complex, and which consequently function in ways which are at least implicitly antagonistic to the dominant fiction.

1. Subjectivity and Ideological Belief

It may seem surprising, in light of more recent theoretical work, that Althusser should have chosen to use Christianity as his ideological model in "Ideology and Ideological State Apparatuses."[3] It is not only that in so doing he is led to posit a structuring element—the Absolute

Subject—which is not easily generalizable to other ideologies, but that he showcases a representational system whose class-bases are far from self-evident, at least within many twentieth-century societies. Nevertheless, there is a crucial reason for giving Christianity center stage. It enjoys its exemplary status because it dramatizes so vividly one of the defining features of all ideologies—the demand for belief. As Althusser remarks, "It is a peculiarity of ideology that it imposes (without appearing to do so, since these are 'obviousnesses') obviousnesses as obviousnesses, which we cannot *fail to recognize* and before which we have the inevitable and natural reaction of crying out (aloud or in the 'still, small voice of conscience'): 'That's obvious! That's right! That's true!'" (171–72).

Belief is frequently assumed to turn upon conscious assent, or as the *OED* puts it, upon "the acceptance of a proposition, statement, or fact, as true, on the ground of authority or evidence." However, in *Lenin and Philosophy*, Althusser suggests that ideological belief may have little to do with consciously held ideas. It can be enacted simply through "kneeling down," "the gesture of the sign of the cross," or the "*mea culpa*."[4] Slavoj Žižek suggests that these rituals may even be performed cynically, without conscious acquiescence, since ideological belief is "radically exterior," like Tibetan prayer wheels.[5] Althusser invokes Pascal's wager by way of illustrating this curious faith: "Kneel down, move your lips in prayer, and you will believe."[6]

We might of course attempt to explain the exteriority of ideological belief according to a performative model, whereby meaningful practices and rituals are understood to produce the assent of the individual who engages in them. Such a reading of *Lenin and Philosophy* would be facilitated by Foucault's *Discipline and Punish*, with its account of the discursive construction of the subject by means of the "calculated manipulation" of the body's "elements," "gestures," and "behavior."[7] Within such a reading, belief would emerge as a kind of spiritual extension or registration of an orchestrated corporeality. However, the main thrust of the Althusserian argument is to locate ideological faith outside *consciousness*, rather than outside the *psyche*. Ideological belief, in other words, occurs at the moment when an image which the subject consciously knows to be culturally fabricated nevertheless succeeds in being recognized or acknowledged as "a pure, naked perception of reality."[8]

Freud accounts for belief in ways which are ultimately more capable of accommodating and even extending the Althusserian paradigm. Like "Ideology and Ideological State Apparatuses," *The Project for a Scientific Psychology* defines belief as a "judgment" or attribution of "reality."[9] And like Althusser, Freud insists that belief proceeds from a site exterior to consciousness. In *The Interpretation of Dreams* he provides a theoretical model which is able to account psychically for this exteriority.[10] In that text, he suggests that the real center of subjectivity is the unconscious, and he demotes consciousness to a kind of receiving-room for stimuli which originate elsewhere, and which have been at the very least psychically worked over. It is consequently not within the domain of consciousness that reality is established, but rather within another scene, closed off from it by repression—that of the unconscious.

Freud also makes clear that psychical reality does not necessarily correspond to objective "fact," and so helps to explain how the subject of ideology can attribute actuality to mere representation. He maintains that events which never literally happened can assume the status of highly significant memories, while occurrences which might seem of the first importance to a biographer may not even figure within the subject's psyche, since it is fantasy rather than history which determines what is reality for the unconscious. In his famous letter of September 21, 1897 to Wilhelm Fliess, Freud was obliged to break with his earlier assumption that female hysteria is caused by literal parental seduction, citing as his reason for doing so the discovery that since "there are no indications of reality in the unconscious," the subject "cannot distinguish between truth and fiction that has been cathected with affect."[11] In the much later "Formulations on the Two Principles of Mental Functioning," he cautions that "one must never allow oneself to be misled into applying the standards of [objective] reality to repressed psychical structures, and on that account, perhaps, into undervaluing the importance of phantasies in the formation of symptoms,"[12] since for the psyche fantasy has all the force of actuality. Laplanche and Pontalis adhere to the spirit, if not to the letter of the passages I have just quoted from Freud, when they claim that "in its strictest sense, 'psychical reality' denotes the unconscious wish and the phantasy associated with it."[13]

If fantasy is in some ultimate sense reality for the subject, that is because it articulates the particular libidinal scenario or tableau through which each of us lives those aspects of the double Oedipus complex which are decisive for us—because it articulates, in short, our symbolic positionality, and the *mise-en-scène* of our desire.[14] In his essay on the uncanny, Freud associates "primitive beliefs"—the "civilized" equivalent of which would seem to be any belief unquestioningly maintained, even in the face of counter-evidence—with "infantile complexes."[15] He thereby suggests that it is ultimately from these complexes that fantasy derives its reality-effect. And in a second letter to Fliess, written on October 15, 1897, and in the context of an overriding concern with narratives of paternal seduction, Freud not only introduces the most important of all infantile complexes, but connects it explicitly to fantasy:

> I have found, in my own case too, [the phenomenon of] being in love with my mother and jealous of my father, and I now consider it a universal event in early childhood. . . . If this is so, we can understand the gripping power of *Oedipus Rex*. . . . Everyone in the audience was once a budding Oedipus in fantasy. . . .[16]

Lacan, too, associates the Oedipus complex with an "intensity of fantasy" in his second seminar.[17] Belief, then, would seem to attach to fantasy insofar as it is a vehicle for infantile complexes, and most particularly for the Oedipus complex, the variable terms of whose enactment provide the subject with a locus or "place."

The issue of belief is also central to the first volume of Proust's *A la recherche du temps perdu*, where it is again linked with the Oedipus complex. The narrator begins an important passage near the conclusion of "Combray" with a cluster of infantile memories, organized around the image of his mother reaching over to proffer him a goodnight kiss. He confides that it is only the objects displayed to him in these memories in which he is able to *believe* or *have faith*. He contrasts them with "the flowers that people show me nowadays for the first time," which "never seem to me to be *true* flowers"[18] (my emphasis). The mnemic traces of his childhood command belief because they constitute the narrator's psychic reality; they provide the "deepest level" of his "mental soil," the "firm ground" on which he "still stands." Significantly, this psychic reality has a libidinal consistency; Marcel characterizes it as "the landscape in which I would like always to live."

A later section of the first novel, "*Noms de pays: le nom*," concludes with a strikingly similar passage, which once again offers a kind of disquisition on belief. The narrator describes himself walking as an adult in the Bois de Boulogne, surrounded by women wearing "Graeco-Saxon tunics, pleated à la Tanagra," and "Liberty chiffons sprinkled with flowers like wall-paper," in whose elegance he has "no faith" (460). He conjures up a very different picture from the time when he "still had faith" (462), the Oedipally resonant image of Mme Swann, walking on foot in the Bois de Boulogne, wearing "an otter-skin coat, with a woollen cap from which stuck out two blade-like partridge-feathers, but enveloped also in the artificial warmth of her own house" (461). In the same passage, Marcel associates belief with "the power," now lost to him, "of imparting reality to new things" (460). In so doing, he acknowledges once again that those "memories" which are most "real" for the subject are those which entertain the most intimate relation with infantile complexes.

Fantasy also passes for reality at the level of the unconscious because it is propelled by desire for the foreclosed real. Although this desire, which is born with language, is fundamentally "a desire for nothing,"[19] fantasy defines it as a desire for something. It posits a given object as that which is capable of restoring lost wholeness to the subject. All of this is implicit within Lacan's formula for fantasy, $< >a$. That formula, which means something like "desire on the part of the barred subject of or for the *objet a*,"[20] posits the desiring subject as a subject who lacks being. (As Lacan remarks in his second seminar, "Desire is a relation of being to lack. This lack is the lack of being properly speaking. It isn't the lack of this or that, but lack of being whereby the being exists" [223].) The subject desires the *objet a* as if its absence were somehow synonymous with this void. *Seminar XI* suggests that the prototypical *objet a* enjoys this status because it is "something from which the subject, in order to constitute itself, has separated itself off as organ," and which therefore "serves as a symbol of the [subject's] lack,"[21] but this status would also seem extrapolatable to other objects. Fantasy might thus be said to confer psychical reality upon the objects which stand in metaphorically for what is sacrificed to meaning—the subject's very "life."

Although this discussion has so far maintained a privileged relation between fantasy and belief, I now want to suggest that the latter category comes into play in relation to a second term, the ego or *moi*. Laplanche and Pontalis maintain that "when Freud speaks of psychical reality ... he means everything in the psyche that takes on the force of reality for the subject,"[22] and there is nothing to which the subject typically attributes greater reality than its "self."[23] Belief is indeed a central part of the *méconnaissance* or self-recognition-misrecognition upon which the ego is founded; Althusser suggests that this transaction induces in the subject a sensation whose verbal translation would be: "*Yes, it really is me!*" (178). However, since the ego is situated from the very beginning in a "fictional direction,"[24] that which commands belief is once again profoundly phantasmagorical.

Jane Gallop has recently proposed that the mirror stage be read according to the future perfect—that rather than locating it between the ages of six and eighteen months, we understand it as an event which comes into play retroactively, from a subsequent moment.[25] One of the compelling advantages of such a reading is that it permits us to get around the theoretical difficulty of positing an initial identification which somehow stands outside the "social determination" of later identifications. What Lacan calls "primary identification" can be seen to be the reconstitution of an earlier event, from a position well within language and sociality. Secondary identification thus in a sense precedes primary identification.

There is also another important gain, and one which is equally relevant to the present discussion: If the mirror stage is something which *will have existed* only from the vantage of a later point in time, the *moi* would seem to emerge decisively only on the other side of lack—to be, as Lacan suggests in *Seminar II*, intimately "tied to the primitive gap of the subject" (210). It would seem to emerge, indeed, precisely as an imaginary compensation for lack or *manque-à-être*— as a structure, much like fantasy, through which the subject seeks to fill the hole induced through language.[26] Like the *objet a*, then, the ego derives its privileged place within psychic reality from its surrogate value; it passes as reality at the level of the psyche because it is that through which the trauma of symbolic castration is denied. Like the object of desire, the ego fills at the level of the imaginary the void which is opened through aphanisis. Here, however, the gap is overcome less through a *having* than a *being*; indeed, the ego can perhaps best be understood as that through which being is imputed to the acephalic or lacking subject.

But what, precisely, is the relation between psychic reality as I have articulated it here, and the topic with which I began this chapter— ideological belief? My project is to show that it is only by successfully defining what passes for "reality" at the level of the psyche that ideology can be said to command the subject's belief. We have been at least partially aware for some time now of the relation between ideology and identity, since the ego comes insistently into play within Althusser's model of ideology. *Lenin and Philosophy* uses Lacan's account of the subject's ceaseless misrecognition of itself within a series of exterior and irreducibly phantasmagorical images with which it can never be equivalent as the basis for its theory of interpellation. Not surprisingly, ideology's claim on belief is never more prominently on display in *Lenin and Philosophy* than when Althusser attempts to describe the process through which a subject is ideologically sutured, which he imagines "along the lines of the most commonplace everyday police (or other) hailing: 'Hey, you there!'" Successful interpellation means taking as the reality of the self what is in fact a discursive construction, or to state the case differently, claiming as an ontology what is only a point of address:

> Assuming that the theoretical scene I have imagined takes place in the street, the hailed individual will turn round. By this mere one-hundred-and-eighty-degree physical conversion, he becomes [an ideological] *subject*. Why? Because he has recognized that the hail was "really" addressed to him, and that "it was *really him* who was hailed" . . . (174)

However, although the concept of interpellation has by now passed into common parlance as a way of accounting for how ideology works upon the subject, we have not yet confronted the full extent to which ideology can penetrate identity. Lacan speaks at one point in his second seminar about epochal identifications—about identifications which represent "essential landmark[s] for the subject, at each historical moment in his life" (165). These epochal identifications would seem to be those which "count," in some ultimate sense—those with the greatest quota of "reality." Laplanche also distinguishes in *Life and Death in Psychoanalysis* between "'primary'" or "founding" identifications, and those which merely "shape and enrich" what has already been put in place.[27] It is generally assumed by readers of Althusser that ideological interpellation involves the latter rather than the former—that it comes *after* the parental identifications through which the subject is constituted as such, and is consequently less primary or secondary than "tertiary." The following discussion will dispute this assumption. I will attempt to demonstrate that even the earliest and the most decisive of the subject's identifications may be ideologically determined—that the dominant fiction may encroach upon the very formation of the *moi*.

Because Althusser's account of ideological interpellation depends almost entirely upon identification, his corpus does not propose a fully elaborated theory of the relation of ideology to fantasy, and so largely neglects the other feature of psychic reality which I have foregrounded here. However, a brief passage from "Marxism and Humanism" proposes the need for such a theory, and provides the initial outlines of one. In the passage to which I refer, Althusser remarks that in ideology "the real relation is inevitably invested in the imaginary relation, a relation that *expresses* a *will* (conservative, conformist, reformist or revolutionary), a hope or a nostalgia, rather than describing a reality."[28] By "real relation," Althusser of course means the subject's relation to the mode of production—its relation to the economic system which exploits it, or from which it profits. Without in any way diminishing the force of this reading, I would like to suggest a supplementary gloss. Within the present context, Althusser's claim that in ideology "the real relation is inevitably invested in the imaginary relation" can also be interpreted as implying that ideology is intimately bound up in the process whereby the subject's relation to the existential real—which is one of castration or loss—is covered over at the level of the imaginary; part of the process, that is, whereby not only the ego, but fantasy, are mustered against the void.

Since will, hope, and nostalgia all represent modalities of desire, the rest of the sentence from "Marxism and Humanism" suggests that the imaginary relation to the economic real which is promoted by a given ideology functions to position the subject in a libidinal relation either to a past, present, or future mode of production. It thereby serves as a crucial reminder that ideology can so fully invade unconscious desire that it may come to define the psychic reality even of a subject who at a conscious level remains morally or ironically detached from it. Žižek has recently extended this implicitly Althusserian insight into a domain that falls outside a classic Marxist purview. "It not enough to say that we must liberate ourselves of so-called 'anti-Semitic prejudices' and learn to see Jews as they really are," he writes; we must rather "confront ourselves with how the ideological figure of the 'Jew' is invested with our unconscious desire" (48). The emphasis which Žižek places on race is extremely welcome. The unconscious articulation of racial and class difference is facilitated, however, by the articulation of an even more inaugural difference, which we also need to conceptualize ideologically—sexual difference.

Stephen Heath has criticized Althusser for failing to account for the psychic specificity of the subject—for failing to distinguish where the constitution of the subject leaves off, and its ideological interpellation begins.[29] The distinction upon which Heath insists implies a false chronology, a kind of "before" and "after" ideology. We will not be able to understand the full extent to which ideology permeates subjectivity as long as we conceptualize that social agency only or even primarily as a carrier of competing class, racial, or even gender values capable of being "grafted" on to an already-formed identity, or a previously articulated fantasmatic structure. We will also be unable to grasp the absolute imbrication of ideology and subjectivity as long as we think in insistently individualizing ways about the psyche. Let us attempt to take Althusser at his word when he tells us both that "the category of the subject is constitutive of all ideology," and that "*ideology has the function (which defines it) of 'constituting' concrete individuals as subjects*"[30] by exploring the subjective bases of social consensus, and the ideological bases of conventional psychic reality.

2. Towards a Psychoanalytic Theory of Hegemony

One of the great virtues of the Althusserian model is that it provides at least the beginning of a psychoanalytic theory of hegemony. Although Althusser claims in "Ideology and Ideological State Apparatuses" that "Gramsci is the only one who went any distance in the road I am taking" since "he had the 'remarkable' idea that the State could not be reduced to the (Repressive) State Apparatus, but included . . . a certain number of institutions from '*civil society*'" (142n), his account of how the members of a group come to accept the same ideological representations as "true" is ultimately more dependent upon Lacan. Hegemony hinges upon identification; it comes into play when all the members of a collectivity see themselves within the same reflecting surface. In his essay on Bertolazzi and Brecht, Althusser reconceives the mirror stage as something that occurs on a mass as well as an individual level; he suggests, in other words, that an entire society might be said in some sense to undergo a perpetual collective captation, and he attributes to that captation the constitution of the society as such. The relevant passage occurs midway through a discussion of the great and seemingly eternal themes of classical theater— "politics, morality, religion, honor, 'glory,' 'passion.'" Pondering the ideological basis of these themes, Althusser asks:

> But what, concretely, is this uncriticized ideology if not simply the "familiar," "well-known," transparent myths in which a society or an age can recognize itself (but not know itself), the mirror it looks into for self-recognition . . . [31]

He thus suggests that social consensus is not a matter of rational agreement, but of imaginary affirmation. And once again that affirmation is synonymous with the very constitution of the subject.

It is perhaps necessary to add that the collective mirror about which Althusser writes provides each subject with more than an image of "self." It also depicts the surrounding environment, the *vraisemblance* which the captated subject inhabits. It is presumably for this reason that Althusser extends the notion of *méconnaissance* beyond the societal self to the "world" in an important passage from "Theory, Theoretical Practice and Theoretical Formation." "Ideological representation," he writes there,

> . . . makes *allusion* to the real in a certain way, but . . . at the same time it bestows only an *illusion* on reality. . . . ideology gives men a certain "knowledge" of their world, gives them a certain "recognition"; but at the same time ideology only introduces them to its *misrecognition. Allusion–illusion* or *recognition-misrecognition*— such is ideology from the perspective of its relation to the real. (29)

In this passage, Althusser insists that ideology constitutes not only the subject, but the world, and that the latter is as much an imaginary construction as the former. Since hegemony depends upon the maintenance of what is at least to some degree a shared universe, it necessarily implies not only a common identification, but a shared "reality," both subordinate to the principle of a recognition which is simultaneously a misrecognition.

But what is the agency through which this double *méconnaissance* is effected? At several points in "Ideology and Ideological State Apparatuses," Althusser maintains that hegemony is instituted through the Ideological State Apparatuses, which are themselves unified beneath the ideology of the ruling class (146, 149). He thereby implies that every member of a given society somehow inhabits the conceptual universe of that group,[32] and that it is finally class which is most "real" for the subject. However, other essays draw a more complex picture. In some of those essays, and even in the 1970 "Postscript" to "Ideology and Ideological State Apparatuses," Althusser indicates that ideology may provide an important site of class struggle, and that hegemony is consequently not the automatic result of one class's preeminence. There are also passages scattered throughout Althusser's *corpus* which suggest that hegemony may not in the final analysis be pegged to class, but rather to something demanding a different specification. Let us move our way slowly toward the second set of passages via the first. In so doing, we will arrive at last at an understanding of the *vraisemblance* as something which is simultaneously in excess of class, and the focal point of the ideological class struggle.

Although "Ideology and Ideological State Apparatuses" is most notorious for its insistence upon the primacy of the ideology of the ruling class, it also gestures in the direction of a greater ideological heterogeneity. At one point in that essay, Althusser grants that although our Ideological Apparatuses are unified beneath bourgeois ideology, they are "multiple, distinct, 'relatively autonomous' and capable of providing an objective field to contradictions which express, in forms which may be limited or extreme, the effects of the clashes between the capitalist class struggle and the proletarian class struggle, as well as their subordinate forms" (149). Although this passage insists upon a narrowly economic reading of ideology, it nevertheless allows for ideological contestation, and so challenges the assumption that one class can simply impose its "reality" upon another. Althusser also speaks about "the class struggle in the ISA's" in the 1970 "Postscript" to "Ideology and Ideological State Apparatuses," although he again insists that this struggle is initiated "elsewhere" (185), i.e. in the economic realm.

A passage from "Theory, Theoretical Practice and Theoretical Formation" goes further. In that passage, Althusser acknowledges that the bourgeoisie, petty-bourgeoisie, and working class may all inhabit different ideological "worlds," and presumably recognize themselves within competing images. He thus problematizes the notion that the ideology of the ruling class by very definition commands general belief. However, Althusser maintains that these contradictory "realities" and images must all be elaborated within the "language" of the presiding ideology. Hegemony resides in this "language," or—as Althusser calls it—this "structure":

> If in its totality ideology expresses a representation of the real des-tined to sanction a regime of class exploitation and domination, it can also give rise, in certain circumstances, to the expression of the *protest of the exploited classes* against their own exploitation. This is why we must now specify that ideology is not only divided into regions, but also *divided into tendencies* within its own social exis-tence ... we thus observe the existence of *different ideological tendencies* that express the "representations" of the different social classes. ... But we should not lose sight of the fact that in the case of the capitalist mode of production these petty-bourgeois and proletarian ideologies remain *subordinate* ideologies, and that in them—even in the protests of the exploited—it is always the ideas of the dominant class. ... which get the upper hand. ... What do we mean when we say, with Marx, that bourgeois ideology domi-nates other ideologies. ...? We mean that working-class protest against exploitation expressed itself *within the very structure of the dominant bourgeois ideology* within its *system*, and in large part with its representations and terms of reference. (30)

Althusser here attempts to explain how ideology can be at the same time a site of class struggle, and an agency of hegemony, a project which is also at the heart of the present discussion. Regrettably, the economic determinism of this passage ultimately vitiates its attempt to account simultaneously for ideological diversity and ideological unity. Within the theoretical formulation it advances, the opposing ideologies always unconsciously replicate the ideology of the ascen-dent class in their signifiers and systematicity because of their subor-dinate class status. Unity thus prevails over diversity.

"The Transformation of Philosophy" proves a more supple model for understanding how ideology can be at the same time the site of contestation and the mechanism through which a society is made to cohere. In that essay, Althusser acknowledges to a far greater degree than usual the kind of give and take to which an ideology must submit in order to achieve consensus. He also suggests that there are extrinsic ideological elements to which a class ideology must accommodate itself if it is to pass hegemonic muster. "It is not simply a question of manufacturing a dominant ideology because you have need of one, by decree," Althusser writes,

> nor simply of constituting it in a long history of class struggle. It must be constructed at the basis of what already exists, starting from the elements, the regions, of existing ideology, from the legacy

of the past, which is diverse and contradictory, and also through the unexpected events that constantly occur in science as well as politics. An ideology must be constituted, in the class struggle and its contradictions ... which transcends all those contradictions, an ideology unified around the essential interests of the dominant class in order to secure what Gramsci called its hegemony.[33]

In the first two sentences of this passage, Althusser suggests that if a class ideology is to command belief it must articulate itself in relation to "what already exists." Significantly, that category includes at least one item which escapes a narrowly economic specification—scientific discovery. A second item—"the legacy of the past"—is more ambiguous in this respect. However, even assuming we are to give it a class inflection, which is by no means certain, it must be read as anachronistic in relation to the existing mode of production, and so to the ideology of the dominant class. It must be understood, that is, as a relic of an earlier mode of production, as the result of uneven development. Althusser thus encourages us to rethink ideological class struggle—to see it as a battle over ideological elements which have no immediate class basis. The dominant class ideology is presumably the one which most fully succeeds in constructing itself in relation to those elements.

These two sentences from "The Transformation of Philosophy" describe the process whereby a social consensus is manufactured in very similar terms to those proposed by Chantal Mouffe in her important rereading of Gramsci. In the text to which I refer, "Hegemony and Ideology in Gramsci," Mouffe claims that a class is hegemonic only "when it has managed to articulate to its discourse the overwhelming majority of ideological elements characteristic of a given social formation,"[34] thereby suggesting that ideological struggle takes place in relation to representational and signifying elements which are not the sole preserve of any one class, but which constitute a kind of *vraisemblance.*

Unfortunately, the passage from "The Transformation of Philosophy" fails to elaborate sufficiently upon the category of "what already exists," and its final sentence reverts to a more classic Marxist paradigm. Hegemony is there synonymous with the ideological regime of the ruling class, and is no longer dependent upon a signifying and representational system which is exterior to all present class ideologies. However, as we will see, both in "Freud and Lacan," and in an important passage from "Ideology and Ideological State Apparatuses," Althusser encourages us to think in more psychoanalytic ways about the ideological reserve upon which belief depends, and thereby further complicates our understanding of the relation between it and ideologies of class.

The rest of this chapter will attempt to define the ideological "reality" with which other ideologies seek to intersect. I will henceforth abandon any pretense that this conceptual conglomeration can be even loosely equated with the ideology of the ruling class. Instead, I will propose that we think of the primary agency of social consensus as a "dominant fiction," and that we understand its core elements to be deployable for class purposes, but not themselves the automatic vehicle of particular class interests. My intent in so doing is not to minimize the importance of class within the ideological domain, but to show that class ideologies cannot by themselves conjure forth the belief upon which they depend. Class ideologies must lean for this purpose upon another ideological system—upon "that which already exists." Within the ideological domain, then, class struggle implies at the most profound level a struggle over this prior "reality," which is in the strictest sense the "always already."

In the pages that follow, I will also be arguing that when Althusser tells us that ideology constitutes the subject, he ultimately means the subject as psychoanalysis conceives it. We must consequently be on guard against any temptation to qualify the psychic specificity of the subject, even when we are attempting to conceive of a collective or societal interpellation. The "familiar," "well-known," and "transparent myths in which a society or an age can recognize itself (but not know itself)" can only in the first instance be those through which it articulates desire and identity. It is thus via a politically sensitive psychoanalysis rather than through some more expressly political or sociological discourse that we must orchestrate the theoretical transition from individual to group subject—via the notions of "secondary" identification, and the typical fantasy.

Secondary identification, as the reader of "The Mirror Stage" will recall, provides the category through which Lacan accounts for social identification. The first and most formative of all such captations are those which hinge upon the parental imago, and which introduce the subject into sexual difference—those which divide the world into "Ladies" and "Gentlemen,"[35] while at the same time constituting two psychic collectivities. The typical fantasy also works to promote a conventional subject. In "Fantasy and the Origins of Sexuality," Laplanche and Pontalis describe this kind of fantasy as a pre-given sequence or structure which intrudes into the subject from outside. It derives from a "spoken or secret discourse," which is "going on prior to the subject's arrival, within which he must find his way."[36] Its initial conduit, as Laplanche suggests in *Life and Death in Psychoanalysis*, is parental fantasy,[37] but it ultimately derives from that wealth of representational and signifying practices which make up the dominant fiction.[38] Within the context of this chapter, fantasy will function as a virtual synonym for the positive Oedipus complex, and *vice versa*. Subsequent chapters will address other, less normative fantasmatic structures, along with their political implications.

3. Ideology and the Symbolic Order

Two theorists—Ernesto Laclau and Jacques Rancière—have recently urged us to think about hegemony in ways that are not rigidly circumscribed by class. Like Althusser and Mouffe, both of these writers suggest that social consensus depends upon a kind of *vraisemblance*. Once again, moreover, this ideological reserve doubles as a mirror. However, whereas in Althusser's work there is some uncertainty about whether insertion into it involves primarily a class or a societal identification, here captation is clearly productive of a broadly societal subject.

In Chapter 3 of *Politics and Ideology in Marxist Theory*, Laclau argues that within capitalist social formations certain antagonisms are determined not by relations of production, but by "the ensemble of political and ideological relations of domination."[39] These antagonisms express themselves through the opposition between "power" and "the people." The ideologies which give voice to this conflict have no fixed class context. In and of themselves, they interpellate subjects only as "the people." Because of the strong identificatory pull exercised by that latter category, however, they provide an indispensable tool for the mobilization of the socius by class ideologies. "Fascism and Ideology" consequently maintains that "the struggle for the articulation of popular-democratic ideology in class ideological discourses is the basic ideological struggle in capitalist social formations" (114). Laclau argues that fascism was successful because it understood this principle, whereas the contemporary working-class movements in Germany and Italy did not.

Since *Politics and Ideology in Marxist Theory* has influenced my thinking about the dominant fiction in many ways, it would seem crucial to indicate the points of congruence and disjuncture between that text and my own. Like Laclau and his occasional collaborator, Chantal Mouffe, whose work on Gramsci prefigures the notion of popular-democratic interpellation, I remain unpersuaded by traditional accounts of ideological domination. The ideology of a particular class cannot simply impose itself upon a socius; in order to command collective belief, it must intersect decisively with the society's "reality," which does not "belong" to any class. I would also like to preserve the notion that the struggle to effect this intersection represents the most fundamental ideological struggle within any social formation. However, while I am prepared to accept many of the claims Laclau makes on behalf of the people/power antagonism, I am not persuaded that it is capable by itself of performing the absolutely pivotal role which "Fascism and Ideology" assigns it. Laclau's formulation makes no provision either for the typical fantasy or the parental imago, and hence fails to account for that phenomenon without which it is impossible to manufacture a social consensus—belief. It fails, that is, to explain how the power/people opposition becomes psychically "real" for the subject. It also locates at the center of the ideological domain a term which more properly belongs at its periphery. The category of "the people" exists in an intimate relation with a much more pivotal element of our "reality"—the family. It is from this element that it derives its affective force.

Rancière advances a more inclusive notion of what constitutes the *vraisemblance*. In an interview with the editors of *Cahiers du Cinéma*, he proposes that we think of a society's ideological "reality" as its "dominant fiction." Like popular-democratic interpellation, the dominant fiction represents primarily a category for theorizing hegemony, and once again it functions as a mirror. Rancière defines it as "the privileged mode of representation by which the image of the social consensus is offered to the members of a social formation and within which they are asked to identify themselves."[40] Whereas Laclau writes about the political uses to which hegemony can be put, Rancière is more concerned with its representational uses; he sees it as "a reserve of images and manipulator of stories for the different modes of configuration (pictorial, novelistic, cinematic, etc.)" (28). He maintains that America's dominant fiction is "the birth of a nation," and that this story of national origin can be staged in several different ways, all of which hinge upon binary opposition—upon the adversarial relation of whites to Indians, North to South, and law to outlaw. Finally, Rancière insists that a community is "able to recognize itself as such" only "by recognizing its Law" (26).

I find the term "dominant fiction" so resonant that I will be appropriating it for my own, rather different purposes. Two other aspects of Rancière's formulation also point in a promising direction, especially when conceptualized in relation to each other. One of these is his assertion that the dominant fiction consists of the images and stories through which a society figures consensus; images and stories which cinema, fiction, popular culture, and other forms of mass representation presumably both draw upon and help to shape. Equally important is Rancière's claim that a society constitutes itself as a society only by *recognizing* its Law. Since it should be evident by now that there is no ideological recognition which is not at the same time a misrecognition, the word I have just italicized encourages us to theorize the dominant fiction as a "bank" of representations for inducing a *méconnaissance* of the Law, or to state the case somewhat differently, for establishing an imaginary relation to it. But what is this Law?

Rancière would no doubt respond that by "the Law" he means something like "the Law of the Land" (in the next paragraph he associates it with "ethics" and "the American town"). But what Law can be said to govern an entire society, irrespective of class and other divisions? An important passage from "Ideology and Ideological State Apparatuses" provides the definitive answer to this question, albeit in a less than direct manner.

In the passage in question, Althusser elaborates upon the economic and ideological functions of the family. He begins by isolating that institution as a crucial Ideological State Apparatus within the capitalist mode of production. At the same time, he acknowledges that it does more than reproduce existing economic relations. "The family obviously has other 'functions' than that of an ISA," he writes. "It intervenes in the reproduction of labor power. In different modes of production it is the unit of production and/or the unit of consumption" (143f.). However, even this expanded definition seems insufficient. A later paragraph, which describes the contribution of the Ideological State Apparatuses to the reproduction of the relations of production, concludes with a curious ellipsis, suggesting that there is something about the family which resists simple assimilation even to Althusser's revised paradigm: "The religious apparatus [contributes] by recalling in sermons and the other great ceremonies of Birth, Marriage and Death, that man is only ashes, unless he loves his neighbor to the extent of turning the other cheek to whoever strikes first. The family apparatus . . . but there is no need to go on" (154). Most surprising of all, when Althusser finally does elaborate more specifically upon the ideological function of the family, class does not provide one of the terms of analysis. Instead, this excursus reads as though it had been lifted right out of Lacan's "Rome Discourse," in import if not in style:

> Everyone knows how much and in what way an unborn child is expected. Which amounts to saying, very prosaically, if we agree to drop the "sentiments," i.e. the forms of family ideology . . . in which the unborn child is expected: it is certain in advance that it will bear its Father's Name, and will therefore have an identity and be irreplaceable. Before its birth, the child is therefore always-already a subject, appointed as a subject in and by the specific familial ideological configuration in which it is "expected" once it has been

conceived. I hardly need add that this familial ideological configuration is . . . highly structured, and that it is in this implacable and more or less "pathological" . . . structure that the former subject-to-be will have to find "its" place, i.e. "become" the sexual subject (boy or girl) which it already is in advance. (176)[41]

I have quoted this passage at length because it accounts in a very condensed way both for the dominant fiction as I will be retheorizing it, and for the Law which subtends it. But let us proceed more methodically.

Only one of the theoretical categories Althusser deploys in this passage—ideology—comes from Marxism. The others derive from Lacanian psychoanalysis, and they are not easily digested by historical materialism. The category which proves most intractable in that respect is of course the symbolic order, here conjured forth through the Name-of-the-Father, and through the notion of an "implacable and more or less 'pathological' . . . structure." Not only is the category of the symbolic resistant to a Marxist model of periodization, but it defies efforts to locate it within a "superstructure." The real problem, of course, is that the symbolic order occupies as determinative a role within Lacanian psychoanalysis as mode of production does within a materialist paradigm, and neither of those categories can be persuasively shown to be an effect of the other. The symbolic order also operates according to a different temporality than does mode of production. It manifests, that is, a far more profound inertia.

Nevertheless, although the concept of the symbolic can only with the greatest difficulty be accommodated within a conventional Marxist discourse, Althusser's language suggests that it may provide the Law for which we are looking. Since that feature of the symbolic which he describes as an "implacable and more or less 'pathological' . . . structure" can only be disclosed if we abandon "the forms of family ideology," it would seem to lie concealed behind them. It thus closely resembles the Law about which Rancière speaks.

Despite the fact that his primary allegiances are clearly Marxist, Althusser meditates at greater length upon the concept of the symbolic in another essay from *Lenin and Philosophy*. That essay, "Freud and Lacan," appears immediately after "Ideology and Ideological State Apparatuses," in the guise of an "Appendix." As if further to subordinate the symbolic order to the mode of production, Althusser warns the English readers of "Freud and Lacan" that "no theory of psychoanalysis can be produced without basing it on historical materialism (*on which the theory of the formations of familial ideology depends, in the last instance*)."[42] In the body of the essay, however, Althusser attributes to psychoanalysis, as to Marxism, the privileged status of a "science."[43] He defines a science as that which "can claim a right to an object of its *own*" (202), and he insists with Lacan that psychoanalysis has such an object: "the *unconscious* and its 'laws'" (204).

Althusser might more appropriately have defined that object as "the unconscious and its Law," since it is about "the Law" that he then goes on to speak. Significantly, the Law turns out to mean the symbolic order. As in the Rancière interview, this Law is assigned a formative role, albeit one which is more insistently bound up with the constitution of the subject than with the constitution of a society:

> Where a superficial or prejudiced reading of Freud has only seen happy, lawless childhood, the paradise of "polymorphous perversity" . . . Lacan demonstrates the effectiveness of the Order, the Law, that has been lying in wait for each infant since before his birth, and seizes him before his first cry, assigning to him his place and role, and hence his fixed destination. . . . (211)

Astonishingly, Althusser not only acknowledges in "Freud and Lacan" that the symbolic Law plays a pivotal part in the formation of the unconscious, but he traces it back to the beginning of social existence—makes it, indeed, the very point of origin. He thereby gives it a transcendental position in relation to Marxism's privileged category, "mode of production":

> . . . any reduction of childhood traumas to a balance of "biological frustrations" alone, is in principle erroneous, since the Law that covers them, as a Law, abstracts from all contents . . . and the infant submits to this rule and receives it from his first breath. This is the beginning, and has always been the beginning, even when there is no living Father (who is Law), hence of the Order of the human signifier, i.e. of the Law of Culture. . . . (212)

As this passage makes clear, the Law to which Althusser refers is a paternal Law. Its privileged signifier is the Name-of-the-Father.

Although I will in a moment challenge the notion that this Law is irreducibly conjoined with the Name-of-the-Father, I want to reiterate and slightly reframe one of Althusser's primary points: The Law which stands outside all ideologies of class, but which provides the underpinning of ideological belief, belongs to the symbolic order rather than the mode of production. At the same time I want to insist, as Althusser implicitly does, that we need the concepts both of the symbolic order and of the mode of production in order to account for subjectivity and the social formation. Finally, I want to emphasize that the integrity of each of these concepts must be maintained—that neither can be read as the consequence of the other. But how is it possible for two such different principles of determination to be operative at the same time, each in its full complexity? Let us return, in an attempt to answer this question, to "Ideology and Ideological State Apparatuses."

As I have already noted, that essay makes it possible to distinguish between the "implacable . . . structure" or symbolic Law, and the "forms of family ideology," the latter serving somehow to conceal the former. Significantly, Althusser associates the process of interpellation more definitively with family ideology than with the Law, as if to suggest that the subject can no more be directly inserted into the symbolic order than into the reality of a particular mode of production, but requires an imaginary mediator or facilitator. He thus advances a formulation very similar to the one with which Rancière defines the dominant fiction; he proposes, that is, that the human subject recognizes-misrecognizes the symbolic Law in the mirror of ideology. An important footnote from "Freud and Lacan" offers a similar argument. In it, Althusser maintains that "the persons inscribed in [the] structures [of the symbolic order] *live* their functions" through "determinate ideological formations" (211). The symbolic order here occupies an analogous position to that of the "world"—i.e. the mode of production—in the more famous Althusserian pronouncement, "ideology is a matter of the *lived* relation between men and their world."[44]

Although ideology would indeed seem to determine our lived relation both to the dominant mode of production, and to the symbolic Law, we need for the moment to forge an artificial distinction between the *kind* of ideology which is primarily responsible in each of those two cases (I say "artificial" because it will not be possible in the final analysis to sustain so absolute a division). The subject's relation to the existing mode of production is lived via the ideologies of gender, class, race, ethnicity, etc.,[45] ideologies which are always imbricated in crucial ways with the core elements of the dominant fiction. Sometimes the imbrication is so profound that elements drawn from those ideologies actually become peripheral components of the dominant fiction over an extended period of history. Our relation to the present symbolic order, on the other hand, is lived via those ideological components which are most central to the dominant fiction, albeit always in ways that are significantly inflected by the ideologies of gender, class, race, and ethnicity.

As should be evident from the foregoing discussion, our present dominant fiction is above all else the representational system through which the subject is accommodated to the Name-of-the-Father. Its most central signifier of unity is the (paternal) family, and its primary signifier of privilege the phallus. "Male" and "female" constitute our dominant fiction's most fundamental binary opposition. Its many other ideological elements, such as signifiers like "town" and "nation," or the antithesis of power and the people, all exist in a metaphoric relation to these terms. They derive their conceptual and affective value from that relation.

4. The Laws of Language and Kinship Structure

We have arrived at a provisional understanding of the dominant fiction, but we have not yet succeeded in specifying the Law which buttresses it. Again I ask: what is this Law? It would appear, first of all, that the Law for which we are looking is not single, but double. On several occasions in "Freud and Lacan," as we have seen, Althusser conflates the symbolic Law with the Name-of-the-Father, thereby giving the latter a kind of definitional status with respect to the former. However, in another passage from the same text, he insists that we must discriminate not only between familial ideology and the symbolic order, but between two different aspects of that order: between "the *formal* structure of language" on the one hand, and "the concrete kinship structures" on the other (217). Althusser thus implies that the symbolic order is organized around *two* Laws, only one of which is at present represented by the Name-of-the-Father—around what might be called the "Law of Language," and the "Law of Kinship Structure."

If, as Althusser suggests, the Law of Language represents "the absolute precondition for the existence and intelligibility of the unconscious," then it can best be understood in terms of the Lacanian binarism, "your meaning or your life"—as the unavoidable castration which every subject must experience upon entering the order of language or signification, its inauguration into a regime of lack.[46] This castration or lack entails both the loss of being, and the subject's subordination to a discursive order which pre-exists, exceeds, and substantially "speaks" it.

The Law of Kinship Structure poses greater definitional difficulties. Although it would seem to consist of the culturally and historically variable elaboration of a universal dictate, the very theoretical texts which have made it possible for me to articulate this distinction invariably read the universal dictate through its local articulation, the Name-of-the-Father. The universal dictate is of course the incest prohibition, which "expresses the transition from the natural fact of consanguinity to the cultural fact of alliance."[47] As Lévi-Strauss explains in *The Elementary Structures of Kinship*, a group within which marriage is forbidden implies another group, with which marriage is allowable or even obligatory. The incest taboo consequently serves to incorporate individual families into larger social units:

> The prohibition of incest is not merely a prohibition . . . because in prohibiting it also orders. Like exogamy, which is its widened social application, the prohibition of incest is a rule of reciprocity. (51)

For Lévi-Strauss, the incest taboo would seem necessarily to imply the exchange of women. Indeed, he argues in "Language and the Analysis of Social Laws" that exogamy can be compared to language because it obliges women to circulate, much like words, between "clans, lineages, or families."[48] In "Structural Analysis in Linguistics and in Anthropology," he toys briefly with the notion of inverting this model, but concludes that "in human society, it is the men who exchange the women."[49] And in *The Elementary Structures of Kinship*, he claims that "the emergence of symbolic thought"—i.e. of culture—depends upon the exchange of women (496).

Like Althusser, both Freud and Lacan conceive of the Law of Kinship Structure more in terms of the Name-of-the-Father than the circulation of women, but Gayle Rubin makes it possible for us to understand the psychoanalytic and anthropological formulations in ways which are almost immediately assimilable to each other. She observes that although the exchange of women "does not necessarily imply that women are objectified," it does imply "a distinction between gift and giver," a distinction which confers symbolic privilege upon the male subject:

> If women are the gifts, then it is men who are the exchange partners. And it is the partners, not the presents, upon whom reciprocal exchange confers its quasi-mystical power of social linkage. . . . As long as the relations specify that men exchange women, it is men who are the beneficiaries of the product of such exchanges—social organization.[50]

The circulation of women can thus be seen to represent the most rudimentary articulation of the Name-of-the-Father—the most basic mechanism for defining men, in contradistinction to women, as the producers and representatives of the social field.

Not surprisingly, given the ideological thrust of his essays on sexual difference, we can see the same kind of universalizing project at work in Freud's account of the symbolic father as we find in Lévi-Strauss's account of the exchange of women. He begins *Totem and Taboo*, the text in which the concept of the Name-of-the-Father makes its first theoretical entrance, with a discussion of the invariability of the incest taboo. But rather than isolating it as the site at which human culture emerges, he subordinates it to a more primordial event, of which it is merely a consequence or extension. Its inception becomes one of the concluding moments in a phylogenetic narrative, a narrative in which a horde of sons murder and incorporate the father, and then elevate the paternal principle to a Law.[51] Freud consequently makes it impossible to conceptualize the incest taboo outside the context of a phallocentric symbolic order. It emerges as the guarantee that the paternal legacy will be transmitted in an orderly way from father to son.

Although he is less concerned with phylogenesis than with the ontogenesis of the subject, Lacan also equates culture with the Name-of-the-Father. "In all strictness the Symbolic father is to be conceived as 'transcendent,' as an irreducible given of the signifier," he observes in his seminar of March/April, 1957.[52] He states the case even more forcefully in "Function and Field of Speech and Language in Psychoanalysis": "It is in the *name of the father* that we must recognize the support of the symbolic function which, from the dawn of history, has identified his person with the figure of the law."[53] Even Juliet Mitchell agrees with Lévi-Strauss and Lacan on this point. In her important pioneering introduction of feminism to psychoanalysis, she maintains that "the systematic exchange of women is definitional of human society."[54] She thereby suggests that the Name-of-the-Father is synonymous with culture.

Neither Lévi-Strauss, Freud, Lacan, nor Mitchell, however, adduces any structural imperative, analogous to the incest prohibition itself, which dictates that it be women rather than men—or both women and men—that circulate in this way, nor can such an imperative be found. We must consequently pry loose the incest prohibition from the Name-of-the-Father so as to insist, despite the paucity of historical evidence for doing so, that the Law of Kinship Structure is not necessarily phallic. As Rubin points out, "the 'exchange of women' is neither a definition of culture nor a system in and of itself" (176).

This is perhaps the moment to note that the kinship structure through which a particular symbolic order articulates the incest prohibition would also seem capable of determining the ideological signifiers through which lack is represented. The dominant fiction, in other words, would seem to interpret *manque-à-être* or the Law of Language in relation to the local form assumed by the Law of Kinship Structure. Such is at least the case within our dominant fiction, which conceptualizes the lack installed through language as the absence of the male sexual organ. It is of course Lacan who provides us with the fullest theoretical account not only of the Law of Language, but of its ideological imbrication with the phallus:

> . . . through his relationship to the signifier, the subject is deprived
> of something[:] of himself, of his very life, which has assumed the
> value of that which binds him to the signifier. The phallus is our
> term for the signifier of his alienation in signification. When the
> subject is deprived of this signifier, a particular object becomes for
> him an object of desire . . . .
>
> The object of desire is essentially different from the object of any
> need [*besoin*]. Something becomes an object of desire when it takes
> the place of what by its very nature remains concealed from the
> subject . . . that pound of flesh which is mortgaged [*engagé*] in his
> relationship to the signifier . . . [55]

Unfortunately, as this passage dramatizes, the phallus often emerges
within the Lacanian text as a universal signifier of desire, rather than
as the variable metaphor of an irreducible lack. It is often depicted,
in other words, as the obligatory unconscious representative of what
is lost to the subject with the entry into language, rather than as one
of a range of possible representatives. The theoretical model which
I am in the process of elaborating depends upon as scrupulous a
maintenance of the distinction between the Law of Language and its
ideological representation as of that separating the incest prohibition
from its specific elaboration.

 Earlier in this chapter, I suggested that the dominant fiction induces
in the subject a *méconnaissance* of the Laws of Language and Kinship
Structure—that it provides the imaginary facilitator whereby we
"live" those two Laws. However, I have not yet sufficiently elaborated
upon the differences between kinship and the family, and—by extension—the symbolic order and the dominant fiction. Here, again, I am
insisting upon a distinction which is not always sustained within my
theoretical sources. Freud reads the Oedipus complex directly off that
structure of kinship which he claims to be universal. In *Totem and
Taboo*, he maintains that in forbidding the killing of the totem and
relinquishing their claim to the father's women, the members of the
original horde "created out of their filial sense of guilt the two fundamental taboos of totemism, which for that very reason inevitably
corresponded to the two repressed wishes of the Oedipus complex"
(143). In making this argument, he assumes the coincidence of the
system of kinship with the human family. Rubin advances a similar
argument in "The Traffic in Women":

> Kinship systems require a division of the sexes. The Oedipal phase
> divides the sexes. Kinship systems include sets of rules governing
> sexuality. The Oedipal crisis is the assimilation of these rules and
> taboos. Compulsory heterosexuality is the product of kinship. The
> Oedipal phase constitutes heterosexual desire. Kinship rests on a

radical difference between the rights of men and women. The Oedipal complex confers male rights upon the boy, and forces the girl to accommodate herself to her lesser rights. (198)

In effect, then, Freud and Rubin equate not only kinship and the family, but the incest taboo and the Oedipus complex.

Lévi-Strauss, however, argues persuasively in "Language and the Analysis of Social Laws" that there can be no coincidence between kinship and the family. These categories cannot be conflated because kinship maps relations *between* rather than *within* families (49). It depends for that purpose upon *simultaneous* relations of descent, affinity, and consanguinity. Its minimal terms are consequently father, son, brother, and sister. The father/son relation inscribes descent, and the brother/sister relation consanguinity. Affinity is inscribed through the husband/wife relation, which is unnamed as such, but is implicit in the brother/sister relation. It is made possible by the brother's surrender of his sister for someone else's (43). (Lévi-Strauss explains that "the relationship between 'brothers-in-law' is the necessary axis around which the kinship structure is built," because its most fundamental principle is exchange [45].) The family, on the other hand— or what I prefer to call the *ideology* of the family—maps relations *within* the family, and its minimal terms are father, mother, and child. It articulates not only the legal, economic, and religious, but the *psychic* ties linking parents and child. As Lévi-Strauss emphasizes in *The View from Afar*,

1. The family originates in marriage.
2. It includes the husband, the wife, and the children born of their union.
3. The members of the family are united among themselves by:
   a. Legal bonds.
   b. Rights and obligations of an economic, a religious, or some other nature.
   c. A precise framework of sexual rights and prohibitions, and a variable and diversified group of feelings, such as love, affection, respect, fear, and so on.[56]

The ideology of the family defines the parents as privileged objects for desire and identification, and so works to eroticize precisely those relationships which kinship, in the guise of the incest prohibition, forbids. It promotes libidinal ties between brother and sister, and parents and children.

All of this is another way of indicating that whereas kinship revolves around the imposition of the incest taboo, the dominant fiction or ideology of the family functions to arouse in the subject conventional

Oedipal desires and identifications. The positive Oedipus complex is consequently the normative psychic response not to kinship, but to the dominant fiction. I am not of course suggesting that there is no relation between kinship and the family, or between the incest taboo and the Oedipus complex. On the contrary, the positive Oedipus complex provides the structure through which we "ideally" live our necessarily imaginary relation to kinship. The positive Oedipus complex functions, moreover, in ways that are only superficially at odds with our Law of Kinship Structure. We must remember that this Law consists not only of an invariable element, the incest taboo, but of a variable one, which is in our case the Name-of-the-Father. Whereas the eroticization of the field of family relations might seem to work against the imposition of the incest taboo, it is indispensable if the subject is to be subordinated to the Name-of-the-Father, since that subordination entails both sexual difference and heterosexuality. The libidinization of the son/mother and daughter/father relations works to guarantee that although the original object must be relinquished, it will provide the model for all subsequent object-choices.

But what, precisely, does it mean to suggest that the positive Oedipus complex provides the structure through which we "ideally" live our necessarily imaginary relation both to the variable and invariable elements of our particular Law of Kinship Structure? It means, first of all, that the incest taboo is lived as paternal prohibition and erotic displacement—as the necessity to substitute erotic objects outside the family for those within. The Name-of-the-Father is also lived by the boy as the paternal legacy which will be his if he renounces the mother, and identifies with the father. It is lived by the girl as the experience of anatomical and cultural "lack"; as a compensatory desire for the father and his surrogates; as a forced identification with a devalued mother; and as contempt for the other members of her own sex.

Although I have characterized the positive Oedipus complex as the result of a normative interpellation into the dominant fiction, it by no means represents the only possible psychic response to the ideology of the family. As subsequent chapters will demonstrate, the psyche can exceed the constraints of the positive Oedipus complex in a variety of ways. There is perhaps no subjectivity which does not escape the straitjacket of that complex to some degree, if only by simultaneously inhabiting its negative counterpart. It is consequently necessary to hold at some theoretical distance from each other not only the Name-of-the-Father and the symbolic order, the symbolic order and the dominant fiction, the dominant fiction and the Oedipus complex, but the Oedipus complex and the psyche.

There are enormous theoretical advantages to be gained from maintaining these distinctions. To insist upon the non-equivalence of the Name-of-the-Father and the symbolic order is to isolate what is irreducible about the second of those categories from what is purely provisional—to separate the Laws of Language and Kinship Structure from their variable articulation. It is thus to grasp both what can and what cannot be changed within our present symbolic order.

In extricating the symbolic order from its conventional cultural representation, we expose the arbitrariness of the particular form assumed by our Law of Kinship, which the dominant fiction generally works to soften and rationalize. We also come to understand not only that the subject lives its relation to the symbolic at the level of the imaginary, through identification and fantasy, but that it is only through those particular identifications and fantasies which are commensurate with ideological belief that this relation is "exemplary," i.e. that the subject is accommodated to the Name-of-the-Father. We are then in a position to see that the dominant fiction and the symbolic order exist in a relation of mutual determination, and that by withholding our belief from the dominant fiction we at the same time jeopardize all that is variable about our symbolic order.

It is more difficult to sustain the distinction between the dominant fiction and the positive Oedipus complex, but it is nevertheless crucial that we grasp the latter as the psychic consequence of a conventional interpellation into the former. Doing so will help us to remember that the positive Oedipus complex represents the primary vehicle through which the subject affirms the "reality" of the family and the phallus, as well as the other ideological elements with which they are intertwined. It provides, in other words, a crucial reminder of the psychic mechanisms through which the dominant fiction solicits our belief.

Finally, holding the psyche at a conceptual remove from the positive Oedipus complex permits us to understand that there are subjectivities which have established a different relation to the family—and, in some cases, even to the Laws of Language and Kinship Structure—than those valorized by the dominant fiction. For these subjectivities, as we will see, psychic reality has a different consistency than that dictated by the dominant fiction. The desires and identifications through which they are constituted may even sustain a disjunctive or oppositional relation to the *vraisemblance*.

I want to emphasize once again that the dominant fiction not only offers the representational system by means of which the subject typically assumes a sexual identity, and takes on the desires commensurate with that identity, but forms the stable core around which a nation's and a period's "reality" coheres. Other ideologies compel belief by articulating themselves in relation to it, since it imparts the illusion of reality to whatever comes into close proximity with it. Because of the interarticulation of the core elements of the dominant fiction with elements drawn from the ideologies of class, race, ethnicity, and gender, the dominant fiction might be said to negotiate between the symbolic order and the mode of production—to be that which permits two very different forms of determination to be lived simultaneously. Finally, the dominant fiction presents the social formation with its most fundamental image of unity, the family. The collectivities of community, town, and nation have all traditionally defined themselves through reference to that image.

5. The Dominant Fiction and the Phallus

It is imperative that we understand that when the Name-of-the-Father organizes the rules determining marriage, reproduction, lineality, abode, and inheritance, the Law of Kinship Structure exists in a contradictory relationship to the Law of Language. The Law of Language dictates universal castration, whereas our Law of Kinship Structure equates the father with the Law, and hence exempts him from it. Our dominant fiction effects an imaginary resolution of this contradiction by radically reconceiving what it means to be castrated.

When I say "imaginary resolution," I mean to suggest not only that it is fictive, and that it involves the production of images, but that it turns upon *méconnaissance.* Our dominant fiction calls upon the male subject to see himself, and the female subject to recognize and desire him, only through the mediation of images of an unimpaired masculinity. It urges both the male and the female subject, that is, to deny all knowledge of male castration by believing in the commensurability of penis and phallus, actual and symbolic father.

By way of showing that this belief is less an effect of consciousness than of identification and fantasy, I want to quote a lengthy passage which simultaneously acknowledges and dramatizes the misrecognition upon which masculinity is founded. This passage, which is taken from an interview with Serge Leclaire on the ostensible topic of homosexuality, entertains an intimate relationship with some of the passages I quoted earlier from Lacan—passages in which Lacan equates the Name-of-the-Father with the symbolic order, and characterizes the phallus as a historically transcendent signifier of desire. Including it here will consequently have the additional advantage of permitting me to specify more precisely the points at which it is necessary to go beyond Lacan's account of symbolic castration:

> Let us call the phallus "God." It's an old tradition. You don't have to see "God," properly speaking, you have no image of him. "God" (the phallus) is invisible; therefore, the relation to the phallus is marked by a nonformalizable relation, a relation of exclusion. At the same time, everything is in relation to the phallus; everything is in relation to "God." Let's suppose that there is a child, Jesus, the son of God, who serves as mediator. Now, let's replace the "child Jesus" with the penis, which happens to be the most convenient representative of the phallus. Because man has in his body a relation with his *penis as the representative of the phallus*, schematically, his natural inclination leads him to forget the fact that the phallus ("God") is invisible, unseizable, unnameable. But woman does not have this representative in her body; therefore, her relation to the phallus is less veiled. She is less tempted to forget the fact that the phallus is absent. Consequently, man's and woman's relations to castration are profoundly different. I am referring to castration as the relation to the phallus, to the Invisible, to an unnameable term. In Lacanian language I would say that it is both signifier and object . . . In the whole evolution and history of woman, nothing has ever come as a screen between the invisible "God," phallus, and the way she speaks. For man, the possession of the penis, which is highly cathected, serves as a screen denying the fundamental character of castration. Man comes to believe that he has not been castrated.[57]

Unlike Freud, Leclaire is quick in this passage to concede that the male subject is as scarred by lack as his female counterpart. He also emphasizes the delusory nature of conventional masculinity—its reliance upon anatomy as a safeguard against castration. In so doing, he seems almost to encourage a feminist analysis of the relationship between the Name-of-the-Father and the Law of Language. Yet as if to illustrate the fact that ideological belief is exterior to consciousness, the rest of the passage enacts an astonishing obfuscation both of the phallus/penis relationship, and of the process whereby the male subject is inducted into *méconnaissance*.

The passage is, to begin with, structured around a major internal contradiction. Its entire argument rests upon the assertion that the phallus cannot be seen, grasped, or named—that it is, in short, *unrepresentable*. However, the penis (which *can* be seen, grasped, and named) is described as both "the most convenient representative of the phallus," and as the latter's incarnation or "son." The relation between the phallus and the penis is thus totally mystified; it seems at the same time miraculous (i.e. beyond rational or secular explanation) and natural (i.e. biologically or ontologically motivated). In either case the relation seems to escape ideological determination. We are told that it just "happens to be."

A similar refusal to admit that the phallus/penis equation might be in any way ideologically circumscribed is evident both in Leclaire's subsequent claim that "man *comes to believe* that he has not been castrated" (in the inference, that is, that this perception is entirely spontaneous), and in his sweeping generalization that "in the whole evolution and history of woman, nothing has ever come as a screen between the invisible 'God,' phallus, and the way she speaks." Sexual difference and the signifiers of paternity are situated in a space beyond ideological causation or political intervention—in a sacred time. The overriding theological metaphor not only contributes heavily to this sense of changelessness, but helps to soften the passage's contradictions into paradox.

Finally, while Leclaire candidly admits that *méconnaissance* motivates the male subject's phallic identification, he never stops to consider what this might cost the female subject. He avoids the necessity of addressing the political consequences of sexual difference by defining the phallus merely as a signifier of what is lost with the entry into language, thereby shearing off its reference to power and privilege. However, once again the theological analogy reveals that more is at issue here than the metaphorization of "being," since that analogy turns upon the question of how best to give representational consistency to what would otherwise remain an abstract theological signifier, i.e. the Name-of-the-Father.

The present discussion shares with Leclaire the assumption that classic male subjectivity rests upon the denial of castration. However, I am concerned in a way that he is not with the consequences for the female subject of this lived relation to the Law of Language. It also seems to me crucial that we understand the ideological bases of the conventional male subject's self-recognition-misrecognition, for far from belonging to a kind of "sacred time," beyond the vicissitudes of ideology and history, the phallus/penis equation is promoted by the dominant fiction, and sustained by collective belief. Moreover, whereas within the Althusserian model belief involves only *one* form of *méconnaissance*, here it requires the support of two others, neither of which represents an immutable condition of subjectivity.

Interpellation provides the model for theorizing the first kind of *méconnaissance* necessary to the maintenance of phallic identification. If we extend the Althusserian paradigm from the domain of Christianity to that of sexual difference, as he encourages us to do, we can see that the latter depends upon a similar process of captation to the former. Like the religious system about which Althusser writes, the dominant fiction offers a seemingly infinite supply of phallic sounds and images within which the male subject can find "himself." There is, however, at least one respect in which this captation differs from that afforded by Christianity: it promotes the fiction of an *ideal ego*. In so doing, it rationalizes man's relation to the Name-of-the-Father, and covers over the lack upon which his access to language depends.

We must turn to Freud in order to identify the other two forms of *méconnaissance* so crucial to belief in the phallus/penis equation. His writings on the psychical implications of the anatomical distinction between the sexes activate another of the French meanings of that crucial Lacanian concept, since they reveal male subjectivity to hinge not only upon a misrecognition, but upon a "failure to recognize." This "failure to recognize" can take two forms, depending upon its object; it can pertain either to the self or the other. The subject classically refuses to recognize an unwanted feature of the *self* by projecting it onto the other, i.e. by relocating it.[58] He or she refuses to recognize an unpleasurable or anxiety-inducing aspect of the *other* by disavowing it, a process which sometimes requires the support of a fetish.

For Freud, disavowal is a typically male defense, which comes into play in the founding drama of sexual difference—the "discovery," on the part of the boy and girl, of anatomical "otherness." Through it, the boy protects himself against the destabilizing knowledge of female castration.[59] However, as is perhaps best revealed by the rhetorical slippage between "glance at the nose" and "shine on the nose" in Freud's essay on fetishism, sexual difference is unthinkable apart from the externalizing displacement of *male castration* onto the *female subject*. The case of the male patient which provides the essay's central example hinges not only upon fetishism, but upon projection, and the latter is shown to be temporally prior to the former. The case in question revolves around a curious fetish—upon the necessity that there be a "shine" or "*glanz*" on the nose of the female erotic object. This "*glanz*" reveals itself on analysis to be the product of a cross-language wordplay. By means of a homonymic translation from English to German, the patient's glance away from the female genitals to the female nose at the initial moment of anatomical revelation is transmuted into the desired "shine" on the love-object's nose, which then functions as the fetish enabling sexual union (152–53).

However, by focusing exclusively on the formation of the fetish, Freud neglects to note that in the transformation of the glance into the shine something is transferred from the male patient to the female subject. In this particular story, that "something" can perhaps best be described as the "flash" of a "wounded" or distraught male look, but Freud's other examples of masculine fetishes encourage us to read that look as the signifier of a more generalized castration—of the sacrifice exacted by language, and subsquently compounded in all kinds of ways by history. Those examples suggest, in other words, that female subjectivity represents the site at which the male subject deposits his lack.[60]

One of those fetishes is an athletic support belt, which covers up the genitals, and so erases all evidence of anatomical difference. Freud writes that this item of clothing not only signifies at the same time "that women [are] castrated and that they [are] not castrated," but "allow[s] of the hypothesis that men [are] castrated, for all these possibilities [can] equally well be concealed under the belt" (156–57). The other example of male fetishism cited by Freud is the Chinese custom of foot-binding. He remarks that implicit in the reverence of the traditional Chinese man for this fetish is his gratitude to the Chinese woman for "permitting" herself to be mutilated. "It seems as though the Chinese male wants to thank the woman for having submitted to being castrated," Freud adds, thereby making clear that the castration which is synonymous with sexual difference is not endemic to the female body, but is emblazoned across it by the male subject through projection. These examples, like that with which the essay on "Fetishism" begins, indicate that conventional masculinity can best be understood as the denial of castration, and hence as a refusal to acknowledge the defining limits of subjectivity. The category of "femininity" is to a very large degree the result.

As we will see, disavowal also has a crucial part to play within the constitution and maintenance of sexual difference. However, whereas the Freudian account of that psychic mechanism explicitly posits it as a male defense against *female* lack, "Fetishism" implicitly shows it to be a defense against what is in the final analysis *male* lack. Since woman's anatomical "wound" is the product of an externalizing displacement of masculine insufficiency, which is then biologically naturalized, the castration against which the male subject protects himself through disavowal and fetishism must be primarily his own. Significantly, Freud himself broadens the concept of disavowal to include as one of its meanings the repudiation of something specific to the subject's own self in "Some Psychical Consequences," although he relies upon a female rather than a male example in doing so. It is, moreover, precisely upon castration that this disavowal is shown to turn. In that 1925 essay, he suggests that the little girl sometimes refuses to accept her anatomical "lack," and "harden[s] herself in the conviction that she *does* possess a penis" (253).

Some of the cinematic texts which will provide my primary focus in the next chapter suggest that there is yet another way in which disavowal comes into play in sexual difference. Those texts show that the "ideal" female subject refuses to recognize male lack, and that disavowal and fetishism provide important mechanisms for effecting this refusal. Indeed, traditional masculinity emerges there as a fetish for covering over the castration upon which male subjectivity is grounded. Those texts also indicate that insofar as the female subject's recourse to disavowal and fetishism can be characterized as "pathological," that pathology must be attributed to the dominant fiction, for we are dealing here with an ideologically induced phenomenon. Films like *Pride of the Marines* (1945), *It's a Wonderful Life* (1946), and—most particularly—*The Guilt of Janet Ames* (1947) summon the female subject to uphold the male subject in his phallic identification by seeing him with her "imagination" rather than with her eyes.

It is imperative that belief in the penis/phallus equation be fortified in the ways that I have just outlined, for it represents the most vulnerable component of the dominant fiction. The male subject's identification with power and privilege is threatened from many directions. It is under siege, first of all, from the Law of Language, to which no fully constituted subject is immune. Projection is a tenuous barrier against this Law, since what has been cast violently away will continue to threaten from without. Oppression experienced in relation to class, race, ethnicity, age, and other ideologically determined "handicaps" may also pose major obstacles in the way of a phallic identification, or may expose masculinity as a masquerade. Finally, history may manifest itself in so traumatic and unassimilable a guise that it temporarily dislocates penis from phallus, or renders null and void the other elements of the dominant fiction with which it is closely imbricated.

Although the family and the phallus constitute the core elements of our dominant fiction, they exist in the closest possible intimacy with many other signifying and representational elements, including those privileged by Laclau and Rancière. Some of these elements, like Christianity, contribute importantly to the definition of the dominant fiction's central terms. Others derive from the ideologies of class, race, ethnicity, gender, and nation, but have come for a time to share the "reality-effect" of sexual difference and the family. Whenever the interarticulation of the primary and secondary elements of the dominant fiction has been particularly successful, a loss of belief in the secondary elements can precipitate a crisis in the primary ones. However, the withdrawal of belief from the core components will *always* jeopardize not only the particular form assumed by the Law of Kinship Structure, but the coherence of the larger social formation. The survival of our whole "world," then, depends upon the preservation of two interlocking terms: the family, and the phallus.

6. Contesting the Dominant Fiction

The reader is no doubt wondering why there has been until now no discussion of the strategies by which the members of a culture might actively intervene in the formation and deformation of the dominant fiction. Is there no concept, analogous to class struggle, by means of which we could theorize the possibility of transforming the ideological system through which we live our relation to the symbolic order, and possibly even the culturally and historically variable elements of that order itself? This is an exceedingly difficult question, to which I can provide only the most tentative and partial of answers.

Let us begin by stressing that the dominant fiction doesn't exist in the abstract. Although I have defined it as a reservoir of sounds, images, and narratives, it has no concrete existence apart from discursive practice and its psychic residue. If representation and signification constitute the site at which the dominant fiction comes into existence, then they would also seem to provide the necessary vehicle for ideological contestation—the medium through which to reconstruct both our "reality" and "ourselves." However, even as I emphasize the capacity of discursive practice to challenge and transform the dominant fiction, I must acknowledge the existence of powerful constraints.

A number of forces conspire against a permanent withdrawal of collective belief from our current dominant fiction. We must reckon, first of all, with the conservatism of the psyche—with its allegiance to the past. Once again I feel impelled to emphasize that ideological belief operates at a level exterior to consciousness, and that the subject can continue to "recognize" itself and its desires within certain kinds of sounds, images, and narrative paradigms long after consciously repudiating them. I am not arguing that every unconscious is organized according to the positive Oedipus complex, nor that every *moi* is the simple product of a normative familial interpellation. Indeed, one of the major premises of this book is that there can be other kinds of subjectivity than those promoted by the dominant fiction. However, I am proposing that there is no subject whose identity and desires have not been shaped *to some degree* by it.

The dominant fiction also derives support from other ideologies. I suggested earlier in this chapter that this ideological system doesn't necessarily serve vested class, racial, or ethnic interests, but that it can be put to other uses. I also proposed that the struggle over access to the dominant fiction's "belief-effect" constitutes the primary form of ideological conflict. Unfortunately, what this means is that a whole host of competing ideologies join forces with respect to one task—the need to preserve the core elements through which belief can be conjured. There are of course ideologies, most notably some operating under the banners of feminism, Marxism, and gay sexuality, which stand outside this struggle, and indeed criticize it, but such a stand is widely—and correctly—perceived to be a tremendous liability. These ideologies are perceived as posing a threat to everything that is most "true" and "real" for the majority of people—as threatening the very "universe" in which they believe.

The dominant fiction or ideology of the family also has economic determinants. Although Juliet Mitchell finds the family redundant within capitalism (411), other Marxist feminists maintain that it plays an important role within that mode of production. Annette Kuhn, for instance, argues that the property relations specific to capital are inscribed not only into the wage form, but into the legal definition of "the marriage relationship":

> . . . a sexual division of labor has a specific effectivity in capitalism . . . mapping itself onto the spatial separation of the site of production of use values (home and family) and that of the immediate production of exchange values (work-place). . . . The patriarchal relations implied in a social/sexual division of labor and in the appropriation of women's labor by men within the family are "worked on" by the forces of capital and re-emerge at each conjuncture as particular forms of social relations.[61]

Kuhn adds that even when women work outside the home, their economic status is defined by their position within the family. Roisin McDonough and Rachel Harrison insist that it is within the family that capitalism reproduces its relations of production.[62] Michèle Barrett makes the same point at greater length; she coins the phrase "family-household system" to refer to the institution of the family, which she sees both as the site for the ideological construction of gender, and as "an important organizing principle of the relations of production of the social formation as a whole" (211). While certain of the functions isolated by these feminists are clearly performed by the dominant fiction, others would seem more an effect of the actual family. However, even the latter are ideologically rationalized and perpetuated. Capitalism would thus seem to "need" the dominant fiction, or—to state the matter more precisely—to constitute one of the important forces sustaining it.

Finally, we come to the symbolic order itself, prime determinant of the dominant fiction. What is at issue here, as we have seen, is less the Laws of Language and Kinship Structure than their particular disposition. It is primarily in the guise of the written and unwritten laws which confer primacy upon the Name-of-the-Father—or, to state the case slightly differently, which dictate that it be men rather than women who constitute society's producers and representatives—that our symbolic order militates against change within the dominant fiction. The current status of affirmative action and abortion in the United States reveals only too clearly how difficult it is to alter these laws in any long-term way.

This last set of constraints may seem absolutely insuperable. However, we must remember that although the symbolic order determines to a significant degree the form which the dominant fiction can take, its survival is nevertheless keyed to that ideological system, which depends in turn upon collective belief. A given symbolic order will remain in place only so long as it has subjects, but it cannot by itself produce them. It relies for that purpose upon the dominant fiction, which works to bring the subject into conformity with the symbolic order by fostering normative desires and identifications. When the dominant fiction fails to effect this interpellation, it is not only "reality," but the symbolic order itself which is placed at risk.

It would consequently be as much of a mistake to assume that our transformative energies should be channeled exclusively in the direction of the symbolic order as to assume that economic battles are the only ones worth fighting. The ideology of sexual difference and the family must remain a crucial site of political struggle, even in the face of the opposing forces I have just enumerated. The moment has come, however, to reframe the terms of that struggle. Rather than seeking access for all subjects to an illusory "wholeness," we need to work at the level of representation and theory to renegotiate our relationship to the Law of Language, and thereby to challenge the dominant fiction at its most vulnerable and yet most critical site: the phallus.

What, precisely, would such a renegotiation entail? It would require that we collectively acknowledge, at the deepest level of our psyches, that our desires and our identity come to us from outside, and that they are founded upon a void. It would involve, as Julia Kristeva suggests, interiorizing *"the founding separation of the socio-symbolic contract"*— introducing "its cutting edge into the very interior of every identity."[63] Renegotiating our relation to the Law of Language would thus seem to hinge first and foremost upon the confrontation of the male subject with the defining conditions of all subjectivity, conditions which the female subject is obliged compulsively to reenact, but upon the denial of which traditional masculinity is predicated: lack, specularity, and alterity. It would seem to necessitate, in other words, dismantling the images and undoing the projections and disavowals through which phallic identification is enabled. This is one of the projects to which *Male Subjectivity at the Margins* is dedicated.

The next chapter will offer a fuller exploration and a more vivid dramatization of the issues which have been raised here. It will examine three films made in Hollywood in the 1940s, all of which attest to a radical loss of belief in the conventional premises of masculinity. I will attribute this crisis of faith to the historical trauma of World War II and the immediate postwar situation. I will at the same time attempt to demonstrate the larger ideological ramifications of the loss of belief in the commensurability of penis and phallus. Finally, the three films in question—*The Best Years of Our Lives, It's a Wonderful Life,* and *The Guilt of Janet Ames*—will provide the occasion for a lengthier analysis of projection, disavowal, and fetishism, and of the role they play within the constitution of "exemplary" male subjectivity.

2

Historical Trauma and Male Subjectivity

The male subject's aspirations to mastery and sufficiency are undermined from many directions—by the Law of Language, which founds subjectivity on a void; by the castration crisis; by sexual, economic, and racial oppression; and by the traumatically unassimilable nature of certain historical events. It has only been very recently that yet another threat has come into play in a politically organized way—that constituted through the representational and sexual practices of feminism and gay liberation. It has, however, been implicit all along, for there have always been individual men who have embraced lack at the level of their unconscious fantasies and identities, and individual women for whom the phallus has not been the signifier of desire. Although subsequent chapters will address some of these libidinal challenges and refusals, my primary concern in this chapter will be to trace the consequences for masculinity of a particular historical upheaval—that of World War II and the recovery period.

A number of films made in Hollywood between 1944 and 1947 attest with unusual candor to the castrations through which the male subject is constituted—to the pound of flesh which is his price of entry into the symbolic order, as well as to the other losses that punctuate his history. *Pride of the Marines* (1945), *Hail the Conquering Hero* (1944), *State Fair* (1945), *Those Enduring Young Charms* (1945), *Lost Weekend* (1945), *The Guilt of Janet Ames* (1947), *Spellbound* (1945), *It's a Wonderful Life* (1946), *Gilda* (1946), and *The Best Years of Our Lives* (1946) all speak in some way to the failure of the paternal function. Moreover, in order to shore up the ruins of masculinity, many of these films are obliged to confer upon a female character the narrative agency which is the usual attribute of a male character, thereby further undermining sexual difference. As a contemporary viewer remarked, "The first thing one has to note about all these films is that the old descriptive term—'boy gets girl'—no longer fits. In *Lost Weekend*, it is the heroine, not the hero who gives the kisses. . . . In *Spellbound* it is *she* who walks into *his* room in the middle of the night. . . . In *Pride of the Marines*, when letters and telephone calls get her nowhere, the heroine resorts to abducting the hero 'bodily' home, there in the face even of his desperate 'Get me out of here!' to insist that they shall be married."[1] Not surprisingly, given their preoccupation with male lack, these films are also characterized by a loss of faith in the familiar and self-evident. The hero no longer feels "at home" in the house or town where he grew up, and resists cultural (re)assimilation; he has been dislodged from the narratives and subject-positions which make up the dominant fiction, and he returns to them only under duress.

About half the films I have just enumerated explicitly attribute the crisis of male subjectivity to the cataclysmic events of the 1940s. In *Pride of the Marines*, *Lost Weekend*, *The Best Years of Our Lives*, and *The Guilt of Janet Ames*, the "hero" returns from World War II with a physical or psychic wound which marks him as somehow deficient, and which renders him incapable of functioning smoothly in civilian life. Sometimes the veteran also finds himself strangely superfluous to the society he ostensibly protected during the war; his functions have been assumed by other men, or—much more disturbingly—by women. These texts thus dramatize the vulnerability of conventional masculinity and the larger dominant fiction to what I will call "historical trauma."

This chapter will discuss three films made during this period, films which adopt very different attitudes toward male castration: *The Best Years of Our Lives*, *It's a Wonderful Life*, and *The Guilt of Janet Ames*. *The Best Years of Our Lives* represents the most extreme and dislocated of these three texts. Its three central male characters, all veterans of World War II, are so scarred by lack that they are incapable of effecting a reentry into the dominant fiction. However, rather than working in any way to neutralize this dangerous situation, *The Best Years of Our Lives* focuses obsessively and at times erotically on the physical and psychic mutilation of the three veterans, whom it explicitly associates with "junk." *It's a Wonderful Life* also emphasizes male castration at the expense of the dominant fiction. Indeed, it shows sacrifice to be the inevitable price of all subjectivity. Only by calling in "heavenly" reinforcements, and by depicting masculine suffering as the prelude to a divine legacy, is the film finally able to convert its hero's social, economic and psychic losses into cultural gains. *The Guilt of Janet Ames* attributes male insufficiency not only to the war, but to the collapse of traditional gender divisions on the home front demanded by the war effort—a collapse for which it holds the female subject responsible. It moves relentlessly toward the reaffirmation of the sexual status quo, but the machinery of that reaffirmation is rusty, and its workings "show." *The Guilt of Janet Ames* thus renders unusually transparent the defensive mechanisms necessary for the construction of an "exemplary" masculinity.[2]

Despite their differing attitudes toward male lack, all three of these films attest to the unraveling of America's "reality" in the mid-forties. Indeed, each is characterized by "ideological fatigue"[3]—by a loss of belief not only in the adequacy of the male subject, but in the family and small-town life. They thus vividly dramatize the centrality of the penis/phallus equation to the survival of our "world." *The Best Years of Our Lives* further signals the crisis of faith in the dominant fiction by making a self-conscious departure from many of the standard representational practices of classic cinema. Although *It's a Wonderful Life* and *The Guilt of Janet Ames* ultimately work to reconfirm the dominant fiction, they, too, must break with certain Hollywood conventions in order to do so.[4]

1. History, Dominant Fiction, and Social Formation

The textual analyses that follow will rely heavily upon two theoretical categories—dominant fiction and historical trauma. "Dominant fiction" is opposed here neither to an ultimately recoverable reality, nor to the condition of "true" consciousness. "Fiction" underscores the *imaginary* rather than the delusory nature of ideology, while "dominant" isolates from the whole repertoire of a culture's images, sounds, and narrative elaborations those through which the conventional subject is psychically aligned with the symbolic order.

But the dominant fiction is more than the ideological system through which the normative subject lives its imaginary relation to the symbolic order. It is also informed by what Ernesto Laclau calls a "will to 'totality'"; it is the mechanism by which a society "tries to institute itself as such on the basis of closure, of the fixation of meaning, of the non-recognition of the infinite play of differences."[5] The dominant fiction neutralizes the contradictions which organize the social formation by fostering collective identifications and desires, identifications and desires which have a range of effects, but which are first and foremost constitutive of sexual difference. Social formations consequently depend upon their dominant fictions for their sense of unity and identity. Social formations also rely for their continued survival upon the dominant fiction; both the symbolic order and the mode of production are able to protect themselves from interruption and potential change only so long as that ideological system commands collective belief—so long, that is, as it succeeds in defining the psychic reality of the prototypical subject.

My second theoretical category, "historical trauma," may seem something of an oxymoron, since it uses an adjective connotative of the public sphere to qualify a noun conventionally associated with the psychic or physiological shock suffered by an individual person. I am, however, relying upon that phrase to describe something which exceeds our usual categories. By "historical trauma" I mean a historically precipitated but psychoanalytically specific disruption, with ramifications extending far beyond the individual psyche. To state the case more precisely, I mean any historical event, whether socially engineered or of natural occurrence, which brings a large group of male subjects into such an intimate relation with lack that they are at least for the moment unable to sustain an imaginary relation with the phallus, and so withdraw their belief from the dominant fiction. Suddenly the latter is radically de-realized, and the social formation finds itself without a mechanism for achieving consensus.

Since Fredric Jameson has also theorized history as a force capable of inflicting injury, it would seem crucial to pause for a moment in order to clarify the relationship between his argument and my own. In *The Political Unconscious*, Jameson describes history as what "hurts"—as "what refuses desire and sets inexorable limits to individual as well as collective praxis, which its 'ruses' turn into grisly and ironic reversals of their overt intention."[6] He attributes the painful or constraining qualities of history primarily to what he calls the "Necessity" of the political unconscious—to the great master narrative which moves us inexorably toward its predestined conclusion, whether we want to go there or not.

Although I, too, am interested in the notion of historical hurt, my theoretical paradigm does not depend upon either a master narrative or an immanent Necessity. The notion of historical trauma represents rather an attempt to conceptualize how history sometimes manages to *interrupt* or even *deconstitute* what a society assumes to be its master narratives and immanent Necessity—to undo our imaginary relation to the symbolic order, as well as to the other elements within the social formation with which that order is imbricated. Let us turn, in our search for a conceptual model capable of accounting both for the social dimensions and the psychoanalytic specificity of historical trauma, to the three texts in which Freud discusses the psychic causes and consequences of war: *Beyond the Pleasure Principle* (1920), "Introduction to *Psycho-Analysis and the War Neuroses*" (1919), and "Why War?" (1933).

Freud conceives of the psychic consequences of war primarily in terms of what he calls "war trauma." At its most manifest level, *Beyond the Pleasure Principle* represents war trauma as a wound or effraction resulting from the exposure of an unprepared psyche to a powerful excitation or "shock." Freud attempts to literalize this concept of a wound, which derives from the pathological definition of trauma, as a break in the cortical layer protecting the psyche against excessive external stimuli. As a consequence of the breach, the mental apparatus is "flooded" with excitation, and its "binding" mechanisms are overwhelmed.[7]

The passages in which Freud puts forward this model encourage us to understand war trauma as an *internal* response to an *external* danger.[8] That external danger is the force of destruction marshaled by war, or to state the case somewhat differently, the social orchestration of mass death. Insofar as the death drive comes into play—and Freud does not hesitate to propose it as the psychic basis for the violence of battle—it would thus seem to do so in a dramatically exteriorized form. The soldier venturing into combat is exposed to the death drive of the Other.

In "Introduction to *Psycho-Analysis and the War Neuroses*," however, Freud wonders whether the excitations responsible for war trauma have a strictly exterior origin; he questions, that is, whether this particular variety of traumatic neurosis does not proceed in some way from "a conflict between the ego and the sexual instincts which it repudiates,"[9] as do other related neuroses. As if pursuing a similar train of thought, Freud compares war trauma to hysteria in *Beyond the Pleasure Principle*, suggesting not only that it exhibits a similar "wealth" of "motor symptoms" (12), but that its victims suffer "mainly from reminiscences" (13).[10] In so doing, he implicitly invokes a model of trauma which hinges upon an internal as well as an external stimulus.[11] Danger would consequently seem to threaten both from the inside and the outside.

Another passage from the same text forecloses even more decisively upon the notion that trauma involves a strictly exterior threat; trauma's perceptual unpleasure is seen to derive either from the conflict between the ego and a repressed wish, or the ego and an external perception which elicits a repressed wish.[12] Again, the enemy dwells within as well as without:

> [Perceptual unpleasure] may be perception of pressure by unsatisfied instincts; or it may be external perception which is either distressing in itself or which excites unpleasurable expectations in the mental apparatus—that is, which is recognized by it as a "danger." (11)

But although *Beyond the Pleasure Principle* continues in the pages that follow to complicate the notion that trauma could ever be the simple result of a psychic response to an exterior stimulus, it also moves increasingly away from the notion of wish-fulfillment. It obliges us to read war trauma in relation not to a repressed desire or thwarted pleasure principle, but to a force which is *beyond* the pleasure principle. In order to establish that relation, and thereby to get at the heart of the historical trauma to which *The Best Years of Our Lives, It's a Wonderful Life* and *The Guilt of of Janet Ames* are a response, we must pay greater attention to the examples through which Freud illustrates this force than he himself does, for this "beyond the pleasure principle" ultimately eludes the theoretical formulation which he advances.

Freud implies that the subject suffering from a war neurosis constantly relives his traumatic experiences as a way of binding those experiences, and so of integrating them harmoniously into his psychic organization. Similarly, he suggests, the child in the *"fort/da"* story reenacts his mother's departures in order to tame the unpleasure they evoke through symbolic and linguistic repetition. Mastery is at the heart of both of these formulations; in each instance, the male subject—and he is manifestly a *male* subject—renegotiates his relation to an event by shifting from a passive to an active position. As Freud notes with respect to his grandson, "At the outset he was in a *passive* situation—he was overpowered by the experience; but, by repeating it, unpleasurable though it was, as a game, he took on an *active* part. These efforts might be put down to an instinct for mastery . . . " (16).[13]

What Freud here calls "an instinct for mastery" is what he will subsequently identify as the "beyond the pleasure principle." He gives it primacy over the pleasure principle because it represents the latter's precondition—because it prepares the mental apparatus for the elimination of an excitation "in the pleasure of discharge" by binding that excitation (62). Curiously, however, Freud insists upon the "compulsive" nature of this repetitive force, a characterization which runs directly counter to the notion of mastery; indeed, the examples which he cites in the same passage all hinge not only upon an involuntary, but upon a *passive* "'recurrence of the same thing.'" "There is the case," Freud writes, "of the woman who married three successive husbands each of whom fell ill soon afterwards and had to be nursed by her on their death beds." He adds that "the most moving picture of a fate such as this is given by Tasso in his romantic epic *Gerusalemme Liberata*. Its hero, Tancred, unwittingly kills his beloved Clorinda in a duel while she is disguised in the armor of an enemy knight. After her burial he makes his way into a strange magic forest . . . He slashes with his sword at a tall tree; but blood streams from the cut and the voice of Clorinda . . . is heard complaining that he has wounded his beloved once again" (22).

Freud's emphasis upon the compulsory and instinctual nature of the "beyond the pleasure principle" also seems at odds with his claim that it represents "cultural achievement" and the renunication of instinct (15), a claim which he makes in the process of discussing the *fort/da* game. Finally, in those sections of *Beyond the Pleasure Principle* which are given over to a discussion of the drives there is no mention of an "instinct for mastery."[14] In fact, Freud explicitly associates the instincts with *unbound* energy, and counterposes them to the "higher strata of the mental apparatus," to which he attributes the control achieved through binding (34–35).

Although the later sections of *Beyond the Pleasure Principle* do not bring the drives into a theoretical alignment with mastery, they do nevertheless link the death drive with the compulsion to repeat. Indeed, that drive is so exclusively defined through its insistence upon a recurrence of the same that it increasingly looks like the "beyond the pleasure principle" for which Freud is looking. Finding an instinctual basis for compulsory repetition, however, only further erodes the connection between it and mastery. The death drive seeks to reduce the organism once again to nothingness, and so poses a radical challenge to the organization of the psyche. If repetition is indeed to be located at the level of the drive, then it must be understood to subvert rather than to consolidate control.

But although the death drive increasingly emerges over the course of *Beyond the Pleasure Principle* as the motivating force behind war trauma and other instances of involuntary and immobilizing repetition, Freud does not sufficiently distinguish it from other kinds of psychic recurrence. Indeed, he at times unwittingly conflates it with forms of repetition to which it is completely antipathetic. Let us attempt to differentiate the death drive from these other types of repetition so as to arrive at a clearer understanding of the role that it plays within historical trauma, and its subset, war trauma.

First, although the death drive often makes itself felt at the level of desire,[15] there is obviously no one-to-one relation between it and that variety of repetition which results from the "fantasmatic" or "stereotype plate,"[16] i.e. from the unconscious fantasy which informs dreams, daydreams, and object-choice. There is no absolute connection, in other words, between the death drive and the scenario or tableau through which desire is articulated. The death drive must also be sharply distinguished from another principle of psychic "sameness," the ego; Freud associates the ego with psychic binding, and the death drive with a radical unbinding.[17] Finally, the death drive must be rigorously differentiated from the repetition which leads to mastery. The death drive can perhaps best be defined as the compulsion to repeat experiences of an overwhelming and incapacitating sort—experiences which render the subject hyperbolically passive. Mastery, on the other hand, results when those same experiences are *actively* repeated—when they are linguistically rather than affectively reprised.

I do not want, however, to effect too extreme a theoretical cleavage between these last two categories. Although mastery and the death drive could not be more antipathetic to each other, they nonetheless coexist in a strangely intimate manner. In the one passage from *Beyond the Pleasure Principle* in which Freud explicitly differentiates between those two phenomena, he also suggests that one can build upon the other. "The manifestations of a compulsion to repeat," Freud writes,

> (which we have described as occurring in the early activities of infantile mental life as well as among the events of psycho-analytic treatment) exhibit to a high degree the instinctual character and, when they act in opposition to the pleasure principle, give the appearance of some "daemonic" force at work. In the case of children's play we seemed to see that children repeat unpleasurable experiences for the *additional* reason that they can master a powerful impression far more thoroughly by being active than they could by merely experiencing it passively. Each fresh repetition seems to strengthen the mastery they are in search of. (35; my emphasis)

Freud here attributes repetition in the first instance to that "'daemonic' force" which I have associated with the death drive, and in the second instance to the process of psychic binding, as if the latter is somehow superimposed upon the former. The repetition through which the subject lays claim to an active position would consequently seem to "[point] back toward—and [to depend] on—something anterior to itself," as Samuel Weber has suggested.[18] Mastery, in other words, exists in a parasitic or anaclitic relation to the death drive. It is hardly surprising that Freud often conflates the two.

But in what precise way can the death drive be said to constitute an internal enemy in war trauma? Freud claims in *Beyond the Pleasure Principle* that the death drive is an indwelling force in every organism.[19] In *The Ego and the Id* he maintains that it is in part "rendered harmless by being fused with erotic components," and in part "diverted towards the external world in the form of aggression."[20] War would seem to provide the ideal vehicle for the collective exteriorization of this dangerous force, and hence to facilitate an emphatic victory over that which threatens the subject. Freud insists, however, upon the impossibility of a complete evacuation of the death drive; indeed, he immediately adds that "to a large extent" it "undoubtedly" continues its "internal work unhindered" (54). He advances a similar formulation in "Why War?." After suggesting that the subject can best protect itself against the death drive by directing it at another, he concludes that even in such a seemingly self-affirming situation, "some portion of the death [drive] remains operative *within* the organism."[21] In the same passage, moreover, he characterizes the death drive as a force "at work in every living creature and striving to bring it to ruin" (211). The soldier thrust into battle would thus seem to face both an internal and an external enemy, each fortified through its consolidation with the other.

In these two passages from "Why War?," the death drive emerges as the carrier of a biological death, and hence conforms closely to Freud's definition of it in *Beyond the Pleasure Principle*. We cannot help but remark, though, that the victim of war trauma does not experience physical extinction. Instead, he is described by Freud as suffering from "strongly marked signs of subjective ailment" and a "general enfeeblement and disturbance of the mental capacities."[22] The war neurotic suffers more precisely from "reminiscences," i.e. from the compulsion to repeat traumatic experiences. The symptoms mentioned by Freud are secondary in relation to this compulsion; they are, in fact, its consequences. If we read those symptoms as part of the "ruination" of the subject by an indwelling death drive, we begin to understand that the nothingness to which it threatens to reduce the subject bears less upon the body than the psyche.

As I have already indicated, *Beyond the Pleasure Principle* associates trauma with the disruption of a bound state. In "Introduction to *Psycho-Analysis and the War Neuroses*," Freud articulates the threat posed to the psyche in war and other traumatic neuroses as a threat to the most important product of psychical cohesion and binding, the ego. He claims that "in traumatic and war neuroses the human ego is defending itself from a danger which threatens it from without or which is embodied in [an internal] shape" (210). He thereby brings into sharp focus that entity which the death drive seeks most to annihilate.

In the larger passage from which I have just quoted, Freud isolates war neuroses from those in which the ego defends itself against the libido. He thus distinguishes, as I have been insisting we must, between those neuroses which are motored by a repressed desire, and are hence obedient to the pleasure principle, and those which are produced in response to an external event which reactivates an earlier trauma. This second kind of neurosis, which is typified by war neurosis, does not depend upon the return of a desire which comes into conflict with the ego. Instead, answerable to a "beyond the pleasure principle" which is in the final analysis synonymous with the death drive, it turns upon the dissolution of the ego or *moi*—upon the death of that through which the subject imputes identity to itself. The subject who is thus robbed of the illusion of presence is brought into a profoundly unpleasurable contact with lack.

It should be apparent by now that I am proposing the death drive as the "insistence" within the subject of a force inimical to the coherence of the ego. I am also challenging Freud's assumption that the death drive leads to the evacuation of tension.[23] If that psychic principle is synonymous with the compulsion to repeat trauma, then its destructive effects on the ego must be attributed to an excess rather than a diminution of excitation, and characterized as a "shattering"[24] rather than a release. Implicit in this formulation is the assumption, which I derive from Jean Laplanche, that the ego is governed not by the so-called "pleasure principle," but rather by the "constancy principle." The ego, in other words, seeks to maintain a *constant* level, not a *zero degree* of excitation—"a veritable energy *Gestalt*," bound by "the very limit of the vesicle."[25] The death drive threatens both to violate that limit, and to raise the energy level above an optimal level, thereby converting *bound* energy into *unbound* energy.

Masculinity is particularly vulnerable to the unbinding effects of the death drive because of its ideological alignment with mastery. The normative male ego is necessarily fortified against any knowledge of the void upon which it rests, and—as its insistence upon an unimpaired bodily "envelope" would suggest—fiercely protective of its coherence. Yet the repetition through which psychic mastery is established exists in such an intimate relation with the repetition through which it is jeopardized that Freud shows himself unable to distinguish clearly between them. Since the kind of traumatic neurosis which is typified by war trauma can only be bound through repetition, yet is itself nothing more than the imperative to repeat unpleasure, disintegration constantly haunts the subject's attempts to effect a psychic synthesis.

Never is the imbrication between "the repetition that links" and "the repetition that erases and destroys,"[26] clearer than in the story about Freud's grandson, a story which Lacan has put to important parabolic uses. Significantly, the protagonist of this anecdote is presented as an exemplary if nascent male subject; Freud puts much emphasis upon his being a "good boy," as evidenced by his refusal to be undone by his mother's absences. The game through which he masters the trauma of her departures, however, proves the vehicle through which that trauma returns, now in a guise which will prove much more significant for his future history. The child puts himself in an active relation to his mother's disappearances by throwing away and then recovering the toy which is her symbolic representative, while uttering the words "*fort*" ("gone") and "*da*" ("there"). In so doing, he deploys language for the first time as a differential system, and so stages the trauma of his own disappearance. His ostensible mastery is consequently based upon a radical self-loss, and upon his subordination to the order of discourse. "If the young subject can practice this game of *fort/da*," writes Lacan,

> it is precisely because he does not practice it at all, for no subject can grasp this radical articulation. He practices it with the help of a small bobbin, that is to say, with the *objet a*. The function of the exercise with this object refers to an alienation, and not to some supposed mastery, which is difficult to imagine being increased in an endless repetition. . . .[27]

Although the trauma of this *aphanisis* is not apparent in Freud's version of this story, it is destined to make itself felt over and over again throughout the history of the normative male subject. That trauma surfaces in the form that will henceforth prove decisive during the castration complex; it manifests itself, that is, in the guise of the anatomical lack to which the female body is subsumed, and with which the male body is threatened. Physical castration consequently provides the form through which the subject is ideologically encouraged to live—or not to live—the loss of being, and all subsequent crises that reprise that loss. It is not surprising, then, that when the male subject is brought into a traumatic encounter with lack, as in the situation of war, he often experiences it as the impairment of his anatomical masculinity. What is really at issue, though, is a *psychic* disintegration—the disintegration, that is, of a bound and armored ego, predicated upon the illusion of coherence and control.

I do not mean to understate the centrality of the discourse of war to the construction of conventional masculinity. Recent work by Klaus Theweleit, Susan Jeffords, and Susan Gubar has made abundantly clear how pivotal that discourse is to the consolidation of the penis/phallus equation,[28] as did media coverage of the Persian Gulf War. However, although the discourse of war works not only to solicit civilian belief in the dominant fiction, but to shape the subjective experience of battle, it does not always manage to fortify the soldier against an introverted death drive. Wilfred Owen describes the "extraordinary exultation" he and others felt in exposing themselves to enemy fire during World War I,[29] and Jean Bethke Elshtain emphasizes how few American soldiers were able to deploy their weapons during World War II:

S.L.A. Marshall, the great American Military historian, concluded, as a result of his extensive study of American rifle companies in action in the Pacific and European theaters of the Second World War, that *"fear of killing, rather than fear of being killed, was the most common cause of battle failure."* Moreover ... only 15 percent of these men actually fired their weapons in battle, even when they were very hard pressed by enemy soldiers.[30]

Sandra Gilbert and Elaine Showalter elaborate upon the literal and symbolic impotence from which veterans of trench battle suffered after the Great War,[31] and Jeffords accounts for recent representations of the Vietnam War precisely as an attempt to relocate the lack which initially attached itself insistently to the returning veteran. Theweleit writes at length about the constant danger of dissolution which threatened the Freicorps soldier, a danger which was more internal than external.[32]

Even under the most auspicious circumstances, moreover, the fiction of a phallic masculinity generally remains intact only for the duration of the war. As long as the soldier remains on the battlefield, he is fortified to some degree by his comrades; the "binding" which can no longer take place at the level of the ego occurs instead at the level of the group. For the civilian society, moreover, the traumatized soldier remains a comfortingly heroic abstraction, which poses no challenge to the *vraisemblance*. But once removed from the battlefront, the traumatized veteran no longer enjoys the support of his comrades-in-arms. All that stands between him and the abyss is the paternal imago, within which he can no longer recognize himself. For the society to which he returns, moreover, he represents a sorry travesty of "our fighting men and boys," a living proof of the incommensurability of penis and phallus.[33] Because of the resulting crisis of faith, "reality" itself is at least temporarily jeopardized.[34]

The many films from the mid-1940s which focus in an obsessive way upon male lack give vivid testimony to the trauma of war. In at least two of those films, *The Best Years of Our Lives* and *It's a Wonderful Life*, that trauma manifests itself in surprisingly explicit ways—as the compulsion to repeat experiences which are so threatening to the coherence of the male ego that they come close to exposing the void at the center of subjectivity. *The Best Years of Our Lives*, moreover, openly links the trauma of war to the death drive, which it defines in terms that are surprisingly close to those I have proposed here: as a force within the subject which seeks to reduce it to a psychic nothingness.

The Best Years of Our Lives, It's a Wonderful Life, and *The Guilt of Janet Ames* speak as well to a second historical trauma threatening

American masculinity—that posed by a social formation which had proven itself capable of managing without the absent soldier, in significant part by mobilizing a female workforce.[35] Like war trauma, the trauma of the male subject's superfluity must be read in relation to earlier losses, which it serves both to reactivate and to compound. Both *It's a Wonderful Life* and *The Guilt of Janet Ames* work to dispel these threats to normative masculinity, the former by bringing in heavenly reinforcements, and insisting upon the irreparable "tear" in the social fabric resulting from the departure of the prototypical male subject, and the latter through male projection and female fetishism.

Hollywood cinema of the mid- to late forties also dramatizes the inevitable process of cultural binding that follows quick on the heels of any general loss of faith in the dominant fiction. The verb "to bind" has a very specific sense in Freud's writings. It refers not only to the circumscription of a homeostatic body of energy within the limits of the ego, but to the process whereby memories characterized by a high degree of affective and sensory intensity are brought within linguistic control—the process whereby they are anchored to signifiers, and consequently to meaning. The memories in question are totally transformed by this binding operation; indeed, it might be more accurate to say that something else is put in place of the original, hallucinatory mnemic traces. That "something else" is a signified, or rather a cluster of potential signifieds.[36]

However, when the process of binding takes place on a larger, cultural level, it involves not only the translation from one mnemic system to another, but also the gradual reaffirmation and reconstitution of the dominant fiction. In the aftermath of World War II, this reaffirmation and reconstitution occurred at the level of a wide range of textual practices, from Hollywood cinema, to advertisements for kitchen appliances, to Dior's "New Look." However, at least within Hollywood cinema, the historical trauma of the war had to be registered before it could be bound, and—as we will see—the resulting disruption is often considerable.

Before turning to *The Best Years of Our Lives*, I want to emphasize that I in no way mean to propose catastrophe as the antidote to a mass *méconnaissance*. Nor do I mean to suggest that World War II, an event of monumentally tragic consequences, provided a privileged agency of social transformation. In fact, as we all know, the opposite has been the case. What I am trying to do by focusing upon three films made in the immediate wake of World War II is to isolate that brief moment in the 1940s when the forces of destruction and dissolution got out of the control of those attempting to orchestrate the war, and served to annihilate less the enemy than the positivities of the masculine "self." My motives are two-fold. First, I hope to show that male mastery rests upon an abyss, and that the repetition through which it is consolidated is radically and ceaselessly undermined by a very different and much more primordial kind of repetition—by that insistence within the present of earlier traumas that I have associated with the death drive. Second, I hope to dramatize the central part which the equation of penis and phallus plays in the maintenance of a certain "reality"—to demonstrate that the continuation of our "world" depends upon a collective belief in that equation. Although I have characterized the occasions on which masculinity and the dominant fiction experience at least a temporary disintegration as "historical," my wish is that every subject's encounter with the death drive might become in time more of an everyday occurrence—that the typical male subject, like his female counterpart, might learn to live with lack.

2. A Film Written by Events

> Characters of this kind have rarely been seen before on the screen. Visionless, at the mercy of any wind, benumbed even in their love-making, they drift about in a daze bordering on stupor . . . It is as if those Innocents had been dragged out of their enchanted universe to face the world as it actually is— a world not in the least responsive to their candid dreams and hopes. The guise of the discharged soldier assures us that they are now average individuals, stunned by the shock of readjustment.
>
> (Siegfried Kracauer)

William Wyler's *The Best Years of Our Lives* is one of the films through which André Bazin most ardently pursues his realist dream. Curiously, like *Bicycle Thief* and *Diary of a Country Priest*, two of the other films which serve as vehicles for that dream, *The Best Years of Our Lives* focuses upon marginal male subjectivity—upon figures who are not equal to the phallic legacy. To a certain extent the case Bazin makes for Wyler also resembles the case he makes for De Sica. In the essay on *The Best Years of Our Lives*, as in the essay on *Bicycle Thief*,[37] he praises what might be called the "authenticity" of the pro-filmic event. But whereas Bazin attributes the realism of De Sica's film to its transparent reflection of the pro-filmic event, he attributes the realism of Wyler's film to the technical difficulties that event created— to the tactical problems posed by the use of a complete, life-sized set and non-theatrical makeup:

> In concentric order of value, I will first of all cite the realism of the decor, built in actual dimension and in its entirety (which I suspect

would complicate the shooting since it would be necessary to raise the "sections" to give the camera proper perspective). The actors wore clothes exactly like those their characters would have worn in reality, and their faces were no more made up than in any town. No doubt this quasi-superstitious but scrupulous regard for the truthfulness of the everyday is uncommonly strange to Hollywood, but its true importance rests perhaps not so much on its tangible convincingness for the spectator, as in the disruptions it must inevitably introduce into the mise-en-scène: the lighting, the camera angle, the direction of the actor.[38]

Bazin thus equates the realism of *The Best Years of Our Lives* with its deviations from a cinematic practice which was no longer capable of passing representational muster after the upheavals of the 1940s. Not only does he argue that the film's break with the formal conventions of Hollywood was motivated by those upheavals, but he claims that "something of the inundation, the cyclone of realities which [the war] had unfurled on the world" finds "interpretation" through it.[39]

Wyler also establishes an intimate connection between World War II and the film's articulation. Indeed, he remarks not only that "the picture came out of its period, and was the result of the social forces at work when the war ended," but that it was "written by events"[40]—i.e. that its enunciation was coerced by an external stimulus. Like Bazin, Wyler distinguishes sharply here between his own film and conventional Hollywood cinema. For those who had seen the corpses at Dachau, he writes, Hollywood seemed not only "divorced from the main currents of our time," but far from "the world" (116). What both Bazin and Wyler make clear is that the American *vraisemblance* was no longer capable of commanding belief in the immediate wake of World War II—that far from standing for the real, it had come to seem that which obstructed access to actuality.

The force of the events which coerced the "writing" of *The Best Years of Our Lives* manifests itself in part through the formal markings (deep focus, the long take) which differentiate that work from most Hollywood films of the period.[41] It also manifests itself through the film's newly redefined realist aim—through its evident desire to connect the viewer with "the main currents of our time." Finally, the historical trauma of the war makes itself felt through the systematic demystification of the "preexisting inherited traditional or sacred narrative paradigms" which had previously organized "reality."[42]

The inherited narrative paradigms which *The Best Years of Our Lives* most systematically demystifies are those which serve to construct the adequate male subject. Like *The Guilt of Janet Ames* and *It's A Wonderful Life*, *The Best Years of Our Lives* opens the curtain on male castration. However, unlike the other two films it never resolves the crisis it sets in motion. *The Best Years of Our Lives* sustains its traumatic revelation for 160 minutes, progressing from one spectacle of loss to another. Male lack is so fully displayed in that film that even four decades after its original release it remains profoundly disturbing, and at times almost unwatchable.

3. A Long Way from Home[43]

As Al Stevenson (Fredric March), Homer Parish (Harold Russell), and Fred Derry (Dana Andrews) fly back to Boone City at the beginning of *The Best Years of Our Lives*, they talk about what it will be like to return to civilian life. Al, an army sergeant, is the only one who goes home to a family and an established job, but he is far from enthusiastic about the prospect. He worries that "everyone's going to try to rehabilitate me," and he later compares his arrival to landing on a beach during a battle. He has to be virtually ordered out of the cab he later shares with the others, and after an uncomfortable reunion with his family he drags his wife Millie (Myrna Loy) and his daughter Peggy (Teresa Wright) to nightclub after nightclub. The evening's debauchery concludes at Butch's Place, where Al reencounters Homer and Fred. His enthusiasm reaches almost hysterical proportions at the sight of his former traveling companions, but while dancing with his wife he seems to forget who she is.[44] The family would no longer seem to be that which Al "cannot *fail to recognize*," or before which he cries: "That's obvious! That's right! That's true!"[45]

Al is not only estranged from the family, but from "free enterprise" and his former "self." The next morning he awakens in a state of total confusion. He throws his slippers out of the window, climbs into the shower with his pajamas on, and bewilderedly compares his mirror image with the pre-war photo of himself he finds on the vanity table (Figure 2–1). His clothes no longer fit him, and his son treats him like a stranger. As time passes, Al returns to his job at the bank, where he is promoted to vice-president in charge of small loans, but like his clothes it no longer seems cut to his measure. He conforms with great difficulty to the bank's guidelines for distributing loans, and holds his expensive briefcase stiffly, as though it were a prop. Al's heavy drinking attests to a continued resistance to the home front, and to the privileges he enjoys there. Like the characters who populate the 1940s films about which Deming writes in *Running Away From Myself* (xiv), Al suffers from a "deep crisis of faith" in the dominant fiction.

Homer, who lost both hands in an aircraft fire during the war, evinces as keen if not as histrionic a sense of estrangement from

Figure 2–1

the "reality" of postwar America. During the flight to Boone City he remains determinedly cheerful, but when the cab pulls up in front of his parents' home he, like Al, is reluctant to descend. His disability, which seemed a minor sacrifice while he was in the service, now assumes a very different meaning. He feels himself the constant object of a horrified gaze, held at a scopic remove from his family, his neighbors, and his girlfriend Wilma (Cathy O'Donnell). Homer's father speaks to his son's estrangement when he tells Wilma: "His mother and I have tried to make him feel at home but he just keeps to himself all the time." As if to reinforce the point, the film shows us Homer alone in his bedroom, surrounded by photographs from his athletic high school years, now incapable of even putting himself to bed—a stranger among the tokens of his own past. He spends his days at Butch's Place, at the drugstore where Fred works, and in the family wood shed, engaged in solitary target practice.

Fred, a former bombardier, is the only one of the veterans who looks forward to civilian life, and who once there seeks assimilation. His dream is the American dream; as he tells Al, "All I want is a good job, a mild future, and a little house big enough for me and my wife. Give me that, and I'm rehabilitated . . . " However, he is also the only one without a home to return to. When he arrives in Boone City he pays a brief visit to his alcoholic father, who lives with his mistress in a dilapidated shack on the wrong side of town. Fred hopes to find his wife there, but learns that she has moved to town and taken a job in a nightclub. He searches for her in vain most of his first night back, unable even to gain entrance to her apartment. Although he does find Marie (Virginia Mayo) the next morning, they are at cross-purposes from the outset, and they separate when his airforce savings run out.

Fred is equally frustrated in his attempts to find a good job, and eventually ends up in the drugstore where he worked before the war. Although his military rank is higher than either Al's or Homer's, and his military affiliation more prestigious, he reenters the civilian world as a member of the working class. His father's poverty and moral "irregularity" conspire against his assimilation into the middle class, as they did before the war. Moreover, not only does he return to an already overcrowded job market, but the skills he learned in the service (dropping bombs) have no civilian equivalent. Indeed, those skills relegate him even more fully to a marginal social position, since like Homer's amputated hands they are the traces of a force totally incompatible with postwar America—of the "inundation" or "cyclone" of which Bazin speaks.

But it is above all at the level of spectacle that *Best Years of Our Lives* breaks with the dominant fiction. Far from obliging the female subject to display her lack to her sexual other, it repeatedly calls upon her to look acceptingly at *his*—to acknowledge and embrace male castration. Although a number of other films from this period also invert the classic scopic paradigm, that inversion is ultimately justified by the physical, psychic, or social restoration of the injured male subject (even *Pride of the Marines*, which is unusually blunt about its hero's blindness, eventually grants him a partial reprieve). *The Best Years of Our Lives*, however, offers no such easy resolution, nor does it account for its deviation from gender orthodoxy by promising that the female subject's healing touch will restore the wounded male subject to his former potency. Instead, it sustains the correlation of masculinity and castration until the very end.

The first of the many scopic traumas which punctuate *The Best Years of Our Lives* occurs in the military airport where Al, Homer, and Fred wait for a flight back to Boone City. Homer reveals his hooks, which have been concealed until now, when he and Fred go to the desk to sign the passenger list. Fred registers shock at the sight of the metal implements (Figure 2–2). Homer exposes his hooks again on board the plane, as he offers cigarettes and a light to Al and Fred (Figure 2–3). This time reactions are much more muted, but Homer begins almost immediately to talk about what it will mean to return to his family and girlfriend without hands. "They don't know what

Figure 2–2

these [hooks] look like," he worries. "It'll be all right—wait and see," responds Al with false reassurance. "Yeah . . . wait and see," Homer says bitterly. "Wilma's only a kid. She's never seen anything like these hooks."

Homer here articulates the thematics of his amputation—the thematics of an intolerable difference, accessible to vision, which defines its carrier as both other and inferior, and which confers upon its viewer an unwanted knowledge. The comparison between Homer's disfigured arms and the female body within the classic psychoanalytic account of sexual difference becomes even more striking when he associates Wilma's scopic ignorance with her youthfulness, and imagines that her affection will be unable to survive the unveiling. Over and over again the film insists upon this equation, making the spectacle of Homer's hooks (and, even more, his stumps) something primal and traumatic, and stressing that to the civilian eye he is a "mutilated creature."[46]

The first and only time we see the amputated limbs is, nevertheless, the moment at which Wilma most ardently embraces Homer. The scene in question begins with Wilma coming into the Parish kitchen where Homer is eating a late-night snack, and pressing him to clarify the terms of their relationship. Homer self-protectively rebuffs her at first, but eventually allows her to go to his bedroom and help him

Figure 2-3

undress (Figure 2-4). After the harness and hooks have been removed, he compares himself to "a baby that doesn't know how to get anything except by crying for it," and averts his eyes from the revulsion he expects. But Wilma's look contains nothing but tenderness, and as she puts him to bed (a ritual earlier performed by Peggy for Fred, and by Millie for Al) the lovers embrace (Figure 2-5).

Homer's lack also situates him in the relational position usually reserved for the female subject within classic cinema. Not only is he the object of a probing social gaze, obliged to account for his appearance to strangers at drugstore counters, but his undressing becomes the occasion for an intense erotic investment. In an essay published in 1947, Robert Warshow remarks upon the sexual charge of the sequence where Homer discloses his stumps to Wilma, and in which she commits herself to being his wife:

> He . . . has lost his hands—and with them his power to be sexually aggressive. . . . Every night, his wife will have to put him to bed, and then it will be her hands that must be used in making love. Beneath the pathos of the scene . . . one feels a current of excitement, in which the sailor's misfortune becomes a kind of wish-fulfillment, as one might actually dream it: he *must* be passive; therefore he can be passive without guilt.[47]

Figure 2–4

For Warshow, this scene not only situates Homer in a classically "feminine" position, but communicates to its male viewer a dangerous fantasy—the fantasy of occupying a subordinate sexual position.

Homer's stumps and compensatory hooks constitute a crisis not only of vision but of representation—a crisis which is the result of combining documentary detail with the spectacle of male castration. As Wyler himself observes, the decision to cast an actual amputee for the part of the disabled sailor gives the image of that character a credibility it would not otherwise have had, and so implicates the viewer more fully than usual in all visual transactions within which it figures ("We wanted Russell himself to play the part, rather than an actor. No matter how good a performance an actor gave of a man without hands, an audience could reassure itself by saying, 'It's only a movie.' With Russell playing Homer, no such reassurance was possible").[48] Warshow makes a similar point, but he complains that the casting gives the film too much authenticity—that it erases the boundary between cinema and life:

> Everything about the sailor is especially affecting because the part is played by a man who really did lose his hands in the war. There was nothing else to be done, I suppose, but this is one of the elements that help to make the movie spill over into the real world, carrying its falsehood with it. (111)

Figure 2–5

Despite their varying assessments of its success, Wyler and Warshow agree that the casting of Harold Russell for the part of Homer Parish was a choice on behalf of belief. There are at least two important issues here, one of which pertains to classic cinema's "impression of reality,"[49] and the other to the defensive processes through which that cinema has traditionally constructed the male subject. Harold Russell's double amputation does not "make the movie spill over into the real world," but it does situate the image of Homer Parish's arms on a different level of representation than the rest of the film. At every other point, including Russell's acting, there is a dimension of performance or simulation to which the stumps and hooks cannot be subsumed. Russell's injury is no more "present" than any other profilmic event; it too is recorded, and its "unfolding" is purely "fictive."[50] However, in this instance the filmic representation exercises a strong referential pull, seeming to point beyond the text and Russell's acting to his body and the traces left there by the war.

Because of this, there is a sort of doubling up of belief, a reinforcement of the disavowal Metz and Comolli identify with the cinematic experience. The image of Russell's stumps and hooks functions further to minimize "the gap which the 'yes-I-know/but-all-the-same' has to fill."[51] It negates the cinematic signifier, inclining the spectacle even more precipitously than usual toward the referent or object. Yet at the same time what most passes for "the real thing" in *The Best Years of Our Lives*—what provokes the representational "lurch" toward the pro-filmic event—is precisely what classic cinema is generally at most pains to deny, and against which it marshals such protective measures as projection, disavowal, and fetishism: male lack. The peculiar doubling up of belief around the castration of the male subject may well be the most traumatic feature of Wyler's intensely traumatic film.

Of course we are no more in direct contact here with lack than we are when confronted with an image of the female genitals. In both cases, it is an imaginary inscription which commands our belief. However, counter-intuitive as such a suggestion might be, it is only through imaginary inscriptions—and hence through recognition/misrecognition—that belief can be generated, since what is at issue here is not rational persuasion but a subject-effect. While historical trauma may work to disintegrate normative masculinity, it is only through representation that we can come to believe in male lack, in the strongest sense of that verb. Because it not only dismantles the defensive mechanisms upon which conventional male subjectivity depends, but provides us with images in which we can recognize-misrecognize male castration, *The Best Years of Our Lives* might thus be said to renegotiate our lived relation to the Law of Language.

Homer is not the only exhibit of male lack in *The Best Years of Our Lives*. Al also makes a spectacle of his alienation from the phallic ideal through his incessant drinking. Since he has institutional and economic supports which are not available to the other veterans, though, his inadequacy never becomes as visible or as obviously incapacitating as Homer's. There are only two occasions when Al seems in danger of missing the safety net held out to him by his wife and employer, and of succumbing to his desire to escape rehabilitation—the night of his return to Boone City, and the night of the bank dinner in his honor.

Al's interactions with his children the night of his return point to a general disintegration of the paternal function, a disintegration which becomes more and more pronounced as the evening wears on. Not only does Al's son seem more knowledgeable than his father about Japanese society, atomic energy, and the future of the world, but he manifests no interest whatever in Al's war experiences or souvenirs. The familial generations become further confused as Peggy chauffeurs her parents from one bar to another, like a chaperone. She herself remarks humorously on the role reversal as she watches them dance ("It's nice to see the young folks enjoying themselves"). Not surprisingly, Fred cannot seem to grasp the relationship between Peggy and her father, even after it has been explained to him three times. "So

Figure 2–6

you're Al's daughter. You don't seem like Al's daughter," he remarks after one of these clarifications. "Actually, I'm not; he's my son by a previous marriage," Peggy responds, supplying an appropriate caption to the spectacle of Al reeling drunkenly on the dance floor (Figure 2–6).

Since the family provides the dominant fiction with its primary image of unity, and since hegemony can only be achieved by those ideologies which successfully articulate themselves in relation to it, we should not be surprised to find the President of the Cornbelt Loan and Trust Company attempting to reincorporate Al by addressing him in its terms. However, once again Al seems strangely out of place within the world of the family, unequal to or—at least unready for—the paternal legacy. At the end of a conversation about the bank's loan policies, Mr. Milton says to him: "You know how I feel about you, and always have. Why, I've always considered you one of the family, so to speak—like my own sss . . . younger brother."

As this rhetorical slippage would suggest, Al's difficulties with fatherhood translate into difficulties at work. Weeks later, on the occasion of the bank dinner, he must fortify himself with nearly a pitcher of martinis before he even leaves home, and he continues to drink heavily throughout the evening. Immediately before Al rises to deliver his obligatory speech, the bank president, Mr. Milton (Ray Collins) offers a toast to the American dream: "Our country must stand today where it's always stood—the citadel of individual initiative, the land of unlimited opportunity for all." Al initially responds to this appeal with a tautological parody of the president's words ("Our country stands today where it stands today"), and an ironic story about a soldier who refused to take a hill without collateral, and so lost the war. However, he concludes with a utopian elaboration of the relation between the Cornbelt Loan and Trust Company and the veterans who apply to it for G.I. loans—with an account of a kinder and gentler capitalism, in which there would be no opposition between "power" and "the people":[52]

> I love the Cornbelt Loan and Trust Company. There are some who say that the old bank is suffering from hardening of the arteries and the heart. I refuse to listen to such radical talk. I say that our bank is alive, it's generous and it's human. And we're going to have such a line of customers seeking and getting small loans that people will think we're gambling with the depositors' money—and we will be. We'll be gambling on the future of this country.

As both a banker and a former soldier, Al embodies the contradictions he attempts to resolve through his speech. Earlier in the film Mr. Milton explains that it will be his job to admit into the financial network of the bank only those returning soldiers who pose no risk to its stability. In effect, he asks Al to help maintain existing economic relations, but to do so in his guise as a veteran, i.e. as the ostensible spokesman of that which challenges those relations. However, in order for Al to do this, he would have to believe as fully in the dominant fiction as Mr. Milton is represented as doing. Instead, he continues to regard America's governing "reality" as a construction rather than as the natural or inevitable condition of social existence. He refuses to suspend his disbelief in its representations, privileged signifiers, and rhetorical formulae, and this disbelief is as disruptive to the operations of the bank as it is to Al's day-to-day functioning. It is only after making a public display of his alcoholism at the bank dinner, and after coming dangerously close to breaking off relations with the Cornbelt Loan and Trust Company, that Al finally manages to perform the requisite act of faith, but he does so only by looking at that institution with his eyes closed.

Fred's castration is on much more permanent display, particularly after he removes his air force uniform. When he finally manages to track down his wife the day after his return to Boone City, she greets him enthusiastically, much taken with the ribbons decorating his chest. Indeed, she responds to him *as spectacle*—as a glamorous and

Figure 2–7

heroic image. "Come on in, honey, where I can take a look at you," she exclaims, "Oh, you're *marvellous*—ribbons!" (Figure 2–7). However, the first time she sees him in civilian clothes she visibly recoils, appalled by his shabby and unfashionable suit, with its working class connotations. She literally begs him to change back into his uniform, exclaiming with satisfaction after he complies: "Now you look wonderful . . . now you look like yourself . . . you know, we're right back where we started."

Fred soon resumes civilian dress, becoming an even more pitiful spectacle when he is forced to return to the drugstore where he worked before the war, and to don the white overcoat of a salesman and soda jerk. On the only occasion we see him at work in the first of these capacities a small boy releases a toy plane into the air above Fred's head, and pretends to shoot it. The plane is an ironic reminder of the heights from which he has fallen since his return. As it noisily circles around the cosmetic counter of the crowded store, it is also indicative of the way in which ideology attempts to recuperate the trauma of history through trivializing representation.

A woman reaches both hands into the air, and grounds the spinning plane. As she does so, the camera cuts to a medium long shot of Peggy, owner of the hands, who has been standing quietly in the background of the scene (Figure 2–8). The expression on her face, which registers

Figure 2–8

both sympathy and bemusement, suggests that her look has taken in all the manifold complexity of the scene. Once again the female subject is given a privileged access to the spectacle of male lack. Here, as in the nocturnal exchange between Wilma and Homer, that spectacle is highly eroticized, saturated with female desire. Later the same day Peggy confides to her parents her plan to break up Fred's marriage to Marie, revealing in the process her investment not only in the former bombardier, but in the disintegration he increasingly comes to represent.

Peggy is introduced to Fred the night of his return to Boone City, when they both turn up at Butch's Place. Because he has no place to sleep, the Stevensons take him home with them, and Peggy gives him her bed. Awakened during the night by Fred's cries, she goes into the bedroom and rescues him from a recurrent nightmare about a burning plane—a nightmare which replays his worst war experience. As she attempts to awaken him, Fred sits bolt upright, his eyes wide open (Figure 2–9a). Peggy's immediate response is to cover his eyes, as if to protect him from an intolerable sight—a gesture which locates him again on the side of the spectacle (Figure 2–9b). She then induces him to lie down, and strokes his face as she whispers over and over: "Go to sleep." Peggy performs these nursing gestures with an even more passionate tenderness than that with which Wilma regards Homer's

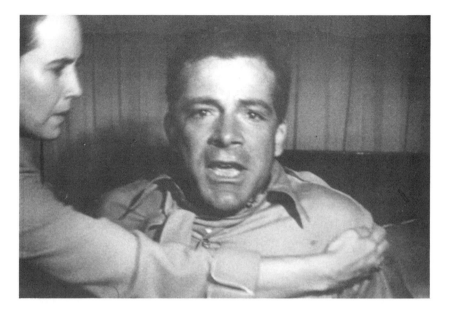

Figure 2–9a

mutilated body. Her desire for Fred can be traced to this moment of unveiling.

Marie adopts a very different attitude toward what she regards as Fred's "difference." She is embarrassed by his nightmares, viewing them as symptoms of psychological abnormality and social failure. They are also further evidence of what she already suspects—that Fred has been "contaminated" by a force antagonistic to the "good times" she seeks. "Are you really alright . . . in your mind?," she irritably asks, "Can't you get those things out of your system? Maybe that's what's holding you back. You know, the war's over. You won't get anyplace till you stop thinking about it. Come on—snap out of it!" Ironically, the film here entrusts Marie with its clearest articulation of the dysfunction which results when the ego is flooded with excessive excitation. The war has indeed infiltrated Fred's "system," and that trauma has not yet been "bound."

When Fred loses his job because of a drugstore brawl, and Marie announces she wants a separation, he decides to leave Boone City. On his way to the military airport he stops by his father's shack to collect the clothes Hortense has washed for him. While there he discards various war souvenirs, including a commendation for distinguished flying. These once-prized possessions have been relegated to the status of junk; they attest to experiences which are not only unassimilable

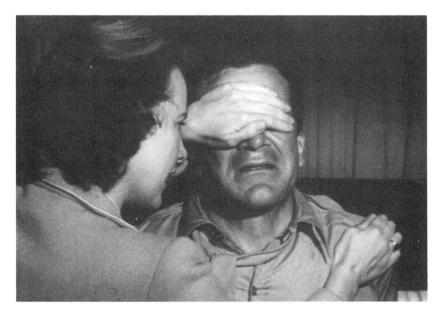

Figure 2–9b

to America's "reality," but threatening to its positivity. After Fred leaves, his father picks up the commendation with trembling hands and reads aloud from it. What emerges is an account of the purest negativity—of a death drive unleashed equally on enemy and self:

> Despite intense pain, shock, and loss of blood, with complete disregard of his personal safety, Captain Derry crawled back to his bomb site, guided his formation on a perfect run over the objective and released his bomb with great accuracy. The heroism, devotion to duty, professional skill, and coolness under fire displayed by Captain Derry under the most difficult conditions reflect the highest honor upon himself and the armed forces of the United States of America.

Immediately before Mr. Derry reads these words, we see Fred arriving at the military airport, trying to catch a plane out of Boone City. When asked whether he wants to fly east or west he says it doesn't matter; because the war has invaded his psyche, his homelessness will be equally acute wherever he goes.

While Fred waits for the next plane he walks down to a field filled with hundreds of World War II bombers. The planes have all been stripped of their engines and propellers, and are waiting to be scrapped. Like Homer and Fred they are disabled and unwanted, a "defilement" which must be jettisoned from the social formation. Fred climbs into one of the planes, and moves through the litter of dust and worn maps to the bombardier's seat. The camera cuts to an exterior reverse shot of the nose, showing Fred through the plexiglass window. As he looks to the viewer's right the camera cuts again, moving with Fred's eyes to one of the outer engine nacelles. It then pans from right to left across the surface of the bomber, pausing momentarily at each of the other three nacelles, as if to emphasize their readiness for departure (Figures 2–10a thru 2–10d). A third exterior shot follows, dollying in rapidly from a extreme long shot to a low-angle close-up of the nose, and then tilting slightly to disclose Fred, still sitting motionless behind the window (Figures 2–11a thru 2–11f). The last two exterior shots effect a di-vision, denying what they at the same time assert. In the first of those shots the absence of engines and propellers is belied by Hugo Friedhofer's musical score,[53] which evokes the sounds of take-off. In the second the low angle of the camera and its head-on approach simulate the movements of a plane preparing for flight, even as the image of the disabled B–17 attests to the impossibility of any such event.

This extraordinary incitement to a divided belief does not so much cover over a lack as push negativity to the limits. When Fred imagines himself aloft once again on a bombing mission, he detonates the dominant fiction. At that moment he escapes social rationality, opting

Figure 2–10a

Figure 2–10b

Figure 2–10c

Figure 2–10d

Figure 2–11a

Figure 2–11b

Figure 2–11c

Figure 2–11d

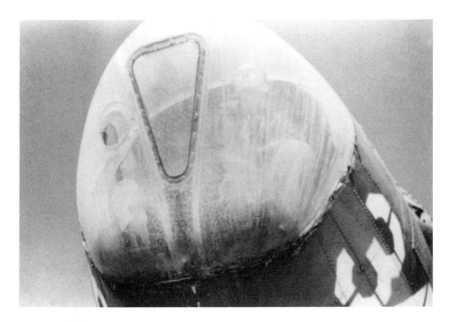

Figure 2–11e

Figure 2–11f

for the non-ego over the ego, the threatening outside over the coherent inside, and death over life.[54] The film throws its formal weight behind this negativity through the di-visions described above. When it pits sound against image, or camera angle and movement against iconic meaning, it too invests in trash, privileging what falls beyond the social pale over what remains within.

In the exterior close-up of the bomber's nose with which the sequence ends, Fred's face seems to have surrendered all consistency, and to have become part of the texture of the plexiglass window. This shot thus attests to a profound psychic disintegration—to the dissolution of the bodily ego or imago. Although Fred is called back to life and work by the salvage man a moment later, he never really leaves the scrapyard. In the final sequence of the film, when Peggy meets Fred at Homer's wedding and remarks that she's heard that he's "in some kind of building work," he responds: "That's a hopeful way of putting it. I'm really in the junk business—an occupation for which many people feel I'm well qualified by temperament and training. It's fascinating work." Moreover, when Fred proposes to Peggy in the concluding moments of the film, he does so entirely through the delineation of his lack, and through what is in effect an assertion of disbelief in the dominant fiction ("You know what it'll be, don't you Peggy? It may take us years to get anywhere. We'll have no

Figure 2–12

money, no decent place to live. We'll have to work . . . get kicked around").

The Best Years of Our Lives ends with one marriage, and with the promise of another. However, those marriages do not have the usual metaphoric value; rather than affirming the cultural order, they further dramatize (and libidinally valorize) male castration. Moreover, the two sets of lovers remain remarkably alone in the middle of this ostensibly social ceremony, an isolation indicative of the distance separating them not only from their families and neighbors, but from the American dream.

When Homer slips the ring on Wilma's finger, and she lovingly places her hand on the cold metal of his hooks, the onlookers recoil from the severely denaturalized spectacle (Figure 2–12). The contact of flesh and steel evokes yet another crisis of vision, eliciting fear, anxiety and pain. Al, standing in rear center frame, holds tightly onto Millie's arm, a gesture which speaks not only to the tension in the room, but to the difficulties in his own marriage, and his barely contained desire to break the phallic contract.

Another scopic exchange occurs in the back of the room, unwitnessed by anyone within the diegesis. Fred (in medium close-up) looks toward Peggy (in long shot), and she reciprocates (Figures 2–13a and 2–13b). This visual transaction resonates with the affect generated

Figure 2–13a

Figure 2–13b

by the "main event"—a displacement motivated in part by Fred's proximity to Homer, and his status as best man, and in part by Peggy's (and the viewer's) knowledge that he too is marked by lack. Since Fred and Peggy effect their scopic reunion during the reading of the marriage vows, those vows also perform double duty, binding them together in anticipation of the kiss and the declaration of ideological disbelief which are soon to follow.

4. Mutilated Creatures

Because they so closely approximate the reactions attributed by Freud to the male subject at the sight of the female genitals, two kinds of critical response to *The Best Years of Our Lives* warrant attention here. One of these responses disavows the conspicuous display of male castration, insisting upon the film's conformity to the classic paradigm. Thus Roger Manvell argues (against a strong but unspecified opposition) that it "staunchly upholds the sacred stability of home and family, and even . . . of free enterprise and the virtues of big business,"[55] while Michael Wood characterizes it as "an evasive and cosy tale."[56] The other response acknowledges not only the film's negativity, but the concentration of that negativity at the site of male subjectivity. However, it defends itself against that unpleasurable spectacle through moral disapprobation—through a horror of the mutilated creatures who populate *The Best Years of Our Lives*. Kracauer, for instance, discovers in Wyler's film "a common man reluctant to heed the voice of reason and a liberal spokesman unable to run the emotional blockade around him" (571). Similarly, Warshow writes that "the sexual relations of the characters form an unusually clear projection of the familiar Hollywood (and American) dream of male passivity. The men are inept, nervous, inarticulate, and childishly willful" (112).

Surprisingly, Warshow identifies Hollywood's male subject with qualities that are more conventionally identified with its female subject, such as passivity and insufficiency. Since these qualities are on prominent display in *The Best Years of Our Lives*, he sees that film as a typical example of Hollywood film, rather than as a text which breaks in certain key respects with the normative model. But even though Warshow feels the equation of male subjectivity and castration to be ubiquitous within American cinema, he has his defenses securely in place against it. Rather than entertaining the possibility that any more heroic version of masculinity must be constructed through the tenuously maintained projection of male lack onto the female subject, he proposes the reverse argument: All lack properly belongs at the site of femininity, but the female subject constantly attempts to disburden herself of it by projecting it onto the male subject. In proposing this argument, Warshow rhetorically re-enacts the exteriorizing displacement through which sexual difference is constituted, and thereby shores up the dominant fiction. That he should have felt impelled to perform this task in 1947 in response not only to *The Best Years of Our Lives* but to Hollywood cinema in its entirety speaks eloquently to the ideological "exhaustion" of that period.

5. History Dramatized

> Yes, the war did affect me. I didn't want to see another cannon go off, I didn't want to see another bomb blow up. War lost its glamor for me. Just to see those trembling people in London during the Blitz, poor sick old ladies crying, dying in terror . . . Children. There's got to be something better than bombing old ladies and children. I lost . . . there's nothing glamorous about war. I didn't want to be a war hero, nothing. That's why I made a movie about an ordinary guy.
>
> (Frank Capra)

> I hope . . . that all together we will try—try out of the memory of our anguish—to reassemble our broken world so firm and so fair that another great war can never again be possible . . .
>
> (*The Story of G. I. Joe* [1945])

It's a Wonderful Life (1946) was the first film Capra made after the war and the *Why We Fight* documentary series he directed for the armed forces—a series he later described as "history . . . dramatized."[57] Yet despite its proximity to the war, *It's a Wonderful Life* does not manifestly concern itself either with that event or with its aftermath. The central character, George Bailey (Jimmy Stewart) is kept out of the military by an ear injury, and so continues throughout the early and mid 1940s to work at his usual job. His wife Mary (Donna Reed) also proceeds with the routine business of producing babies and maintaining the family home. The military support services George and Mary perform in addition to their regular activities are compressed into a brief montage sequence, and the war seems over almost as soon as it has begun. Even the setting of *It's a Wonderful Life* conspires to limit the viewer's vision to a seemingly undisturbed civilian society; the only time the camera ever leaves the claustrophobic confines of Bedford Falls is when it tilts "upward" toward the simulated heavens, site of an even more serene timelessness.

Capra's remarks about the film suggest that it represented for him not only an abrupt departure from the *Why We Fight* series, and hence from "history," but a retreat from the trauma of death and destruction. In an interview with Richard Glatzer he attributed his desire to make a movie about "an anonymous man in a small town" to a revulsion against the disruption of war: "I didn't want to see anything more of war—the brutality of it so upset me and so filled me with a feeling of the incompetence of the human race" (38).

Elsewhere Capra writes that *It's a Wonderful Life* grew out of his felt need to restore belief in the dominant fiction, a belief which he situates emphatically outside consciousness:

> People are numb after the catastrophic events of the past ten to fifteen years. I would not attempt to reach them mentally through a picture, only emotionally. Anything of a mental sort, anything apart from the purely human will have to be incidental ... the individual ... must be built up in his beliefs, his hopes and his aspirations and then as a matter of course you will find the new world we all talk about developing in the larger way.[58]

A surprising number of Capra's critics also argue that *It's a Wonderful Life* turns in some crucial way upon the restoration of belief in the governing "reality." Leland A. Poague, for instance, describes the film as "a celebration of community life and the bonds of faith and trust that tie the community together";[59] Peter Roffman and Jim Purdy characterize it as a "hard-won assertion of Capra's faith"[60] in Bedford Falls, the family, and the Bailey Building and Loan; and Charles J. Maland refers to its reaffirmation of "the society's dominant cultural values."[61] Moreover, like Capra, James Agee and Richard Griffith insist that the film touches not so much the "mind" as the "heart"—that it manages to command ideological belief despite rational doubt or misgivings.[62]

Yet despite the film's apparent distance from the horrors of war, and its final triumphant reaffirmation of the dominant fiction, at least two contemporary critics were convinced that a nightmare haunts the American dream in *It's a Wonderful Life*. Deming remarks that in Capra's texts, as in a number of other postwar films, "there erupts some really harrowing moment of violence ... The jugular vein, pierced, spurts its blood directly at us, spurts, it almost seems, straight from the screen ... The camera cannot take its fill of that face, where teeth bite lips, eyes suddenly roll in a swoon ... [It] voluptuously involves us in the destructive moment, moves in too close and dwells overlong, inviting us to suffer the ecstasy of dissolution, the thrill of giving it all up" (10). Deming thus seems to suggest that the death drive surfaces almost directly in certain Hollywood films of the 1940s.

While this is an impossible claim, it is nonetheless true that at a key moment in *It's a Wonderful Life* the central character not only contemplates suicide, but gives verbal expression to the desire that he had never been born. The subsequent twenty-five minutes of that film are, moreover, dedicated to the dramatization of this astonishing premise.

Kracauer also implicitly associates *The Best Years of Our Lives* and *It's a Wonderful Life* with the death drive, this time by isolating in those films the two phenomena through which historical trauma most powerfully manifests itself within our social formation—male castration and the failure of ideological belief:

> . . . do not the "progressives" in these films combat prejudice and ignorance? No doubt they do. And yet their efforts seem to be ineffectual. Something emasculates them, adding to the weakness I have already described. (570)

> . . . there is a strange inconsistency in all these "progressive" films. Upon closer inspection one cannot help noticing that they reveal the profound weakness of the very cause for which they try to enlist sympathy. (568)

A more recent critic, Robert B. Ray, echoes Kracauer's second point, arguing that "the evident strain involved in achieving the film's happy ending implie[s] that what had once been guaranteed as part of the American landscape itself, now rest[s] only on the most precarious faith."[63]

Both sets of critics are of course correct. *It's a Wonderful Life* does ultimately manage to reaffirm the dominant fiction, but only by forcing upon George an identification with a "weak" father, an identification which would seem to challenge in every respect the normative representations of the Oedipal drama with which Hollywood provides us. It thereby emphasizes the irreducible distance separating the actual father from the symbolic father or paternal position. It also makes startlingly apparent that male subjectivity, like its female counterpart, consists of the compulsory repetition of unpleasurable experiences. *It's a Wonderful Life* succeeds in realigning penis and phallus only by invoking a sacred temporality within which the male subject's lack will finally be made good.

Before turning to an analysis of the film, I want to emphasize that a number of its details permit us to associate the negative force operative within *It's a Wonderful Life* not only with the death drive, but with World War II. Most importantly, the film's diegetic present is situated immediately after that event, on Christmas Eve 1945. That day is also the occasion when George's younger brother Harry (Todd

Karns) returns from the war with a congressional medal of honor—
the occasion when Bedford Falls makes contact with what will remain
forever unassimilable to its cozy "truths." Moreover, Harry stands in
for George (Jimmy Stewart) in his guise as war hero, not only because
George has repeatedly sacrificed himself so that Harry can have a life
elsewhere, but because George has for years passionately desired a
similar escape. The accelerated montage by means of which *It's a
Wonderful Life* represents World War II thus serves less to marginalize
than to repress that event. Finally, the film addresses in a surprisingly
direct form the anxiety elicited in the returning veteran by his apparent "redundancy." In dramatizing the crucial part played by George
Bailey in the world of Bedford Falls, *It's a Wonderful Life* shows every
male subject to be both indispensable and irreplaceable, and so attempts to neutralize the historical trauma of civilian reentry.

6. The Celestial Suture

It's a Wonderful Life opens at a moment of extreme crisis, and one
which threatens to disclose the lethal nature of the Oedipal legacy.
George Bailey has been asked to make so large a self-sacrifice that it
seems to him synonymous with suicide. He has been shackled with the
responsibility for an $8000 deficit created by his Uncle Billy (Thomas
Mitchell). Since he doesn't have the money, he sees no way out of his
dilemma but death. However, George must be taught that he cannot
"take" his own life, because it belongs to his culture. (One of the
residents of Bedford Falls later tells him that "It's against the law to
commit suicide around here," and Clarence, George's guardian angel
warns that "It's against the law where I come from too.")
    This potentially very dangerous situation is cinematically con-
tained through a "celestial" suture; we are given an implied shot/
reverse shot between the roofs of the town's houses and the heavens
above (Figures 2–14a and 2–14b). This visual formation is supple-
mented by an equivalent sound formation, in which we hear first the
voices of George's family and his friends praying for him, and then
the voices of the answering angels. The film's immediate recourse to
supernatural assistance suggests that without it there would be no
possibility of cultural reintegration for George. It also implies that
the real crisis in George's life (and in Capra's film) has been generated
by the loss of belief, and that the emergency situation will end only
with the restoration of faith. Clarence (Henry Travers) is sent to earth
to assist with that restoration, but before he leaves heaven he is
introduced to George through a montage of scenes from the latter's
past.

Figure 2–14a

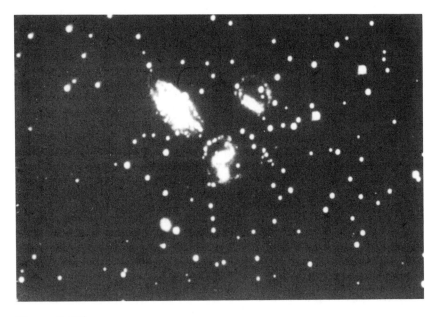

Figure 2–14b

The second of these scenes begins in the drugstore where George works as a soda jerk and delivery boy. Standing behind the soda fountain, he flourishes a handful of travel brochures at his diminutive customer, Mary,[64] and announces his intention to see the world, marry multiple wives, and have several harems. Mary gives voice a moment earlier to the ideological norm which will ultimately restructure these desires.[65] As the pharmacist's youthful assistant leans down to scoop up some ice-cream, she reaches over and whispers: "George Bailey, I'll love you till the day I die." George's desires are thus shown from the very outset to point beyond the boundaries of Bedford Falls and the bourgeois family. He discloses the source of these exploratory and accumulatory desires, to which he returns again and again throughout the film, when he proudly announces that he has been nominated for a membership in the National Geographic.

The travel fantasies articulated by the National Geographic discourse are by no means entirely incompatible with the dominant fiction. Indeed, they belong to the general pool of narratives upon which American popular culture repeatedly draws—safaris, expeditions to the North Pole, mountain climbing, etc. However, *It's a Wonderful Life* treats these fantasies as though they were somehow unpatriotic, deflecting vital energy away from the home front. It suggests that the desire to travel is at best the sanctioned fantasy only of a very young man, and it thrusts adulthood upon George before he has even come of age. The severe attitude adopted by the film toward the National Geographic discourse is part of its defensive reaction against anything that might be reminiscent of the war or of the world beyond Bedford Falls. The dominant fiction undergoes a kind of constriction as a consequence of this phobic avoidance.

George is called away from the soda fountain to take a prescription to a patient, and sees the pharmacist mistakenly fill the prescription with poison. Perplexed about how best to act, George glances at an advertisement on the wall which features a cigar-wielding patriarch and the words "Ask Dad"[66] (Figure 2–15). Responding promptly to this cultural command, George goes in search of his father. However, when he arrives at his destination he is confronted with a second view of paternal insufficiency. Peter Bailey's business has incurred a $5000 deficit, leaving him vulnerable to public humiliation at the hands of his enemy Potter (Lionel Barrymore). In a frenzy of filial distress, George attempts to close the obvious gap between the actual and the symbolic father. He shouts: "[My Dad's] the biggest man in the whole town . . . bigger'n [Potter] . . . bigger'n everybody!"

Despite George's protestations to the contrary, the spectacle of his father's shame clearly precipitates a castration crisis, albeit one orga-

Figure 2–15

nized again around male rather than female lack. Like the male subject in Freud's account of that crisis, George disavows the spectacle of lack that greets his unhappy gaze when he opens the door of his father's office. And like that other male subject he acknowledges what he has seen only later, when he feels himself exposed to a similar fate, i.e. when his father asks him to carry on the family business. Unlike Freud's male subject, though, George understands castration entirely in terms of cultural insufficiency; his crisis has no anatomical motivation. Indeed Potter, the figure against whom Peter Bailey is measured, is a childless cripple. His superiority is monetary rather than physiological—he is known as "the richest man in town."

Potter emphasizes the lethal nature of the cultural debt which George will eventually be asked to assume when he remarks: "Peter Bailey was not a businessman; that's what killed him. He was a man of high ideals." And long before the final crisis George anticipates Potter's sentiment, telling his father: "I just feel like if I don't get away, I'd bust." However, the continuation of the Bailey Building and Loan, of Bedford Falls, and—by implication—of small-town American life, is shown to depend upon George remaining precisely where he is. When, during the nightmare sequence, he finally "escapes," the town undergoes a demonic metamorphosis.

This, then, is the film's dilemma: Unable to conceal the castrations through which the paternal position is consolidated, *It's a Wonderful Life* is at the same time committed to the preservation of the dominant fiction, and so to the succession of father by son. As a result, it must bully George into occupying a position from which he recoils. Not surprisingly, the transfer of the paternal legacy does not happen punctually in Capra's first postwar film, but must be repeated over and over again. Each time it hinges upon the same narrative paradigm: First, George voices a set of desires which are not part of the sanctioned reality of Bedford Falls. A crisis is then engineered which requires George to step into his father's shoes. He rebels for a time, and then succumbs to the ideological address.

Thus it is that on the evening of George's long-anticipated trip around the world, equipped with a suitcase large enough for one thousand and one nights, Peter Bailey calls upon him to take over the family business. George energetically declines the "offer," but he never does leave on his journey since later the same night his father suffers a fatal heart attack. Peter Bailey's death leaves a culturally inadmissible vacuum or "hole" which George is temporarily obliged to fill.

After putting his father's affairs in order, George prepares to leave for college, but the Bailey Building and Loan board votes to keep the institution in business only if he will take over for Peter Bailey as executive secretary. George has no choice but to remain in Bedford Falls. *It's a Wonderful Life* cuts at this point to the sunny day four years later when Harry returns from college, ostensibly to take over as executive secretary for the Bulding and Loan. George, who is waiting for him on the train tracks, shows Uncle Harry the travel brochures for the trip he now plans to take. "You know what the three most exciting sounds in the world are?," he confides, " . . . anchor chains, plane motors, and train whistles." But Harry returns with a wife and an offer for a job elsewhere, and George has no choice but to continue on at the Building and Loan.

Mrs. Bailey (Beulah Bondi) responds to George's obvious unhappiness on the night of his brother's homecoming by helping to introduce him into a marriage of his own, and thereby incorporate him more fully into the paternal position. She describes Mary Hatch (Donna Reed) as "the kind [of woman] that will help you find the answers," and she points him in the direction of the latter's house. When George arrives at his preordained destination, Mary "hails" him from the balcony, in a reprise of their earlier encounter after a school dance.[67] Indeed, she quite painstakingly reconstructs that scene through two strategically chosen props: an embroidered rendition of George lassoing the moon, and a recording of "Buffalo Gals." These props also represent part of the film's larger project of relocating George's desires

Figure 2–16

within the confines of the family—of convincing him that the only frontier worth conquering is that of the home, and the most celestial of bodies is already sitting by his side. (Much later, by way of announcing to him that he is soon to be a father, Mary tells him: "George Bailey lassoes stork.")[68]

George indicates that he does not at all like the position into which he has been so skillfully inserted. He squirms unhappily in Mary's living room, and when her mother asks him what he wants there he angrily responds: "Not a thing. I just came in to get warm." This refusal to invest in the obligatory heterosexual narrative, and to have "needs" which only the family can satisfy, cannot be tolerated. George's desires are subsequently orchestrated with terrifying precision. Mary tells her mother that "He's making violent love to me," and then coerces him into doing just that through an ingenious deployment of triangulation, in which the Althusserian metaphor is brilliantly literalized.[69]

Mary receives a phone call from Sam Wainwright, a childhood friend and suitor. Feigning a rather exaggerated enthusiasm, she summons George to the receiver, which she holds between them (Figure 2–16). Sam (Frank Albertson) is full of news about his nascent plastics business, but after a moment or two neither Mary nor George listens to anything he says. He figures only as a rival through whom George's desire for Mary is forcibly mediated; thus although he ostensibly invites George to enter the world of high finance, he in fact helps to interpellate him into the heterosexual scenario the other has resisted for so long. But even as he is being involuntarily inserted into the paternal position, George rebels once again against the notion that his desires must come to him from the dominant fiction. He throws down the phone, grabs Mary, and shouts his protest against the imperatives of capital and the family: "I don't want any plastics, I don't want any ground floor, and I don't want to get married—ever—to anyone . . . I want to do what *I* want to do!"

The next shot shows George and Mary becoming man and wife. He has now been cut off from a number of what the film insists are wayward ambitions—the adolescent dream of harems and polygamy as well as the more "mature" dreams of going to college and becoming an architect—and integrated into a second familial organization. But Bedford Falls insists upon a further renunciation. At the very moment of seeming cultural integration, when George has finally been recruited to a life of responsible heterosexuality, he is obliged to relinquish one last unacceptable desire—his long-cherished wish to see the world.

As he and Mary drive away from the church in which they have just been married, George waves a wad of bills in the air and describes to the cab driver how they plan to spend it—a week in New York and then another in Bermuda, with "the highest hotels," the "oldest champagne," the "richest caviar," and the "hottest music." Later that day the wad of bills has been reduced to a "papa dollar" and a "mama dollar," and George retires to the tumble-down building which will thereafter be his home. He and Mary never arrive in either New York or Bermuda, because on the way to the airport there is a run on the Bailey Building and Loan, and they must return to save the family business with their honeymoon money.

This last sacrifice seems in excess of what even a culture predicated on renunciation could demand of its subjects. However, the film insists upon the premise that "all you can take with you is that which you've given away," as the slogan beneath Peter Bailey's portrait tells us in the bank-run scene—a premise which is absolutely central to its ultimate reaffirmation, via Christianity, of the penis/phallus equation. George's honeymoon money, like his school money, shows that somehow a personal profit has been made, and that profit must be relinquished. He is therefore called upon to reinvest the money immediately in socially productive (and reproductive) ways. *It's a Wonderful Life* also suggests that George is still guilty of overvaluing the world beyond Bedford Falls, a mistake which can only be rectified by ex-

Figure 2–17a

pending all of his libidinal reserves within its borders. Consequently, at the end of his wedding day he is escorted back to the dilapidated old house beneath which he earlier confided his determination first to see the Parthenon and the Colosseum, and then to build skyscrapers "a hundred stories high," and given to understand that henceforth it will be the locus of his desires.

Mary has transformed the interior of that house into a comic condensation of all the locations George has dreamed of visiting: travel posters cover the walls (Figure 2–17a), red-checked curtains adorn the windows, and Mary (a veritable incarnation of the Buffalo gal) is roasting chickens over an open fire (Figure 2–17b). This sequence represents the triumph of the (constricted) dominant fiction over the National Geographic discourse, a triumph which is consolidated in the accelerated montage which follows. That montage shows George engaging in various forms of social service connected with the war, most of which revolve in one way or another around salvage.

At this juncture, George has been successfully interpellated into the position of the castrated father. When Potter offers him a better-paying job with travel benefits, he even manages to decline the job, although he is strongly tempted. However, George still doesn't like his position, and his continued resistance to the ethic of self-sacrifice threatens to disrupt the entire town. His refusal to absorb the $8000

Figure 2–17b

deficit incurred by Uncle Billy on the day of the film's opening suggests that more drastic measures must be taken to contain him—measures that will teach George to take pleasure from the pain of his cultural renunciations and responsibilities. The suffering male subject must be metamorphosed into the masochistic male subject.

Under the guise of fulfilling George's dream of escape (a dream which has reached such intensity that it is now articulated as the desire never to have been born), the film has Clarence lead him on a tour through a strangely defamiliarized Bedford Falls,[70] isolating him in the process from all the objects he has never learned to value sufficiently—his family, his house, his neighbors, the Building and Loan, and all the other landmarks that define his home town. As George moves through Bedford Falls, now become Pottersville, no one calls out to him or "hails" him; indeed, no one seems to know him.[71] He has been deprived not only of Mary, his children, his home, his business, and his town, but of his subjectivity (or so Clarence would have him believe). At a critical moment in the nightmare sequence George's guardian angel tells him that outside Bedford Falls he has no identity: "You're nobody . . . You have no papers, no cards, no driver's license, no 4F card, no insurance policy." This form of terrorism proves so effective that George literally begs to be re-interpellated, no matter what the cost. "I don't care what happens to me. Get me back . . . to my wife and kids," he pleads, " . . . please—I want to live again!"

The chief aim of the nightmare sequence is to reconcile George (and the viewer) to the dominant fiction by proving that there is no life outside its boundaries—by demonstrating that the desire for escape is finally nothing more than the desire for extinction. *It's a Wonderful Life* thus seemingly holds out the dominant fiction as a refuge from the death drive. George, if not the viewer, is persuaded. Threatened with non-representation, he longs for the return of the "reality" he has previously scorned. In so doing, however, he embraces lack.

The first thing we ever learn about George is that he lost the hearing of one ear when he saved his brother from drowning in an icy pond. This injury constitutes only one of the many "splittings" or castrations upon which his subjectivity is shown to depend. Those castrations include not only the negation of his dreams of travel, education, and architectural success, and Uncle Billy's loss of the $8000, but assorted minor injuries, such as ZuZu's broken flower, the cut he suffers on his lip during a bar fight, and the bannister knob that always comes off in his hand as he goes upstairs to his bedroom. All these cultural wounds are miraculously healed during the nightmare sequence, disappearing as completely as George's identity. Consequently, when he is inserted into the paternal position once again he shouts for joy to discover that his face is bleeding once again; searches excitedly for the petals of ZuZu's flower; kisses the broken bannister knob; and pronounces the Bailey residence to be a "wonderful old drafty house." George even welcomes the seeming outcome of Uncle Billy's negligence ("I'll bet it's a warrant for my arrest. Isn't it wonderful—I'm going to jail," he responds to the sheriff). He not only accepts these "wounds" as the necessary condition of cultural identity, but takes pleasure in the pain they induce in him. George thus steps over the narrow boundary separating exemplary male subjectivity from masochism, or to state the case slightly differently, the masculine norm from its perversion.[72]

7. All You Can Take With You

So open a display of wounds would normally be totally incompatible with an affirmation of the dominant fiction and its phallic representations. It is only by giving Christianity an authoritative position that *It's a Wonderful Life* is able to accommodate the spectacle of George's castration and masochism within an ideological system predicated upon the equation of penis and phallus, since that discourse not only acknowledges the distance separating the actual from the symbolic father, but makes renunciation and suffering the necessary path leading from the former to the latter. As I suggested earlier, the slogan under Peter Bailey's portrait—"All you can take with you is that which you've given away"—provides the crucial road map for that journey. *It's a Wonderful Life* relies upon this paradox as a mechanism for transforming George's debt into a handsome credit, his self-sacrifice into exaltation, and his lack into plenitude.

Significantly, Christianity is also the discourse chosen by Althusser to illustrate the point that subjectivity is always the effect of interpellation. He suggests that it interpellates its subjects by setting up a mirror relation between them and an Absolute Subject (i.e. Christ):

> ... the Absolute Subject occupies the unique place of the Centre, and interpellates around it the infinity of individuals into subjects in a double mirror-connection such that it *subjects* the subjects to the Subject, while giving them in the Subject in which each subject can contemplate its own image (present and future) the *guarantee* that this really concerns them and Him, and that since everything takes place in the Family (the Holy Family . . .), "God will *recognize* his own in it," i.e. those who have recognized God, and have recognized themselves in him, will be saved. (180)

At first glance, *It's a Wonderful Life* conforms with startling precision to the model described by Althusser; it too delineates a series of mirror relationships between heaven and earth, all of which take place "in the Family." However, on closer examination the situation becomes much more complex, and obliges us to qualify the terms of the Althusserian paradigm.

At both the film's heavenly and earthly levels a "father" calls upon a "son" to undergo a number of trials and tribulations whereby the latter will earn what is jokingly described as his "wings." This is a familiar Christian paradigm, but it is not elaborated in the usual way. Instead of equating Peter with God, and George with Christ, *It's a Wonderful Life* equates Peter with Joseph, and George with Clarence. At the same time, the more "exalted" models of God and Christ are constantly evoked by the film.

"Joseph" is of course the name of the New Testament figure who takes Mary as his wife, and who thereby stands in for God as the father of Christ. He occupies the paternal position, but is never equal to it. Joseph thus represents the actual rather than the symbolic father. The angel Joseph in *It's a Wonderful Life* enjoys an analogous status; in sending Clarence to earth on a mission of salvation, he stands in textually for God, who did the same with Christ. The subsequent equation of Peter Bailey with Joseph thus serves to isolate him, too, from the symbolic father.

Similarly, although details like the temptation scene in Potter's office or the celebration of Christmas at the end of the film align

Figure 2–18

George with Christ, that relation is mediated through the figure of Clarence. The latter parodically reenacts Christ's incarnation and descent to earth. He also performs a divinely commissioned task, although on a much smaller scale than the original. Clarence is the type of the good Christian, who despite temptations like alcohol perseveres in the attempt to accommodate himself within a narrative that exceeds him. He enjoys this paradigmatic status because of his ideological *belief*; as one of the angels says at the beginning of the film, even though he has "the I.Q. of a rabbit," he has the "faith of a child."

The degree to which even the heavenly figures of Joseph and Clarence fall short of the paternal ideal is nowhere more evident than in the sequence which immediately follows the celestial suture—a sequence which relies heavily upon an extended cinematic metaphor. As preparation for his earthly mission, Joseph invites Clarence to a "screening" of selected images from George's past. However, when Clarence first looks at the screen all he sees is a blur. Since he doesn't know how to operate the apparatus, he is obliged to wait until Joseph has adjusted the focus before proceeding with the "show."

Joseph, on the other hand, seems in perfect control of the screening situation. Not only does he adjust the focus, but at one point he freezes a frame so that Clarence—and the viewer—can take a good look at George (Figure 2–18). Nevertheless, Joseph is not permitted to

Figure 2–19

intervene at the level of production. His position is analogous to that of a projectionist, in charge of running the machine which delivers the images to the screen, but unable to participate in the construction of those images. The enunciative role within this schema is reserved for God, who remains unrepresented.

As this example would suggest, Christianity's mediations serve to distance the creation from the creator, the actual father from the symbolic father, and the spoken subject from the speaking subject. In so doing, it manages to free the latter from all of the linguistic, material, and diachronic pressures which threaten to capsize the former. By identifying the phallus with God, much as Serge Leclaire does,[73] *It's a Wonderful Life* represents it as immune to those forces which so insistently threaten earthly masculinity—the Law of Language; racial, sexual, and economic oppression; and historical trauma.

However, even as the film stresses the abyss which separates the the penis from the phallus, it spans the abyss through a flexible system of figuration which promises that the first of those terms will find fulfillment through the second—that the divine family will make good the insufficiencies of the earthly family, and that the symbolic father will convert the actual father's lack into a divine plenitude. The figures of Joseph and Clarence "fill in" the distance isolating Peter and George Bailey from their ultimate prototypes, like links in a chain.

Thus *It's a Wonderful Life* does not so much cancel as *defer* the phallic legacy. As George stands between the Christmas tree and his neighbors' largesse at the end of the film, with Mary at his side and a child in his arms, he seems finally to have taken his place within the figural chain which leads to the paternal pot of gold (Figure 2–19). The result is not only an advance on George's divine inheritance, but a resounding reaffirmation of faith in male subjectivity, the family, and small-town American life.

8. Word-Pictures

As we have seen, *The Best Years of Our Lives* and *It's a Wonderful Life* suffer in varying degrees from ideological fatigue, induced by the historical trauma of World War II and the recovery period. Like a number of other Hollywood films from the same period, they attest to the forced confrontation of the male subject with castration, as a consequence of his massive exposure to the unbinding power of the death drive. They also dramatize his resulting dislocation from the paternal position, and hence from the dominant fiction. Wyler's film registers a particularly overt loss of faith in the pieties of masculinity, the family, and capitalism. Rather than marshaling the usual defenses against the spectacle of male castration, moreover, it saturates that spectacle with affect, and calls upon the female subject to embrace it. *It's a Wonderful Life* ostensibly enacts the triumph of belief over disbelief. However, it is characterized throughout by the "interpellative urgency" which Michael Renov associates with propaganda,[74] an urgency which speaks eloquently to a crisis of faith. Furthermore, it manages to "bind" the unpleasurable excitations which threaten to overwhelm the male subject only by eroticizing them in the guise of a masochism which is antipathetic to mastery. Henry Levin's *The Guilt of Janet Ames*, on the other hand, attempts to neutralize the trauma of the war and the veteran's re-entry into a society to which he is no longer central by an energetic gearing up of ideological belief. Strenuously devoted to the reaffirmation of male adequacy, and female lack, this little-known but symptomatically important film openly relies for that purpose upon the psychic mechanisms best suited for the purpose of denial, but it puts them to uses not anticipated by Freud.

Like the other texts discussed in this chapter, *The Guilt of Janet Ames* is set in America in the postwar period, and it attempts to resolve a crisis which was somehow precipitated by that event. The title character, played by Rosalind Russell, is the widow of a man who threw himself on a grenade two years earlier in order to save the lives of the other men in his platoon. This woman is obsessed with her husband's death, which she persists in regarding as both unnecessary and unjust. She decides at the beginning of the film to find out whether even one of the survivors is equal to her husband's "little finger," and equipped with a list of their names she sets out to track them down.

It is not only in her capacity as a kind of "lack sensor," but in her capacity as an "independent woman" that Janet threatens to capsize the five veterans. As the widow of a man to whom she refused to provide either children or a home, she provides the demonic incarnation of the civilian society that somehow managed to do without the men who were giving their lives to protect it, and to which those men are consequently "superfluous."[75] An elaborate ideological machinery is put in motion to neutralize this double danger, and by the end of the film Janet has not only testified to the worthiness of all five men, even in the face of evidence to the contrary, but has assumed responsibility for her husband's death.

In the opening scene of the film, Janet is shown hesitating outside the bar where one of the survivors works. Twice she starts to cross the street to enter the bar, but is knocked down by an automobile on her second attempt. She is taken to a hospital where she is found to be incapable of walking. Since the doctor can't find any physical injury, he diagnoses Janet's paralysis as hysterical. He delivers this opinion irritably, as if to suggest that the injured woman is a self-indulgent malingerer; indeed, he tells her at one point that the only reason she can't walk is that she doesn't want to.

Rummaging through Janet's handbag at the reception desk, the police and hospital attendants are unable to determine her identity. All they find there is a congressional medal of honor and a list of five male names. One of those names—Smithfield Cobb—is familiar to all present; it belongs to a journalist who used to work the hospital beat, but who is presently unemployed, spending most of his time at Danny's Bar. He is contacted there, and summoned to the hospital to identify the "mystery woman."

Smithfield Cobb (Melvyn Douglas) or "Smitty," as he is generally called, was a successful journalist before the war, but came back a ruined man. He refuses to talk to anyone about what happened to him during that period until the very end of the film, when he confesses that he was the commanding officer who ordered Janet's husband to throw himself on the grenade. When Smitty arrives at the hospital he is shown the congressional medal and the list of names. Not only does he seem to know the identity of the "mystery woman," but he rebuffs a rival journalist with the territorial claim: "This is an old story with me; I'm just writing the finish."

The hospital staff seems quite willing to relinquish Janet to Smitty. The doctor discusses her "case" in front of him, and a nurse permits him to take Janet into a private room so that he can take care of some "private bookkeeping." Once alone with her, he prescribes a peculiar variation on the talking cure, which he offers to supervise. Inexplicably, she agrees. For most of the remainder of the film, Smitty draws a number of "word-pictures" for Janet, who attempts to visualize what he describes. Through these word-pictures she is introduced to one after the other of the men on her list. In each case the same procedure is followed: Sitting immobile in her wheelchair and looking directly in front of her, Janet listens to Smitty's voice until she is able to "see" what he relates. As soon as the image comes into focus the hospital room disappears, and we (along with Janet and Smitty) enter the world of one of the war survivors. The camera does not return to the diegetic present until each of these narratives is complete, although periodically both Smitty and Janet speak "over" the image track, reminding us that they too are onlookers.

Janet appears in each of the word-pictures. She is thus on the side of the spectacle as well as on the side of the gaze, in an unusual literalization of the position to which classic cinema consigns the female viewing subject. That split is intensified by the emphasis upon Janet's appearance. In the first of Smitty's stories she is afflicted by the feeling that she has lost something—by a sense of loss which presumably pertains to her husband's death, but which she finally attributes to a misplaced earring. Much later, within the frame story, Smitty confirms that she has in fact lost an earring, but assures her that its absence gives her "an engagingly lopsided look." In the fourth and final inner narrative, Smitty adorns Janet in diamonds, which he declares to be "her" jewel, and takes her to dinner. During this fantasmatic rendezvous Janet and her diamonds are a major topic of conversation, a conversation that eventually leads her to conclude that she is wearing one bracelet too many. Thus although she is the most important diegetic viewer of Smitty's word-pictures, Janet feels herself to be on constant display.[76] She sees herself being seen. Both in the case of the earring and the diamond bracelet, moreover, "less" is "more"; female desirability is established through absence or removal.

The imposition of this notion of female desirability upon Janet is part of the normalization to which the film subjects her, a normalization that turns precisely on specularity. In contrast to the glittering image she presents in the final narrative insert ("Oh my goodness, look at me," she coyly invites), the opening sequence of the film depicts Janet as self-absorbed and indifferent to the look of an aggressive admirer (Figure 2–20). Not only does she fail to register the stranger's attentions, but she reserves for herself the right to initiate what is

Figure 2–20

finally the most important scopic transaction in the film—the scopic transaction between herself and the surviving men. As she later confides to Smitty, "I wanted to *see* them all . . . I wanted to know if [my husband's] death was the awful waste I think it was." As if in just punishment for these sins of the eye, Janet is struck down by a driver who doesn't register her presence until it's too late; temporarily deprived of the use of her legs; and given what might be called "vision therapy." That therapy teaches her to "recognize" male sufficiency and her own guilt.

Janet's split subjectivity is not the only way in which she resembles a film viewer. Her immobility, the darkness into which she is plunged during an electrical storm, and (above all) the coercion of her look all align her with the cinematic spectator. The point of transition from the frame story to the first of the inner narratives makes that coercion quite explicit; it also depicts Smitty as a kind of projectionist, and his "word-pictures" as moving images. As Smitty describes the first of the survivors—Joe Burton—and the bar where he works, the camera zooms in from a point slightly above and behind Janet's head to a close-up of the window directly in front of her. The window immediately yields, by way of a dissolve, to an exterior shot of the bar. The window of the hospital room thus serves at the outset as a kind of screen for the projection of Smitty's flickering images (Figures 2–21a thru 2–21d).

Figure 2–21a

Figure 2–21b

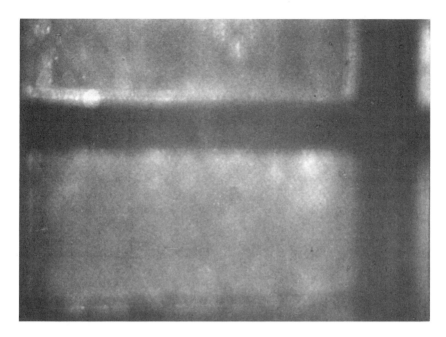

Figure 2–21c

Figure 2–21d

Figure 2–22

The fact that those images so clearly belong to the realm of "make-believe" further establishes the filmic analogy. Smitty's word-pictures seem as artificial in relation to the frame narrative as the latter seems in relation to the three-dimensional continuum of everyday life. They show characters moving through extremely stylized and overtly two-dimensional sets where conventional representational logic no longer obtains (on one of those sets, for instance, no walls separate inside from outside; on another human shadows substitute for people—Figure 2–22). At the same time the word-pictures have a hallucinatory intensity which the images from the frame narrative completely lack. They thus conform with great precision to Metz's characterization of the cinematic signifier as "unaccustomed perceptual wealth, but at the same time stamped with unreality to an unusual degree,"[77] (Figure 2–23).

This foregrounding of the "unreality" of the word-pictures might seem to undermine the larger project of *The Guilt of Janet Ames*—to work against the suspension of disbelief in male adequacy. However, Metz himself emphasizes that the cinematic viewer is never "duped by the diegetic illusion," but that there is nevertheless a "credulous person . . . seated *beneath* the incredulous one . . . who disavows what he [or she] knows" (72). He also maintains that cinema's belief-effect

Figure 2–23

hinges in a paradoxical way precisely upon its obvious unreality, since its signifiers, "already imaginary in [their] own way . . . [play] more into the hands of the diegesis . . . [tend] more to be swallowed up by it, to be credited to its side of the balance-sheet by the spectator" (67). However, in the case of this 1947 film the situation is even more complex, for Janet (and by implication the film's female spectator) must be brought to the point where her belief requires no external support—to the point where she, like Freud's fetishist, will "see" the phallus even when face to face with male castration.

Each of the word-pictures conveys Janet to one of the survivors' homes or his place of business. However, once there she is more likely to meet a girlfriend, a wife, or a daughter than the survivor himself. On the first of her imaginary journeys she encounters Joe's girlfriend, Katie, before she sees him, while on the third of those journeys she visits for some time with the small daughter of another survivor, Frank Merino, before he appears on the scene. She never even makes the acquaintance of Eddie Pierson, the second man on her list, but speaks only to his wife, Suzy. Afterwards, though, she confidently claims to know what kind of man he is.

Each of these female characters orients herself entirely in relation to male desire. Katie "doesn't belong" at Barney's Place, but she stays because Joe works there. Suzy has submitted to a similar dislocation for her husband's sake, leaving a pleasurable city life for the remote desert landscape his research requires. And when Janet defiantly asks Smitty what makes Frank better than her husband, he shows her Frank's daughter Emmy, who at the age of four or five has already mastered enough domestic arts to stand in for her dead mother. Smitty focuses primarily upon these three female figures because it is crucial for the film's resolution that Janet learn to look through their eyes at her husband's former companions. Joe, Eddie, and Frank are ultimately shown to be entirely an effect of the way in which they are viewed by the women around them. Their girlfriends, wives, and daughters confer the phallus upon them by "refusing" to see their inadequacy. Janet, on the other hand, precipitates a collective castration crisis; far from aiding in the general reconstruction of the postwar male subject, she undermines him even further by insisting upon his "unworthiness."

We are first encouraged to read male lack as an extension of female disbelief by the proximity of the scene where Janet starts to cross the street with the one in which Smitty's shortcomings are most fully and publicly displayed. Because the journalist's alcoholism and professional decline are revealed immediately after Janet is taken to the hospital, that revelation seems somehow to have been precipitated by her search. The film goes to great pains to reinforce this reading, both by making Smitty's restoration consequent upon Janet's "willingness" to believe in him, and by developing its own metadiscourse of disavowal.

We learn early in *The Guilt of Janet Ames* that Smitty is given to conversing with his bartender about Peter Ibbetson, a prisoner who was able "to go any place he desired—all over the world, even into his past—all in his mind," and in so doing to escape "from the ugly reality of his life on the wings of his imagination."[78] Smitty invokes Peter Ibbetson once again when he proposes his unusual "cure" to Janet. When she objects that Ibbetson only fantasized that he could overcome time and distance, Smitty enunciates the film's theory of belief, a theory which is startlingly congruent with that put forward in the previous chapter: "At first he did, until it finally became reality."

The word-pictures attribute an even greater effectivity to belief. As soon as Janet enters Barney's Place, the first of the hallucinatory locales, she hears Katie singing the lyrics: "Without imagination there's no reality." Katie's position, which the film strongly endorses through constant repetition, is that "If you don't believe in it, it can't happen." In other words, she maintains that *méconnaissance* necessarily precedes and is in fact capable of producing reality. Janet, on the other hand, adopts a staunchly materialist view of determination. Not surprisingly, Katie and Janet come into sharpest conflict over what is perhaps the most sacrosanct item on the American shopping list—a home of one's own. For Katie, the only prerequisite to having such a home is "the wish to live in it with someone." Janet argues that one can't have a home until one has a lot. She attempts to prove her point by blowing over the house of cards Katie and Joe have built on one of the bar tables. This action is greeted by a chorus of voices saying: "Shame on you!"

Janet encounters an even more vehement response when she challenges another privileged component of the American dream. As she walks toward the front of Barney's Place, she sees Joe dealing encouragingly with a drunk who claims he can fly. When Janet asserts the contrary, she is met by a trio of resisting male voices. The drunk complains that she's made him lose confidence in himself; Joe admonishes her that "the worst thing you can do [is to] make a man lose confidence in himself"; and Smitty's voice-over adds: "He's right. That's the worst thing you can do. Shame on you!" The film thus makes the reaffirmation of the dominant fiction entirely dependent upon an unquestioning faith—a faith incapable of being in any way shaken by material considerations such as the need for land, or "hard" facts such as gravity. Nor does *The Guilt of Janet Ames* make any attempt to demonstrate Smitty's excellence as a journalist or Joe's ability to raise money for a house. Instead, the case for male subjectivity and the ideological system which sustains it is elaborated entirely at the level of fantasy. Not surprisingly, given the theological resonances of this appeal to faith, the female subject is made responsible for every failure of the male subject to conform to the phallic ideal.

Janet "returns" from the third of her imaginary journeys skeptical about the motives behind Smitty's experiment. She begins to interrogate those motives twice, but backs away from direct confrontation each time. What she finally says is somewhat more oblique, but nonetheless extremely revealing of the film's ideological operations: "You were going to show me five worthy men. Instead of that, you've turned this gradually into an attack on me." Actually, Janet has been under attack since the first moment of the film. As she stands on the street in the opening scene she is twice harassed by a stranger. When she attempts to cross the street she is struck by a car. At the hospital the doctor scolds her for wasting time with imaginary symptoms when emergency cases require his attention, a nurse disputes that anything is wrong with her, and Smitty characterizes her mourning for her dead husband as self-indulgent. In the first of the narrative inserts Janet is subjected to a chorus of disapproving voices, while in the second she is chastized for having robbed her husband of the desire to live. The third word-picture concludes with an even more sweeping attack: Frank claims that Janet makes "everybody unhappy" through her selfishness.

The final criticism (which marks the point of Janet's revolt) is puzzling, since everyone in Smitty's stories has been shown to be extraordinarily happy. Each of his stories dramatizes the triumph of true love over all possible odds—over amputation, poverty, parental disapproval, and death. However, what Smitty reveals at the end of the film is that the lives of the five veterans read quite differently from the stories he has told about them. Instead of a heroic amputee, Joe is just "a tough guy in a saloon." Far from becoming an idealistic scientist, Eddie has opted to live off his rich father-in-law. Frank and his daughter reside with his grandmother, rather than in their own house and garden. Sammy, who is depicted as a popular comedian in the fourth of the word-pictures, in fact spends most of his time at the races. Finally, Smitty himself has degenerated from a successful journalist to an unemployed alcoholic. What these last-minute disclosures make clear is that an abyss separates each of the men on Janet's list from the paternal ideal. She makes "everyone unhappy" because she threatens to expose that abyss—to reveal the culturally inadmissable spectacle of male lack.

Janet continues to insist that houses require lots and that humans are subject to gravity until the end of the third word-picture, but when Smitty threatens her with the prospect of never walking again, she is finally "persuaded" to suspend her disbelief in the worthiness of the five men on her list. In the fourth and final inner narrative, Janet goes with Smitty to a fantasmatic nightclub where she obediently declares that there is champagne in her empty glass and that pearls are the food of love (Figure 2–24). More importantly, she claps enthusiastically when Sammy, the last veteran, performs his comic routine. (That character indicates how much is at stake in her approval when he thanks her for giving him his "chance.") However, she is still unable to walk when Smitty has turned off the imaginary projector, and he calls upon her to "confess" the "truth" he claims she is withholding.

The Guilt of Janet Ames cites no psychoanalytic, social, economic, or political reasons for the postwar disintegration of the five men whose lives David spared. Indeed, it provides no explanation whatever for the failure of Joe, Eddie, and Frank. The only reason Smitty ever suggests for his own unemployment and alcoholism is that he ordered David to jump the grenade that he should have jumped himself— that he was, as he puts it at one point, "selfish enough to live." The implication is that if he were not responsible for his subordinate's

Figure 2–24

death, he would indeed be what he passes himself off as being in the final word-picture—a "campaigning journalist."

By means of the externalizing displacement of this responsibility from himself to Janet, Smitty ultimately achieves precisely this enviable status. However, that displacement is not secure until Janet "voluntarily" assumes the burden of guilt which has been repeatedly laid at her feet. I say "voluntarily" because Janet produces her "confession"[79] only after she has been prompted to do so by Smitty, and told that it is the precondition for leaving her wheelchair:

> I've been blaming five men for David's death when I should have blamed myself. I felt guilty . . . I was trying to blame anyone but myself . . . I let him die with all his dreams unfinished. It was I who refused to plan a house . . . It was I who made him stay in that dull job he hated because I was selfish . . . afraid to risk my security . . . David *did* want a child—he wanted it very much . . . But my greatest shame is that I married him and I never loved him at all.

In this speech Janet assumes sole responsibility not only for her husband's death, but for the weakening of the dominant fiction—for the loss of belief in the family, the American home, romantic love, and the phallic male subject.

It is not until Janet has testified to her own lack that Smitty admits to her both his own contribution to her husband's death, and the fictive basis of the word-pictures. At last she grasps what is expected of her, and gives a dazzling demonstration of her ability to conform to his expectations. She absorbs Smitty's guilt ("I don't think David even heard what you were saying to him . . . He was already on his way to that grenade. He chose to die because he himself had so little to live for"); denies that the five survivors are in any way insufficient ("I still see [all of them] just as you showed them to me because that's what they really are if you look at them with your understanding and not just your eyes"); and affirms her belief both in Smitty's phallic attributes and in those elements of the American dream that she had earlier repudiated ("Close your eyes and try to see [the future]: Smithfield Cobb is a crusading journalist with a wife who adores him").

9. The Female Fetishist

In his 1927 essay on fetishism, Freud maintains that the fetish always reveals itself upon analysis to be "a substitute for the woman's (the mother's) penis that the little boy once believed in and—for reasons familiar to us—does not want to give up."[80] This formulation would seem to exclude the female subject definitively from the position of fetishist. It would also seem to situate the lack in relation to which the fetish is mustered emphatically at the site of the female genitals. Fetishism emerges quite simply as a male defense against woman's castration.

In an influential essay from 1982, Mary Ann Doane also claims that fetishism is alien to female subjectivity, although for different reasons than those stated by Freud. Doane situates that psychic operation in the gap opened up between "the visible and the knowable" in the male subject's relation to the female genitals—in the capacity Freud attributes to him for disavowing what he has seen.[81] For woman, on the other hand, there is no distance between seeing and understanding, and this "mode of judging 'in a flash'" is "conducive to what might be termed an 'over-identification' with the image." She has no capacity to "speculate" about what she sees.

However, Lacan throws a wrench into both of these arguments by insisting that the penis itself can assume the status of a fetish—by maintaining, that is, that the ostensible referent or base-term within the fetishistic scenario may be no more than a supplement or prop disguising a lack which is no longer conceived in strictly anatomical terms. Woman "finds the signifier of her own desire in the body of him to whom she addresses her demand for love," he writes. "Perhaps it should not be forgotten that the organ that assumes this signifying function takes on the value of a fetish."[82] Although this is a characteristically obscure passage, one detail emerges with absolute clarity: the position of fetishist within this tableau is occupied by the female rather than the male subject.

Lacan does not specify whose lack it is that the penis serves to conceal, man's, or woman's. It is consequently unclear whether we are to conceptualize the female subject as a fetishist in relation to the male subject's lack, or in relation to her own. Freud gestures in the direction of the second of these possibilities in "Some Psychical Consequences of the Anatomical Distinction Between the Sexes"; although he is no closer in that essay than in the one under discussion to proposing that there are female fetishists, he does acknowledge that the female subject may fortify herself in a relation of disavowal to her own lack (253).

A series of texts by Sarah Kofman, Elizabeth L. Berg, and Naomi Schor have advanced a similar account of female fetishism. In *Enigma of Woman*, Kofman argues that the bisexuality of the hysteric resembles fetishism, in that each hinges upon a fundamental undecidability.[83] Expanding upon this insight, Berg suggests that the female subject's bisexuality permits her to "take pleasure in both a feminine and a masculine mode,"[84] and that for the woman who is able to affirm both modes, "sexual difference is seen as undecidable, producing an irresolvable oscillation" with respect to castration (19). In a provocative reading of the novels of George Sand, Schor also pursues the notion that bisexuality—or, as she prefers to conceptualize it, "bisextuality"—provides the most appropriate basis for theorizing female fetishism.[85]

However, *The Guilt of Janet Ames* suggests that *male* castration may ultimately be the more conventional object of feminine denial. That film's central character, who so clearly stands in for the female spectator, is ideologically recruited to invest at least a partial belief in the images of an ideal masculinity which are conjured forth for her by pitting "heart" against "mind," faith against evidence. She is "cured," in other words, by learning to disavow male lack. The most important and exemplary scene in *The Guilt of Janet Ames* is consequently the final one, in which Janet manifests the "divided attitude" of the fetishist—in which she dramatizes, that is, Mannoni's "I know very well, but all the same . . ."[86] Sitting in Danny's Bar surrounded by empty glasses and the torn ticket which should have taken him to Chicago and a fresh start that night—surrounded, in short, by the palpable traces of his castration—Smitty says to Janet: "Look at me. What do you see?" And Janet, in complete disregard of the conflicting visual evidence, responds: "Smithfield Cobb, crusading journalist."

Although Janet does not know until the end of the film that Smitty's narratives are pure fabrications, and so cannot be said technically to be a fetishist until the moment that she affirms that character's adequacy in the face of his alcoholism and failed career, the same cannot be said of the film's female spectator, who is made privy to the journalist's disintegration from the very start. This viewer is encouraged to invest ideological belief in Smitty's narratives and hence in male sufficiency in spite of the palpable "unreality" of the image track, and—by extension—the dominant fiction. Significantly, the word-pictures are so palpably artificial that they can be best described in the terms Stephen Heath reserves for the fetish. Each one is "a brilliance, something lit up, heightened, depicted, as under an arc light, a point of (theatrical) representation." Since Janet is so visibly "installed (as at the theater or at the movies) *for* the representation,"[87] moreover, the female viewer cannot fail to see herself similarly positioned. The film thus gives her "knowledge" of her situation, just as it ultimately does for Janet, yet works at the same time to engage her belief. I feel once again impelled to invoke Metz's "credulous person . . . seated *beneath* the incredulous one," now not merely as a general reminder that ideological belief operates at a level radically exterior to consciousness, but as a very precise characterization of the female spectator projected by Levin's film.

Not only does *The Guilt of Janet Ames* appeal to the female viewer to invest belief in its manifestly artificial images of male adequacy, but it insists that the continuation of the American *vraisemblance* depends upon her doing do. Female fetishism thus emerges in that film not as the manifestation of a rare perversion, but as the precondition for "reality" itself. Only through the belief of a good woman, the film maintains, can the "broken world" be once again assembled.

I have attempted to demonstrate that *The Best Years of Our Lives*, *It's a Wonderful Life*, and *The Guilt of Janet Ames* enact a range of responses to the historical trauma of World War II, and to the difficult reentry of the veteran soldier into postwar American society. Wyler's film attests eloquently to the consequences for masculinity of a massive exposure to trauma, but rather than attempting to shore up phallic identification, it repeatedly reveals and even privileges male lack. *It's a Wonderful Life* not only addresses the crisis in postwar male subjectivity, but dramatizes its implications for the dominant fiction and the larger social formation. It attempts to resolve that crisis by engineering a renewal of ideological belief, but it is able to do so only by effecting the male subject's identification with a castrated father, and by eroticizing his compulsory repetition of unpleasure as masochism. Although *The Guilt of Janet Ames* might seem the least conventional of the three films, or at least the one which most breaks with realist representation, its response to the historical crisis of World War II is by far the most normative. By drawing attention to the contrived nature of its representations, it cleverly acknowledges and even gives the impression of participating in the ideological exhaustion of postwar America, while at the same time engaging its viewer in an efficacious "make-believe" with respect to the most privileged elements of the *vraisemblance*.

This chapter and the previous one have challenged the phallic identification upon which masculinity depends by insisting upon the lack at the heart of all subjectivity, and by isolating historical trauma as a force capable of unbinding the coherence of the male ego, and exposing the abyss that it conceals. Chapter 3 will showcase the male subject's unavoidable specularity. It will also enforce an absolute distinction between the gaze and the look. Finally, it will demonstrate that the male subject is no more in possession of the first of those apparent perquisites than is his female counterpart. Although the theoretical framework of Chapter 3 will be insistently psychoanalytic, ideology will once again provide one of the central terms of analysis.

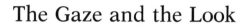

The Gaze and the Look

3

Fassbinder and Lacan: A Reconsideration of Gaze, Look, and Image

This chapter will differentiate the gaze from the look, and hence from masculinity. It will also provide a theoretical articulation of the field of vision[1] within which every subject is necessarily held. Although the paradigm which it will advance differs in many respects from that which has dominated film theory over the past fifteen years, my aim is less to displace than to complicate the latter, whose resources are still far from exhausted. Lacan is of course central to this double project. However, since the distinctions that I will attempt to draw depend as fully upon the cinema of Rainer Werner Fassbinder as they do upon *Seminar XI*, it is with that cinema and its exemplary refusals that I shall begin.

Although the descriptive phrase "aesthetics of pessimism" derives from Fassbinder himself,[2] it might well have been coined by one of his critics, who have commented in a variety of ways on the negativity which suffuses his texts. Tony Pipolo complains that Fassbinder's films do not "work to dispel that sense of helplessness so pervasive in the present atmosphere," that they generate an "enveloping negativity of affect," and that in them "conditions are generally depicted as virtually unchangeable and characters are denied the personal redemption of classical tragedy."[3] Richard Dyer accuses Fassbinder of left-wing melancholy, and worries that "hardly anywhere" in his films "is there a notion of working-class, or women's, or gay, struggle, whether in the form of resistance . . . or revolution."[4] More interestingly, Wilfred Wiegand characterizes Fassbinder's cinema as "post-revolutionary," in that "it no longer steers a course for the naive pre-revolutionary dream of a better world, but . . . has absorbed the fragments of a negative historical experience."[5] And Thomas Elsaesser, as always Fassbinder's most astute reader, writes that identity in his films is "a movement, an unstable structure of vanishing points, encounters, vistas, and absences"—that "it appears negatively, as nostalgia, deprivation, lack of motivation, loss," and that characters "only know they exist by the negative emotion of anxiety."[6]

What all of these accounts point toward, although only Elsaesser manages to theorize it, is Fassbinder's radical refusal to *affirm*, his repudiation of positivity in any shape or form. His aversion to the fictions which make psychic and social existence tolerable is perhaps best dramatized by those films which put such fictions temporarily into play. *The Marriage of Maria Braun* (1978), for example, has been hailed as the story of a "strong and believable" woman, who "comes to personify the triumph of the will,"[7] and whose life "stands as a symbol that another kind of life is possible."[8] However, the end of the film detonates this fantasy of the self-made woman, less through the match which Maria lights in her gas-filled kitchen than through the belated revelation of Oswald's arrangement with Hermann, an arrangement which hinges upon the exchange of a woman between two men, i.e. that transaction which Luce Irigaray has shown to be at the center of the existing symbolic order.[9] *Jail Bait* (1972) also puts the torch to positivity, this time in the guise of the romantic love which ostensibly binds the adolescent protagonists to each other, and motivates the murder of Hanni's father. Encountering Franz outside the courtroom where he is to stand trial for their joint crime, Hanni announces the still-birth of their child, and dismisses their relationship as "only physical." *Mother Küsters Goes to Heaven* (1975) enacts a similar collapse of belief in the capacity of the left to deal adequately with an event like the murder by Hermann Küsters of one of his factory bosses, and his subsequent suicide, providing in the process a searing portrait of political *méconnaissance* on the part both of the Thalmanns, wealthy members of the Communist Party, and Knab, the anarchist.

However, few of Fassbinder's other films deviate even to this degree from an uncompromising negativity, occasionally irradiated but in no way mitigated by an extreme and irrational joy. More is at issue here than a a refusal to provide affirmative representations of women, blacks, gays, or the left, although that is already a great deal given the intense preoccupation of Fassbinder's cinema with precisely those sexual, social, and political groupings. What is thus placed at risk is identity itself, which is no longer able to secure an "interior" foothold.

Identity, as psychoanalysis has taught us, necessitates the internalization of a series of things which are in the first instance external. Freud insists upon this principle with respect both to the ego and the super-ego, defining the former as the psychic mapping of what is initially a bodily image,[10] and the latter as the introjection of parental authority, in the guise, for instance, of the father's voice.[11] Lacan's account of the mirror stage further elaborates this notion of an exteriority which is taken within the subject, first in the guise of its mirror image, subsequently in the form of parental imagoes, and later yet in the shape of a whole range of cultural representations, the *moi* becoming over time more and more explicitly dependent upon that which might be said to be "alien" or "other."[12] What Lacan designates the "gaze" also manifests itself initially within a space external to the subject, first through the mother's look as it facilitates the "join" of infant and mirror image, and later through all of the many other actual looks with which it is confused. It is only at a second remove that the subject might be said to assume responsibility for "operating" the gaze by "seeing" itself being seen even when no pair of eyes are trained upon it—by taking not so much the gaze as its effects within the self. However, consciousness as it is redefined by Lacan hinges not only upon the internalization but upon the elision of the gaze; this "seeing" of oneself being seen is experienced by the subject-of-consciousness—by the subject, that is, who arrogates to itself a certain self-presence or substantiality—as a seeing of itself seeing itself.[13]

What happens within Fassbinder's cinema is that both the gaze and the images which promote identity remain irreducibly exterior, stubbornly removed from the subject who depends upon them for its experience of "self." Elsaesser has touched upon the first of these exteriorizations in "Primary Identification and the Historical Subject: Fassbinder and Germany," although his emphasis falls more fully upon the exhibitionism of Fassbinder's characters than upon the gaze on which they depend:

> Their endless waiting wants to attract someone to play the spectator, who would confirm them as subjects, by displaying the sort of behavior that would conform to the reactions they expect to elicit. The audience is inscribed as voyeurs, but only because the characters are so manifestly exhibitionist. Substantiality is denied to both characters and audience, they derealize each other, as all relations polarize themselves in terms of seeing and being seen . . . to be, in Fassbinder, is to be perceived, *esse est percipi*. (542)

The film through which Elsaesser pursues his thesis—and upon which Judith Mayne also focuses in her account of specularity in Fassbinder[14]—is *Ali: Fear Eats the Soul* (1973), but there are many other texts in that filmmaker's oeuvre where characters display themselves in this way to whomever will look, and in which subjectivity is consequently shown to depend upon a visual agency which remains insistently outside. "We are watched on all sides," the singer, Tripelli (Barbara Valentin) warns in *Effi Briest* (1974), a curse which turns into a lost source of sustenance when the socius finally looks away from Effi. The gaze is similarly omnipresent in *Mother Küsters Goes to Heaven*, represented this time precisely through the camera to which Lacan compares it in *Four Fundamental Concepts*. The passage to which I refer, which insists once again upon the alterity of the gaze, provides the basis for what I have elsewhere theorized as "the photo session,"[15] i.e. the clicking of an imaginary camera which photographs the subject and thereby constitutes him or her. "What determines [the subject], at the most profound level, in the visible," remarks Lacan, "is the gaze that is outside. It is through the gaze that [the subject enters] light and it is from the gaze that [he or she receives] its effects. Hence it comes about that the gaze is the instrument through which light is embodied and through which . . . [the subject is] *photographed*."[16]

Among the characters in *Mother Küsters Goes to Heaven*, only Corinna (Ingrid Caven) has reason to celebrate the illumination into which she is thrust, since she alone is able to meet the gaze halfway by offering herself as a spectacle to it. *Mother Küsters Goes to Heaven* thus suggests that some limited power is available to the subject who recognizes her necessary subordination to the gaze, but finds potentially transgressive ways of "performing" before it. The title character (Brigitte Mira), on the other hand, repeatedly places herself guilelessly in front of a camera, confident that it will record her "true" essence and feelings, only to be constructed anew, and in ways which never cease to appall her.

In a film made a year earlier than *Mother Küsters Goes to Heaven*, *Fox and His Friends* (1974), Fassbinder himself plays a character who is virtually haunted by the gaze, as if to call dramatically into question his own position of apparent visual control. That film begins with a crane shot down from the sky above a circus to the window of a police car waiting near the stage, where Fox the Talking Head (Fassbinder) and a group of female strippers are being introduced to the audience by Klaus (Karl Scheydt), the "ring-master." We thus look initially at Fox from the point of view of the police officers inside the car, whose eyes might be said to "stand in" for the gaze. After Fox wins the lottery, it is Max (Karlheinz Böhm), the antiques dealer, who takes over this function. He is shown conspicuously and at times ceremonially looking on while Fox meets Eugen (Peter Chatel) and Philip (Harry Baer), takes a mud bath at a man's gym, and breaks up with Eugen. Max's presence is particularly resistant to a naturalistic reading on the last of these occasions; it is, indeed, inexplicable in any terms other than the specular. He silently accompanies Fox and Eugen as they descend the blue neon-lit escalators of what is presumably a subway station, sometimes following at a distance, sometimes positioning himself in proximity to one of the other two characters, but always a necessary but diegetically redundant witness.

At least two other Fassbinder films suggest that it is no more possible to die without a confirming gaze than it is to assume an identity. Having fallen asleep in one of the empty offices in Saitz's apartment building, the central character of *In a Year of Thirteen Moons* (1978) is awakened by the entrance of a man attaching a rope to the ceiling of the room in order to hang himself. That man invites Erwin (Volker Spengler) to watch him die, and as he falls limply from the rope the camera holds on Erwin's attentive face, back-lit against a lurid red. Similarly, the "Epilogue" to *Berlin Alexanderplatz* (1980) builds to a crescendo with the crucifixion of Franz Biberkopf (Günther Lamprecht), an event which assumes the status of a specular extravanganza. Here it is not only the film's protagonist who is "on stage," but the gaze itself, dispersed across the crowd assembled around the cross in a range of historical costumes, their eyes and hands raised theatrically to the dying man.

Elsaesser argues that what is articulated through this constant foregrounding of the look is a subjectivity specific to fascism, whose prototype is "the German petit-bourgeois, identifying himself with the State, and making a public spectacle of his good behavior and conformism" (544). While I am reluctant to minimize any argument which facilitates an historical understanding of subjectivity, it does seem to me that this curious solicitation of the gaze has less to do with fascism than with Fassbinder's refusal to commute exteriority into interiority—his refusal, that is, to naturalize identity by concealing its external scaffolding.

Fassbinder's cinema does more than exteriorize the gaze; it also separates it from its usual support, the look, a dislocation which has extreme consequences for sexual difference. No character within that cinema, male or female, is ever represented as possessing the gaze, regardless of how central his or her look happens to be to the articulation of the visual field. What films like *Ali: Fear Eats the Soul* and *Fox and His Friends* oblige us to see is that although the look of a character or a group of characters may masquerade as the gaze for another character, that imposture is made possible only through the propping of the look upon the gaze. *Four Fundamental Concepts* stresses not only the otherness of the gaze, but its distinctness from what Lacan calls the "eye," or what I have been calling the "look." (The French language does not, of course, sustain my distinction, offering only one word—*le regard*—in place of the two primary English signifiers of vision: look and gaze.)

Although the gaze might be said to be "the presence of others as such,"[17] it is by no means coterminous with any individual viewer, or group of viewers. It issues "from all sides," whereas the eye "[sees] only from one point." Moreover, its relationship to the eye is sufficiently antinomic that Lacan can describe it as "triumph[ing]" over the look.[18] The gaze is "unapprehensible,"[19] i.e. impossible to seize or get hold of. The relationship between eye and gaze is thus analogous in certain ways to that which links penis and phallus; the former can stand in for the latter, but can never approximate it. Lacan makes this point with particular force when he situates the gaze outside the voyeuristic transaction, a transaction within which the eye would seem most to aspire to a transcendental status, and which has consequently provided the basis, within feminist film theory, for an equation of the male voyeur with the gaze.[20] *Four Fundamental Concepts* suggests, on the contrary, that it is at precisely that moment when the eye is placed to the keyhole that it is most likely to find itself subordinated to the gaze. At this moment, observes Lacan, "a gaze surprises [the subject] in the function of voyeur, disturbs him, overwhelms him and reduces him to shame" (84). The subject who thus "feels himself surprised," Lacan adds, is the subject who is "sustaining himself in a function of desire" (85). What this crucial passage from *Four Fundamental Concepts* suggests is that if the gaze always exceeds the look, the look might also be said to exceed the gaze—to carry a libidinal supplement which relegates it, in turn, to a scopic subordination. The gaze, in other words, remains outside desire, the look stubbornly within.

Fassbinder does more than distinguish between the gaze and the characters who at times function as its representative. He goes so far at times as to suggest an equation between "look" and "lack," thereby further complicating our understanding of cinema's scopic regime. His films oblige the look to acknowledge itself not only as a carrier of libido, but as a signifier of castration. They refuse to cover over the void which is at the core of subjectivity, a void which gives rise not only to anxiety, but to desire. In *Ali: Fear Eats the Soul*, for instance, to which I will return in a few moments, there are characters whose look functions less to confirm or deny another's identity by standing in for the gaze than to express an erotic yearning. It is in this way that the women stare at Ali in the bar he frequents, and that Emmi watches him when he takes a shower in her apartment. Even more striking in this respect are the looks directed toward the figure of Franz (Harry Baer) in *Gods of the Plague* (1969), not only by Johanna (Hanna Schygulla) and Margarethe (Margarethe von Trotta), but by the waitress in the cafe he visits at the beginning of the film.

As Franz enters the cafe, the camera adopts a position to the waitress's immediate right, the viewfinder so close to her face as almost to graze her skin (Figure 3–1a). Franz stands at the counter to her left, using the telephone, behind her in the frame. Although the waitress only turns to look directly at Franz once in this lengthy shot (Figure 3–1b), she is covertly watching him all the time, and the camera insists upon showing what she "sees." Her look is foregrounded again a few shots later as she places the fresh coffee on a table. Franz inserts a few coins in the jukebox, and the affect which has been produced through this foregrounding of the look finds expression with the first bars of "Here We Go Again," to which he and the waitress dance.

Beware of a Holy Whore (1970), which is organized almost entirely around one-way visual transactions, is another film in which the look circulates independently of the usual sexual boundaries, and without any power to subordinate. Babs (Margarethe Von Trotta) and the make-up "girl" watch two men absorbed in conversation; Eddie Constantine watches Hanna (Hanna Schygulla); Irm (Magdalena Montezuma) watches Jeff (Lou Castel); Jeff watches Ricky (Marquard Bohm); and Ricky watches an unknown woman (Ingrid Caven) at the bar. The camera meanders from person to person, and group to group, sometimes by means of a cut, and at other times through some aleatory movement which parallels the libidinal "drift." However, the syntactic element which most brilliantly evokes the operations of desire also anchors it intimately to the human look. The element to which I refer—a fast zoom in on the face of a watching character at a moment of pleasure, excitement, or shock—constitutes a reversal of one of the conventional signifiers of vision, a zoom in on what is seen. This reversal, which focuses attention upon the look rather than its object, brings the look emphatically within spectacle. The turning of the look back upon itself—the mimicry on the part of the camera of a scopic drive made suddenly to go "backward"—also suggests its inability both to reach and to subjugate its object, and so inverts the usual scopic paradigm.

Whereas classic cinema equates the exemplary male subject with the gaze, and locates the male eye on the side of authority and the law even when it is also a carrier of desire, *Beware of a Holy Whore* not only extends desire and the look which expresses it to the female subject, but makes the male desiring look synonymous with loss of control, dramatized in the film through hysterical outbursts and the reckless consumption of alcohol. It might thus be said doubly to "feminize" erotic spectatorship, and this despite the fact that the male character who is placed most emphatically on the side of desire is also the director of the film within the film. When, near the conclusion of *Beware of a Holy Whore*, the cameraman comes to the director, Jeff,

Figure 3–1a

Figure 3–1b

and asks him for instructions about the next day's "shoot," Jeff shows him by holding an imaginary viewfinder in his fingers. Here is the male eye standing in once again for the gaze, but off-handedly and even irritably, as if asked to perform a role in which it can no longer believe. For most of the film Jeff is either engaged in histrionic displays worthy of Petra von Kant—displays which locate him decisively on the side of the spectacle—or impotently looking at and brooding upon the one figure who eludes his amorous calculations.

Fassbinder further denaturalizes identity by emphasizing at every conceivable juncture its imaginary bases. Thus he never misses an opportunity to point the camera at a character's mirror reflection rather than at the character himself or herself, and he shoots almost compulsively through windows, as if to deny any possibility of a direct or immediate access to the object of the camera's scrutiny. In *Despair* (1977) and *Nora Helmer* (1973) the windows are lavishly etched, this ornamentation working against the illusion of depth which represents such an important part of the cinematic *vraisemblance*—against that "impression of reality" to which the classic film aspires. A dazzling series of shots from *Chinese Roulette* (1976) complicates the paradigm further by substituting glass display cases for windows, thus giving glass a three-dimensionality which the characters themselves lack.

As Elsaesser remarks, Fassbinder's characters also "endlessly try to place themselves or arrange others in a configuration that allows them to reexperience the mirror stage" (543). One thinks in this respect not only of Erwin's excitement upon seeing the photograph of himself in the magazine which publishes his interview, a photograph which affords a momentary conviction of identity, but the desperate attempts on the part of Veronika Voss (Rosel Zech) to orchestrate lighting and music in such a way as to create the impression that she "really" is the star which her publicity stills declare her to be. There is also the celebrated moment in *Lili Marlene* (1980) when Willi (Hanna Schygulla) lying on the bed in her newly acquired white apartment, and basking in the borrowed glory of her stage persona, kisses her own image in the mirror in a euphoric double *méconnaissance*.[22] In a much earlier film, *The American Soldier* (1970), a homosexual gypsy named Tony El Gitano (Ulli Lommel) attempts to seduce Ricky (Karl Scheydt), the Killer, without recourse to the usual lures of touch, smell, or taste. Instead, he undresses in front of a mirror, with his back to Ricky, as if to suggest that he is offering his image in place of his body (Figure 3–2). Significantly, El Gitano's subsequent death is recorded as precisely the loss of this reflection; as Ricky fires his gun, El Gitano falls to the bed, leaving his fantasmatic murderer in sole "possession" of the mirror.

Figure 3–2

However, it is *Gods of the Plague* which holds subject and ideal image at the most extreme distance from each other, and which hence attests most eloquently to the latter's recalcitrant exteriority. Pinned on the wall over Margarethe's bed is an enormous poster of a blonde woman's face, presumably a blown-up advertisement. The face bears a sufficiently close resemblance to Margarethe as to make evident even to the casual viewer that the poster represents the mirror in which that character sees herself. However, whenever Margarethe appears in the same frame as the larger-than-life woman, she is not only dwarfed, but diminished by the comparison (Figure 3–3). This image is also central to the film's libidinal transactions. At a key moment in the film, Günther (Günther Kaufmann), Franz, and Margarethe form an intimate grouping in Margarethe's bedroom prior to having sex, and talk about traveling to Greece. "We don't need money," says Franz, and Günther adds: "Because we're in love." As Günther utters these words, he embraces the poster above the bed, his body held in a spread-eagle position against the female face (Figure 3–4). This telling gesture suggests that it is not just Margarethe who views herself through that idealizing portrait, but Gunther and Franz

Figure 3–3

as well—that *it* is the cause and support of love, the terrain across which the two men meet.

Margarethe is not the only character in *Gods of the Plague* who sustains her identity through constant reference to an external representation. Johanna (Hanna Schygulla), who is a chanteuse in a bar called the Lola Montes, keeps a movie poster in her dressing room which depicts a still photograph of Marlene Dietrich, prototype of all of Fassbinder's torch singers, in what would appear to be *The Devil Is A Woman* (Figure 3–5). Later in the film Franz and Margarethe go into a shop to buy a poster which they pin up in the hall of their apartment, and which henceforth serves as *his* narcissistic support—a poster, that is, of King Ludwig, an epicene historical "personality" whom Baer, the actor playing Franz, would subsequently go on to perform in Syberberg's film, *Requiem for a Virgin King* (1972).

The insistent specularization of the male subject in Fassbinder's cinema functions not only to desubstantialize him, but to prevent any possibility of mistaking his penis for the phallus, a dislocation which is at the center of Fassbinder's "aesthetics of pessimism." There is ultimately no affirmation more central to our present symbolic order,

Figure 3–4

yet at the same time more precariously maintained, than the fiction
that the exemplary male subject is adequate to the paternal function.
This affirmation rests upon the negation of the negativity at the heart
of all subjectivity—a negation of the lack installed by language, and
compounded in all sorts of ways by sexuality, class, race, and history.
Fassbinder not only refuses to give us male characters who might in
any way be eligible for "exemplariness," focusing always upon figures
who are erotically, economically, and/or racially marginal, but he
obsessively de-phallicizes and at times radically de-idealizes the male
body, a project which at least in one film—*In a Year of Thirteen
Moons*—leads to a corresponding psychic disintegration expressive of
the absolute annihilation of masculinity.

   Although an extremely early film, *Gods of the Plague* is in this respect
fully congruent with Fassbinder's later texts. Franz Walsh, innova-
tively rendered by Baer, can perhaps best be characterized as a "limp"
male subject. He holds himself as though he were literally bereft of
"backbone," whether walking on the street or sitting at the dinner
table, and at one point he huddles on the floor in an infantile posture
for at least three minutes of screen time, listening to a nonsensical
children's record. As is so frequently the case in Fassbinder's films,

Figure 3–5

Franz's character is metaphorically reinscribed through an inanimate object, a rag doll which hangs lifelessly from the ceiling of Margarethe's hall (Figure 3–6).

An important scene near the beginning of the film speaks even more eloquently to Franz's flaccidity. Rescuing him on the street from a group of angry assailants, Magdalena takes him home with her and attempts to seduce him. Franz remains completely inert, despite Magdalena's best efforts, but eventually she maneuvers him onto the bed, where she struggles with his remaining items of clothing. Two extraordinary shots describe what is in effect a sexual pietà: In the first one, Franz sprawls on the bed to the left of Magdalena, his legs on her lap. A reverse shot follows, unmotivated by any diegetic look; in it, the camera takes up a position on the other side of the bed, so that Franz's head occupies the right front frame, and Magdalena's the left rear frame. This second shot accentuates the unnatural, almost Mannerist deployment of the male body, which connotes a passivity akin to death. Franz's eyes are turned away from the woman who holds his lower limbs, and, as both shots indicate, his penis is completely detumescent (Figure 3–7a thru 3–7b).

Ali: Fear Eats the Soul articulates the marginality of its central male

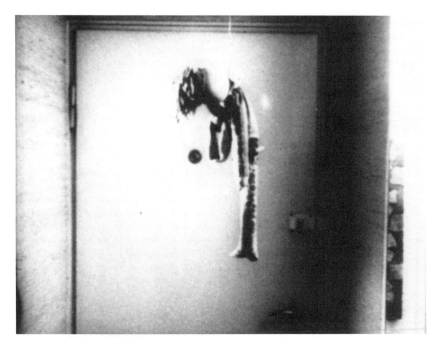

Figure 3–6

character according to a different logic than does *Gods of the Plague*, focusing upon an Arab *Gastarbeiter* rather than a member of the German underclass. However, once again it is the male rather than the female body which constitutes the object of cinematic fascination, and once again that body is stripped of the usual accoutrements of masculinity. *Ali: Fear Eats the Soul* displays both to the diegetic and the extra-diegetic eye a body which is barred, by virtue of its skin pigmentation, from representing the phallus, at least within the film's contemporary German context. However, if that body is the privileged object of the gaze, it has the same status for the look; it is the locus, that is, of libidinal investment as well as a kind of social surveillance. (The same, I should note, could also be said of Franz in *Gods of the Plague*, whose "limpness" paradoxically makes him the cynosure of all female eyes.)

In a crucial scene late in *Ali: Fear Eats the Soul*, the camera takes up residence in the bathroom of Emmi's apartment while Ali (El Hedi Ben Salem) takes a shower. Although we are made visual accessories to that event, we are never permitted to glance directly at Ali; the film shows only the image of his body reflected from the thighs up in an obliquely angled mirror hanging on the wall next to the medicine

Figure 3–7a

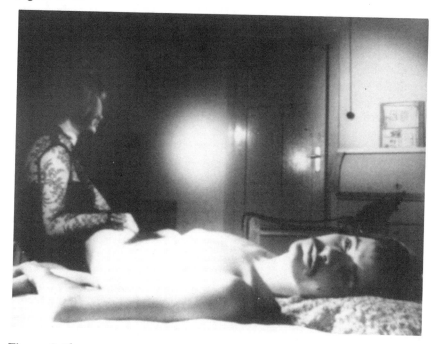

Figure 3–7b

Figure 3–8

cabinet (Figure 3–8). As in *The American Soldier, Ali: Fear Eats the Soul* thus suggests that it is not so much the body itself as the representation of the body which constitutes erotic spectacle, and once again the form which that representation takes is almost classically feminine. This shot of Ali's mirror reflection is repeated four times, with slight variations. After its first citation, which remains unclaimed by any diegetic onlooker, Emmi (Brigitte Mira) enters the room, and what we see is henceforth what she ostensibly sees (Figure 3–9). Her only remark—"You're very handsome"—makes explicit the desire in her look. Ali smiles at her in the mirror, with the modesty of someone whose pleasure in himself is entirely dependent upon the pleasure another takes in him, in a re-enactment of that peculiarly non-narcissistic "narcissism" which Freud associates with the classic female subject. (In one of his metapsychological essays, Freud observes of "such women" that they love themselves "with an intensity comparable to that of the man's love for them.")[23]

The second scene which works both to specularize and to sexualize Ali occurs after he and Emmi return from their vacation, and in it the desiring look is complexly imbricated with the gaze. Emmi invites two of her co-workers up to her apartment, and introduces them to

Figure 3–9

her husband. The women circle around Ali, touching his biceps while murmuring, "Terrific . . . and such nice, soft skin" (Figure 3–10). It is not only the attention which they lavish on the black man's body which de-phallicizes him—an attention which strays far from the organ to which male identity is pinned, dispersing itself across the entire body in a reprise of female sexuality—but the way they exchange him amongst themselves. If many of Fassbinder's other films abound with scenes over which "Women on the Market" might well be emblazoned, this scene should surely be entitled "Man on the Market."

The film's tone toward all of this is heavily ironic, but the camera itself insists upon Ali's specular status in a closely adjacent scene. Distressed by his treatment at the hands of Emmi and her colleagues, he abruptly leaves home, ending up at the apartment of Barbara (Barbara Valentin), owner of the Arab bar. The first shot inside that apartment shows him, in extreme long shot, sitting on Barbara's bed, his head downcast. Because the camera is situated in the hallway, outside the doorway of the bedroom, and because the bed is placed in front of orange curtains which frame both it and a wide window, Ali is doubly framed, even—one might say—"on-stage" (Figure 3–11).

Figure 3–10

In the next shot of the same room, which represents a later point in time, Ali lies on the same bed, face down. As Barbara enters the apartment, and goes into the bathroom to wash, Ali stands, undresses, and faces the camera with his arms slightly raised, as if offering himself up to the gaze (Figure 3–12). Barbara enters the frame from the left, turns off the light, walks over to Ali, briefly embraces him, and falls down on the bed with him. Illuminated by a shaft of light, Ali can be seen to lie passively on top of her. The shot continues for approximately sixteen more seconds, during which nothing moves but Barbara's arm.

A number of questions pose themselves with a certain insistence at this juncture: What is the relationship of the erotic specularization of Ali to the gaze which both sustains him as subject, and appears as the agency of his social oppression? Is it a simple extension of that gaze, or a form of resistance to it? And how are we to read the conclusion of the film, which reunites Emmi to Ali only by confining the second of those characters to a hospital, apart from its obvious reference to the final scene of Douglas Sirk's *All That Heaven Allows* (1955)?

I suggested earlier that unlike the gaze, the look foregrounds the

Figure 3–11

desiring subjectivity of the figure from whom it issues, a subjectivity which pivots upon lack, whether or not that lack is acknowledged. In the scene involving Emmi's co-workers, the look attempts to deny the void upon which it rests both through a sadistic identification with the gaze, and through the projection of insufficiency onto Ali. However, in the scene in Barbara's apartment the gaze, as inscribed through the elaborately framing shots of a camera which initially insists upon its autonomy from human vision, is redefined through its alignment with Barbara's desiring and accepting look. Although the film specularizes and eroticizes Ali, and in the process further feminizes a character who is already, by virtue of his blackness, estranged from dominant representation, it also directs desire toward him, through the agency of the look.

I say "directs desire toward him" rather than referring to Ali as the "object of desire" because that latter rhetorical construction has encouraged what seems to me a gross misunderstanding of how women are represented within dominant cinema, a misunderstanding that I am reluctant to extend to the figure of Ali. If feminist theory has reason to lament that system of representation, it is not because

Figure 3–12

woman so frequently functions as the *object* of desire (we all function simultaneously as subject and object), but because the male look both transfers its own lack to the female subject, and attempts to pass itself off as the gaze. The problem, in other words, is not that men direct desire toward women in Hollywood films, but that male desire is so consistently and systematically imbricated with projection and control. *Ali: Fear Eats the Soul* begins to make it possible to distinguish between those two things, by differentiating as it at times does between the look and the gaze.

It is perhaps obvious by now to the reader that there is still a missing term in this analysis, a term capable of accounting for the social meaning which is assumed by Ali's body even at moments when there is no diegetic viewer present, such as the hallway shot I discussed a moment ago. The gaze confirms and sustains the subject's identity, but it is not responsible for the form which that identity assumes; it is merely the imaginary apparatus through which light is projected onto the subject, as Lacan suggests when he compares it to a camera. We have yet to account for that agency which determines what the viewer sees when he or she adopts a position behind the "camera," if I may extend Lacan's metaphor—for what makes Ali, for instance, the very "picture" of social and sexual marginality. My search for this missing term leads me always back to the same three diagrams from *Four Fundamental Concepts* (see 91 and 106), diagrams which also further clarify the relation of subject to gaze:

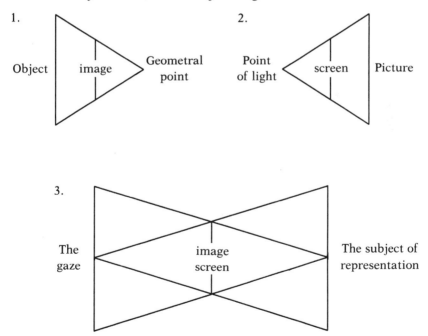

Diagram 1 appears at first to offer a very familiar paradigm, one perfectly in keeping with traditional accounts of geometrical perspective. The site marked "geometral point" would seem to designate the place from which the artist would survey the object to be painted through the mediating frame of the image. Alberti, whom one can imagine deploying exactly the same diagram, would account for the image as that transparent pane of glass through which the Renaissance artist was to see the object, and onto which—the pane of glass turning into a canvas—he was to draw it.[24] This account of geometrical perspective conflates eye and gaze; the artist serenely surveys the world, whose optical laws he commands.

Lacan, however, whose work stands as a monumental challenge to all such notions of mastery and immediacy, clearly wants us to understand both image and geometral point rather differently. Diagram 1, which articulates the field of vision from the point of view of the one-who-looks, situates the looking subject at the site marked "geometral point." In occupying this position, the eye emerges from what Lacan calls the "function of *seeingness*" (82), which both precedes and antedates it, and which thus always exceeds it. Rather than representing the locus of mastery, the geometral point is only a "partial dimension in the field of the gaze" (88), one constituted by the straight lines along which light moves. Lacan further diminishes the importance of the perspectival model by suggesting that it has so little to do with vision that it could be understood by a blind man—that it has less to do with vision than space. He also goes on to stress the irradiating properties of light over those which ostensibly convey the object to the viewer. Finally, as we will see, he shows the intervening image to have nothing in common with Alberti's pane of glass. Consequently, to the degree that the viewer imagines him or herself the agent of vision, he or she is caught within the snares of a scopic Cartesianism, held prey to the belief that "seeing" constitutes "being" (86).

A peculiar feature of geometrical perspective encourages a further deconstruction of the Albertian paradigm, and one which is very much in the spirit of *Four Fundamental Concepts*. That visual system works by inverting the triangle articulated in diagram 1. Whereas the latter fans out from the geometral point, the constitution of depth of field within visual representation requires that linear planes which are widely separated in the foreground converge at a seemingly distant vanishing point. That vanishing point might thus be said to reinscribe the geometral point into the "far" reaches of the representation. In so doing, it calls radically into question the possibility of separating vision from the image—of placing the spectator *outside* the spectacle, in a position of detached mastery. The gaze thus gives way to the eye, and the eye, perhaps even more drastically, to the geometral point, for at the juncture where planar lines converge within a perspectival painting, drawing, or photograph, it is precisely the viewer him or herself who might be said to "vanish" or "fade away." All that remains is the inverted inscription of that triangle which pre-and post-dates the subject, what might be called the viewer as function. Lacan's reading of Holbein's *The Ambassadors* thus provides an implicit meta-commentary not only on the irreducible alterity of the gaze, but on the disappearance of the viewing subject at the perspectival vanishing point. Holbein's painting, he explains, "makes visible for us . . . the subject as annihilated in the form . . . of castration . . . It reflects our own nothingness, in the figure of the death's head" (88–89, 92).

Lacan does not say whether diagram 1 is to be understood primarily as a mapping of the viewer's visual relation to the object, or as a mapping of his or her relation to the image. However, since it is impossible to see the object except through the image, both are presumably at issue. Diagram 1 would thus seem to constitute a vehicle for articulating the viewer's relation both to "reality," and to that by means of which we apprehend it.

Diagram 2 represents the subject no longer as a viewer standing at the site of the gaze or geometral point, but rather as the object of the gaze. (It is crucial to understand that for Lacan it is impossible to occupy the first of these triangles without being imbricated at the same time in the second, which is the chief reason why he superimposes them in diagram 3.) In diagram 2, the gaze is indicated through the radically disembodying and de-anthropomorphizing phrase, "point of light," which conjures up once again the metaphor of the camera. Although the point of light occupies the apex of the second triangle, as does the geometral point in triangle 1, the two are not to be equated. Diagram 2 *inverts* diagram one, situating the subject at the *wide* end of the triangle. In positioning the subject at the site of the "picture," Lacan thus indicates that he is now concerned with that figure as *spectacle* rather than as viewer.

Intervening between gaze or "point of light" and subject or "picture" is something which corresponds spatially to the "image" in diagram 1, but which Lacan dubs the "screen." Although *Four Fundamental Concepts* does not here explicitly invoke Alberti, one of the definitions it offers of the screen opposes it implicitly to the latter's transparent pane of glass. The screen, Lacan insists, is opaque, and hence intraversible (96). The subject who occupies the site of the picture thus seemingly has no choice but to assume the shape predetermined by the screen. (As *Seminar XI* puts it, "if [the subject is] anything in the picture, it is always in the form of the screen" [97].) In a later passage, Lacan characterizes the screen in terms which are directly reminiscent of the mirror stage, as an "imaginary" mapping (107). At the same time, though, *Four Fundamental Concepts* makes clear that more is at issue here than the dyadic relation of the subject to its literal reflection. Diagram 2 is instead centrally concerned with the process whereby the subject assumes the form of a representation, or—to state the case somewhat differently—*becomes a picture*, a process which involves *three* rather than *two* terms: subject, screen, and gaze.

The screen cannot be understood apart from the closely linked concept of mimicry, which Lacan loosely derives from Roger Caillois. In "Mimicry and Legendary Psychasthenia," Caillois attempts to account theoretically for the process whereby certain insects assume the morphology and coloration of other insects or plant life. Since predators are not deceived by this mimicry, Caillois dispenses quickly with the notion that it serves defensive purposes. He argues instead that it attests to a "disturbance in the perception of space."[25] The "overwhelming tendency to imitate" found in primitive organisms (27) speaks to a "*depersonalization by assimilation to space*," hence to a "decline in the feeling of personality and life" (30). For the author of "Mimicry and Legendary Psychasthenia," mimicry involves taking a step backward in the chain of being, retreating toward a "reduced existence" (32).

Significantly, Caillois at one point describes mimicry as a photography at the level of the object rather than at that of the image—as "a reproduction in three-dimensional space with solids and voids: sculpture-photography or better *teleplasty*" (23). Although he here omits to indicate the apparatus through which this unusual photography occurs, his account of the process whereby an organism assumes the appearance of something external to itself resonates within *Four Fundamental Concepts*. Lacan also at one point illustrates mimicry, and hence the subject-screen relation, through an example which is drawn directly from Caillois:

> Let us take an example chosen almost at random . . . that of the small crustacean known as *caprella* . . . When such a crustacean settles in the midst of those animals . . . what does it imitate? It imitates what, in that quasi-plant animal known as the briozoaires, is a stain—at a particular phase of the briozoaires, an intestinal loop forms a stain, at another phase, there functions something like a colored centre. It is to this stain shape that the crustacean adapts itself. It becomes a stain, it becomes a picture, it is inscribed in the picture. This, strictly speaking, is the origin of mimicry. And, on this basis, the fundamental dimensions of the inscription of the subject in the picture appear infinitely more justified than a more hesitant guess might suggest at first sight. (99)

Finally, Lacan emphasizes, with Caillois, that mimicry serves no inherently protective purpose. As the passage I have just quoted would suggest, however, the uses to which *Four Fundamental Concepts* puts the concept of mimicry exceed Caillois's model.

In the first of the senses in which Lacan uses the word, mimicry signifies not assimilation to space, or the loss of individuation, but rather a *visual articulation*. As diagram 2 indicates, that visual articulation is effected at the moment that the subject is "photographed" in the guise of the screen. Lacan says of this kind of mimicry not only that it involves the reproduction of an image, but that "at bottom, it is, for the subject, to be inserted in a function whose exercise grasps it" (100). He thereby suggests that it hinges less upon parody or deformation than upon the passive duplication of a preexisting image.

Four Fundamental Concepts posits a second kind of mimicry, but one which is presumably fully available only to the subject capable of acknowledging the split between its "being" and its "semblance," or, to put the matter somewhat differently, between its "being" and its specular image. Whereas Lacan extends the first kind of mimicry to the entire animal kingdom, he maintains that the second kind, which he associates with "travesty, camouflage, [and] intimidation" (99), is limited to the human subject: "Only the subject," we are told, "—the human subject, the subject of the desire that is the essence of man—is not, unlike the animal, entirely caught up in this imaginary capture. He maps himself in it. How? In so far as he isolates the function of the screen and plays with it. Man, in effect, knows how to play with the mask as that beyond which there is the gaze. The screen is here the locus of mediation" (107).[26] This passage reiterates the defining and structuring role of the screen, while at the same time implying that it might be possible for a subject who knows his or her necessary specularity to exaggerate and/or denaturalize the image/screen; to use it for protective coloration; or to transform it into a weapon. *Four Fundamental Concepts* thus provides one of those rare junctures within the Lacanian oeuvre where it becomes possible to impute to the subject some kind of agency, albeit one hedged about with all kinds of qualifications and limitations, not the least of which is the impossibility of that subject ever achieving either self-presence or "authenticity."

Lacan's third diagram explicitly conflates the image in diagram 1 with the screen in diagram 2. The slippage between those two terms suggests to me that by "screen" he in fact means the image or group of images through which identity is constituted. What we are asked to understand by this last diagram is that it is at the level of what is variously called the "image" and the "screen" rather than at that of the gaze that the subject's identity is established. Since the gaze is ultimately no more than what diagram 2 calls a "point of light," it has no power to constitute subjectivity except by projecting the screen on to the object. In other words, just as Lacan's infant can see him or herself only through the intervention of an external image, the gaze can "photograph" the object only through the grid of the screen.

Although *Four Fundamental Concepts* does not do so, it seems to me crucial that we insist upon the ideological status of the screen by describing it as that culturally generated image or repertoire of images through which subjects are not only constituted, but differentiated in relation to class, race, sexuality, age, and nationality. The possibility of "playing" with these images then assumes a critical importance, opening up as it does an arena for political contestation. Lacan indicates some of the forms which that contestation can assume when he defines the screen through one of those proliferating catalogues of nouns of which he is so fond. It is, we learn, "something . . . like a mask, a double, an envelope, a thrown-off skin, thrown off in order to cover the frame of a shield," which "the being *gives of himself*, or *receives from the other* [my emphasis]"[27] (107). *Four Fundamental Concepts* thus suggests once again that the screen can assume the status of a shield or defensive weapon. Alternatively, it can become a "lure" or a tool of seduction in a battle of friendlier persuasion. Elsewhere in the same passage, Lacan maintains that mimicry can even assume the proportions of a "struggle to the death" (107).

It is imperative that we keep in mind when reading *Four Fundamental Concepts* that the subject can only be "photographed" through the frame of culturally intelligible images. Those attempts at a collective self-redefinition which rely upon masquerade, parody, inversion, and bricolage will consequently be more successful than those aimed at the *ex nihilo* creation of new images, since they work upon the existing cultural imaginary. It is presumably for this reason that Lacan speaks of "playing" with the screen rather than replacing it with a new one. In positioning its practitioners so tensely in relation both to dominant representation and the gaze, these strategies also work to maintain a productive distance between the subject and its "self," a distance which is indispensable to further change.

The third diagram goes even further in its deconstruction of the eye than I have so far suggested, necessitating in the process a still more drastic reformulation of the paradigms through which we have recently theorized cinema's scopic regime. Lacan speaks at one point in *Four Fundamental Concepts* about the "pulsatile, dazzling and spread out function of the gaze" (89), a function which is implicit in the latter's status as light, and which helps to explain why it must be represented not only as the narrow end of one triangle, but as the wide end of the other. But more is at issue here than the dispersibility of light. Diagram 3 insists once again upon the non-coincidence of the look and the gaze, now not simply by showing the former to be at most a representative of the latter, but by situating the one at the opposite pole from the other. Lacan actually goes so far as to locate the gaze at the site of what the first diagram has shown to be the *object* of vision, and the verbal text provides additional confirmation that this is indeed how we are to read the superimposed triangles of the subsequent diagram. "The phenomenologists have succeeded in artic-ulating with precision, and in the most disconcerting way," remarks Lacan in "Anamorphosis," "that I see *outside*, that perception is not in me, that it is *on the objects that it apprehends* [my emphasis]" (80). Elsewhere in *Seminar XI*, Lacan makes clear that what is at issue in diagram 3 is the conflation of gaze and spectacle, a conflation which is made on the basis of what might be called the spectacle's "lit up" quality. Through the luminousness which imparts specularity to the object, it in effect looks back at the viewer, much like the sardine can in Lacan's anecdote:

> . . . can we not . . . grasp that which has been eluded, namely, the function of the gaze? I mean, and Maurice Merleau-Ponty points this out, that we are beings who are looked at, in the spectacle of the world. . . .
> The spectacle of the world, in this sense, appears to us as all-seeing. (74–75)[28]

Lacan goes on a moment later, in a passage of staggering implica-tions for film theory, to compare the gaze not to the male look, but to woman-as-spectacle:

> At the level of the phenomenal experience of contemplation, this all-seeing aspect is to be found in the satisfaction of a woman who knows that she is being looked at, on condition that one does not show her that one knows that she knows.
> The world is all-seeing, but it is not exhibitionistic, does not provoke our gaze. When it begins to provoke it, the feeling of strange-ness begins too. (75)

What this passage makes clear is that since the gaze always emerges for us within the field of vision, and since we ourselves are always being photographed by it even as we look, all binarizations of specta-tor and spectacle mystify the scopic relations in which we are held. The subject is generally both, as indicated by the right-hand side of diagram 3. Moreover, although our look can never function as the gaze for ourselves, it can have that metaphoric function for others, even at the moment that we emerge as spectacle. Exhibitionism unsettles because it threatens to expose the duplicity inherent in every subject, and every object—to reveal the subject's dependence for definition upon the image/screen, and his/her capacity for being at the same time within the picture, and a representative for the Other of the gaze. It is thus possible to superimpose in an inverted form not only diagram 1 on diagram 2, but my diagram 3 on your diagram 3, which is presumably why Lacan speaks more than once about the immanence of the gaze within the picture ("in the picture, something of the gaze is always manifested" [101]).

Diagram 3 suggests that if the viewer cannot see the object without the intervention of the image/screen, neither does he or she have a direct visual access to the gaze. In both cases the relationship is mediated by a "mask, double, [or] envelope," and in both instances "misrecognition" would seem to be the inevitable outcome. Foucault has made it possible for us to apprehend some of the cultural representations of the gaze which have been put in place since the end of the eighteenth century, representations which are complexly bound up with the medical and penal institutions.[29] Feminist film theory has foregrounded a number of others through its interrogation of the male look.[30] However, the interrogation has not always been pushed far enough. We have at times assumed that dominant cinema's scopic regime could be overturned by "giving" woman the gaze, rather than by exposing the impossibility of anyone ever owning that visual agency, or of him or herself escaping specularity.

According to the reading of diagram 3 which I have proposed here, the field of vision puts all three of the Lacanian registers into play. The gaze occupies two domains simultaneously; in its capacity as light, and as that which is foreclosed from the subject, it partakes of the real,[31] but in its status as "the presence of others as such," it clearly belongs to the symbolic. The relationship of subject to screen, on the other hand, is articulated within the domain of the imaginary. However, "captation" can occur only with the complicity of the gaze; the subject can only achieve an invisible join with those images or screens through which the gaze in its capacity as "others as such" looks at him or her. That most apparently claustral of all psychic transactions—"self-recognition" is thus mediated by a third term.

Foucault's account of the gaze does not generally intersect with Lacan's, but it enriches *Four Fundamental Concepts* immeasurably when it suggests that the field of vision may have been variously articulated at different historical moments. *Discipline and Punish* distinguishes between two "modalities of power" according to their very different scopic regimes. Within the earlier of these modalities, which was organized around the sovereign and his force, "power was what was seen, what was shown and what was manifested . . . Those on whom it was exercised could remain in the shade." Privilege, in other words, was concentrated at the site of the spectacle rather than that of the gaze. (Twentieth-century fascism has often deployed spectacle in a similar way, as Elsaesser suggests in his discussion of Fassbinder.) However, within the next great power modality, which Foucault associates with discipline, specularity implied subjection; power exercised itself through its invisibility, while "at the same time [imposing] on those whom it [subjected] a principle of compulsory visibility" (187).

Although it cannot be immediately reconciled to the Foucauldian paradigm, J.C. Flugel's notion of the Great Masculine Renunciation also encourages us to think in historically specific ways about our present scopic regime. It is Flugel's contention that prior to the late eighteenth century, masculinity aligned itself with sartorial extravagance—that given the social and economic possibility to do so, it invariably chose to "command" rather than to "lay claim" to the gaze. However, since that time, phallic "rectitude" has increasingly associated itself with sobriety of dress, and the male subject's specularity and exhibitionism have been projected onto his female counterpart.[32]

These two accounts do more than alert us to the historical vicissitudes of the field of vision. They further denaturalize the alignment of masculinity with the gaze. They also indicate that power can invade spectacle, and disinvest from the gaze—that spectacle, in other words, can function phallically. Feminism must consequently demand more than the "return" of specularity and exhibitionism to the male subject. What must be demonstrated over and over again is that all subjects, male or female, rely for their identity upon the repertoire of culturally available images, and upon a gaze which, radically exceeding the libidinally vulnerable look, is not theirs to deploy.

I have indicated some of the ways in which Fassbinder's cinema anticipates the political program that I have just outlined. Not only does it show subjectivity to be at all points dependent both upon gaze and image/screen, but it demonstrates that the look, male or female, is itself within spectacle. It also works to transform the images or screens through which we see the male subject. This last struggle is conducted very much at the level of corporeal representation, suggesting that although the phallus is not the penis, it nonetheless derives its material support from that organ. We do not remember often enough that in "Subversion of the Subject and Dialectic of Desire"

Lacan himself defines the phallus as "the image of the penis."[33] Fassbinder's films work to ruin or deface that image.

Texts like *Ali: Fear Eats the Soul, Fox and His Friends, In a Year of Thirteen Moons* and *Berlin Alexanderplatz* consequently make the male body the point at which economic, racial, and sexual oppression are registered. As Wiegand has remarked, Fassbinder—perhaps more than any other filmmaker—"has understood the human body as an arena of social conflict,"[34] and it seems to me that this is precisely how we are to interpret the ulcer which afflicts Ali at the conclusion of the film which bears his name, Hans's heart attack in *The Merchant of Four Seasons* (1971), and the symptoms from which Fox suffers in *Fox and His Friends*.

Fassbinder's curious response to the racism of contemporary Germany—a response which evacuates the masculinity and insists upon the vulnerability of the *Gastarbeiter*—might seem indicative of precisely that left-wing melancholy of which Dyer has accused him.[35] The crucial point to grasp here, however, is that he refuses to treat the Arab guest worker differently from his white male protagonists—that he refuses to confer upon that figure a positivity which he eschews elsewhere. Fassbinder is unwilling even for a moment to countenance the notion that a black or third world man operates out of an existential plenitude or a self-sufficiency denied to the first world white man, or that such a figure is any less riven by anxiety or desire. Nor is he ever prepared to forego his assault on the phallus, even within a text which is given over as fully as *Ali: Fear Eats the Soul* to a critique of racism.

Fassbinder's cinema also seems to me exemplary in the particular way in which it approaches the issue of the mediating image/screen. The risk implicit in any politics devoted to what might be described as a "representational contestation" is that it will give fresh life to the notion that what is needed are "positive images" of women, blacks, gays, and other disenfranchised groups, images which all too often work to resubstantialize identity, and even at times to essentialize it. Fassbinder's films refuse simply to resituate the terms of phallic reference. Instead, they evacuate both those terms and the *moi* which is their imaginary correlate. At its most extreme, Fassbinder's cinema might almost be said to model itself on Holbein's *The Ambassadors*, with its anamorphosic death's head—to seek to induce in the viewer a recognition of him or herself as "annihilated in the form . . . of castration."

Since Freud, we have grown accustomed to thinking about lack according to a specular logic, or to state the case rather differently, as the *absence* of a particular visual term. One of the crucial features of Lacan's redefinition of castration has been to shift it away from this obligatory anatomical referent to the void installed by language. But Lacan might also be said to "visualize" castration, albeit in very different terms from those suggested in "Some Psychical Consequences of the Anatomical Distinction Between the Sexes" or "Female Sexuality." Despite its failure to factor the look into the three diagrams, *Seminar XI* repeatedly locates lack at the level of the eye, defining castration as the alterity of the gaze. Lacan remarks at one point, for instance, that the gaze is "symbolic of what we find on the horizon . . . namely, the lack that constitutes castration anxiety" (73), and at another that the gaze, "*qua objet a*, may come to symbolize this central lack expressed in the phenomenon of castration" (77). *Four Fundamental Concepts* thus extends castration to the male as well as the female subject, and in an ultimately much more satisfactory way than a text like "The Signification of the Phallus" manages to do. *Seminar XI* also makes it possible for us to understand that if the gaze exceeds the look, the look introduces a term in excess of the gaze.

It is Fassbinder rather than Lacan, however, who assists us in conceptualizing a look which would acknowledge its lack rather than seeking to deny it. Films like *Ali: Fear Eats the Soul*, *Gods of the Plague*, and *Beware of a Holy Whore* work as strenuously to maintain castration at the site of the look as they do to situate it at the level of the male body. As I have already suggested, *Beware of a Holy Whore* even articulates a new formal element—a zoom in on the look rather than its object—for enacting something that might best be described as the reverse of that visual transaction described by Freud at the beginning of his essay on fetishism,[36] a look which, rather than locating castration definitively elsewhere, becomes itself the locus of insufficiency.

As a result both of their oppression, their specularization and their forced confrontation with their own lack, Fassbinder's male characters acquire the capacity to become something other than what the male subject has classically been—to slip out from under the phallic sign, away from the paternal function. They may even approach that condition of "beauty" which Fassbinder associates with victimized women.[37] However, his cinema also at times valorizes the suffering which produces these effects, and it is here that his "aesthetics of pessimism" becomes both most politically dangerous and most libidinally complex.

While *Gods of the Plague* presents the viewer with a "limp" male subject, and *Ali: Fear Eats the Soul* with one who escapes from the gaze to the look only at the cost of a further feminization, neither violates the integrity of that corporeal "envelope" which constitutes the male body. In two subsequent films, though, *In a Year of Thirteen Moons* and *Berlin Alexanderplatz*, the assault upon the male body assumes much more aggressive forms. Within the terrifying confines of those two texts, the male body is subjected to sex-change surgery, amputation, torture, and crucifixion, now at the behest of a negativity which is no longer content merely to exteriorize the necessary supports of identity, but which demands a much more corporeal eradication. Chapter 6 will speak at length about the ruination of masculinity within these two films. It will also explore the masochism which alone makes Fassbinder's negativity endurable, generating those moments of ecstasy to which I alluded earlier.

There is, however, much theoretical ground to cover before we return to Fassbinder. Our immediate concern continues to be the distinction between the look and the gaze, a distinction which the novels of Henry James will help us to refine further. Chapter 4 will attempt to demonstrate that when the male look is contextualized within the framework of the primal scene, it represents the site of trauma and dispossession. The next chapter will also map out the terms of a male subjectivity which is very much at odds with the dominant fiction—a male subjectivity located at the intersection of the positive and negative Oedipus complexes, and deprived of conventional sexual "means."

4

Too Early/Too Late: Male Subjectivity and the Primal Scene

A curious phrase recurs again and again in the "Prefaces" to the New York edition of Henry James's work, a phrase which is absolutely central to his theory of the novel. James repeatedly speaks of "going behind" a particular character, by which he means us to understand that he adopts that character's conscious "focus" or point of view. Several writers have persuasively demonstrated that James constructs his persona through this delegated consciousness—that it is given as somehow representing him, and that he in turn authorizes it. David Carroll, for instance, observes that "essential to James's theory of the novel . . . is the presence of the author at its source—the fictional universe has its center in the consciousness of a fictional subject behind which stands the 'true origin' and subject of the novel: the author and his consciousness."[1]

Were we to accede to James's equation of himself with this originating consciousness, he would emerge as the very embodiment of the traditional author, and so—by extension—as an "exemplary" male subject. This chapter, however, will attempt to demonstrate that James's authorial subjectivity has a very different consistency—that it is determined less by the refinements of his consciousness than by the imperatives of his unconscious fantasy. James's "vision of the behind," as Peter Brooks would say,[2] opens decisively onto the primal scene, and accommodates desires and identifications which are in every respect antipathetic not just to his preferred self-image, but to conventional masculinity. Moreover, although this James, like the one who occupies the house of fiction, occupies an emphatically spectatorial position, his look exercises no control over the field it surveys; it is instead the point of entry for an alien and traumatic sexuality. Finally, the James who is conjured forth by his authorial fantasmatic defies specification according both to a strictly heterosexual, and to a classically homosexual paradigm. He is consequently an almost hyperbolically marginal male subject.

James's preconscious defenses are securely in place against such an unwelcome discovery. One can scarcely help remarking that the artist who stands at the window of the house of fiction has no intention of turning around to see what lies within, but looks resolutely outward.[3] James shows himself even more armored against unwanted self-knowledge in the "Preface to 'Lady Barbarina,'" in which he makes the uncharacteristic admission that his work is determined by forces beyond his conscious control, but then voices his firm determination not to consider what those forces might be. Significantly, he declines self-knowledge through the very phrase with which he habitually describes his assumption of a particular point of view—i.e. through the phrase "to go behind." James in effect refuses to "go behind" his desire to "go behind" certain fictional characters:

> The subject . . . pressed upon the artist is the necessity of his case and the fruit of his consciousness; which truth makes and has ever made of any quarrel with his subject, any stupid attempt to go behind *that*, the true stultification of criticism. The author of these remarks has in any case felt it, from far back, quite his least stupid course to meet halfway, as it were, the turn taken and the perceptions engendered by the tenor of his days. Here it is that he has never pretended to "go behind"—which would have been for him a deplorable waste of time.[4]

We will have many occasions to return to James's predilection for rear subject-positions. First, however, let us consider what it would mean to "go behind" this (or for that matter any other) authorial matrix.

1. Authorial Subjectivity and the Fantasmatic

In considering James's authorial relation to characters like Isabel Archer, Fleda Vetch, and Lambert Strether, at least one critic has felt impelled to invoke the essay in which Freud elaborates his *ars poetica*, "Creative Writers and Day-Dreaming."[5] That essay, we recall, presents the fiction writer as someone who is able to disguise and generalize his or her daydreams in such a way that they succeed in gratifying the reader's own unconscious desires without inducing guilt. What is it about this aesthetic paradigm which fails to satisfy, particularly in the case of a writer like James? It is not that there are no points of coincidence between his work and the pulp novels upon which Freud bases his theoretical model; as James himself acknowledges, there is often an element of the potboiler about his stories. However, the psychic drama which those novels and stories play out has little to do with the one described in "Creative Writers and Day-Dreaming":

> One feature above all cannot fail to strike us about the creations of these story-writers: each of them has a hero who is the center of interest, for whom the writer tries to win our sympathy by every possible means and whom he seems to place under the protection of a special Providence. If, at the end of one chapter of my story, I leave the hero unconscious and bleeding from severe wounds, I am sure to find him at the beginning of the next being carefully nursed and on the way to recovery; and if the first volume closes with the ship he is in going down in a storm at sea, I am certain, at the opening of the second volume, to read of his miraculous rescue . . . through this revealing characteristic of invulnerability we can immediately recognize His Majesty the Ego, the hero alike of every day-dream and of every story.[6]

Far from being under the protection of a special providence, the prototypical Jamesian character is the one who, like Lambert Strether, gets nothing for him or herself "out of the whole affair"[7]—the one who is, moreover, precisely marked by vulnerability. That character also bears scant resemblance to the exuberantly active hero described by Freud; he or she often stands to one side of the "action," watching rather than participating in the flow of events. Indeed, in this one respect, the paradigmatic Jamesian character bears an uncanny resemblance to the artist evoked by the author himself in the "Preface to *A Portrait of a Lady*," the artist who looks onto a scene from which he or she is somehow excluded.

But what is least satisfying for me about Freud's *ars poetica*, especially when it is juxtaposed with James's work, is its crude notion of wish-fulfillment—its assumption that what manifests itself in daydreams and novels will always be what in the final analysis serves to "crown" or aggrandize the ego. A theoretical abyss separates "Creative Writers and Day-Dreaming" from later essays like " 'A Child Is Being Beaten' " or "The Economic Problem of Masochism," with their much more complex understanding of both pleasure and fantasy.

"The Economic Problem of Masochism" is corrective primarily with respect to the issue of pleasure, elaborating as it does three categories of voluptuous or exquisite pain.[8] The first of these categories, "erotogenic masochism," underlies the other two, and designates that pleasure which attaches itself to the traumatic infraction of an organ, whether that organ be physical or psychic, as in the case of the ego. Freud associates the second of these categories with fantasies and sexual practices involving bondage and ritual punishment. It is so named because it enacts a hyperbolic dramatization of female subjectivity, although the patients upon which Freud bases his account are all men. As I will argue in Chapter 5, this form of masochism can be read as a phallic divestiture. The last of Freud's categories, moral masochism, poses perhaps the most direct challenge to "Creative Writers and Day-Dreaming" in that it turns upon the abasement and castigation of the ego. Moral masochism occurs when the ego begins to enjoy and indeed to provoke the super-ego's severity. Any artistic text functioning as even the indirect "trace" of masochistic desire, whether it be "feminine" or "moral," would put certain obstacles in the way of an easy transition from injury and humiliation to recovery and exaltation.

" 'A Child Is Being Beaten' " not only delves more deeply into what Freud would later call "feminine" masochism, but theorizes fantasy in ways which enormously complicate the 1908 formulation.[9] It insists much more strenuously than "Creative Writers and Day-Dreaming" on the link between daydreams and their unconscious counterpart. Indeed, whereas the earlier essay is prepared to connect daydreams only to infantile memories, " 'A Child Is Being Beaten' " insists that conscious fantasies are merely another phase of unconscious ones. It also indicates that the pleasure towards which unconscious fantasy aims may depend in some very profound way upon passivity, punishment, loss, or pain. Finally, whereas "Creative Writers and Day-Dreaming" focuses primarily upon narrative reversal in its attempt to uncover authorial desire, " 'A Child is Being Beaten' " places its emphasis rather upon the scene. It suggests that unconscious desire generally assumes the form of a visual tableau or narrateme like the one indicated by the repressed version of the female beating fantasy, which Freud transcribes with the sentence "I am being beaten by my father." (Even the two conscious versions of the beating fantasy have this same scenic quality. The female version, for instance, has the girl watching while a group of boys is whipped.)

But no summary of Freud's views on the relation of fantasy to art would be complete without some reference to "Leonardo da Vinci and a Memory of His Childhood," an essay whose focus is much more explicitly visual, and whose pursuit of authorial desire in assorted texts by Leonardo leads him to two privileged scenes. The first of these scenes, which was consciously "remembered" by the artist, but which Freud insists was a fantasy transposed onto infancy, is recounted by Leonardo in his scientific notebooks, and misquoted in several key details in *The Standard Edition*:

"It seems that I was always destined to be so deeply concerned with vultures [kites]; for I recall as one of my very earliest memories that while I was in my cradle a vulture [kite] came down to me, and opened my mouth with its tail, and struck me many times with its tail against my lips."[10]

The second scene is constructed by Freud in the course of his unorthodox analysis of Leonardo, and is posited as the unconscious fantasy hidden behind the conscious fantasy of the kite. In it the infant Leonardo sucks upon the breast/penis of a phallic and self-sufficient mother. Freud finds in this second scene the structuring psychic principle behind not only Leonardo's sexuality—his repressed homosexuality—but the *Mona Lisa*, *Saint Anne with Two Others*, and a remarkable anatomical drawing of the sexual act.[11] Leonardo's libidinal apparatus, according to Freud, sustained two erotic objects, both of which were present within the unconscious fantasy: the non-castrated mother of his infancy, and the male youth capable in some way of mirroring or replicating the child he himself once was.[12]

At issue here is what Freud was in an essay written two years after "Leonardo da Vinci and a Memory of His Childhood" to call a "stereotype plate . . . which is constantly repeated—constantly reprinted afresh—in the course of the person's life, so far as external circumstances and the nature of the love-objects accessible to him permit. . . . "[13] This concept has been suggestively elaborated and refined by Laplanche and Pontalis under the more appropriate rubric of the "fantasmatic" or "structuring action" which shapes and orders the whole of psychic life.[14] A fantasmatic is an unconscious fantasy or group of related fantasies which underlies a subject's dreams, symptoms, repetitive behavior, and daydreams. It also provides what is in my view the best point of entry into authorial subjectivity.

In organizing my discussion of Jamesian authorship around the fantasmatic, I will be distinguishing in a way that Freud does not between the author "outside" the text and the author "inside" the text.[15] The author "outside" the text can perhaps best be described as an "origin under erasure"—as a site which is simultaneously productive of desire, and devoid of authorial "substance" or presence. He or she in some sense "gives rise" to the author "inside" the text, but is at the same time constituted as authorial subject only through that construct. The author is thus simultaneously "the place from which the set of representations are ordered and organized," and the point "toward which they are channelled back."[16] Since it is in large part the shadow cast "outside" the text by the author "inside" the text which constitutes what we conventionally think of as the author, it is with the latter that we should begin our interrogation of authorship, rather than with the wealth of biographical detail that supports most traditional archaeologies. This is not to say that the theorist should bracket the biographical author's race, class, historical moment, or socially assigned gender; on the contrary, authorial subjectivity assumes much of its political force and meaning from its relation to these crucial elements. Rather than automatically assuming, as Freud does, that there will be a direct match between the biographical author and the authorial fantasmatic, however, we should be prepared to see elements within the latter which are excessive, transgressive, or reactionary with respect to the former—to read the authorial fantasmatic, when it is appropriate to do so, *against* the class, race, gender, or historical moment of the biographical author, and the class, race, gender, or historical moment of the biographical author *against* the fantasmatic.

Before attempting to determine more precisely the contours of the fantasmatic which structures James's work, I want to stress with Laplanche and Pontalis that more is involved here than a "thematic." The fantasmatic is what *The Language of Psycho-Analysis* calls a "*mise-en-scène* of desire," a dramatization of a scene or scenario in which the subject always has a part to play. It can undergo syntactical changes, as it does from one phase to another of " 'A Child Is Being Beaten,' " and roles can be reassigned within it. It also facilitates "the most primitive of defense processes, such as turning round upon the subject's own self, reversal into the opposite, negation and projection" (318).

2. The Primal Scene

> It is almost as though that prying, peeping child, who is at the psychological core of all these morbidly and sexually curious observers during this period of Henry James's work, had at long last gained entrance to what has been called "the primal scene" of his parents' sexual intercourse.[17]

Since Foucault, the signifiers "knowledge" and "power" have been frequently linked as a compound noun.[18] In James's fiction, however, they are often placed in stark opposition. Nothing could speak more eloquently to the inadequacy of an intractably Foucauldian reading of that fiction[19] than the climactic scene in *The Ambassadors*, where Lambert Strether, spending a quiet day in the French countryside, catches a glimpse of Mme de Vionnet and Chad Newsome boating alone together on the river, and has forced upon him an unwanted and incapacitating knowledge. He responds with a social version of that most classic of all psychic defenses—disavowal; he pretends, or as the novel puts it, he "make[s]-believe" that he hasn't understood what he has seen (313). Only later, in a deferred action, does he acknowledge to himself what he is unable to face at the time.[20]

What is it that Lambert Strether so unpleasurably discovers during his day in the country? He learns that the relationship between Chad and Mme de Vionnet isn't, as he has hitherto assured himself, virtuous—he learns, as James puts it, that those two figures are "expert, familiar, frequent"—that "they [know] how to do it," and that "this wouldn't at all events be the first time" (307). I do not think I am stretching a point in suggesting that what is enacted here is in effect a primal scene, albeit one in which the generations are strangely confused. Strether, as he tells us in his celebrated speech to Little Bilham at Gloriani's house, after meeting Mme de Vionnet for the first time, is out of synchronization with what he sees, much like the child who "watches" his or her parents having coitus. Whereas the child is "too early" with respect to sexual knowledge, however, Strether is "too late." "Live all you can," he tells Little Bilham,

> . . . it's a mistake not to. It doesn't so much matter what you do in particular, so long as you have your life. If you haven't had that what *have* you had? This place and these impressions . . . of Chad and of people I've seen at *his* place—well, have had their abundant message for me . . . I see it now. I haven't done so enough before— and now I'm old; too old at any rate for what I see. Oh I *do* see, at least. . . . It's too late. And it's as if the train had fairly waited at the station for me without my having had the gumption to know it was there. (132)

As we discover in *The Notebooks*, this speech, with its insistence upon Strether's status as a spectator, and his marked isolation from what he sees, was the "germ" of the entire novel.[21]

Like the primal scene, moreover, what Strether sees on the river is strongly marked precisely *as a scene*. Interestingly, he is himself "in the picture," albeit at the edges, much like the watching child in the larger context of the primal fantasy; indeed, James has recourse to a very insistent representational metaphor in describing Strether's sense of himself as he wanders around the village. Not once, we learn, does he "[overstep] the oblong gilt frame," which "[draws] itself out for him, as much as you please" (305):

> For this had been all day at bottom the spell of the picture—that it was essentially more than anything else a scene and a stage, that the very air of the play was in the rustle of the willows and the tone of the sky. The play and the characters had, without his knowing it

till now, peopled all his space for him, and it seemed somehow
quite happy that they should offer themselves, in the conditions so
supplied, with a kind of inevitability. (306)

Eventually Strether sits down in a small pavilion by the water—a
space clearly differentiated from the river tableau—and awaits the
play to unfold within the picture frame.

The pictorial inflection which James gives to the scene in the French
countryside also makes a special kind of sense when we recall that
the primal scene occurs not so much in "reality" as in fantasy—that
it is a construction after the fact, subsequent to an event with which
it is by no means commensurate. The primal scene, in other words,
never actually "happens" as such, but is either constituted through a
deferred action much like that through which Strether reacts to what
he has seen on the river, or constructed as a fantasy on the basis of
some remembered detail. It is consequently "marked" as an image.

But what precisely is the primal scene, and what range of possible
desires and identifications does it sustain? In "Some Psychical Consequences of the Anatomical Distinction Between the Sexes," Freud
describes it as a "primal fantasy" which is activated by the sounds of
parental copulation, and which is capable of producing sexuality
within the child (". . . analysis shows us in a shadowy way how the
fact of a child at a very early age listening to his parents copulating
may set up his first sexual excitation, and how that event may, owing
to its after-effects, act as a starting point for the child's whole sexual
development").[22] In his much more extensive treatment of the primal
scene in *From the History of an Infantile Neurosis,* Freud focuses upon it
initially as a literal spectacle whose significance is only subsequently
understood, but later suggests that it is a fantasy loosely based upon
the observation of animal coitus.[23] The primal scene thus routes sexuality along the axes of vision and hearing, privileging image and sound
over smell, touch, or taste.

The watching/listening child is separated from the parental embrace by more than age. As Christian Metz suggests, voyeurism always
"*concretely represents the absence of its object* in the distance at which
it maintains it and which is part of its very definition: distance of the
look, distance of listening."[24] Within the primal scene this distance
implies an isolation both from genitality and from the tumult of
passion, except—and this is a crucial qualification—at the level of
identification.

I will return to this last point in a moment, but first I want to note
that whereas within the Metzian definition the distance between the
the voyeur and his object facilitates mastery and sadism (59–63),
here it is conducive instead of passivity and masochism. Far from

controlling the sounds and images of parental sexuality, the child held captive within the crib is controlled—indeed, overwhelmed—by them. Adult sexuality invades him or her through the eyes and ears, puncturing, as it were, those vital organs. As Laplanche remarks in *Life and Death in Psychoanalysis*, "the child, impotent in his crib, is Ulysses tied to the mast of Tantalus, on whom is imposed the spectacle of parental intercourse . . . the passive position of the child in relation to the adult is not simply passivity in relation to adult activity, but passivity in relation to the adult fantasy intruding within him."[25] Because the relation of the spectating subject to the scene of passion conforms to the logic of the "too early" or "too late," moreover, the spectacle of parental sexuality elicits a sense of exclusion and inadequacy. The mastering, sadistic variety of voyeurism discussed by Metz can perhaps best be understood as a psychic formation calculated to reverse the power relations of the primal scene—as a compensatory drama whereby passivity yields to activity through an instinctual "turning around" and reversal.

Like the distance separating the viewer from the cinematic screen, the distance separating the child or his adult equivalent from the scene of passion paradoxically promotes identification with its actants. Here, again, the look functions less to consolidate than to undermine masculinity, for the spectacle of the primal scene encourages identifications which are in excess of sexual difference. Freud notes in "Some Psychical Consequences of the Anatomical Distinction Between the Sexes" that the primal scene fantasy opens onto both the positive or heterosexual, and the negative or homosexual versions of the Oedipus complex[26]—that it promotes, in other words, desire for the father and identification with the mother, as well as desire for the mother and identification with the father. In addition, it disposes of anatomical lack in ways that are profoundly disruptive of conventional masculinity.

Freud writes that at one unconscious level, the Wolfman declines the "knowledge" which would permit him to distinguish clearly between himself and his mother, and so forecloses altogether upon castration; he refuses, in other words, to acknowledge woman's anatomical otherness. His unconscious sexuality is, in addition, largely organized around an erotogenic zone which is undecidable with respect to gender, i.e. the anus. The imaginary position which he there occupies attests to a further collapse of the distance separating him from femininity. Because of the privileged status given by the Wolfman to various anally coded memories of servant women, his obsessive preoccupation with Christ's anus during a childhood period of deep fascination with that figure, and various symptoms relating to disorders of the bowels, Freud deduces that his patient's primal scene fantasy revolves around *coitus a tergo*. He also establishes that the Wolfman identifies strongly with the mother's position in this scene, and dreams of being anally used by the father in the same way (57, 77–79).

At a second unconscious level, the Wolfman deviates even more sharply from the scenario described in "Some Psychical Consequences of the Anatomical Distinction Between the Sexes." He acknowledges the mother's "castration," but refuses to renounce his identification with her. Recognizing her "wound" as the "necessary condition of intercourse with his father" (46), he accepts it as his own sexual lot, and "console[s]" himself "with femininity as a compensation" (85). The fantasy of the primal scene thus deprives the male subject not only of the visual but the anatomical accoutrements of masculinity; he is what Freud in his case history of Dora calls "a man without means."[27]

Only in his conscious sexual fantasies and practices does the Wolfman both acknowledge and abominate woman's "castration." Even these fantasies and practices turn upon a blurring of the distinction between the vagina and the anus, however—upon the possibility of the former standing in for the latter (hence his intense excitement when glimpsing the female form from behind, in a floor-scrubbing attitude). And although he consciously assumes the position occupied by the father within the primal scene, and "takes" women sexually from behind, this identification is never very strong, and is radically undermined by his very different unconscious desires (110–11).

Finally, at the unconscious level at which the Wolfman is able to entertain the notion of lack, he attaches it not only to the mother and himself, but to the father. Freud writes that like every male participant in the positive Oedipus complex, he views his father as the agency of castration, and so directs toward him an "intense unconscious hostility." At the same time, however, and presumably as a concomitant of the negative Oedipus complex, the Wolfman regards his father "as the one who had been castrated and as calling, therefore, for his sympathy" (87). Although Freud neglects to do so, it would seem crucial to point out that if castration is the insignia of sexual receptivity, then to attribute castration to the father is in a sense to "go behind" him, i.e. to position him as a potential penile receptacle. As we will see, James's authorial fantasmatic also articulates this possibility.

3. A Man Without Means

Who can fail to remember, in the context of the present discussion, that Strether is preeminently a man without (economic) means, who must be financed by Mrs. Newsome? That he feels himself to be at home in Woollett's "society of women," something which he himself acknowledges to be "an odd situation for a man" (213)? That he is given to sudden sharp identifications with Mme de Vionnet, who occupies the place of the mother within his primal scene, identifications which are described by the novel as "queer displacement[s] of his point of view" (235)? Or that he shrinks from the position of "hero" (265), preferring to be "behind the scenes" (262)?

It seems to me that subjectivity in James's corpus is bound up in some very fundamental way with the primal scene—that it indeed constitutes one of his authorial fantasmatics, if not indeed the primary one. There is, first of all, James's extraordinary obsession with the scenic principle, an obsession which reaches its apotheosis in *The Awkward Age*, but which also surfaces quite explicitly in his constant self-exhortations to "dramatize, dramatize," and in the organization of *The Tragic Muse*. "The whole thing has visibly, from the first, to get itself done in dramatic, or at least scenic conditions," writes James in the "Preface" to that last novel,

> —though scenic conditions which are as near an approach to the dramatic as the novel may permit itself and which have this in common with the latter, that they move in the light of *alternation*. This imposes a consistency other than that of the novel at its loosest, and, for one's subject, a different view and a different placing of the center. The charm of the scenic consistency, the consistency of the multiplication of *aspects*, that of making them amusingly various, had haunted the author of "The Tragic Muse" from far back, and he was in due course to yield to it all luxuriously, too luxuriously perhaps, in "The Awkward Age". . . .[28]

The effect of conceiving the novel as a series of "scenes" is to position the author emphatically as an onlooker, even when he is not closely identified with a fictional "perceiver."

James's novels and short stories also return again and again to situations which, like Strether's visit to the French countryside, somehow reprise that fantasmatic moment where the child is first made aware of adult sexuality. The most crucial scene in *The Portrait of a Lady*, for instance—at least insofar as Isabel's consciousness is concerned—is surely the one in which, hesitating on the threshold of her Italian drawing room, she catches sight of Madame Merle and Gilbert Osmond immersed in an intimate colloquy. As in *The Ambassadors*, there is nothing explicitly carnal in what she sees, but the glimpsed tableau bristles with an assumed privacy whose effect is to make the spectator suddenly aware of a sexual secret from which she has been barred:

> What struck Isabel first was that he was sitting while Madame Merle
> stood; there was an anomaly in this that arrested her. Then she
> perceived that they had arrived at a desultory pause in their ex-
> change of ideas and were musing, face to face, with the freedom of
> old friends who sometimes exchange ideas without uttering them.
> There was nothing to shock in this; they were old friends in fact.
> But the thing made an image, lasting only a moment, like a sudden
> flicker of light. Their relative positions, their absorbed mutual gaze,
> struck her as something detected.[29]

Here, too, the spectacle assumes its full force only later, after it has
been internalized as representation. Isabel sits up late the same night,
thinking about her husband, and gazing at the "remembered vision"
of him and Madame Merle "unconsciously and familiarly associated"
(434).

The Princess Casamassima builds toward a structurally identical
scene, to which Hyacinth Robinson has a more classically readable
response. Furtively watching the Princess get out of a cab and go into
her house with Paul Muniment, he has "a very exact revelation of the
state of feeling of those who love in the rage of jealousy. If he had been
told half an hour before that he was capable of surreptitious peepings
in the interest of that passion he would have resented the insult; yet
he allowed himself to be checked by his companion just at the nearest
point at which they might safely consider the proceedings of the
couple who alighted."[30] This is perhaps the earliest example of an
interesting variation on the usual primal scene, a variation to which
James was to return more than once in his later work. Hyacinth is
joined in his look-out point—indeed brought there—by Prince Casamassima, so that the cast of characters includes four rather than the
usual three. This doubling up of the figure of the spectator foregrounds
the voyeurism of the scene. It also places Hyacinth and the Prince
emphatically onstage, albeit at the margins rather than at the center
of the spectacle:

> "What does he say? What does *she* say?" hissed the Prince; and when
> he went on the next moment, "Will he go in again or will he go
> away?" our striken youth felt a voice given to his own sharpest
> thought. The pair were talking together with rapid sequences, and
> as the door had not yet been opened it was clear that, to prolong the
> conversation on the steps, the Princess delayed to ring. "It will make
> three, four hours he has been with her," moaned the Prince.
>   "He may be with her fifty hours!" Hyacinth laughed as he turned
> away ashamed of himself. (445–46)

The last chapter of the novel contains a matching tableau, except
that its spectator is solitary. Rejected by the Princess Casamassima,

and confronted with the painful obligation to perform an assassination for a political cause in which he no longer believes, Hyacinth goes in search of Millicent at the shop where she works. When he at last finds her, she is standing with her back to him, but with her face to Captain Sholto, ostensibly modeling a fashionable dress for the latter's inspection, but in fact offering up her body to his visual delectation:

> In spite of her averted face he instantly "spotted" Millicent; he knew her shop-attitude, the dressing of her hair behind and the long grand lines of her figure draped in the last new thing. She was showing off this treasure to the Captain, who was lost in contemplation . . . his eyes travelling up and down the front of their beautiful friend's person. . . . (506)

Sholto catches sight of Hyacinth, but fails to acknowledge him; he only gives the young man a "hard" look, intimating the privacy of his negotiations with Millicent.

And then there is *The Golden Bowl*, which is in many ways an extended primal scene, and which does not fail to conjure forth an image which brings home with particular force to Maggie Verver that, as James puts it elsewhere in the novel, "Amerigo and Charlotte [are] arranged together," whereas she "[is] arranged apart."[31] That image, which is curiously displaced with respect to the moment at which Maggie learns of her husband's adultery, is produced for her one day as she returns home. Waiting for her on the balcony are Charlotte and Amerigo, in a display whose calculated publicity is unable to conceal their private understanding—a display that "might almost have shocked the decency of Portland Place":

> . . . the pair were perched together in the balcony, he bare-headed, she divested of her jacket, her mantle, or whatever, but crowned with a brilliant brave hat, responsive to the balmy day. . . . They were gay, they were amused, in the pleasant morning. . . . The group on the pavement stared up as at the peopled battlements of a castle. . . . Maggie's individual gape was inevitably again for the thought of how the pair would be at work. (358–59)

I must not omit from this brief catalogue three James texts which turn the spotlight away from the primal scene itself to its spectator— *The Turn of the Screw*, *What Maisie Knew*, and *The Awkward Age*. The governess in the first of those works manifests a veritable obsession with the question of what the children know and what they have seen of the compromised (and compromising) Peter Quint and Miss Jessel. What she *herself* knows and sees has of course become the crux of the critical controversy about the *nouvelle*.[32] *What Maisie Knew* and *The Awkward Age* similarly focus on a girl who is visually or verbally "exposed" to adult sexuality, and in each case the interrogation of her knowledge forms the central drama of the book. In both instances, knowledge leads not to power and social integration, but to loss and isolation. Nanda is obliged to leave her parent's world for the celibacy of Longdon's country estate at the end of *The Awkward Age*, and the eponymous heroine of *What Maisie Knew* is ejected from all of her various family circles and left to the devices of Mrs. Wix at the end of the novel. The consequences for the child-spectator are even more severe in *The Turn of the Screw*; when Miles is finally brought to the point of uttering Peter Quint's name, his heart stops.

A surprising number of Jamesian characters, moreover, are—like the infantile voyeur—conspicuously either too early or too late with respect to sexuality. Miles, Flora, Nanda, and Maisie are all out of temporal alignment with the sexuality they somehow hear or see. Like Lambert Strether, Mr. Longdon of *The Awkward Age* comes to sexual awareness only when he is too old for that awareness to make an experiential difference. Even Isabel Archer encounters sexuality in the form of Caspar Goodwood's "white lightning" kiss only after she has married the passionless Gilbert Osmond.

But the most explicit and complex dramatization of the temporality specific to the primal scene is surely "The Beast In the Jungle." John Marcher has all the curiosity and scopic urgency of the spectating child, and his voyeurism is reinforced by May Bartram's; for decades they wait and watch together, both of them "peep[ing]" as James puts it, through the same "apertures"[33] at Marcher's life. They both live "to see what would *be* to be seen," but their joint look meets a specular void. At first glance it seems as though the heterosexual couple—the protagonists of the primal scene—have repositioned themselves as the onlookers, leaving an empty space at center stage. However, it is primarily Marcher who occupies the spectatorial position; he is very emphatically coded as the man apart, the man "to whom nothing on earth [is] to [happen]" (535).

Eve Sedgwick has recently suggested that the "real truth" of Marcher's "predicament" is repressed homosexuality, and that this is why he is unable to marry May Bartram.[34] Although her reading is in many respects not only seminal but persuasive, she is obliged to discount the ending in order to secure it. She asks us to "imagine" the story without the "enforcing symmetry" of Marcher's revelation that heterosexuality would have provided both Bartram and himself with an "escape" from aridity and lifelessness (200). Within Sedgwick's analysis, moreover, the figure of Bartram is a structural excrescence, at least with respect to the operations of male homosexual desire; although she is the prototype of "the woman . . . who has not only the most delicate nose for but the most potent attraction toward men who are at crises of homosexual panic" (209), she has herself no place within Marcher's—or James's—libidinal economy.

It would seem important to find a way of reading the many signifiers of homosexuality within this story without refusing its conclusion, something that can only be done by isolating the components of the primal scene within it. I want to emphasize once again that Marcher is in every important sense comparable to the watching child within the Freudian account. Not only is he strongly marked precisely as a spectator, but the spectacle for which he waits is something "rare and strange, possibly prodigious and terrible"—something that will "overwhelm" or even "annihilate" him (490–91). Here again is voyeurism with a difference, voyeurism which bears no relation to that mastering vision which has been so exhaustively interrogated within film theory.[35] Marcher is also a man without sexual means, foreclosed from start to finish from the scene of passion, *except through identification*. Finally, at the point that knowledge comes to him—knowledge, that is, of his own libidinal isolation—it frightens and sickens him:

> This horror of waking—*this* was knowledge, knowledge under the breath of which the very tears in his eyes seemed to freeze. Through them, none the less, he tried to fix it and hold it; he kept it there before him so that he might feel the pain. That at least, belated and bitter, had something of the taste of life. But the bitterness suddenly sickened him, and it was as if, horribly, he saw, in the truth, in the cruelty of his image, what had been appointed and done. He saw the Jungle of his life and he saw the lurking Beast. . . . (536)

The same cannot be said of the only other two characters in the story, May Bartram and the stranger Marcher encounters in the graveyard, even though the former may seem at times to occupy the structural position of the watching child. Although it is only retrospectively that the image of Bartram's sick face speaks to Marcher of wasted desire, that meaning is available to the attentive reader much earlier, and is made almost explicit on the occasion of the visit Marcher later remembers. James writes that on the afternoon of a cold April day shortly before her death it became "suddenly, from her movement and attitude, beautiful and vivid to [Marcher] that she had something more to give him . . . they continued for some minutes silent, her face shining at him, her contact imponderably pressing" (519). The stranger's visage is even more expressive; there is "a kind of hunger in his look," which even after he has passed continues to "flare" for Marcher like a "smoky torch" (533–34).

It occurs to me that what we have here is a curiously fragmented and dispersed primal scene, recuperable primarily from his graveyard encounter, with its insistence on specularity, and its odd evocation of sexuality. It is not only that the stranger is "scarred" with "passion," but that he is twice described as "showing" (and James italicizes this word the second time) his deeply ravaged features (533–34). Something in this spectacle "profane[s] the air," "rouse[s], startle[s]" and "shock[s]" Marcher, and induces him to look after it with the "envy" (534) of one excluded from a privileged transaction.

Because the dead lover for whom the stranger mourns is never represented except through a strong structural parallel to May Bartram, the latter in effect stands in for the former. Together Bartram and the stranger comprise the passionate heterosexual couple of the classic primal scene, although they are in no way present to each other; they designate, in other words, the passionate man and the passionate woman. Lest this reading seem unduly strained, it should be noted that Marcher imagines himself loving only through identification with the stranger's desire for the unknown woman who is herself a projection of Bartram:

> No passion had ever touched him, for this was what passion meant; he had survived and maundered and pined, but where had been *his* deep ravage? . . . The sight that had just met his eyes named to him, as in letters of quick flame, something he had utterly, insanely missed, and what he had missed made these things a train of fire, made them mark themselves in an anguish of inward throbs. He had seen *outside* his life, not learned it within, the way a woman was mourned when she had been loved for herself: such was the force of his conviction of the meaning of the stranger's face. . . . (534)

Like the child in the primal scene, sexual consciousness is implanted in Marcher only through what is in effect an Oedipal triangulation.

As I indicated earlier in this essay, that scene opens onto the negative as well as the positive Oedipus complex, and it may at times be said to superimpose one of those triangles on top of the other. The Jamesian fantasmatic effects just such a superimposition, as a result of which there are two imaginary points of entry into it. One of these points of entry is that designated by Freud in *From a History of an Infantile Neurosis*, i.e. identification with the "mother," and the desire to be used by the "father" as she is. This imaginary access implies, as we have seen, either a blurring of the distinction between anus and vagina, and/or the communication of "lack" from the female to the fantasizing male subject. It also constitutes a classic rendition of the negative or homosexual Oedipus complex.

The second point of entry into James's primal scene is constituted through what can perhaps best be described as a "sodomitical identification" with the "father," an identification which permits the fantasizing subject to look through that figure's eyes and to participate in his sexuality by going "behind" him. At the risk of violating a fundamental tenet of James criticism—the tenet that no matter how luridly suggestive the Master's language, it cannot have a sexual import—I would like to invoke at this point a passage from *The Art of the Novel* which locates the erotic relay I have just described within *The Tragic Muse*, and to insist that at least on this occasion we should take James at his word. "I never 'go behind' Miriam," he writes, "only poor Sherringham goes, a great deal, and Nick Dormer goes a little, and the author, while they so waste wonderment, goes behind *them*" (91). This convergence of desire for the father and identification with his penetration of the mother attests to something which psychoanalysis has not yet prepared us to conceptualize, i.e. the possibility of assuming a subject-position at the intersection of the positive and the negative Oedipus complexes.

In neither the classic working out of the negative Oedipus complex, nor in this second, more complex situation, is the "mother" dispensable. In the first instance she designates the point of interpellation, as Althusser would say,[36] and in the second she is the necessary third term within a relay which seems to begin with the fantasizing subject, who stands at the level of imagination "behind" the "father," but which in fact begins with the "father's" penetration of the "mother." The Jamesian fantasmatic can thus be said to enclose homosexuality within heterosexuality, and heterosexuality within homosexuality.

But let us return to "The Beast in the Jungle." Sedgwick has already commented upon the "cruisiness" of the graveyard scene (210), an observation with which I am in fundamental agreement. However, I also want to draw attention to a surprising rhetorical reversal that occurs in that scene, and that attests to the two desires which the Jamesian fantasmatic sustains—the desire to be sodomized by the "father" while occupying the place of the "mother," and the desire to sodomize him while he is penetrating the "mother." When the stranger first appears to Marcher in the cemetery, he looks at the latter with "an expression like the cut of a blade" that goes "so deep down that [Marcher] wince[s] at the steady thrust" (532, 533). The second time the two men encounter each other, the wound has been displaced from Marcher to the stranger:

The most extraordinary thing that had happened to him . . . took place, after his immediate vague stare, as a consequence of this

impression. The stranger passed, but the raw glare of his grief remained, making our friend wonder in pity what wrong, what wound
it expressed, what injury not to be healed. What had the man *had*,
to make him by the loss of it so bleed and yet live? (534)

Whereas in the first passage the stranger is the one who penetrates
Marcher with the knife of his vision, in the second passage he has
become the one who is penetrated, and, in the process, feminized.
The former marks the maternal point of entry into the Jamesian
fantasmatic—that turning, in other words, upon identification with
the "mother"—and the latter the point of entry which occurs through
what I have called "sodomitical identification" with the "father."

I cannot help but think, here, of those two passages in *From the
History of an Infantile Neurosis* where Freud remarks upon the contradictory "currents" within the Wolfman's psyche, one of which led the
latter at times to see his own castration as the necessary condition of
sexual satisfaction from his father (46, 85), and the other of which
prompted him to regard his father as "the one who had been castrated,
and as calling, therefore, for his sympathy" (87). The movable castration of which Freud speaks in these two passages closely resembles
the displaceable wound in "The Beast in the Jungle." James's text,
however, metaphorizes the wound in a way that the Freudian text
fails to, making it a consequence not of anatomy, but of subject-
position.

4. Going Behind

By way of concluding my discussion of the author "inside" James's
work, I want to turn to a novel which is seemingly the least "subjective" of his major works, the one which is most fully realized according
to dramatic principles, and which involves a minimum of "interioriza-
tion." I refer, of course, to *The Awkward Age*, a text which consists
almost entirely of conversation; which is composed of a series of
admirably constructed "scenes"; and which builds up to a highly
theatrical "climax." I propose to demonstrate that it is in fact one of
the *most* "subjective" of James's novels in the sense in which I have
been using that word—that it is a virtual showcase for his authorial
fantasmatic.

The Awkward Age revolves around the issue of Nanda's sexual knowledge—around the question of what she has learned about all the illicit
couplings that are a constant topic of adult conversation: Petherton
and the Duchess, Aggie and Petherton, Harold and Lady Fanny, Lady
Fanny and her other paramours, Mrs. Brook and Van. The other source

of possible "corruption" is the racy reading material the adults constantly exchange, most particularly the French novel which is first mentioned in Book I, and which resurfaces again in Book VIII. Given that Nanda is ultimately shown to know "everything," as she is fond of putting it, the whole of *The Awkward Age* could be said to be an extended primal scene, albeit one in which hearing is much more fully privileged than vision. ("And yet to think that after all it has been mere *talk*!" is how Van describes the sexuality to which Nanda has been "exposed.")[37]

Nanda's knowledge, as I have already mentioned, results in loss and and isolation rather than in gain or social integration. It is the result, moreover, of adult sexuality and conversation rather than of Nanda's own intellectual efforts, so that it is difficult to conceptualize what she learns as mastery. She compares herself at one point to a drain pipe through which "everything" flows, an image suggestive of passivity as well as contamination. Mitchy counters with a more graceful metaphor, likening Nanda instead to " 'a little aeolian harp set in the drawing-room window and vibrating in the breeze of conversation' " (243). The romantic tradition behind this metaphor does little to mitigate the impression created by the earlier image, however—the impression, that is, that Nanda is less acting than acted upon. Finally, although it is here the adults who are traumatized by the child's knowledge rather than the child herself, that knowledge continues to be generative of disruption and crisis.

The Awkward Age also contains a number of more compactly organized—albeit equally unconventional—primal scenes. One of these scenes occurs "off-stage," as it were, and is conveyed to us through a chorus of speculating voices. I refer to the occasion, late in Book VIII, when Petherton and Aggie engage in an erotic tussle over possession of the French novel in a room apart from the one in which everyone else is gathered, listening. The observing child has been replaced by a group of adult auditors, while the child herself has taken her "mother's" place within the primal scene. Significantly, during his erotic struggle with Aggie, Petherton must literally "go behind" her since she sits on the French novel he seeks to secure.[38]

The climax of the novel is, moreover, a veritable inversion of the primal scene. The adulterous grown-ups gather around Nanda to force out of her the confession that she has read the incriminating French novel, and that she is consequently fully capable of understanding the libidinal intrigues that are going on all around her. They thereby make a spectacle out of the bystander's knowledge. It is of course Mrs. Brook who precipitates this crisis, and she does so to prevent a repetition of the Aggie/Petherton affair—to prevent the daughter from usurping the mother within a second erotic conjunction, that involving herself and Van. Surely the most astonishing feature of this late Victorian novel, and the one pointing most unwaveringly to the Jamesian version of the primal scene, is the twice-repeated convergence of mother and daughter upon the same erotic object—the narrative literalization, on the part of the spectating "child," of a maternal identification.

Unlike Aggie, however, Nanda does not succeed in supplanting her mother with Van, or in entering the world of adult sexuality. The information which she derives from reading, watching, and listening guarantees her permanent exclusion from the scene of passion. At the moment that her illicit knowledge is exposed, Van turns away from both daughter and mother. Like Lambert Stether, then, and the other fictional inscriptions of the author "inside" James's texts, Nanda gets nothing sexual for herself.

As if James's authorial fantasmatic were not already sufficiently encoded into *The Awkward Age*, the novel even goes so far as to equip Nanda with a primal scene "memory," a "memory" which assigns both her and the adult protagonists a more classic positionality. "I verily believe she's in love with you," Nanda says of her mother to Van on the occasion of his final visit to her,

> You're more to her, I verily believe, than any one *ever* was. I hate to have the appearance of plotting anything about her *behind her back* [my emphasis]; so I'll just say it once for all. She said once, in speaking of it to a person who repeated it to me, that you had done more for her than any one, because it was you who had really brought her out. It *was*—you did. I saw it at the time myself. I was very small, but I *could* see it. (342)

It should also be noted that the libidinal economy attributed to Nanda is itself explicable only in relation to the structure of that scene. She rejects the amorous Mitchy for the indifferent Van because she "positively *like[s]* to love in vain" (243)—because the subject-position which she occupies within the Jamesian fantasmatic is precisely the one which is always set apart from genital sexuality, forever out of synchronization with the passion it witnesses.

There is yet another inscription of James's authorial fantasmatic in *The Awkward Age*, an inscription which includes the negative or homosexual Oedipus complex as well as its positive or heterosexual version. I refer here to the triangle which extends outward from Longdon, and which has at its other two points Nanda and Van. Like the central character in *The Ambassadors*, Longdon is out of temporal alignment with the world he enters at the beginning of the novel, and leaves at the end. Not only is he "too late" to be part of the sexual intrigues he witnesses, but—more remarkably—he is "too early" to be included in the erotic union which he never in fact sees, but which he might be said to "fantasize": the erotic union of Van and Nanda. Near the conclusion of *The Awkward Age* he is described as a much younger person than Nanda, and as much less "old-fashioned" than Van (368). He is psychically positioned, in other words, as their child. He is also situated as spectator in relation to those characters; as he remarks at one point to Van, "I've watched you both" (186).

Longdon is thus another of James's "observers," manifesting the same hyperdevelopment of hearing and vision as Nanda, although— as I have just suggested—the primal scene which engrosses him is less the one he sees than the one he attempts to bring about. After the Duchess has informed him of Nanda's love for Van, he "conceives" (a signifier with unavoidably erotic connotations) the "desire" (181) to pair them up sexually. This desire eventually becomes so palpable that Van is prompted to exclaim: "How awfully you want it!" (186).

Longdon's "wants" are, it seems to me, extremely complex. The intensity of his desire to bring Van and Nanda together indicates that more is at issue than a paternal interest in the latter's happiness. His attraction to Nanda is frequently documented over the course of *The Awkward Age*; not only is she metonymically connected to the dead woman whose memory he cherishes, but he comes eventually to be "a man of her own." He sends her flowers and books, goes everywhere with her, and takes her off to live with himself at the end of the novel. As the girl herself remarks at several points, they are "one of the couples who are invited together" (154).

Van also figures centrally within Longdon's erotic economy. Mitchy declares at a key point that "[Longdon] likes [Van] not a whit less than he likes [Nanda]" (254), and this account of the elderly man's desires is borne out by other details in the text as well. It is not only Nanda, but Van, who benefits from what might be called a "libidinal legacy"; if she functions as a replacement for her grandmother, he does the same for his mother, who was also loved by Longdon in the past. There is even a moment of telling censorship when Nanda narrowly avoids confronting Longdon with his desire for Van, and that moment, interestingly enough, is precisely when she herself has been brought for the first time to acknowledge her own feelings for that character. "It would be good for me—by which I mean it would be easier for me—if you didn't quite so immensely care for him," Mr. Longdon says to her.

"Oh!" came from Nanda with an accent of attenuation at once so precipitate and so vague that it only made her attitude at first rather awkward. "Oh!" she immediately repeated, but with an increase of the same effect. After which, conscious, she made, as if to save herself, a quick addition. "Dear Mr. Longdon, isn't it rather yourself most—?" (365)

This exchange suggests that Longdon's relationship with Nanda is predicated not only on attraction, but upon a structural identification. It indicates, in fact, that Longdon participates at an imaginary level in Nanda's desire for Van, much as Nanda does in her mother's—that the primal scene which he seeks to bring about is one which would permit him, through identification, to occupy her position, and thereby to effect an erotic convergence with the young man.

Longdon is also represented as entertaining a double relation with Van; once again, in other words, he identifies with what he desires. He says of the fortune which he proposes to put at Van's disposal if the latter marries Nanda, "My dear boy, I *back* you" (182), and the verb resonates through many other scenes. It is thus not only that Longdon wishes to be used by Van as he fantasizes Nanda being used, but that he is bound to the young man through a sodomitical identification analogous to that which binds Marcher to the stranger in "The Beast in the Jungle"; he wants, that is, to go "behind" the union of Van and Nanda, and in so doing to make imaginary love to her *through him*. Longdon's fantasmatic is structured both by his imaginary aspiration to occupy the place of the mother within the primal scene, and by his desire to become the man whom he also wishes to possess, a desire which is at the same time homosexual and heterosexual, in that it encompasses the "mother" as well as the "father."

In the "Preface to *The Awkward Age*," James writes that the "objectivity" of that novel comes "from the imposed absence of that 'going behind,' to compass explanations and amplifications, to drag out odds and ends from the 'mere' story-teller's great property-shop of aids to illusion: a resource under denial of which it was equally perplexing and delightful, for a change, to proceed."[39] This apparent refusal, for once, to look through a character's eyes, and experience the force of his or her desires, is, however, belied by the photograph which serves as the frontispiece to the New York Edition of *The Awkward Age*. That photograph represents Longdon's country home with an image of James's own house in Rye.[40] It thus provides a startlingly frank acknowledgment that authorial subjectivity is concentrated at those sites marked by the signifier "Longdon" as well as those marked by the signifier "Nanda," and that the identifications and desires which

I have attributed to that character are more properly indicative of the author "inside" the text.

The action of "going behind," with all of its sodomitical ramifications, would thus seem to be as constitutive of authorial subjectivity in *The Awkward Age* as it is in *The Tragic Muse* or "The Beast in the Jungle." However, given that it is worked through the characters of Aggie and Mrs. Brook, as well as Nanda and Longdon, the desire to be on the receiving end of that action would appear to exercise an even stronger force within the psychic theater of *The Awkward Age*. Either way, all libidinal roads seem to lead to Van. It is not only Longdon and Nanda who desire that character, but Mrs. Brook. Even Mitchy wants to help Longdon provide Van with financial "backing." Mrs. Brook thus clearly speaks for the author as well as the others when she says to her husband, at the end of *The Awkward Age*: "we were in love with him" (311).

5. Sodomitical Identification

What I have been calling "sodomitical identification" is a variant of narcissistic object-choice, the libidinal economy which Freud most frequently associates with homosexuality.[41] Narcissistic object-choice can assume a number of different forms, including love for what one once was, love for what one would like to be, love for someone who was once part of oneself, or—quite simply—self-love.[42] It is primarily the third of these possibilities, where what one would like to be coincides with what one would like to possess, that I would associate with sodomitical identification. The latter implies, in other words, the convergence of identification and desire upon the same object, an object which is in this case the "father." Sodomitical identification also permits the subject to participate at an imaginary level in the "father's" phallic sexuality—to penetrate by identifying with the one-who-penetrates. It is thereby a mechanism through which a subject who is profoundly marked by passivity and lack can lay temporary claim to an *active* sexual aim.

However, sodomitical identification is at the same time radically de-substantializing, in that it is entirely subsumed within the conditional tenses of the verbs "to be" and "to possess." The subject of whom I speak—the subject who occupies a male position only through an imaginary conflation with the "father" whom he also desires—would consequently seem incapable of effecting that *méconnaissance* so crucial to normative masculinity, i.e. of mistaking his penis for the phallus. Nor, it would seem, could he unblushingly assume himself to be the point of (sexual) origin. He would be only too alert to further syntagmatic possibilities, including that of being used as he imagines himself using the father. The receptive position, in other words, is the overdetermined site of pleasure.

Sodomitical identification with the fantasmatic father is the only means whereby the Jamesian "hero" can approximate a masculine position, and as we have seen that position is only very briefly sustained in "The Beast in the Jungle."[43] It represents an even more elusive goal in *The Awkward Age*, since the figure who occupies the position of the "father" in the imagined primal scene is himself incapable of entertaining an active sexual aim, at least with respect to Nanda. Van is at no point in the present tense of the novel marked by any of the passion that "scars" the face of the stranger in "The Beast in the Jungle," or that of Spencer Brydon's alter ego in "The Jolly Corner." There is not even anything to validate Nanda's childhood "memory" of Van "bringing out" her mother. *The Awkward Age* thus ultimately attests as much to the impossibility of "actual" sexual penetration as to the desire to be both on the "giving" and the "receiving" end. Appropriately, the novel concludes with the self-imposed exile from society of those two characters—Longdon and Nanda— who have been most insistently coded as watching children, their retreat from "real" sexuality to the world of Beccles and fantasy.

James himself comments eloquently on the strangely marginal position occupied by many of the characters who function as the centers of (un)consciousness in his novels. He speaks of a "particular *vice* of the artistic spirit against which vigilance had been destined from the first to exert itself in vain" (and here, too, I would argue for a greater attentiveness to James's language), "the effect of which was that again and again, *perversely, incurably*, the center of my structure would insist on placing itself *not*, so to speak, in the middle," but to one side (my emphasis).[44] The archness of James's "self-indictment" does not prevent this passage from functioning simultaneously as a testimony to the fantasmatic which organizes his work, and as an acknowledgment of the radical heterogeneity of his authorial subjectivity to the proprieties of sexual orthodoxy.

Despite the ostensible gender of the biographical Henry James, the author "inside" his texts is never unequivocally male; situated at a complex intersection of the negative and positive Oedipus complexes, that author is definitively foreclosed from the scene of passion except through identifications which challenge the binarisms of sexual difference. He aspires to knowledge only under the sign of masochism, and is unable to grasp castration as a condition exclusive to woman. Finally, his recourse to vision is more generative of trauma than of power. The author "inside" James's stories and novels bears so little resemblance to what is popularly thought of as the "Master" that I can only think of that Jacobite specter as a compensatory construction of the author "outside" the text.

Because it provides such a fertile terrain for the exploration of identity and unconscious desire, authorial subjectivity will be an ongoing concern of the pages that follow. We will return to that topic next in Chapter 6, which will attempt to show that the author inscribed by Fassbinder's films represents values which are radically antipathetic to the biography of the historical director, and which will explore in some detail the relationship between the author "inside" and the author "outside" the text. Before doing so, however, we need to look closely at the psychic economy and ideological ramifications of male masochism.

Masochism

5

Masochism and Male Subjectivity

Perversion: Turning aside from truth or right; diversion to an improper use. . . .
(*OED*)

What is the "truth" or "right" from which perversion turns aside, and what does it improperly use? The *OED* goes some way towards answering these questions when it quotes, by way of illustration, part of a line from Francis Bacon: "Women to govern men . . . slaves freemen . . . being total violations and perversions of the laws of nature and nations." According to this grammatically "deviant" citation, perversion turns aside from both biology and the social order, and it does so through the improper deployment or negation of the binarisms upon which each regime depends—binarisms that reinforce each other in the case of gender, if not that of class. The "truth" or "right" which is thus subverted is the principle of hierarchy.

Freud's account of perversion also stresses its diversionary and decentering character. "Perversions," he writes in *Three Essays on the Theory of Sexuality*, "are sexual activities which either (a) extend, in an anatomical sense, beyond the regions of the body that are designed for sexual union, or (b) linger over the intermediate relations to the sexual object which should normally be traversed rapidly on the path towards the final sexual aim."[1] Here, in utter disregard for Western metaphysics, the "true" or "right" is heterosexual penetration. All other sexual activities belong either to the category of "fore-play," in which case they are strictly subordinated to "end-pleasure," or perversion.

Coitus is "ideally" a reprise in miniature of the history of infantile sexuality, a history that begins with oral gratification and culminates with genital desire for an object of the opposite gender. Here too the subject is exhorted to keep his or her eyes on the finish line, and to move as expeditiously as possible through the preliminary stages. But in both cases perversion intrudes as the temptation to engage in a different kind of erotic narrative, one whose organization is aleatory and paratactic rather than direct and hypotactic, preferring fore-pleasures to end-pleasures, and browsing to discharge. Since every external and internal organ is capable of becoming an erotogenic zone, sexuality need not even be limited to the three stages Freud decreed for boys, or the four he ordained for girls. Infantile sexuality is polymorphously perverse, and even in the erotic activities of the most "normal" adult there are "rudiments which, if they had developed, would have led to the deviations described as 'perversions.' "[2]

I do not mean to suggest that polymorphous sexuality is more "natural" than genital sexuality. There is no form of human sexuality which does not marginalize need or substitute a fantasmatic object for the original and nutritive object. As Laplanche explains, "Sexuality is . . . a localized, autoerotic pleasure, a pleasure of the organ 'in place,' in opposition to a functional pleasure with all which that term implies of an opening towards the object . . . Thus a natural, functional rhythm (that of rutting) disappears, while elsewhere there emerges a different kind of sequence, which is incomprehensible without calling into play such categories as repression, reminiscence, work of elaboration, 'deferred action.' "[3]

The notion of a deferred action has a particular relevance within the present discussion, since infantile sexuality assumes the narrative coherence of "stages" only after the fact, from the vantage-point of the Oedipus complex. The concept of perversion is equally unthinkable apart from the Oedipus complex, since it derives all its meaning and force from its relation to that structuring moment and the premium it places upon genital sexuality. It is in fact something of a misnomer to characterize infantile sexuality as "polymorphously perverse" since sexuality only becomes perverse at the point where it constitutes either a retreat from Oedipal structuration, or a transgressive acting out of its dictates. Perversion always contains the trace of Oedipus within it—it is always organized to some degree by what it subverts.

Those writers who have engaged theoretically with the topic of perversion tend to emphasize one of these aspects at the expense of the other. For Foucault, who stands at one extreme, perversion has no subversive edge; it merely serves to extend the surface upon which power is exercised. He insists in *The History of Sexuality* that "polymorphous conducts [are] actually extracted from people's bodies and from their pleasures" by what might be called "the society of the panopticon"—that perversion is "drawn out, revealed, isolated, intensified, incorporated, by multifarious power devices."[4] At the other extreme there is a volume like the polysexuality issue of *Semiotext(e)*,[5] which heaps perversion upon perversion with wild abandon in the vain hope of burying Oedipus altogether. Neither position is adequate to the complexities of the issues involved.

Ironically, it is a rather hateful book by Janine Chasseguet-Smirgel—a book which consistently comes down on the side of the father, "mature" sexuality, and a well-fortified ego—that seems best to intuit the challenge that perversion poses to the symbolic order. Its author cautions that "The pervert is trying to free himself from the paternal universe and the constraints of the law. He wants to create a new kind of reality and to dethrone God the Father."[6] Chasseguet-Smirgel's reading of perversion suggests that its significance extends far beyond the domain of the strictly sexual (if, indeed, such a domain ever existed)—suggests, that is, that it turns aside not only from hierarchy and genital sexuality, but from the paternal signifier, the ultimate "truth" or "right." As I will attempt to demonstrate later in this chapter with respect to masochism, at certain moments perversion may pose such a radical challenge to sexual difference as to enact precisely the scenario condemned by Bacon.

The theoretical interest of perversion extends even beyond the disruptive force it brings to bear upon gender. It strips sexuality of all functionality, whether biological or social; in an even more extreme fashion than "normal" sexuality, it puts the body and the world of objects to uses that have nothing whatever to do with any kind of "immanent" design or purpose. Perversion also subverts many of the binary oppositions upon which the social order rests: it crosses the boundary separating food from excrement (coprophilia); human from animal (bestiality); life from death (necrophilia); adult from child (pederasty); and pleasure from pain (masochism).

Of course not all perversions are equally subversive, or even equally interesting. It is unfortunate but not surprising that the perversion which has commandeered most of the literary and theoretical attention—sadism—is also the one which is most compatible with conventional heterosexuality. (The first thing that Freud says about sadism in *Three Essays* is that "the sexuality of most male human beings contains an element of aggressiveness—a desire to subjugate." He adds that the "biological significance" of this combination

> seems to lie in the need for overcoming the resistance of the sexual object by means other than the process of wooing. Thus sadism would correspond to an aggressive component of the sexual instinct which has become independent and exaggerated and, by displacement, has usurped the leading position. [157–58]

The Ego and the Id describes sadism's combination of cruelty and eroticism as a "serviceable instinctual fusion.")[7] The work of Sade commands enormous intellectual prestige—something inconceivable with the novels of Leopold von Sacher-Masoch, rescued from oblivion by Deleuze.[8] One thinks in this respect not only of Bataille,[9] Barthes,[10] and Gallop,[11] but of the massive double issue of *Obliques* dedicated to Sade, which includes materials from Benoît, Klossowski, Blanchot, Robbe-Grillet, Sollers, Paulhan, Breton, Mandiargues, Masson, and Labisse, to name only a few of its contributors.[12]

The focus of this essay is the perversion which is most commonly linked with sadism, sometimes as its complement and at other times as its instinctual opposite. I refer of course to masochism,[13] variously described by Freud as an unusually dangerous libidinal infraction,[14] and as one of the "kindliest."[15]

1. Three Kinds of Masochism

In his last work to deal extensively with masochism, Freud distinguishes between three forms of that perversion: "erotogenic," "feminine," and "moral."[16] However, no sooner are these distinctions enumerated than they begin to erode. Erotogenic masochism, which Freud defines as "pleasure in pain," provides the corporeal basis both for feminine and moral masochism. The tripartite division thus gives way rather quickly to one of those dualisms of which Freud is so fond, with both feminine and moral masochism "bleeding" into each other at the point where each abuts into erotogenic masochism.

The adjective "erotogenic" is one which Freud habitually links with "zone," and with which he designates a part of the body at which sexual excitation concentrates. Implicit, then, in the notion of masochism, whether feminine or moral, would seem to be the experience of corporeal pleasure, or—to be more precise—corporeal pleasure-in-pain. This stipulation poses no real conceptual difficulties with respect to the first of those categories; erotogenic masochism would seem to be literally "at the bottom" of feminine masochism, which Freud associates with fantasies of being bound and beaten, and with the desire to be "treated like . . . a naughty child."[17] It is far less clear how moral masochism could be said to have a necessary corporeal substratum, until we recall that the ego is for Freud "first and foremost a bodily ego"[18]—or, as Strachey explains in an authorized gloss, "derived from bodily sensations, chiefly from those springing from the surface of the body."[19] If, as "The Economic Problem of Masochism" suggests, the "true" masochist "always turns his cheek whenever he has a chance of receiving a blow" (165), the moral masochist's cheek is the ego. That is the erotogenic zone of choice, the site where he or she seeks to be beaten.

Curiously, after characterizing feminine masochism as "the one that is the most accessible to our observation," Freud announces that owing to the "material at [his] command," he will limit his discussion of that libidinal economy entirely to male patients.[20] The inference is obvious: feminine masochism is a specifically *male* pathology, so named because it positions its sufferer as a woman. Freud in fact says as much:

> . . . if one has an opportunity of studying cases in which the masoch-istic phantasies have been especially richly elaborated, one quickly discovers that they place the subject in a characteristically feminine situation; they signify, that is, being castrated, or copulated with, or giving birth to a baby. For this reason I have called this form of masochism, *a potiori*, as it were . . . the feminine form, although so many of its features point to infantile life.[21]

The reader is likely to object at this point that only five years earlier Freud had clearly identified the beating fantasy primarily with women. (Of the six patients upon whom he bases " 'A Child Is Being Beaten,' " four are female, and only two male.)[22] And from *Three Essays* until *New Introductory Lectures*, Freud was to maintain, albeit with certain crucial qualifications, the connection between femininity and masochism.[23] Yet "The Economic Problem of Masochism" is not the only major work on masochism to focus primarily upon male patients. Richard von Krafft-Ebing, who gave masochism its name and its first definition, cites thirty-three cases of male masochism, and only four of female.[24] (He also names masochism after a male masochist, Sacher-Masoch.) Theodor Reik's research had similar results, leading him to conclude that "the male sex is more masochistic than the female."[25] In his study of cruelty, Deleuze not only focuses exclusively on the novels of Sacher-Masoch, but elaborates a theoretical model of mas-ochism in which the suffering position is almost necessarily male. What is to be made of this anomaly, whereby Freud designates as "feminine" a psychic disorder whose victims are primarily men? While I would certainly dispute Reik's notion that men are more masochistic than women, it does seem to me that it is only in the case of men that feminine masochism can be seen to assume pathological proportions. Although that psychic phenomenon often provides a cen-trally structuring element of both male and female subjectivity, it is only in the latter that it can be safely acknowledged. It is an accepted—indeed a requisite—element of "normal" female subjectivity, provid-ing a crucial mechanism for eroticizing lack and subordination. The male subject, on the contrary, cannot avow feminine masochism without calling into question his identification with the masculine position. All of this is another way of suggesting that what is acceptable for the female subject is pathological for the male. Freud indicates as much when he tells us that whereas the beating fantasy can be effortlessly accommodated within the little girl's *positive* Oedipus complex, it can only be contained within the little boy's *negative* Oedipus complex.[26] Feminine masochism, in other words, always implies desire for the father and identification with the mother, a state of affairs which is normative for the female subject, but "deviant" for her male counterpart.

The disruptive consequences of male masochism are also underscored by an extraordinary passage from Reik, in which he distinguishes the masochistic fantasies of women from those of men:

> Compared with the masculine masochism that of women shows a somewhat attenuated, one could almost say anemic character. It is more of a trespassing of the bourgeois border, of which one nevertheless remains aware, than an invasion into enemy terrain. The woman's masochistic phantasy very seldom reaches the pitch of savage lust, of ecstasy, as does that of the man. Even the orgy in the phantasy does not ascend in so steep a curve. There is nothing in it of the wildness of the chained Prometheus, rather something of Ganymede's submission. One does not feel anything of the cyclonelike character that is so often associated with masculine masochism, that blind unrestricted lust of self-destruction. The masochistic phantasy of woman has the character of yielding and surrender rather than that of the rush ahead, of the orgiastic cumulation, of the self-abandonment of man. (216)

Reik suggests here that even the clinically masochistic woman does not really exceed her subjective limits; she merely stretches them a bit. The male masochist, on the other hand, leaves his social identity completely behind—actually abandons his "self"—and passes over into the "enemy terrain" of femininity. I will have more to say later about the "shattering"[27] qualities of male masochism, but suffice it to note here that the sexual fantasies cited by Reik fully bear out these characterizations, as do those included by Krafft-Ebing.

Not only does it turn out that feminine masochism doesn't have very much to do with women, but that moral masochism doesn't have very much to do with virtue. Although the moral masochist seems to be under the domination of a hyperdeveloped conscience, his or her desire for punishment is so great as to pose a constant temptation to perform "sinful" actions, which must then be "expiated." Freud warns that moral masochism is in fact capable of swallowing up conscience altogether, of perverting it from within.[28] This invisible sabotage occurs through the complete reversal of the process whereby the Oedipus complex was earlier "dissolved," i.e. of the operation whereby the paternal voice and imago were internalized as the super-ego. By deriving erotic gratification from the super-ego's censorship and punishment, the morally masochistic ego not only assumes an analogous position to that adopted by his or her more flamboyantly "feminine" counterpart in fantasy or actual sexual practice, but reactivates the Oedipus complex.[29]

Significantly, what flares up with renewed intensity is that form of the Oedipus complex which is positive for the female subject, but negative for the male—the form, that is, which turns upon desire for the father and identification with the mother. Freud is quite explicit about this:

> We were able to translate the expression "unconscious sense of guilt" as meaning a need for punishment at the hands of a parental power. We know that the wish, which so frequently appears in phantasies, to be beaten by the father stands very close to the other wish, to have a passive (feminine) sexual relation to him and is only a regressive distortion of it. If we insert this explanation into the content of moral masochism, its hidden meaning becomes clear to us. (169)

Thus through moral masochism the ego is beaten/loved by the father, a situation which—once again—is "normal" for the female subject, but "abnormal" for the male.

It would consequently seem that moral and feminine masochism develop out of the same "fantasmatic," to borrow a word from Laplanche and Pontalis[30]—out of the same unconsciously structuring scenario or action. However, the moral masochist remains oblivious to the passion for self-destruction that burns ferociously within; Freud observes that whereas the sadism of the super-ego "becomes for the most part glaringly conscious," the masochism of the ego "remains as a rule concealed from the subject and has to be inferred from his behavior."[31] With the feminine masochist, on the other hand, the beating fantasy assumes a shape which is available to consciousness, albeit not necessarily to rational scrutiny.

Let us look rather more closely at these two categories of masochism, and at the forms they assume in both conscious and unconscious life.

2. Moral Masochism

With a frankness which is more alarming than engaging, Freud acknowledges in *The Ego and the Id* that under certain circumstances the super-ego promotes a "pure culture of the death [drive]" (53). The stronger that psychic entity—i.e. the more thoroughly the subject has been subordinated to prohibition and denial—the greater the possibility that the ego will be driven to the last extremity. In moral masochism the super-ego assumes titanic proportions, but even under much more auspicious conditions its authority and severity are so considerable as to call fundamentally into question the notion of a "healthy" subject, let alone one who might be said to be in a position of mastery or control. Since conventional subjectivity so closely adjoins moral masochism, I want to examine it briefly through the grid of Freud's late topography before turning once again to its pathological correlate.

We recall that the super-ego is the agency whereby the Oedipus complex is neutralized, but its effects indefinitely prolonged. It is formed through the fantasmatization and introjection of what cannot be possessed in reality, and must consequently be renounced—the parents. This process of introjection is a complex one, more hinted at than specified in *The Ego and the Id*, but clarified somewhat in *New Introductory Lectures on Psycho-Analysis*.[32] It develops out of two sets of relationships, one of which is synonymous with the positive Oedipus complex, and the other of which is equivalent to the negative Oedipus complex, a point to which I will return in a moment. The super-ego would also seem to involve two different kinds of introjection, one of which I will characterize as "imaginary" and the other as "symbolic." What I mean by imaginary introjection is the psychic process whereby once-loved figures are taken into the self as subjective models or exempla, i.e. with the formation of that image or cluster of images in which the ego sees itself as it would like to be seen. Symbolic introjection, on the other hand, designates the psychic process whereby the subject is subordinated to the Law and the Name-of-the-Father. Although the category of the super-ego subsumes both kinds of introjection in Freud, it more specifically designates the product of symbolic introjection. Imaginary introjection, on the other hand, results in what is strictly speaking the ego-ideal.

Because the subject usually goes through a negative as well as a positive Oedipus complex, he or she enters into two sets of identifications at the end of that complex: one with the imago of the mother, and the other with the imago of the father.[33] One of these identifications is generally much stronger, and so tends to eclipse the other. If all goes according to cultural plan, the stronger identification conforms to the positive Oedipus complex. Nevertheless, both have a part to play in the agency which they form within the ego, an agency which Freud describes as the "ego ideal or super-ego," but which is more usefully designated by the first of those appellations.

The ego-ideal, I would maintain, represents one area or function of the super-ego but not its entirety, that "face" of each parent which is loved rather than feared. It articulates the ideal identity to which the ego aspires, and by which it constantly measures itself, but in relation to which it is always found wanting. It is the mirror in which the subject would like to see itself reflected, the repository of everything it admires.

Freud argues in *The Ego and the Id* that the introjection of these parental images desexualizes them, with the positive Oedipus complex canceling out the object-choice of the negative complex, and the negative Oedipus complex canceling out the object-choice of the positive complex. Desire for the father, in other words, gives way to identification with him, and desire for the mother to identification with her:

> The father-identification will preserve the object-relation to the mother which belonged to the positive complex and will at the same time replace the object-relation to the father which belonged to the inverted complex: and the same will be true, *mutatis mutandis*, of the mother identification. (34)

This desexualization has grave consequences for the ego, since it results in an instinctual defusion; when object-libido changes to narcissistic libido (that is, when love changes to identification), the aggression which was earlier commingled with that libido also loses its purchase, and turns around upon the subject's own self. No longer in the protective custody of eros, that aggression falls under the jurisdiction of the super-ego, which directs it against the ego (54–55).

Freud says some very inconsistent things about the gender of the super-ego. At some points in *The Ego and the Id* he associates it with both parents, as we have seen, but at other points he connects it exclusively with the father. In one particularly important passage, in which he places great emphasis upon the paternal identity of the super-ego, he refers to the "double aspect" of that psychic entity, an aspect which he equates with two mutually exclusive imperatives: "You *ought to be* like this (like your father)" and "You *may not be* like this (like your father)—that is, you may not do all that he does; some things are his prerogative" (34). The first of these commands clearly issues from the ego-ideal, whose function is to promote similitude between itself and the ego, but where does the second command come from?

It comes, as Freud's reference to a "double aspect" would suggest, from another component of the super-ego, and one whose gender is much more delimited than that of the ego-ideal. This other component is formed through the introjection of the symbolic father rather than his imaginary counterpart—through the internalization of the father as Law, gaze, voice-on-high. This element of the super-ego has no necessary relation to any historical figure, but its gender is irreducibly masculine, at least within the present social order. It is, quite simply, the paternal function, and the ego is always-already guilty in relation to it—guilty by virtue of Oedipal desire.

Curiously, in light of the double parental complex, with the expectation it creates that both parents would have a part to play in the constitution of the super-ego, Freud asserts in *The Ego and the Id* that this entity is always "a substitute for a longing for the father" (37). The context in which he makes this observation indicates that he is speaking not about the ego-ideal, but about what, in the strictest sense of the word, is the super-ego. Freud adds that the psychic entity which replaces desire for the father "contains the germ from which all religions have evolved," and produces "the self-judgment which declares that the ego falls short of its ideal." This passage from *The Ego and the Id* consequently has staggering implications. It suggests that what is really at issue in the dissolution of the male Oedipus complex—what really motivates Freud to insist so strenuously upon its definitive terminus—is the male subject's *homosexual attachment to the father*. The relationship of the male ego to the super-ego would seem to grow out of, and "ideally" undo, the romance between father and son—or, to be more precise, the libidinal economy of the negative Oedipus complex, which hinges upon desire for the father and identification with the mother.[34]

The situation is even more explosive than I have so far shown it to be. There is a fundamental impossibility about the position in which the male subject is held, an impossibility which has to do with the self-canceling structure of the Oedipal imperative. The only mechanism by which the son can overcome his desire for the father is to transform object libido into narcissistic libido, and in so doing to attempt to *become* the (symbolic) father. However, this metamorphosis is precisely what the super-ego prohibits by decreeing: "You may not be like [your father] . . . you may not do all that he does; some things are his prerogative." The paternal law thus promotes the very thing that its severity is calculated to prevent, a contradiction which must function as a constant inducement to reconstitute the negative Oedipus complex.

It is hardly surprising, in view of all this, that the relationship of the ego to the super-ego should be susceptible to sexualization; eros is in fact never far away. But what form does this "sexuality" take? Freud leaves us in no doubt on this particular point. In *Civilization and its Discontents* he describes a situation where the ego comes to take pleasure in the pain inflicted upon it by the super-ego—where fear of punishment gives way to the wish for it, and where cruelty and discipline come to stand for love:

> The sense of guilt, the harshness of the super-ego is . . . the same thing as the severity of the conscience. It is the perception which the ego has of being watched over in this way, the assessment of the tension between its own strivings and the demands of the super-ego. The fear of this critical agency (a fear which is at the bottom of the whole relationship), the need for punishment, is an instinctual manifestation on the part of the ego, which has become masochistic under the influence of a sadistic super-ego; it is a portion . . . of the instinct towards internal destruction present in the ego, employed for forming an erotic attachment to the super-ego. (136)

This description conforms precisely to what Freud was somewhat later to name "moral masochism." However, the condition it describes differs from "normalcy" only in degree and erotic intent. The prototypical male subject oscillates endlessly between the mutually exclusive commands of the (male) ego-ideal and the super-ego, wanting both to love the father and to be the father, but prevented from doing either. The morally masochistic male subject has given up on the desire to be the father, and may in fact have turned away from the paternal ego-ideal to the maternal one, and from identification with the father to identification with the mother. However, he burns with an exalted ardor for the rigors of the super-ego. The feminine masochist, to whom I shall return later in this chapter, literalizes the beating fantasy, and brings this cruel drama back to the body.

3. Christian Masochism

Theodor Reik's exhaustive study of masochism warrants some attention at this point, both because it has been so extensively mined by Deleuze and others, and because it manifests so extreme a sensitivity to the formal features of that pathology. Although it begins with a discussion of masochism as a sexual perversion—a discussion studded with some quite compelling fantasies, to one of which we will circle back later—its chief focus is moral (or what Reik calls "social") masochism. *Masochism in Sex and Society* characterizes that psychic economy as closed and self-referential, and associates it with exhibitionism or "demonstrativeness," revolutionary fervor, and "suspense"—a surprising catalogue at first glance. As I will attempt to demonstrate, certain parts of this definition clearly pertain to that model of moral masochism which Freud associates with the ego/super-ego dynamic, but other parts point toward a rather different paradigm.

Like Freud, Reik stresses that in moral or social masochism the subject functions both as the victim and as the victimizer, dispensing with the need for an external object. Even when punishment seems to derive from the external world, it is in fact the result of a skillful unconscious manipulation of "adverse incidents" (304). The psychic economy of moral masochism is therefore strikingly self-contained:

> ... social masochism springs from the intermediate phase of the development of phantasy, during which the pain-inflicting and the pain-enduring person are identical, *impersonating* simultaneously object and subject [my emphasis]. Also in the masochistic attitude toward life there is generally no object discernible that imposes the suffering and is independent of the ego. It is certainly extant in phantasy, but it does not appear in reality and remains in the twilight where it merges into the ego. This type of masochistic character behaves almost autoerotically. (333)

However, Reik does not foreground the role of the super-ego in moral masochism; the internal agency of punishment remains curiously unspecified in his text. He also gives fantasy a more privileged position within moral masochism than does Freud; indeed, he maintains that it plays as centrally structuring a role there as it does in what he calls "perverse" masochism. Here, again, the emphasis falls exclusively on the ego; even when other figures appear in these fantasies, they are in effect stories with a single character (314). Finally, Reik claims that the fantasies at the heart of masochism remain strictly unconscious, and that they always express the same desire—the desire to be rewarded for good behavior. Consequently, although they invariably dramatize the sufferings and defeats of the fantasizing subject, that is "only to make the final victory appear all the more glorious and triumphant" (315).

Both in its exclusive focus upon the ego, and in its apparent impulsion towards the "enhance[ment]" of that psychic entity, Reik's moral masochism would seem to differ significantly from Freud's. We will, however, discover more substantive differences between the two forms of moral masochism than those I have already noted. The latter will also evaporate upon closer scrutiny. Ultimately, the moral masochism identified by Reik occupies a theoretical position somewhere between Freud's version of that pathology and feminine masochism, manifesting aspects of both.

The second of the qualities enumerated above—exhibitionism or "demonstrativeness"—is one which Reik claims to be an indispensable feature not only of moral or social masochism, but of all masochism:

> ... in no case of masochism can the fact be overlooked that the suffering, discomfort, humiliation and disgrace are being shown and so to speak put on display ...
>
> In the practices of masochists, denudation and parading with all their psychic concomitant phenomena play such a major part that one feels induced to assume a constant connection between masochism and exhibitionism. (72)

As we will see later in this chapter, the demonstrative feature occupies a prominent place within Reik's account of feminine or "perverse" masochism. However, many of the most striking examples of exhibitionism that he cites are drawn from moral or social masochism. Once again, this places him in opposition to Freud, who claims that whereas the super-ego's desire to inflict injury is usually "glaringly" obvious in moral masochism, the ego's desire for punishment generally escapes the attention both of others and of the subject itself. What are we to make of this discrepancy?

A quick survey of Reik's examples suggests that his attention may be focused upon a different variety of moral masochism than that spotlighted by Freud—that his concern may ultimately be with Christian masochism, even when he is discussing more secular instances. Not only does he devote a whole chapter to "the paradoxes of Christ," but most of the other cases of moral masochism that he cites are drawn from the lives of saints and martyrs. As in Freud's account of moral masochism, Reik's typical subject seems ardently given over to self-mortification of one kind or another (one particularly commodious sentence functions as a kind of display-window, disclosing "Benedict rolling himself in thorn hedges, Macarius sitting naked on an ant-hill, [and] Anthony flagellating himself incessantly" [351]), but the psychic dynamics are otherwise quite different.[35] To begin with, an external audience is a structural necessity, although it may be either earthly or heavenly. Second, the body is centrally on display, whether it is being consumed by ants or roasting over a fire. Finally, behind all these "scenes" or "exhibits" is the master tableau or group fantasy—Christ nailed to the cross, head wreathed in thorns and blood dripping from his impaled sides. What is being beaten here is not so much the body as the "flesh," and beyond that sin itself, and the whole fallen world.

This last target pits the Christian masochist against the society in which he or she lives, makes of that figure a rebel, or even a revolutionary of sorts. In this particular subspecies of moral masochism there would thus seem to be a strong heterocosmic impulse—the desire to remake the world in another image altogether, to forge a different cultural order. The exemplary Christian masochist also seeks to remake him or herself according to the model of the suffering Christ, the very picture of earthly divestiture and loss. Insofar as such an identification implies the complete and utter negation of all phallic values, Christian masochism has radically emasculating implications, and is in its purest forms intrinsically incompatible with the pretensions of masculinity.[36] And since its primary exemplar is a male rather than a female subject, those implications would seem impossible to ignore. Remarkably, Christianity also redefines the paternal legacy; it is after all through the assumption of his place within the divine family that Christ comes to be installed in a suffering and castrated position.

The demonstrative feature, as I have been implicitly arguing, works very much against Reik's premise that the driving force behind moral masochism is the victory and reward of the ego. Reik suggests at one point that the moral masochist seeks to be "raised on an invisible pedestal" (315), but the passage I quoted a moment ago thoroughly belies this formulation. In that passage, Reik not only associates all forms of masochism with exhibitionism or self-display, but he acknowledges that what is thus rendered visible is the subject's "suffering," "discomfort," "humiliation," and "disgrace" rather than its grandeur or its triumph. The demonstrative feature also runs counter to the notion that moral masochism is an entirely self-contained system, since at least within Reik's Christian examples the gaze comes dramatically into play, either in a heavenly or an earthly guise. There are also other ways in which moral masochism opens onto the world on which it ostensibly forecloses, whether it assumes the form described by Freud, or that theorized by Reik. The super-ego is produced through the introjection of the paternal function, and the ego through the subject's identification both with its own corporeal imago, and with a whole range of other external images. The interior drama is thus the refraction of a familial structure, which itself interlocks with the whole social order. Christian masochism, as we have seen, involves a similar identificatory system.[37]

The last of the qualities associated by Reik with moral masochism—suspense—would seem to be at the center of all forms of masochism, in addition to being one of the conditions out of which conventional subjectivity develops. Reik rings some complex changes on this word, which he connects with uncertainty, dilatoriness, pleasurable and unpleasurable anticipation, apparent interminability, and—above all—excitation. Masochism exploits all these themes in one way or another because it always seeks to prolong preparatory detail and ritual at the expense of climax or consummation. Since in moral masochism this implies the endless postponement of the moment at which suffering yields to reward, and victory to defeat, suspense clearly works to prioritize pain over pleasure, and so to further undermine the ego.

The larger thesis that Reik pursues over the length of his study is that the masochist is apprehensive about end-pleasure because it is so fully associated with punishment, and therefore seeks to delay it as long as possible ("The . . . characteristic of the masochistic tension-curve is the tendency to prolong the tension, while we meet with the opposite intention, of resolving the tension, in normal sexual life" [60]). However, Reik also maintains elsewhere in *Masochism in Sex and Society* that the masochist rushes toward the punishment he or she fears in order to get it over with as quickly as possible. Through this "flight forward" the normal sequence of pleasure and pain is reversed, and the latter is experienced before the former. This is how Reik accounts for the suffering in masochism, to which he claims the subject would never submit except as the "price" of what is always fundamentally a sexual gratification.

There is a basic contradiction here: if the masochist rushes to experience the necessary punishment *before* indulging in a pleasure so as to thereby assure an untroubled enjoyment of it, why should he or she then delay the moment of gratification for as long as possible out of fear of the consequences? This contradiction is part and parcel of Reik's refusal to admit that the masochist in fact *seeks out* punishment, of his inability to entertain the possibility that for some individuals pleasure might actually inhere in pain and in the psychic destabilization to which it leads.

Such an eventuality would represent the radical perversion of the pleasure principle, which "endeavors to keep the quantity of excitation present in [the mental apparatus] as low as possible or at least to keep it constant."[38] It would indicate, that is, that pleasure (and specifically sexual pleasure) can accompany an excruciating increase in such tension. Freud himself has of course prepared us for such a development. He remarks on more than one occasion that pain "trenches" into pleasure, a verb which the *OED* glosses as "to 'cut' into, to enter into so as to affect intimately." *Three Essays* includes the observation that "nothing of considerable importance can occur in the organism without contributing some component to the excitation of the sexual instinct" (205), and "The Economic Problem of Masochism" adds that "the excitation of pain and unpleasure would be bound to have the same result too" (163). However, Freud's theory of pleasure is closely imbricated with his account of the way in which identity is formed, i.e. with what he has to say about the secondary process and the maintenance of a quiescently cathected ego. As Leo Bersani points out in *The Freudian Body*, the introduction of large quantities of excitation into the psychic economy can only have a "shattering" effect upon this coherence, pitting the pathology of masochism (which for him means sexuality *tout court*) against identity itself:

> ... the pleasurable unpleasurable tension of sexual excitement occurs when the body's "normal" range of sensation is exceeded, and when the organization of the self is momentarily disturbed by sensations or affective processes somehow "beyond" those compatible with psychic organization ... Sexuality [i.e. masochism] would be that which is intolerable to the structured self ... Sexuality ... may depend on the *décalage* or gap, in human life, between the quantities of stimuli to which we are exposed and the development of ego structures capable of resisting or ... binding those stimuli. The mystery of sexuality is that we seek not only to get rid of this shattering tension but also to repeat, even to increase it. (38–39)

What masochism really "suspends," then, is not just the pleasure principle, but the libidinal and psychic constancy that principle supports.

But what are the forms that this suspense takes in moral masochism? The Christian, of course, lives his or her life in perpetual anticipation of the second coming. The figural meaning which this anticipation implants in present sufferings makes it possible for them to be savored as future pleasures, with time folding over itself in such a way as to permit that retroactivity to be already experienced now, in a moment prior to its effectivity. Such is the fundamentally perverse nature of Christian suspense and the pain it sanctifies and irradiates, a suspense which works against anything approximating psychic coherence.

Freud's moral masochist also lives in suspense, but without the promise of a redemptive end-pleasure. Here suspense has a double face. It signifies both the endless postponement of libidinal gratification, and the perpetual state of anxiety and apprehension which is the result of that renunciation and of the super-ego's relentless surveillance. Of course these forms of suspense are not limited to the moral masochist; they are also part of the cultural legacy of even the most conventionally structured of subjects. All that distinguishes the former from the latter is that his or her ego seeks to increase rather than decrease that tension, whether through the commission of misdeeds which will then elicit punishment, or—more classically—through the punctiliousness of its obedience. Freud warns us that the more perfectly the ego conforms to the super-ego's mandates, the more ferocious and exacting that censoring mechanism becomes.[39] It would thus seem that the ego's "goodness" can actually become a request to be beaten. The moral masochist, in short, seeks to intensify both forms of the suspense which is so (seemingly) intolerable to the "ordinary" subject. Freud is quite explicit about the challenge which this poses to the stability and robustness of the ego, remarking in "The Economic Problem of Masochism" that "In order to provoke punishment from [the super-ego], the masochist must do what is inexpedient, must act against his own interests, must ruin the prospects which open out to him in the real world and must, perhaps, destroy his own real existence" (169–70).

4. Feminine Masochism

Let us now turn to feminine masochism via "'A Child Is Being Beaten,'" which is without a doubt the most crucial text for understanding that perversion. Significantly, although Freud focuses primarily upon female patients there, he manages to articulate the masochistic desire he attributes to them only through recourse to one of his male patients, who gives voice to what they cannot—the second phase of the beating fantasy.[40] Let us effect a reverse displacement, and approach the male version of the beating fantasy through its female counterpart. Doing so will permit us to see how fully that fantasy subverts sexual difference.

The female fantasy consists of three phases, the first and third of which are available to analysis, but the second of which remains unconscious. Here is the complete sequence, after it has been "doctored" by Freud (the phrases within square brackets represent either his interpolations, or additions made by the patient at his prompting):

> Phase 1: "My father is beating the child [whom I hate]."
> Phase 2: "I am being beaten by my father."
> Phase 3: "Some boys are being beaten. [I am probably looking on.]"

Freud says of the first phase that it is neither sexual nor sadistic, but "the stuff from which both will later come" (187). He adds that it may not even constitute part of the fantasy proper, but may simply be a memory out of which the fantasy subsequently develops. It is savored for the erotic value it retroactively assumes, a value which Freud translates with the phrase: "My father does not love this other child, *he loves only me.*"

Oedipal desire and its prohibition intervene between phase 1 and 2 of the fantasy. By inserting herself into the imaginary scene in the position earlier occupied by the other child, the girl submits herself to punishment at the hands of the father, and so atones for her incestuous guilt. This new fantasy evokes intensely pleasurable feelings, however, pointing to an erotic as well as a punitive content. Phase 2—"I am being beaten by my father"—thus functions as a mechanism for bringing about a regression to an earlier stage of sexuality; the desire which is blocked at the genitals, in other words, finds expression instead at the anus.

On account of its prohibited content, phase 2 undergoes repression. It is replaced at the level of consciousness by the third variant, which disguises the identity both of the person being beaten and of the one administering the punishment. A group of boys now replaces the little girl, and a paternal representative supplants the father. The fantasizing subject is inscribed into this scenario as an ambiguous spectator.[41] Phases 1 and 3 are ostensibly sadistic. Only phase 2 is unequivocally masochistic.

In a move equivalent in daring to Monsieur D's open concealment of the purloined letter in Poe's short story, Freud disarms his critic by acknowledging what might otherwise have been discovered about phase 2: he admits, that is, to having fabricated that sequence in the fantasy upon which he bases his entire interpretation:

> This second phase is the most important and the most momentous of all. But we may say of it in a certain sense that it has never had a real existence. It is never remembered, it has never succeeded in becoming conscious. It is a construction of analysis, but it is no less of a necessity on that account. (185)

Every time I read this passage, I find myself momentarily paralyzed both by the audacity of the confession, and by the realization that to challenge Freud's right to speak in this way *for* his female patients would be to place my rhetorical weight on the side of the "real" as against the "constructed," the "authentic" against the "inauthentic."

Yet, struggle as I inevitably do against this paralysis, I can find nothing to dispute in Freud's account of phase 2, apart from the fact that he finds what he is looking for in one of his male patient's case histories. The change from the active to the passive form of the verb "to beat"—from phase 1 to phase 3—can only have been effected through the mediation of the instinctual vicissitude indicated in phase 2. In other words, the transition from phase 1 to phase 3 moves the subject from heteroaggression to what appears to be sadism, and hence from the dimension of simple self-preservation to that of sexuality. As Laplanche has compellingly argued, that movement necessitates not only the propping of sexuality upon aggression (i.e. upon the death drive), but the turning around of that sexualized aggression upon the fantasizing subject's own self (85–102). It is only in a second movement that the now eroticized aggression can be redirected outward once again, this time in the form of sadism. I would therefore agree with Freud that what he identifies as phase 2 is behind phase 3, and that implicit in the later moment is a masochistic identification with the beaten children.

At the same time, I do not think that phases 2 and 3 can be completely collapsed, or that the wish for pleasurable pain exhausts the latter's meaning. Greater attention should be paid here to the manifest content of the conscious fantasy, and to its substitution of boys for a girl. The final phase attests to three transgressive desires, not one of which Freud remarks upon, but which clamor loudly for my attention: to the desire that it be boys rather than girls who be loved/disciplined in this way; to the desire to be a boy while being so treated by the father; and, finally, to the desire to occupy a male subject-position in some more general sense, but one under the sign of femininity rather than that of masculinity.

These three desires clearly converge around one thing: a narcissistic investment in a subject-position which it would be transgressive for a man to occupy, but which is almost unthinkable for a woman, since it implies an identification with male homosexuality. Why should this identification fall so far outside the social pale? Because even what generally passes for "deviance" is held to a recognizable and "manageable" paradigm, i.e. to one that reinforces the binary logic of sexual difference, despite inverting its logic. Thus when a woman doesn't identify with a classically female position, she is expected to identify with a classically male one, and *vice versa* in the case of a man. The female version of the beating fantasy, then, attests to the desire for imaginary variations that fall outside the scope of the psychoanalytic paradigm.

Freud comes close on two occasions to commenting upon the last of the wishes enumerated above, but both times he pulls back from what he is on the verge of discovering. At the end of Section IV he observes that

> When [girls] turn away from their incestuous love for their father, with its genital significance, they easily abandon their feminine role. They spur their "masculinity complex" . . . into activity, and from that point forward only want to be boys. For that reason the whipping-boys who represent them are boys too. (191)

Here the contradiction between having a "masculinity complex" and representing oneself as a group of "whipping-boys" goes unnoted by

Freud. In a subsequent passage, however, he points out that the girl's identification with the male position does not imply an identification with activity ("[the girl] turns herself in phantasy into a man, without herself becoming active in the masculine way" [199]).

In Section VI of " 'A Child is Being Beaten,' " Freud suggests that the female subject occupies not only one, but *two* unconventionally masculine positions in phase 3 of the beating fantasy. In the course of describing the various shifts that occur over the history of the beating fantasy, he explicitly states that in phase 3 the girl turns herself into the group of boys (196). A few pages later, however, he indicates that in her capacity as onlooker of the beating scene, the girl occupies another position indicative of a masculinity under erasure. After observing that the girl "turns herself in phantasy into a man without herself becoming active in the masculine way," he adds that she is "no longer anything but a spectator of the event which takes the place of a sexual act" (199).

The first of these masculine positions—that of (passive) male homosexuality—is the position into which the male subject inserts himself in the masculine version of the beating fantasy, and there it has an emphatically maternal significance; Freud maintains that it is "derived from a feminine attitude toward his father" (198), i.e. from the negative Oedipus complex. The male subject thus secures access to femininity through identification with the mother. By turning herself in fantasy into the "whipping-boys," the female subject is in turn given imaginary access to this "borrowed" femininity through the image of the male body. Femininity is thus both radically denatured, and posited as the privileged reference point by means of the curious relay that is set up between these two versions of the beating fantasy. But there is also an ineluctable difference at work here, since it is clearly not the same thing, socially or even psychically, for the girl to be loved/beaten by the father as it is for the boy. Through her identification with the "whipping-boys" in phase 3, the girl establishes an imaginary connection not only with a feminized masculinity, but with that difference. Is not this the beginning of a sexual relation?

It is perhaps less evident how the girl's spectatorial position in phase 3 also aligns her with an "unmanly" masculinity. Voyeurism has been heavily coded within Western culture as a male activity, and associated with aggression and sadism. Here, however, masculinity, aggression, and sadism are definitively elsewhere in the scene, concentrated in the figure of the punishing father-surrogate. Like the child in the primal scene,[42] the shadowy onlooker is more mastered than mastering. The tentativeness with which Freud's female patients insert themselves into this position ("I am probably looking on") points to the irresolute character of the position itself, which is less the site of a controlling gaze than a vantage point from which to identify with the group of boys.

Before leaving the female beating fantasy, I want to note that the pronoun "I" is conspicuously missing from those parts of it which are available to consciousness, except in the adumbrative qualification about spectatorship, and in fact figures prominently only in that phrase which is "a construction of psychoanalysis"—a detail which Chapter 6 will attribute to heteropathic identification. Heteropathic identification is the obverse of idiopathic identification; whereas the latter conforms to an incorporative model, constituting the self at the expense of the other who is in effect "swallowed," the former subscribes to an exteriorizing logic, and locates the self at the site of the other. In heteropathic identification one lives, suffers, and experiences pleasure through the other.[43] In phase 3 of the female beating fantasy, that other is of course the male subject.

Within the male sequence, all three phases, including the conscious one, begin with the assertion of pronominal possession. The subject-position which each phase maps out, however, bends that "I" in a "feminine" direction:

Phase 1: "I am being loved by my father."
Phase 2: "I am being beaten by my father."
Phase 3: "I am being beaten by my mother."

The beating fantasies confided to Freud by his male patients have also been subjected to far less censorship and distortion than those recorded by his female patients. The only significant difference between the conscious scenario (phase 3) and the unconscious scenario (phase 2) bears upon the identity of the person administering the punishment; the conscious fantasy translates into the verbal formula "I am being beaten by my mother," whereas the unconscious one reads "I am being beaten by my father" (198). Even this disguise is lightly worn, since the beating woman manifests such aggressively masculine qualities as to unmistakably resemble the paternal figure she replaces. (Phase 1, which is presumed to lie concealed behind phase 2, is not available to consciousness.)

Finally, although some effort is made to conceal the *homosexual* content of the conscious fantasy, no corresponding attempt is made to hide its *masochistic* content; the two male patients discussed by Freud, like those cited by Krafft-Ebing, Reik, and Deleuze, openly "flaunt" their desire for punishment and degradation both within their conscious fantasies and within their sexual practices. We clearly have an extreme instance here of what Reik calls the "demonstrative feature." In the conscious fantasies of the four female patients, on the other hand, masochism is concealed behind sadism, even though it is more compatible with their cultural position.

What is it precisely that the male masochist displays, and what are the consequences of this self-exposure? To begin with, he acts out in an insistent and exaggerated way the basic conditions of cultural subjectivity, conditions that are normally disavowed; he loudly proclaims that his meaning comes to him from the Other, prostrates himself before the gaze even as he solicits it, exhibits his castration for all to see, and revels in the sacrificial basis of the social contract. The male masochist magnifies the losses and divisions upon which cultural identity is based, refusing to be sutured or recompensed. In short, he radiates a negativity inimical to the social order.

All of this is spectacularly visible in one of the more highly elaborated of the male fantasies included in *Masochism in Sex and Society*. The fantasy in question was told to Reik by a thirty-seven-year-old (married) man, who depended upon it for his sexual potency:

> To an ancient barbaric idol, somewhat like the Phoenician Moloch, a number of vigorous young men are to be sacrificed at certain not too frequent intervals. They are undressed and laid on the altar one by one. The rumble of drums is joined by the songs of the approaching temple choirs. The high priest followed by his suite approaches the altar and scrutinizes each of the victims with a critical eye. They must satisfy certain requirements of beauty and athletic appearance. The high priest takes the genital of each prospective victim in his hand and carefully tests its weight and form. If he does not approve of the genital, the young man will be rejected as obnoxious to the god and unworthy of being sacrificed. The high priest gives the order for the execution and the ceremony continues. With a sharp cut the young men's genitals and the surrounding parts are cut away. (41)

Unlike the male masochists Freud discusses in " 'A Child Is Being Beaten,' " the author of this fantasy is not its overt "star." He is, however, bound to the scenario through a complex imaginary network. His immediate point of insertion occurs via the young man who will be next to fall victim to the priest's knife, but that figure himself identifies closely with the victim presently suffering the mutilation. Reik writes that "the patient shares every intensive affect of this victim, feels his terror and anxiety with all the physical sensations since he imagines that he himself will experience the same fate in a few moments" (42). This peculiar identificatory transfer, which is once again indicative of the heteropathic impulse implicit in feminine masochism, compounds the specularity of the scene, making it possible for the prospective victim (and so for the fantasizing subject himself) to see how he will be seen when the weapon falls on his genitals. It speaks not only to the demonstrative feature of masochism—to the premium it places upon self-display—but to the "I saw myself seeing myself" of classic femininity,[44] and to the mirror staging that underpins all subjectivity.

What is of course most immediately striking about what Reik designates the "Moloch phantasy" is the literalness with which it enacts the "theme" of castration, the way it grounds what is normally a symbolic event at the level of the body. Once again the reader is reminded both of the terms under which the female subject enters representation, marked by the stigmata of a corporeal lack, and of the "pound of flesh"[45] which is the price each of us must pay for our access to language. But even more is "at stake" in this sacrificial drama; the stipulation that each victim must conform to a phallic ideal means that what is really being defaced or disfigured in this fantasy is the paternal imago, and that what is cut off and thrown away is the male subject's symbolic legacy.

So far I have mentioned only one part of the Moloch fantasy. Later in *Masochism in Sex and Society*, Reik describes the dramatic sequel to the dismemberment: the castrated victims are placed on a red-hot grate until they are thoroughly singed, and then dropped into the fire beneath (61–63). In this fantasy nothing is salvaged, and nothing is redeemed. It is a narrative of the darkest pain, negativity, and loss.

The Moloch fantasy also dramatizes some of the other features Reik associates with masochism. It plays with suspense, for instance, in a number of complex ways. First, there is the thrillingly terrifying anticipation built into a situation where the subject imagines himself the second person in line to suffer various atrocities, and must first watch what will later happen to himself. Then there is a narrative structure which works to defeat the apparent climax of castration by making that event only the prologue to even more profound sufferings. Suspense is literalized through the grate mechanism, which dangles the victims over the engulfing fire, and further incorporated as a dramatic device through the mandate that they be adequately singed before being dropped into the flames. The key question at this juncture—a question which pushes the suspense to an almost unbearable level of intensity—is whether the victims will be able to sustain the pain, and remain on the grate until they are ceremonially ejected, or whether they will instead fling themselves onto the fire so as to achieve a quick death. A variation which is sometimes built into the middle of the fantasy further compounds the fearful tension: two of the prisoners are obliged to tend the fire which will subsequently consume them.

The "author" of the Moloch fantasy coordinates it with coitus; provided that the "synchronization" works, ejaculation occurs at the precise moment that the suspense becomes unbearable, and the victim with whom he identifies finally surrenders himself or is subjected to death. Like the other feminine masochists discussed by Reik, this patient seems to increase the psychic tension until there is a veritable physiological explosion. This dramatic escalation of anxiety and apprehension violates Freud's notion of the pleasure principle fully as much as does the actual implementation of sexual or religious torture, suggesting once again the shortcoming of any theoretical account of pleasure which stresses constancy over rupture, and coherence over "shattering." It is no wonder that the patients whom Reik actually managed to "cure" complained to him afterwards that life had lost all its color and intensity (378).

The elaborate preparations which make up the early stages of the Moloch fantasy and the seemingly interminable delay in reaching a conclusion produce an erotic narrative which conforms closely to Freud's definition of perversion; here as there, libidinal interest extends far beyond "the regions of the body which are designated for sexual union," and the "path" leading toward "the final sexual aim" is traversed far from quickly. Moreover, although ejaculation does occur, there is no representation of it within the fantasy, which always ends immediately prior to that event. (This is regularly the case with the masochistic fantasies Reik describes, as well as the masochistic practices Krafft-Ebing enumerates; there seems to be no place within either script for the ostensible goal of all fore-pleasure.) The male genitals do figure prominently here, but not at the grand finale; that part of the fantasy which is given over to their inspection and excision occurs around the middle, and constitutes at most a "false climax." Thus the Moloch narrative does more than linger over "the intermediate relations to the sexual object"; it actually relegates castration to the status of foreplay.

The propensity for impersonation is even more marked in feminine masochism than it is in moral (or at least Christian) masochism, which is not surprising given that it is centrally concerned with subject-positioning and gender "roles." We have already looked closely at one quite flamboyant mental masquerade, a masquerade which changes its "author's" age, his historical moment, and his national identity, as well as the circumstances of his life (and death). The creator of the Moloch fantasy generates other identities for himself as well, including one where he is a Portuguese prisoner of the Aztecs who is first forced to watch a number of other men be skinned alive, and is then subjected to the same fate. Krafft-Ebing recounts numerous cases of male masochists who act out the part of a slave or a page, and others where the preferred role is that of a dog, a horse, a slaughter animal, a count, a surface (such as a floor) on which women walk, and a receptacle for urine, excrement, and menstrual blood. The "hero" of Sacher-Masoch's *Venus in Furs* assumes the disguise of a servant for much of that novel, and—near the end—that of a bull.[46]

The sexual practitioners of feminine masochism generally extend the masquerade to include the person inflicting the pain or humiliation as well, and indeed the entire "scene" of the erotic adventure, in effect remaking the world. This heterocosmic impulse is particularly pronounced in the Moloch and Aztec scenarios to which I referred above, which relocate the fantasizing subject in another time and place altogether. It is also strikingly evident in *Venus in Furs*, where Severin and Wanda actually leave the country in which they are living for one in which they will be better able to pass as mistress and slave. The crucial question to ask here is whether the heterocosmic impulse exhausts itself altogether in the boudoir, or whether the "play" spills over into social intercourse as well, contaminating the proprieties of gender, class, and race.[47]

Freud maintains that it is not only at the level of his sexual life, but at that of his fantasmatic and his *moi* that the male masochist occupies a female position. In " 'A Child Is Being Beaten,' " he writes that femininity assumes the status of a "subjective conviction" for the male masochist (197); he suggests, that is, that the male masochist believes himself to be a woman at the deepest level of his desire and his identity. Near the end of " 'A Child Is Being Beaten,' " he also notes that the fantasy of corporal punishment manifests itself only in "unmanly boys" and "unwomanly girls," and that it is "a trait of femininity in the boy and of masculinity in the girl which must be made responsible" for the construction of the fantasy (202). The degree to which this femininity manifests itself in the conscious existence of the male masochist depends, of course, upon the strength of the "masculine protest"[48] which he brings to bear against it—upon whether or not he fortifies himself against the "woman" within. It is, however, a significant fact that phase 3 of the male version of the beating fantasy makes no attempt to disguise the masochistic position of the fantasizing subject, although it is somewhat more reticent about the latter's homosexuality. Ironically, moreover, the transformation of the agent of punishment from the father to the mother actually functions to accentuate the male masochist's femininity, since it effects so dramatic a reversal of traditional gender roles.

Freud makes the astonishing observation in " 'A Child Is Being Beaten' " that there is no trace within the masochistic unconscious, whether male or female, of the wish to be loved by the father—of the taboo desire from which the entire condition of masochism ostensibly derives. In regressing back to the anal stage of sexuality, the masochist apparently manages to erase all record of that variant of Oedipal genitality which is generally held to be positive for the girl, and negative for the boy:

> Whatever is repressed from consciousness or replaced in it by something else remains intact and potentially operative in the unconscious. The effect of *regression* to an earlier stage of the sexual organization is quite another matter. As regards this we are led to believe that the state of things changes in the unconscious as well. Thus in both sexes the masochistic phantasy of being beaten by the father, though not the passive phantasy of being loved by him, lives on in the unconscious after repression has taken place. (199–200)

If Freud is to be believed on this point, male masochism constitutes a veritable hermeneutic scandal. The passage I have just quoted suggests that the first phase of the male beating fantasy ("I am being loved by my father") is *entirely* a construction of psychoanalysis, and in a much more extreme sense than the second stage of the female sequence can be said to be. It also suggests that the unconscious significance of the fantasy is *completely* exhausted by phase 2, which as I have already noted differs from phase 3 only with respect to the gender of the person administering the punishment. Here there is no radical divide of manifest from latent content. The door to the unconscious need not be picked; it is already slightly ajar, and ready to yield at the slightest pressure.

There are other implications as well. If no record can be found within his unconscious of the desire to be genitally loved by the father, the male masochist cannot be domesticated by substituting the penis for the whip. His (barely) repressed desire runs directly counter to any reconciliation of father and son, attesting irrefutably to the violence of the familial and cultural contract. His sexuality, moreover, must be seen to be entirely under the sway of the death drive, devoid of any possible productivity or use value. It is no wonder that Freud pulls back from promising a psychoanalytic "cure" in the case of the feminine masochist (197).

5. The Mother in Male Masochism

The moment has come to do more than refer in passing to Deleuze's extremely interesting study of masochism, with which this chapter has a good deal of sympathy. Deleuze argues that masochism is entirely an affair between son and mother, or to be more precise, between the male masochist and a cold, maternal, and severe woman whom he designates the "oral mother." Through the dispassionate and highly ritualized transaction that takes place between these two figures, the former is stripped of all virility, and reborn as a "new, sexless man," and the latter is invested with the phallus. (Although the mother assumes a dominant position within this scenario, Deleuze stresses that she is "formed" by the son [21].) What is beaten in masochism is consequently not so much the male subject as the father, or the father in the male subject. Masochism works insistently to negate paternal power and privilege:

> A contract is established between the hero and the woman, whereby at a precise point in time and for a determinate period she is given every right over him. By this means the masochist tries to exorcise the danger of the father and to ensure that the temporal order of reality and experience will be in conformity with the symbolic order, in which the father has been abolished for all time. Through the contract . . . the masochist reaches towards the most mythical and most timeless realms, where [the mother] dwells. Finally, he ensures that he will be beaten . . . what is beaten, humiliated and ridiculed in him is the image and likeness of the father, and the possibility of the father's aggressive return. . . . The masochist thus liberates himself in preparation for a rebirth in which the father will have no part. (58)

This argument offers a "utopian" rereading of masochism.[49] There is an obvious danger that it be taken literally, as designating the standard form of that perversion, rather than its visionary reconfiguration. It is crucial to grasp that although Deleuze does in fact claim that masochism has nothing to do with the father, he obviously knows full well that this is not the case. His account of that libidinal infraction cannot be understood apart from the mechanism of disavowal, which he not only places at the center of *its* organization, but *himself deploys* throughout his study whenever he refuses to acknowledge the place of the father within masochism. In a key passage, Deleuze asserts that masochism "proceeds from a twofold disavowal, a positive, idealizing disavowal of the mother (who is identified with the law), and an invalidating disavowal of the father (who is expelled from the symbolic order)" (60). He thereby clearly indicates that within the masochism about which he speaks paternal power and the law are present only negatively, through their repudiation—that the masochism he celebrates is a pact between mother and son to write the father out of his dominant position within both culture and masochism, and to install the mother in his place.

The contract between Wanda and Severin is one dramatization of that erasing *écriture*, but *Masochism: An Interpretation of Coldness and Cruelty* is itself another. The fact that both Deleuze and his male masochist are so busy disavowing the father's phallus and the mother's lack clearly indicates that both inhabit an Oedipal universe which only the force of a radically heterocosmic imagination can unmake, and not—as one recent writer suggests—a pre-Oedipal realm from which all masochism derives.[50] Deleuze himself tells us all this in a brilliant account of disavowal and fetishism:

> Disavowal should perhaps be understood as the point of departure of an operation that consists neither in negating nor even destroying, but rather in radically contesting the validity of that which is: it suspends belief in and neutralizes the given in such a way that a new horizon opens up beyond the given and in place of it . . . fetishism is first of all a disavowal ("No, the woman does not lack a penis"); secondly it is a defensive neutralization (since, contrary to what happens with negation, the knowledge of the situation as it is persists, but in a suspended, neutralized form); in the third place it is a protective and idealizing neutralization (for the belief in a female phallus is itself experienced as a protest of the ideal against the real; it remains suspended or neutralized in the ideal, the better to shield itself against the painful awareness of reality). (28–29)

Deleuze thus makes it possible for us to see that the mother not only stands in for the father in phase 3 of the male version of the beating fantasy, but usurps his prerogatives. In inviting the mother to beat/ and or dominate him, the feminine masochist transfers power and authority from the father to her, remakes the symbolic order, and "ruins" his own paternal legacy. And that is not all. As Freud remarks of those two patients in " 'A Child Is Being Beaten,' " the conscious fantasy of being disciplined by the mother "has for its content a feminine attitude without a homosexual object-choice" (199). It thereby effects another revolution of sorts, and one whose consequences may be even more transformative than the male subject's fantasy of being beaten by the father—it constitutes a feminine yet heterosexual male subject. As with phase 3 of the female beating fantasy, phase 3 of the male beating fantasy wreaks havoc with sexual difference.

While it is true that the father is left holding the whip at the level of the unconscious fantasmatic, it is also the case that the son does not there manifest any desire to fill his boots. The mother functions as the crucial site of identification in all of the variants of the male beating fantasy. The male masochist as he is presented by Freud in " 'A Child Is Being Beaten' " thus not only prefers the masquerade of womanliness to the parade of virility, but he articulates both his conscious and his unconscious desires from a feminine position. And although he seems to subordinate himself to the law of the father, that is only because he knows how to transform punishment into pleasure, and severity into bliss. This male masochist deploys the diversionary tactics of demonstration, suspense, and impersonation against the phallic "truth" or "right," substituting perversion for the *père-version* of exemplary male subjectivity.

Although I have stressed the heterocosmic tendencies of feminine masochism, I do not mean to erect it as the model for a radically reconstituted male subjectivity. As I have already remarked more than once, masochism in all of its guises is as much a product of the existing symbolic order as a reaction against it. Although in its masculine variants it shows a marked preference for the negative over the positive Oedipus complex, it nevertheless situates desire and identification within the parameters of the family. Moreover, by projecting a cruel or imperious authority before whom he abases himself, the feminine masochist acts out in an exaggerated, anthropomorphic, and disruptive way the process whereby subjects are culturally "spoken." Until our dominant fiction undergoes a radical metamorphosis, however, subjectivity will always carry the imprint of the family. And even in the event of such a metamorphosis, the subject will still be defined by lack and alterity. We can not, then, start from zero with subjectivity; we can only hope to negotiate a different psychic relation to the Laws of Language and Kinship Structure than that dictated by the dominant fiction. Male masochism represents one way of doing so.

In the next chapter, we will return to the cinema of Rainer Werner Fassbinder, which functions as a virtual showcase for male masochism. As we will see, films like *In a Year of Thirteen Moons* and *Berlin Alexanderplatz* are committed to the utter ruination of masculinity. At the same time, they make the process of experiencing and observing that ruination conducive of a pleasure bordering on ecstasy. Our exploration of these two films will provide the occasion for an extended discussion of that suicidal variety of identification which I have linked with feminine masochism—the heteropathic. Chapter 7, "White Skins, Brown Masks: The Double Mimesis, or With Lawrence in Arabia," will introduce yet another category of male masochism, one commensurate with virility and with the paternal legacy. It will also explore some of the implications of feminine masochism for race and class.

6

Masochistic Ecstasy and the Ruination of Masculinity in Fassbinder's Cinema

> ... every imaginary relation comes about via a kind of *you* or *me* between the subject and the object. That is to say—*If it's you, I'm not. It it's me, it's you who isn't.*[1]

In April 1978, Rainer Werner Fassbinder terminated his relationship with his lover of three years, Armin Meier, an actor and former butcher. Some time in the week of May 31, Meier swallowed the contents of four bottles of sleeping pills, and an unknown quantity of alcohol. His decomposing body was found a week later in the kitchen of the apartment he had shared with Fassbinder. Between July 28 and August 28, Fassbinder made a film, the script of which he wrote in the wake of Meier's death. That film, *In a Year of Thirteen Moons*, focuses upon the last five days in the life of a transsexual prostitute, and one-time butcher. Fassbinder not only scripted and directed the film, but assumed during its making a whole series of functions that he typically assigned to others.

Because of its narrative, its broodingly funereal atmosphere, and the terms of its production, *In a Year of Thirteen Moons* would seem unusually susceptible to a biographical analysis, and hence to a gay reading.[2] However, the film is as sharply critical of homosexuality as it is of heterosexuality, and the only "same-sex" union it ever dramatizes is that facilitated through Fassbinder's self-immolating identification with the figure who stands in cinematically for Armin Meier, a figure who is the object of the film's relentless brutalization. To state the case rather differently, *In a Year of Thirteen Moons* articulates a homosexual erotics which is entirely dependent upon imaginary divestiture, a divestiture with crucial authorial ramifications.

From June 1979 to April 1980, Fassbinder shot the footage destined for inclusion in *Berlin Alexanderplatz* (1980), another film marked by a powerful autobiographical imperative. Like *Effi Briest* (1974) and *Bolwieser* (1976/77), *Berlin Alexanderplatz* is closely based upon a literary text, a 1929 novel by Alfred Döblin, and would consequently seem far less "personal" a film than *In a Year of Thirteen Moons*. However, in the same year as the television release of his magnum opus, Fassbinder confided in *Die Zeit* that during his first reading of *Berlin Alexanderplatz* he found himself "breathing in, gulping down, devouring the words," and that he felt as though "I was no longer reading so much as living, suffering, despairing, fearing."[3] A subsequent encounter with the novel revealed to Fassbinder that "nearly all of what I regarded as *my* attitudes, *my* feelings, part of myself, were none other than those described by Döblin in *Berlin Alexanderplatz*" (3). And much later, while rewatching a large number of his films over the period of three days, the German director found himself "literally knocked out by the realization that my work was quite simply jammed with what were more often than not unconscious borrowings from *Alexanderplatz*" (4).

It will be a central premise of this chapter that more is at issue here than "influence" or even casual identification. In "Man's Cities and His Soul," the essay published in *Die Zeit*, Fassbinder suggests that his identity was substantially constructed through the psychic incorporation of Döblin's novel. "*Berlin Alexanderplatz* [not only] affected my head, [but] my flesh, my whole body and soul," he confides there (1). He thus encourages us to read his cinematic adaptation of Döblin's novel as the interrogation of his "own" subjectivity.

While Fassbinder's authorial alignment with the Döblin text obviously depends to some degree upon the specificity of that text's language and narrational structure, the character of Franz Biberkopf occupies the primary site of narcissistic investment. Not only is "Franz Biberkopf" the name which Fassbinder gives the character he portrays in *Fox and His Friends* (1975), and a name which he partially reprises in a number of other films, but the title to the "Epilogue" of *Berlin Alexanderplatz* ("My Dream of the Dream of Franz Biberkopf") effects an overt condensation of himself with Döblin's protagonist. In attempting to describe the suturing effect of Döblin's text upon his adolescent subjectivity, moreover, Fassbinder characterizes that text as "the story of two men whose mean little lives slowly fall apart as they fail to face up to, or even recognize that in a strange and uncommunicable way they love each other" (2). He adds that the novel "enabled me to admit the agonizing fears which almost paralyzed me, to admit my homosexual desires" (3), in an explicit acknowledgment of his structuring identification with its protagonist. "Man's Cities and His Soul" thus suggests that in a very profound way Fassbinder *is* Franz Biberkopf, and that the masculinity which *Berlin Alexanderplatz* works to demolish is his "own."

In Chapter 3, I attempted to demonstrate that films like *Gods of the*

Plague (1969), *Fox and His Friends* (1975), and *Ali: Fear Eats the Soul* (1973) militate against paternal identification and play havoc with cinema's established scopic conventions by dramatically exteriorizing the visual supports of all subjectivity, image, and gaze. *In a Year of Thirteen Moons* and *Berlin Alexanderplatz* push the assault on male subjectivity even further. Both films take as their initial project the subordination of the male body to physical degradation and literal dismemberment, as if to suggest that masculinity can only be abolished by eradicating its corporeal referent. In so doing, they remind us that although the phallus and the penis are discrete terms, the latter derives its symbolic value from the former, which it in turn "props."[4]

In subjecting the central characters of *In a Year of Thirteen Moons* and *Berlin Alexanderplatz* to castration and amputation, Fassbinder also violates the integrity of what Henri Wallon would call the "body-schema," that visual and postural composite which traces the corporeal outlines of the "self."[5] Moreover, not content merely to effect a radical and ultimately unreadable reconfiguration of its protagonist's "literal" body, *In a Year of Thirteen Moons* insists upon dismantling as well its virtual image, the *moi*. That film is so relentlessly de-idealizing in the scrutiny it brings to bear both upon body and ego that the male psyche is stripped not only of symbolic, but of libidinal support.

This de-idealization represents both Fassbinder's attempt to demonstrate just how bereft of narcissistic sustenance a subject like the central character of *In a Year of Thirteen Moons* would be within the present cultural order, and the means by which that film further dismantles male subjectivity. In other words, the film critiques our existing system of sexual differentiation for its inability to accommodate a figure who can be assimilated neither to masculinity nor to femininity, while at the same time maximizing the intransigence of these categories in such a way as to undermine utterly any gesture on its protagonist's part toward the recovery of a phallic identification. For this reason, *In a Year of Thirteen Moons* entertains a highly ambivalent relation to the pain it dramatizes.

Unlike the film with which I am pairing it, *Berlin Alexanderplatz* never manages to move its central character into a space definitively beyond normative male subjectivity. That text is caught in a complex double bind; although it is unwaveringly committed to the annihilation of conventional masculinity, it is also profoundly pessimistic about the possibility of achieving that goal. *Berlin Alexanderplatz* thus works at the same time to negate male subjectivity, and to negate the possibility of that negation. The end result is a kind of arrestation at the site of suffering. Not surprisingly, in both *In a Year of Thirteen Moons* and *Berlin Alexanderplatz* that site is susceptible to an extreme eroticization.

In pursuing Fassbinder's negativity to its outer limits, we will consequently find ourselves transported, from time to time, into certain "pleasure zones"—lifted up and out of despair into a kind of delirious joy which is that negativity's other side, and which alone makes it endurable. Both the absolute refusal of Fassbinder's cinema to provide affirmation, and the access which it periodically yields to a masochistic ecstasy or psychic sublation, locate it in some curious way within a utopian trajectory, one leading not so much to another place as to another corporeality. I will attempt to chart that trajectory after some preliminary discussion of masculinity and its ruination in *Berlin Alexanderplatz* and *In a Year of Thirteen Moons*.

First, however, I want to suggest that although those two films will here constitute my primary textual "objects," I also have a theoretical agenda. The pages that follow will distinguish between two very different kinds of identification, one of which sustains conventional masculinity, and the other of which is at the heart both of classic female subjectivity, and of feminine masochism. The first of these two forms of identification insists upon the principle of the "self-same" body, and functions to consolidate the ego. Through the second, which operates at the expense of the *moi*, the subject surrenders its own corporeal frame of reference for that of the other. I will explore the political implications of each of these two identificatory modalities, as well as the uses to which Fassbinder puts them.

1. "In a Year of Thirteen Moons"—Castration and De-idealization

Leo Bersani has recently claimed that "the rectum is the grave in which the masculine ideal . . . of proud subjectivity is buried," and that it should be "celebrated for its very potential for death."[6] While committed to a similar internment, *In a Year of Thirteen Moons* advocates far more draconian measures; it demands the literal sacrifice of that pound of flesh to which masculinity is keyed, and it insists that this sacrifice be unmotivated by any underlying "sympathy" with the anatomical conditions of femininity. Its central character, Erwin, goes to Casa Blanca to have his penis removed for no other reason than that the man he loves prefers women to men. In other words, he becomes a transsexual without ever having previously felt himself to be a "woman" in a man's body. *In a Year of Thirteen Moons* thus denaturalizes his castration—if such a contradictory formulation can be rhetorically sustained—and requires that it be a loss experienced *at the site of male subjectivity.* This character must give up his claim upon masculinity without thereby gaining the body corresponding to some inner "essence." Everything about his subjectivity is placed at risk, and the film goes to considerable lengths to maximize his anatomical loss.

Erwin submits to this mutilation out of desire for another man, a point whose importance cannot be overemphasized. However, whereas in *Berlin Alexanderplatz* homosexuality, in the guise of sado-masochism, is the primary mechanism for forcing a phallic dis-location, here its status is more ambiguous. Far from accommodating or sustaining the castrato, the various homosexualities represented within *In a Year of Thirteen Moons* present that character with a hostile terrain. He is as out of place there as he is within the heterosexual sites mapped out by the text. Fassbinder thus uses Erwin as the pretext for critiquing all of our existing sexual categories. At the same time, he relies upon the intractability of those categories in order to inflict yet more suffering upon the figure of the transsexual, and thereby further to deplete the male ego. That suffering, moreover, not only helps to bury whatever might remain in the way of a proud subjectivity, but provides the occasion for a highly irregular pleasure.

In a Year of Thirteen Moons opens with what is ostensibly a homosexual pick-up, orchestrated to the music of Mahler's *Fifth Symphony*, which is itself mediated through Visconti's *Death In Venice* (1971). This mediation is extremely complex, since the two films could not be more antipathetic. The homosexuality in *Death In Venice* turns upon a hyperbolic idealization of the erotic object, Tadzio, and upon a corresponding libidinal sublimation in which Eros passes itself off as a passion for Truth and Beauty.[7] It is consequently perfectly in harmony with the romantic yearning of Mahler's music. The pick-up in Fassbinder's film, on the other hand, is more in keeping with the variety of homosexuality imputed by Freud to the "ancients," in that it privileges "Eros" or "the drive itself" over the erotic object.[8] The juxtaposition of Mahler's *Fifth Symphony* with an anonymous sexual transaction between two people dressed as men speaks to the distance separating the positivity of romantic love from the implacably grim world of *In a Year of Thirteen Moons*.

The first entirely intelligible image to emerge from the faint dawn light in which the pick-up occurs shows money passing from the hand of one of the participants to that of the other (Figure 6–1). Their two bodies converge, clothes are ripped off, and a mouth is applied to unrecognizable body parts. The hustler's hand gropes at the ass of the other man, undeterred by the silk underwear exposed to our view. First with one hand, and then, more urgently, with the other, he

Figure 6–1

attempts to locate the penis on the front of his "client's" body. Enraged by the absence of the desired organ, he calls to a fellow hustler, and together they strip and beat the unfortunate "john." They assume that figure to be a woman, but their assumption is based upon a simplistically binarized account of sexual difference, one which *In a Year of Thirteen Moons* will show to be totally inadequate to account for the castrato. That character, played by Volker Spengler, has no stable sexual identity within the diegetic present of the film, and should ideally be designated through the double name "Elvira/Erwin," or an equivalent pronominal compound.[9]

In its search for an organ which cannot be found, the opening scene might well be titled "Something's Missing." Erwin is judged and found wanting, much as woman is within the classic Freudian scenario (it is, indeed, on the basis of his "client's" penile "lack" that the hustler is led to exclaim accusingly in Czech, "You're a woman"). This scene indicates that within that variant of homosexuality represented by the hustler, sexual difference is still sharply drawn, and along lines which are all-too-familiar.

Erwin, on the other hand, is in the opening scene defined much more fully through the anus; first glimpsed from behind, his elaborate undergarments doubly veil and thereby eroticize that orifice (beneath the silk panties can be glimpsed a second item of clothing, consisting

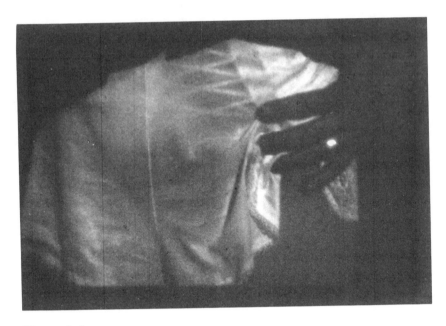

Figure 6–2

primarily of lacing (Figure 6–2). He is thus much closer to the model of homosexuality theorized by Guy Hocquenghem, which, in its foreclosure of identity, largely erases the distinction between "man" and "woman." "All homosexuals," Hocquenghem writes,

> share with women a deep identity disorder; or, to be more accurate, they have a confused identity. Only the phallus dispenses identity; any social use of the anus, apart from its sublimated use, creates the risk of a loss of identity. Seen from behind we are all women; the anus does not practice sexual discrimination.[10]

Although this passage aptly describes Erwin, it is an optative construction with respect to homosexuality. Engaging as Hocquenghem's formulation is, the fact remains that male homosexuality, in all of its present guises, almost invariably specifies that the erotic object possess a penis, regardless of the latter's psychic subject-position, or his preferred sexual position—that this organ be in place beneath the skirts of the transvestite, on the other side of the body from the orifice which is being penetrated, or beneath the mouth which sucks the penis. (It is simply not the case, as Hocquenghem would have it, that there is "an infinity of directions and possibilities for plugging in, with no set places" [97].) Erwin is consequently shown to pose a profound challenge to male homosexuality at the level of the body, which, as *Querelle* (1982) also implies, may well be its point of greatest intractability.[11]

Because of his predilection for sexual masquerade, Erwin would seem more easily assimilable to the world of gay camp than to that of anonymous cruising. However, *In a Year of Thirteen Moons* goes to considerable lengths to dispel this illusion. In an important scene late in the film Erwin pays a visit to the office of Anton Saitz (Gottfried John), the man on whose behalf he underwent the operation in Casa Blanca, and is obliged to participate in a game of mimicry. That game requires its participants to imitate the characters played by Jerry Lewis, Dean Martin, and a group of female actresses in the Hollywood film, *You're Never Too Young*, as they perform a group dance. The premise of the film is that "Jerry" has mistakenly enrolled in a girls' school, and must take on the gestures and mannerisms of "femininity." The scene which Saitz and his men are watching when Erwin enters, and which they subsequently reenact, is the one where the school has a "coming out" party for "Jerry." Wearing a child-like sailor suit, he is shown first dancing with the girls, and then jumping into Dean Martin's arms.

As should be evident even from this brief description, the film itself already turns upon mimicry—not only upon "Jerry's" imitation of the schoolgirls, but (at least implicitly) upon the imitation of behavior and mannerisms of a "gay" man imitating the schoolgirls. When Saitz mimics Jerry's performance he grossly exaggerates this last dimension of the performance, so that what in effect emerges is a heterosexual imitation of gay camp (Figure 6–3). At the same time, of course, this game, which has clearly been played on numerous previous occasions, facilitates intense homoeroticism within a group of ostensibly "straight" men. Saitz and his male cohorts might thus be said to "have it both ways."

This doubleness—or, to use Susan Sontag's rather too morally weighted word, "duplicity"[12]—is also a feature of gay camp renditions of femininity. Implicit in those renditions is the possibility of "taking off" what has been so flamboyantly and humorously "put on," and of thereby revealing the organ whose presence functions as an irrefutable claim upon anatomical masculinity. That organ is never put at risk; on the contrary, it perhaps inevitably functions as the "reality" beneath the construction, and hence as a kind of ironic facilitator. As Daniel Harris has recently observed, camp is only effeminacy in quotation marks, "something that can be donned like formal wear for occasions of state and similarly doffed when the situation demands a

Figure 6–3

low profile."[13] Sontag's definition of camp as "the love of the exaggerated, the 'off,' of *things-being-what-they-are-not*" thus has a very specific pertinence here.[14]

For Erwin, on the other hand, there can be no ironic distance between "appearance" and "actuality," for the simple reason that there
is in his case no term capable of passing itself off as "actuality."
Although the way in which he is dressed in this scene has all the
"over the edge" quality of high gay camp, expressive not only of
extravagance but of extreme artifice, no penis is concealed beneath
the *haute couture* dress. Erwin is thus "out of step" both with Saitz's
parody of femininity, and with his parody of homosexuality, a metaphor which is literalized by the second or two which separates Erwin's
movements from those of the others when they imitate the dance from
You're Never Too Young.

If Erwin cannot be assimilated to homosexuality, he is equally
remote from heterosexuality. Here he is marked less by a corporeal
lack than by a corporeal excess. That excess is not localized in the
way that lack might be said to be; it is dispersed across his entire
body in the form of a general "largeness" which only increases over
time, and which, to the heterosexual male eye, connotes "maleness"
and hence "abnormality." In the painful verbal exchange which takes
place in the second scene of the film, Christoph returns obsessively to

the topic of Erwin's size: "... you drink and get fatter and fatter until even your face gets so bloated and ugly its disgusting, like it was some kind of degenerative disease.... Who knew what you'd turn into later, that you're a loser, that you'd get more and more like a man, big and flabby like a walrus ..." Even in full feminine regalia, Erwin has access only to two visual female identities, both of which situate him outside the boundaries of heterosexual eroticism—that of the dumpy matron whom he appears to be while visiting the video arcade, Soul Frieda's, and the convent, dressed in a black and white jersey dress; or that of the transvestite man connoted by the black hat, veil, high heels, and hour-glass dress he wears in the scene at Saitz's office. Erwin is equally implausible as a heterosexual man; he never looks more like a woman than when "courting" Irene (Elisabeth Trissenaar) at the end of the film, dressed in a suit, tie, and cropped hair.

It is not only within the world of anonymous cruising represented by the opening of the film that idealization is shown to be impossible. Prostitution provides the dominant metaphor of heterosexuality within *In a Year of Thirteen Moons*, and the money which crosses hands between Saitz and Zora in the final scene provides a very precise analogue to that which is exchanged between Erwin and the hustler at the beginning. But Fassbinder is not content merely to portray the repeated de-idealization of Erwin by the other members of his world. He also insists upon dramatizing the disintegration which such a de-idealization would precipitate at the level of the ego or *moi*.

We do not remember often enough that the ego is sustained only through libidinal investment. As Laplanche observes at one point in *Life and Death in Psychoanalysis*, "exactly like an external object, the ego is a love object, charged with libido."[15] The libidinal cathexis of the ego is, moreover, "inseparable from [its] very *constitution*" (67). This love relation depends upon two things—upon the subject being able to "find" itself within ideal images, which necessarily implies being "photographed" or "seen" through those images; and upon the subject not relinquishing all of its love to another, without reciprocity.[16] *In a Year of Thirteen Moons* lays siege to the psyche it imputes to Erwin from both directions.

Within the Lacanian account, the mirror stage is the one period in the subject's life when, through a radical *méconnaissance*, it merges so effortlessly with a beloved image as to believe itself "ideal." It is hardly surprising, given the terms of this captation, that Lacan's infant experiences "jubila[tion]."[17] *In a Year of Thirteen Moons* enacts a very different mirror stage. Early in the film, in an act of unmitigated aggression, Erwin's lover, Christoph, drags him into the bathroom and forces him to look in the reflecting glass on the wall. "Know what

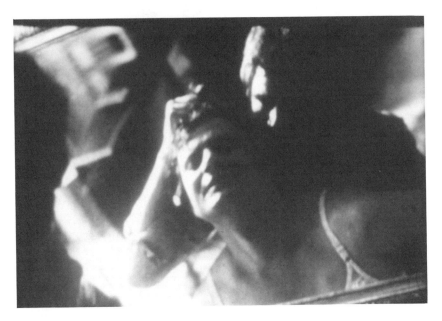

Figure 6–4

you're afraid of?," he asks, "You're afraid of your own messed-up face. Look at yourself in the mirror, go on!" (Figure 6–4).

Whereas within the classic enactment of the mirror stage the mother's look not only stands in for the gaze, facilitating the join of infant and image, but contributes to the idealization of the image, Christoph's look here functions as the carrier of loathing and disgust. The identification which it coerces is consequently productive more of pain than pleasure. Significantly, moreover, what Erwin sees when he looks in the mirror is an image evacuated not only of ideality, but of love—his own, as well as that of his surrounding world. For what this scene makes clear is that Erwin represents a subject who has surrendered all of his libidinal reserves to another. To Christoph's taunts, he responds only: "I see myself loving you," as though desire is all that remains of his subjectivity.[18] If, in addition to being a composite of images, the ego is also a libidinal reservoir, as Freud tells us, Erwin's fictive reservoir has shrunk to a virtual nothingness.[19]

The brutality of this erasure of the male ego seems incomprehensible as long as we read the figure of Erwin as a simple representative of Armin Meier. As I will attempt to demonstrate later in this chapter, however, he stands in for Fassbinder as well. *In a Year of Thirteen Moons* provides a veritable case history of that form of identification which Freud associates with sado-masochism, an identification by means of which a psyche can come to inhabit, and even experience the pain of, other bodies. Fassbinder constitutes himself as the author "inside" the text of that film precisely through such a corporeal estrangement.

2. "Berlin Alexanderplatz"—Amputation and Sado-Masochism

Fassbinder's *Berlin Alexanderplatz*, like Döblin's, dramatizes the enactment of considerable violence upon the female body. A crucial sequence early in the film, which begins and ends with a meditation on a photo of the dead prostitute, Ida (Barbara Valentin), depicts in quick succession the rape of Minna (Karin Baal), and, as a flashback, the murder of Ida. The second of those events is reprised again and again during the first thirteen parts of the film, but always with a different verbal text, so that it remains impossible either to forget or to assimilate. Much later in the film, when Franz (Günther Lamprecht) thinks that Mieze (Barbara Sukowa) has fallen in love with someone else, he beats her almost to the point of death, an event which *Berlin Alexanderplatz* represents in "real time," and whose brutality it does nothing to minimize. Finally, in Part XII, Mieze is strangled by Reinhold (Gottfried John) in Freienwalde, after a protracted struggle.

Despite its obsession with the brutalization of the female body, *Berlin Alexanderplatz* is in no way complicit with the heterosexual aggression it depicts, which it never ceases both to interrogate and critique, and which it at no point eroticizes. However, the film entertains a very different relation to the male body. It is not only the narrative, but the discourse of *Berlin Alexanderplatz* which works to annihilate that body—in part through the camera's attentiveness to Franz's loose flesh and amputated limb; in part through the constant extra-diegetic recourse to the metaphor of a slaughterhouse animal; and in part through the two-hour fantasy which breaks free from Döblin's novel, in which the protagonist is straitjacketed, beaten, humiliated, and crucified. Once again, that body is subjected not only to pain and dismemberment, but to a relentless de-idealization. At a certain point in the film, as we will see, the violence which is enacted upon Franz's body becomes sexualized in the guise of homosexual sado-masochism, at which point it assumes much of the ecstatic potential which also comes to inhere in Erwin's sufferings.

As Eric Rentschler has remarked, "*Berlin Alexanderplatz* stands out as a film preoccupied with the force, possibility, and vulnerability of the human body within the constellations of modernity."[20] Not surprisingly, then, the first experience of its central protagonist, Franz Biberkopf, as he emerges from prison at the beginning of Part I, is precisely a corporeal one—the invasion of his ears by unfamiliar sounds, sounds which are shown to elicit from him the sensation of physical pain. His second experience, an extreme psychological disorientation, is communicated to the viewer through a double 360–degree pan around the apartment buildings surrounding a central courtyard. Rescued by Nachum (Peter Kolleck), and taken to a friend's apartment, Franz falls to his hands and knees on the floor, in the position of the four-legged creatures to whom he will so frequently be compared, and rocks rhythmically back and forth. In so doing, he might be said to perform in reverse that action which Freud makes synonymous with the "elevation" of the individual to a cultural condition.[21] Although Franz almost immediately recovers the use of his feet, and even draws attention to them (as he leaves the apartment to which Nachum has taken him, he announces that "Nobody's cut them off yet"), he never manages to achieve anything approximating phallic rectitude.

As Franz wanders around the streets of Berlin after leaving Nachum's rooms, he looks at two movie posters—one of a woman nude from the waist up, and a second of a woman lying on a flight of stairs and clinging to the feet of the man who stands above her (Figures 6–5a and 6–5b). A second shot of the latter poster moves vertically down the man's body to the woman beneath, emphasizing the man's spatial superiority (Figure 6–6). These images elicit two from Franz's own mnemic reserve, but in both he must stoop to conquer; he visualizes himself first bending over Ida to apply his mouth to her neck, and then leaning down to beat her with the deadly cream-whipper.

The immediately following scene between Franz and a prostitute functions further to diminish the male body, not only because Franz is once again unable to achieve uprightness, or because of the infantilization to which the prostitute subjects him ("putt, putt, putt, my little chick, putt, putt, putt, my rooster," she croons), but because of the film's marshaling of the medical discourse. Propping Franz up on her shoulder, she reads out loud to him from a popular magazine a scientific account of sexual potency and its failure (Figure 6–7): "Sexual potency depends on the combined action of 1) the internal secretory system; 2) the nervous system; and 3) the sexual apparatus. The glands contributing to potency are: the pituitary, thyroid, suprarenal and prostate gland. . . . However, before leaving the brain, the stimulus has to pass the brakes of the inhibitions, those predominantly psychic inhibitions which, as a fear of humiliation. . . . " This medical account works to demystify male erection, both in its matter-of-fact insistence upon a bodily "mechanics," and in its concluding emphasis upon an incapacitating sexual anxiety, of whose effects Franz is the

Figure 6–5a

Figure 6–5b

Figure 6–6

Figure 6–7

immediate demonstration. Issuing as it does from the mouth of a woman, it functions as a virtual castration of the male subject, who has been decreed both by dominant culture and Hollywood cinema not only to be the one in control of sexuality, but to be the usual purveyor of scientific information, often at the expense of the female body.[22]

This is not the only occasion when *Berlin Alexanderplatz* has recourse to a discourse of science. Franz will ultimately be held captive by it, literally imprisoned in a mental institution, and force-fed by one of the doctors in a scene which expresses perhaps the most extreme revulsion against the male body ever communicated through film. (After the doctor finishes spooning the bowl of gruel into Franz's mouth, the unappreciative patient spits out the food all over himself. Meanwhile, in another corner of the room a second inmate sits grunting on the toilet.) *Berlin Alexanderplatz* also deploys the discourse of science in its first portrayal of Ida's murder, but so very differently from either of these other examples as to warrant some brief attention.

In the scene to which I refer, Fassbinder's voice speaks over a series of consecutively ordered images depicting the quarrel between Franz and Ida; the protracted physical struggle culminating in Ida's death, during which Franz hits her repeatedly with a shaving-cream whipper; and the entrance into the room of Frau Kast (Figures 6–8a thru 6–8h). This voice bears no relation whatever to the disembodied male voice-over of the traditional documentary or fiction film;[23] it is characterized less by its omniscience than by its patent inability to grasp anything that is crucial about this event. Ostensibly providing an official or semi-official summary of the murder, it passes blithe judgment on the inconsequentiality of Ida's Christian name, reports the medical damage inflicted on her body in such a way as to suggest that it assumed significance only within the subsequent trial, and invokes physics to explain the impact of a cream-whipper on her rib cage:

> Franz killed his fiancée Ida, her last name doesn't matter, in the flower of her youth. . . . The following organs of the woman were slightly damaged: the skin on the end of her nose, the bone underneath, which was not noticed until later in the hospital, and then took on a certain importance in the court records. Furthermore, the right and left shoulders, which sustained light bruises with a loss of blood. All he had in his hand was a small wood cream-whipper. And with a powerful lunge, twice repeated, he brought this cream-whipper into contact with the rib cage of Ida. . . . At the first blow she cried "ouch" and no longer called him "dirty bum" but "Oh man." The second encounter with the cream-whipper occurred after a quarter turn to the right. Whereupon Ida said nothing at all, but

Figure 6–8a

Figure 6–8b

Figure 6–8c

Figure 6–8d

Figure 6–8e

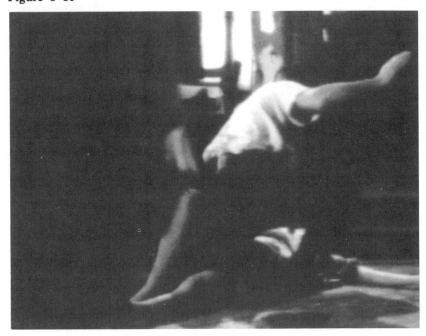

Figure 6–8f

Figure 6–8g

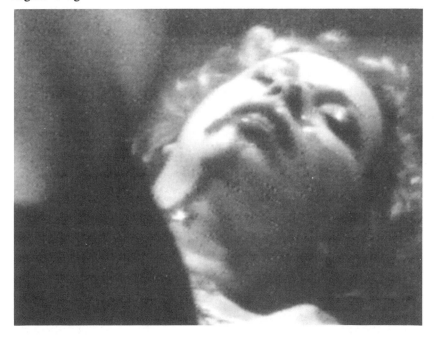

Figure 6–8h

simply opened her mouth in a strange cry. What happened to the woman's rib cage has to do with the laws of rigidity, elasticity, shock and resistance. It is impossible to understand without a knowledge of these laws. Newton's first law: every body tends to remain in a state of rest as long as no external force causes it to change that state. . . . Newton's second law of motion: change of motion is proportional to the force applied and the direction in which it is applied. . . .

At times the actions described by the voice-over are those which the film simultaneously depicts, but more often there is a slight delay at the level of the image track. However, even when sound and image are both ostensibly presenting the same action, they are held at an irreducible distance from each other, the one wrapped in the impenetrable shadow of death, and the other issuing from a discursive space given over to the catalogue of "facts," and the elaboration of "rational" explanations. A complex irony operates within the interval thus opened up, one which inverts the usual hierarchy of sound over image, and scientific discourse over the female body. The image track and the affect which it generates in the viewer are privileged over and against the male voice-over, with its "objectivity" and its invocation of Newtonian laws. Indeed, the emotional "rush" of this scene only increases with the voice-over's increasing recourse to physics, as if to compensate for the inadequacy of that science to represent or account for Ida's death.

The second of the memories recalled by Franz as he stands looking at the movie posters the evening of his release from Tegel—the memory, that is, of sucking on Ida's neck—anticipates numerous subsequent occasions on which he will similarly appropriate the female body (Figure 6–9). As he explains to a startled Lina later in the film after applying his mouth energetically to her neck, "That's the way I do it." It is this vampire-like kiss rather than his penis which represents the privileged signifier of Franz's (hetero)sexuality, a displacement which speaks both to Fassbinder's desire to negate the signifiers of normative male subjectivity, and to his pessimistic negation of that negation. For although *Berlin Alexanderplatz*'s protagonist is thereby given a new erotogenic zone, that zone immediately becomes another site for mastery. Franz's love of women prominently exhibits precisely that feature which Freud associates with infantile orality; it seeks to abolish the "separate existence" of the erotic object through incorporation.[24] Significantly, within the sado-masochistic reveries of the "Epilogue," which seek to return to Franz the violence which he has repeatedly inflicted upon the female body, he is frequently positioned as a domestic animal in the throes of slaughter, i.e. as potential meat.

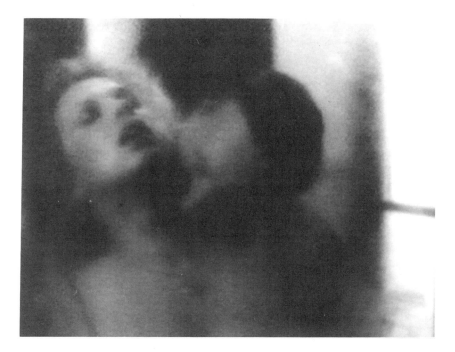

Figure 6–9

However, despite the fact that Franz's orality proves an ideal vehicle for his sadism, it does facilitate a certain dephallicization. *Berlin Alexanderplatz* abounds with scenes attesting to Franz's all-consuming orality, from the one where he dramatizes the conversation between glasses of schnapps and glasses of beer to virtually all of Part IV, where he retreats to a boarding house, and makes the consumption of alchohol his sole activity. Like the later scenes involving Franz's incarceration in a mental institution, those set in the boarding house enact an extreme corporeal degradation, radically incommensurate with the paternal function. Obscenely bloated, Franz sits at the window of his room for hours on end, drinking whole bottles of beer in a single gulp and belching furiously afterward. He vomits all through the night, leaving it to others to clean both the room and his own filthy body. At one point Eva tracks him down, and finds him sitting on the floor with shaving cream applied days earlier smeared grotesquely over his face (Figure 6–10).

I use the word "grotesquely" advisedly, because the corporeal model theorized by Bakhtin is not without relevance to the present discussion. As in that model, Franz's mouth might be said to "[dominate] all else," to be a "wide-open bodily abyss."[25] And like the grotesque

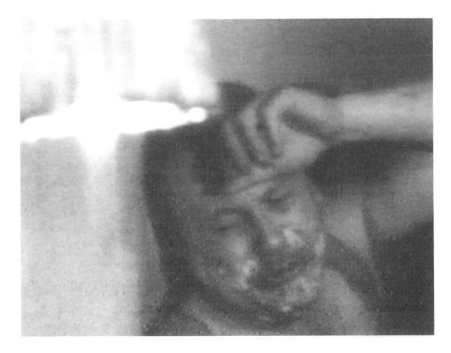

Figure 6–10

body, Franz's is "a body in the act of becoming," a body which is "never finished, never completed" (317), and hence a signifier of change. However, within *Berlin Alexanderplatz* transformation never leads to anything new, only to a terrifying repetition of the same; that utopian principle is shown only to reside in the moment of destruction, never in what follows afterwards.

The most dramatic of the corporeal mutations suffered by Franz is that inflicted upon him by Reinhold, when the latter pushes him out of the speeding car. Franz loses his right arm as a consequence of this "accident," a loss which the film overtly thematizes both as a castration and an erotic event. As is made absolutely manifest by the astonishing scene in Part IX where Franz visits Reinhold and unveils his stump, homosexuality is the only agency within *Berlin Alexanderplatz* capable of "unmanning" Franz because it is synonymous with the eroticized return to the site of his body of all of the cruelty he has directed against women.

After some initial jockeying for position between the two men, Franz's visit to Reinhold begins with the latter's account of his "rerun" with Cilly. "When I haven't had a girl for a few months, then I can have her again," he explains. This confidence, manifestly intended to dissipate the erotic tension which pervades this scene from the moment Reinhold opens the door, only intensifies it further; as the viewer understands full well by now, sharing women with Franz is Reinhold's way of establishing sexual contact with him, and if he was able to "have" Cilly once again, that was because she had been with Franz in the interim.[26] It is now Franz's turn to elaborate *his* erotic relationship with Reinhold, and he does so by projecting "inward" what can perhaps best be described as the "image" of his mutilated body—by speaking for himself a psychic condition which is commensurate with the wound inflicted upon him by Reinhold. Standing in front of a window illuminated with a peculiar orange light, Franz makes clear that at least in his relationship with that other man, his aggression has only one possible target—himself:

> ... actually, I ought to kill you ... but that's only what the others think, I don't want that at all ... What do I mean, anyway? I don't know nothing. I can't do nothing ... [I'm] not a man at all. I'm just spineless.

Overcome with an erotically charged curiosity, Reinhold asks to see Franz's stump, and the latter obligingly complies. The close-up shot which discloses his withered remnant is expressive less of the vagina invoked by Rentschler in his discussion of this scene[27] (the vagina, after all, can be "seen" only by virtue of a speculum, and its form is concave rather than convex) than of the highly loaded terms deployed by Freud to describe the clitoris ("mutilated," we recall, is the adjective he uses to characterize the bearer of that organ),[28] and hence—to return the analogy emphatically and irreversibly to its source—of a castrated penis (Figure 6–11). Once again, then, we find Fassbinder insisting upon the importance of masculinity's anatomical referent. Reinhold's initial response is fascinated horror ("It looks pretty sickening"), followed by an hysterical attempt to disavow what he has seen. With trembling eagerness, he stuffs Franz's right jacket sleeve with socks and underwear so as to construct an artificial arm (Figure 6–12). This way, he explains, "you won't be running around with a loose sleeve," and "people can't tell right away." What he hopes thereby to disguise is obviously not just Franz's lack, but the homosexual desire it communicates.

That desire assumes an even more extreme and self-annihilating form a moment later. "I can't stand a cripple," Reinhold energetically asserts, after abandoning his plan to fill Franz's sleeve, "When I see a cripple I always say, better to do away with him altogether." He sits down beside Franz, a gesture of intimacy which, as the rest of the exchange makes clear, is in no way incompatible with the destructive

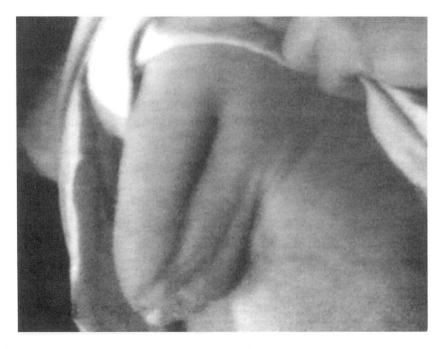

Figure 6–11

force of his words. "Actually, that's what I think too," Franz surprisingly agrees, "You're right there . . . when a guy's a cripple, he can't do what he wants any more." He concludes with what can only be understood as an invitation to Reinhold to push the violence much further: "Then maybe it's better to get rid of [the cripple] altogether." As is so frequently the case in *Berlin Alexanderplatz*, the importance of this exchange is underscored through repetition, this time verbal:

> Reinhold: "That's what I said."
> Franz: "Yeah, that's what you said, and you're right, too."

After these words, both men fall silent, Franz looking frame left, and Reinhold down at the floor. Several seconds later, Reinhold stands up, walks out of frame and lies down on a bed reflected in the armoire mirror behind Franz. The camera tracks left to a close-up of him on the bed, locus not only of his amatory triumphs, but of the libidinal displacement from Franz to the women they share. Thus, although Reinhold might be said literally to walk away from Franz's request to be killed/loved by him, his destination attests eloquently to his own answering desire.

It is of course Mieze rather than Franz who falls victim to Reinhold's

Figure 6–12

sexually charged aggression, whose corporeal signifier is the anvil tatooed on his chest. However, throughout the scene in the Freien-walde woods, Franz is the constant reference point. Mieze agrees to go walking with Reinhold in order to extract information from him about Franz, and Reinhold is obsessed with bringing Mieze to re-nounce her love for Franz, and to attach his own name to the pronoun "my." Here, for example, is a characteristic exchange:

> Mieze: "How long have you known Franz?"
> Reinhold: "Your Franz?"
> Mieze: "Yes."
> Reinhold: "Is he still yours?"
> Mieze: "Who else's?"
> Reinhold: "And who am I?"

What is perhaps most striking about the conversation between Mieze and Reinhold is how imperative it is for the latter, both at the level of his sexuality and identity, that he occupy a subject-position which either has been, still is, or is yet to be, occupied by Franz—the existential crisis into which he is thrown when Mieze refuses to relinquish Franz for himself. One way of explaining this crisis would be to account for the relationship between Franz and Reinhold in terms of imaginary rivalry.[29] However, to do so would be to overlook the complex play between homosexuality and heterosexuality which is so central to *Berlin Alexanderplatz,* and so germane to the issue of identity there. The film makes patently clear that Reinhold can only establish his heterosexual identity by dominating the woman who is the object of his desire at any particular moment, a domination which implies the total exclusion of Franz. (Thus we see him, for instance, demanding not only that Mieze kiss the anvil on his chest, but renounce the man she loves.) But Reinhold can only invest libidinally in a woman who is soon to be, recently has been, or still is desired by Franz, a requirement which is tantamount to an admission of his repressed homosexuality. Reinhold's heterosexuality is thus a kind of dependent clause to his homosexuality, while the latter remains unimaginable for him as a conscious subject-position. The question he poses to Mieze—"And who am I?"—consequently remains completely unanswerable.

The situation is further complicated by the necessity, within the heterosexual paradigm which functions to cover over Reinhold's unconscious homosexuality, of identifying with Franz. An implicit psychic transaction goes on "behind" the requirement that the woman who is the current object of Reinhold's desires also be at some moment in time the object of Franz's, and that transaction is Reinhold's shift from desiring Franz to desiring what he desires. Slippages of this kind point to an unconscious predilection for narcissistic object-choice— to the convergence of desire and identification upon the same object, which is one of the psychic conditions which Freud associates with homosexuality.[30] However, Franz represents values like lack and passivity which are anathema to Reinhold, and which consequently serve to intensify his murderous impulses toward that character. All of this adds up to a very potent cruelty, whose usual target is female, but which at least once before the "Epilogue," as we have seen, finds more immediate expression.

The "Epilogue" might be said to act out openly the unconscious desires which the rest of *Berlin Alexanderplatz* attributes to its two central male characters. Not only does it several times reenact the "accident" in which Franz loses his arm, that event through which Reinhold comes closest to acknowledging his desire for Franz, but it makes Reinhold the driver of the car on one of those occasions. The "Epilogue" also stages a number of highly theatrical tableaux in which the latter humiliates and/or injures the former. In the first of these tableaux, Reinhold, wearing black clothes and heavy makeup, beats Franz with a rag and verbally abuses him while Pums and his gang look on. In the second, Franz is thrown onto a pile of naked bodies lying on the floor of a slaughterhouse, and is first struck with a hatchet by Reinhold, and then trussed, suspended from the ceiling, and scraped with a knife by other members of Pums's gang. In a subsequent scene from the "Epilogue," Reinhold poses as an executioner demanding Franz's heart, a demand which makes absolutely explicit the lethal nature of the erotic contract between the two men.

The sequence which speaks perhaps most eloquently to the sadomasochistic nature of the desire binding Franz to Reinhold is the one which poses those two characters in boxing clothes in front of a front-projected loop showing out-of-scale spectators speeding by in such a way as to create the impression that the boxing ring is itself moving in circles. Upon first catching sight of Reinhold, Franz noisily berates him, but his anger quickly modulates into affection ("You scum, yeah, that's what you are! No rain could ever clean you off, you bastard, you murderer, you criminal! It's a good thing you've come, I really missed you"). Reinhold returns the abuse, but not the affection, concluding with the challenge "Now let's see you fight me! Show me who you are, little Biberkopf!" The "fight" takes the surprising form of a passionate embrace between the two men, from which they are roughly extricated by the referees, as if from a "clinch" (Figure 6–13). As they are pulled apart, Franz falls to the floor, apparently knocked out. "Who's on top now, who's the victor, Franz?," taunts Reinhold. As the camera cuts to a close-up of Franz's bleeding face, he responds: "I'm not the victor. I know that—I'm not the victor" (Figure 6–14).

Given *Berlin Alexanderplatz*'s insistence upon the dangerous consequences of sexual repression, one might be inclined to read the sadomasochism of the "Epilogue" as a simple commentary on Reinhold's inability to express his homosexual desire for Franz in a more "direct" form. This, I think, would be a mistake, for there are other reasons as well why the "Epilogue" should give such consistent priority to scenes of erotic violence. Through the foregrounding of those tableaux, the violence which for Fassbinder inevitably accompanies heterosexuality is both redirected and contained, and Franz's masculinity is brutally expunged. The sado-masochism of the "Epilogue" also provides the vehicle whereby Reinhold can express his desire to "be" Franz as well as to "possess" him, for that sexual formation works to privilege masochism, and thereby to facilitate identification with it, a point to which I will return.

Significantly, the film's emphasis upon the cruelty through which Reinhold expresses his desire for Franz is one of the textual features which separates it from the novel, a detail pointing to Fassbinder's own libidinal investment in masochism. Although Döblin's text in-

Figure 6–13

cludes the scene where Franz shows Reinhold his arm, it is much more compressed, and when Reinhold expresses his revulsion against cripples, Franz only "nods and listens," and "begins to tremble."[31] That character's acquiescence to his own death at Reinhold's hands represents Fassbinder's addition, as does, of course, most of the "Epilogue."

When I suggested earlier that Franz's stump elicits from Reinhold a response not unlike that attributed by Freud to the male child when first glimpsing the female genitalia, I did not mean to imply that *Berlin Alexanderplatz* equates Franz's stump with the clitoris. Indeed, I suggested at the time that the film encourages us to read it precisely as a castrated penis. Sexual difference does not have the same value in Fassbinder's magnum opus that it has within the classic cinematic text; here the female body is quite explicitly defined as "whole" until the moment when rough male hands injure or break it. (Fassbinder's voice-over during the first reenactment of Ida's murder says of her body after it was struck by the cream-whipper that it was "no longer quite intact," as if to suggest that it had been before.) In this world in which virtually every female character is, or has been, a prostitute, "femininity" signifies less anatomical "deficiency" than exchangeabil-

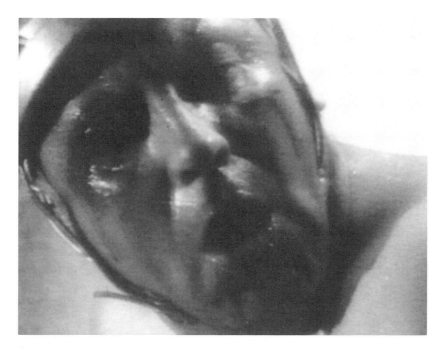

Figure 6–14

ity. It means, in other words, to circulate between men as the carriers
of their unacknowledged homosexuality.

Since "femininity" ultimately implies standing in for a man in relation to another man, it may even refer back in some ultimate way to
the male rather than the female body. An important scene late in
the film seems almost to demand that we effect such a conceptual
rearticulation. After the disappearance of Mieze, Franz dons a woman's garter and hat, and smears lipstick crudely over his lips. Smiling
into a mirror, and puckering up his lips as if offering a kiss, he treats
his own reflection as that other which in fact it is; he constitutes his
mirror image as the woman whom he imagines to have left him
(Figure 6–15). The gesture is tellingly solipsistic; if Franz is able to
kiss his reflected image as though it were Mieze, we are encouraged
to imagine that he has perhaps always kissed her as if she were
himself. His identification with the "feminine," in other words, constitutes an attempt less to recover the dead woman than to retrieve some
aspect of his own subjectivity which he has displaced onto her.

As Franz engages in this maudlin and self-pitying masquerade,
orchestrated to the melody of a favorite record—a masquerade which
effectively forecloses not only upon Freienwalde, but upon Mieze her-

Figure 6–15

self—Fassbinder's voice-over engages in a ferocious anti-blazon calculated to keep alive the viewer's recollection of Mieze's death, and to
remind us once again that what it means to be a woman in the world
of *Berlin Alexanderplatz* is not to signify corporeal "lack," but to be the
depository for all the love and violence which men desire to direct
towards and receive from each other:

> Her face is smashed,
> Her teeth are smashed,
> Her mouth, her lips,
> Her tongue, her throat,
> Her body, her legs, her lap.
> I'm yours, you're supposed to comfort me,
> I feel sick, come on,
> We're almost home, I'm yours.

3. The Wish to Love

Given the unremitting negativity of the cinema to which this chapter is addressed, "utopia" is perhaps the last word one would expect

to fall from Fassbinder's lips. However, he invariably introduced either that signifier or the logic specific to it into interviews about his work. In a 1974 conversation with Wiegand, for instance, he offered the following "confession":

> Generally speaking, history doesn't interest me. What interests me is what I can understand about my possibilities and impossibilities, my hopes and utopian dreams, and how these things relate to my surroundings, that interests me. I'm interested in solidarity, and the potential I might have to overcome the things that bother me, fear and all that, much more than theory. I don't think theory is important to me as a TV watcher, but only as a reader of books. As a television or film spectator, what's important to me is what can activate my dreams in one way or another.[32]

In an interview from the next year, Fassbinder maintained that the goal of his films is to awaken in the viewer the desire to change his or her "reality,"[33] a point which he elaborated more fully in 1977 with respect to *Chinese Roulette* (1976). "Do the numerous mirror shots in the film express the longing for things to be reborn?," the interviewer asked, to which Fassbinder responded: "I hope so. That's how I see it: the rituals go on in the mirrors, where they are broken up, and one hopes that these fractures are so pronounced that the audience unconsciously prepares itself to break with rituals of this kind."[34] Years later, in an interview given shortly before his death, Fassbinder spoke pessimistically about the possibility of personal or social transformation ("You can change yourself a lot, but even when you have understood and know something, you hardly ever succeed in acting accordingly in real life"), but clung nonetheless to the *thought* of transformation ("That doesn't mean, however, that you should stop thinking of the revolution altogether"). More extraordinarily, he derogated love itself while hanging on to what he called the *"wish* for love":

> I think . . . that this system we live in is no system in which you really can love. Because this is a system of exploitation; this system is also made to exploit love and, to be sure, that's exactly how it functions in every case. This is something rather dreadful. On the one hand, and this is of course my wishful thinking, there's something you could call love. I can recommend the wish to love, but not love itself. The *wish* to love should always be emphasized, always made clearer—then perhaps something will happen.[35]

Like Fassbinder's extra-cinematic discourse, his films themselves are shot through with a curious kind of utopianism. Those films sometimes give way at the unlikeliest moments to a kind of "rapture," a signifier suggestive not only of "ecstatic delight or joy," but of "the act of conveying a person from one place to another" (*OED*). I think in this respect of *Katzelmacher* (1969), Fassbinder's second feature-length film, which periodically ruptures its own systematicity (stationary frontal shots of characters engaged in mechanical sex and conversation, from which all affect has been drained) with backward dolly shots of characters, usually female, walking in the sun to the accompaniment of extra-diegetic music. Significantly, the characters who are thus set in motion almost always talk about "feelings"—about love, loneliness, jealousy—as though they had been conveyed not so much from one "place" as from one psychic "state" to another, and the light and music convey the viewer there as well. But even within the emotionally immobilized world projected by the stationary shots there are characters who express the wish to be elsewhere, either physically or psychically, and who might thus be said to embody the principle of utopia. Jorgos, for instance, speaks to Marie about the country to which he wants to take her in words whose primary function is to convey affect, not meaning ("Love good. Eyes like stars. Much love. You come to Greece"). The viewer's knowledge that things would not, after all, be so very different in Greece from the way they are in provincial Germany in no way discredits this little speech, whose value within the Fassbinderian *Weltanschauung* resides not in its accuracy, but in its yearning for something other than what has been given. Despite the fact that Fassbinder himself plays the part of the "guest" worker, Marie represents a position even closer to the one the director ultimately came to espouse; repeating over and over throughout the film the words "I love you," she represents less love than the wish for love.

In a crucial scene from *Gods of the Plague* (1969), Johanna, Franz, and Günther, sitting in front of the poster of the larger-than-life face, speak in turns about going to live on an island where "the sun always shines and it never rains." Greece is once again the imaginary setting of this place which is in fact nowhere. However, while there is scarcely a Fassbinder film in which there is not a yearning for escape from psychic, social, or economic entrapment, the characters in the later films seldom speculate about a geographical "elsewhere." Even when they might be said to "drop out," as do the terrorists in *The Third Generation* (1979), or Hermann Hermann in *Despair* (1977), they never leave Germany, nor do they work to transform the culture into which they were born. Instead, we see these characters chipping away at their specular identities: dying their hair, assuming another person's clothes, undergoing a sex-change operation. Moreover, the utopian

moment comes increasingly to coexist with—indeed, to be inseparable from—loss and suffering. Fassbinderian bliss derives less, in other
words, from the sudden overcoming of limits than from the turning
of those limits to a thrilling advantage; from pleasure seized against
all odds because of a desire which will not cease making its always
exorbitant demands.

4. "Something's Missing"

I suggested earlier that the opening scene of *In a Year of Thirteen
Moons* introduces a thematics of "something's missing," a thematics
which obviously comes into play in *Berlin Alexanderplatz* as well at
the moment that Franz loses his arm. That phrase was not innocently
chosen. It derives from Brecht's *Mahagonny*, and it is used by Ernst
Bloch to account for the impetus behind utopian thinking; as he
remarked in a conversation with Adorno, "each and every criticism
of imperfection, incompleteness, intolerance and impatience already
without a doubt presupposes the conception of, and longing for, a
possible perfection."[36] Since Fassbinder's cinema corresponds with
such surprising precision to this definition, it would seem worth pursuing further its relation to Blochian utopianism. Let us look briefly
at the latter before returning to the former.

Bloch's discourse has nothing in common with that variety of utopian writing which seeks to recover a lost paradise; it is, on the
contrary, extremely hostile to recollection, which it associates with
repetition and changelessness. The yearning after perfection, Bloch
maintains, properly directs the subject away from the past, and toward the future. Indeed, Fredric Jameson suggests that the "ontological pull" of the future is so strong in Bloch's writing that he might be
said to displace the category of the unconscious from the past to the
future.[37]

The chief feature of the Blochian subject is knowing how to "postu-
late ethically beyond a bad existence"—being able, in other words, to
think the future differently from the past.[38] The agency of this utopian
thought is imagination, an intellectual faculty which Bloch opposes
to recollection. But imagination should not function as invention pure
and simple; it must be subordinated to a kind of reality principle,
reined in by the "real potentiality" for "otherness" implicit within
"existing facts."[39] Art is utopian when it casts "anticipatory illumination" on the future which lies concealed within the present, imperfect
world, and in so doing awakens in the viewer or reader a "conscious,
known hope."[40]

In explaining this utopian function, Bloch has recourse to the figural model of interpretation which has proven to be so indispensable to twentieth-century Marxist thought, from Ignazio Silone and Walter Benjamin to Fredric Jameson, and which also provides one of the organizing principles of Fassbinder's *Berlin Alexanderplatz*. His particular figural paradigm turns upon the assumption that the world as it presently exists harbors an unrealized potential or essence. Like all imperfect prototypes of something more perfect which is as yet to come, it might be said to be a figure or a host of figures seeking fulfillment. Utopian art pushes this figure or host of figures to its "entelechical border." Since in so doing, it might be said to "complete the world," it constitutes a fulfillment of sorts.[41] However, since this fulfillment occurs only at an imaginary level, what utopian art in fact offers is another set of figures, more superior than the first, which await realization in the real. Anticipatory illumination shows us not how to leave behind the world we presently inhabit—to soar incorporeally above it—but how to remake it so that it is truer to itself, a truth which has an intractably material dimension.

One of the forms which anticipatory illumination assumes in Bloch's writings is directly germane to Fassbinder's cinema, and will later serve to highlight both the similarities and the differences of their two discourses. In "The Representation of Wish-Landscapes in Painting, Opera, and Poetry," Bloch contrasts the complacent bourgeois interiors of paintings by Vermeer, Metsu, and de Hooch, which project worlds that are complete unto themselves, with the spatial articulation of longing in paintings by Van Eyck, Leonardo, and Rembrandt, where a seductive landscape, opening up behind the figures or buildings in the foreground, can be glimpsed in the distance. Sometimes, he argues, as in Leonardo's most famous painting, the values of that landscape even communicate themselves to the figure in the foreground ("The nature of distance permeates the portrait of Mona Lisa itself. . . . For Mona Lisa herself reproduces the form of the landscape in the ripples of her gown, the weightiness of the dream in her eyelids, the congealed, uncanny, paradoxically nontransparent ether in her smile"). These works by Leonardo, Van Eyck, and Rembrandt, Bloch maintains, work to delineate a lack, to suggest that something is missing from the world which is depicted in the foreground, and hence to create desire for another, different, landscape.[42]

Bloch also demonstrates a strong predilection for unfinished works, and even goes so far as to extend to all great art the status of the fragment. The fragment draws attention to its own partial status, and so opens up a space within which desire for completeness can operate. Like paintings which include a distant "wish-landscape," the unfinished poem or sculpture suggests that there is more to be had, and so directs us beyond the world we presently inhabit.[43]

So far, I have stressed only those features of Bloch's thought which point toward what lies ahead. Fassbinder's cinema clearly has little in common with this utopian trajectory. However, a strong counter-impulse also manifests itself within a text like "Art and Utopia." The penultimate section of that essay, which celebrates the fragment, does not always orient the reader toward a better future. Art's utopian function sometimes seems to reside simply in its capacity to mirror the insufficiency of the world we presently inhabit.

Thus we find Bloch asserting that "the *aesthetic utopian meanings* of the beautiful, even of the sublime . . . reveal their conditions" only at those places where an artistic text opens a "hollow space within an *unrounded immanence*"—wherever it shows itself to be "ruptured, unsealed, [and] unfolded by its own iconoclasm" (150)—at those sites, in effect, where it denies its own adequacy, thus modeling itself upon the present. Moreover, in the same essay Bloch associates the utopian impulse of a work not so much with anticipatory illumination as with the "cipher[ing] of the actual":

> Only what is broken in the art work silenced by the tone of the gallery that has made it into a mere *objet d'art*, or, better yet, only the already formed openness in great art works, provides the material and the form for the great cipher of the actual. (150)

There is clearly a tension in Bloch's work between two utopian impulses, one of which gladly surrenders to the positivity of prefiguration, but the other of which narrows the optical field to the imperfect present. The second of these impulses always seems to contaminate the first, and thereby to triumph over it. The present, in other words, not only prefigures the future, but functions as its prototype, for the latter is no sooner imagined than it is discovered to be inadequate. Utopia becomes an endlessly displaceable goal, a receding horizon which can never be reached. As Jameson suggests, "hope is *always* thwarted [in Bloch's discourse], the future is always something *other* than what we sought to find there, something ontologically excessive and necessarily unexpected" (137).

But although the Blochian future has a way of turning over and over again into the insufficient present, it is endlessly reconstituted through hope. The subject survives by sustaining belief in the possibility of something other than what is and has been, despite mounting knowledge to the contrary. Bloch's negativity is reabsorbed "back into the positive, not as facile consolation, but as a kind of *via crucis* of hope itself, an enlargement of our anticipations to include and find satisfaction in their own negations as well."[44] Gramsci's "pessimism of the intellect, optimism of the will" would thus seem a better characterization of the Blochian utopist than the latter's own appeal to the "unimpaired reason of a militant optimism."[45] To state the case slightly differently, this variety of utopianism would ultimately seem to inhere both in a radical refusal of the present which spills over onto the future, and in an irrational but ever-renewed belief in the possibility for a transfigured world.

5. Fassbinder's "Vicious Circles"

Fassbinder's cinema reiterates Bloch's refusal, but withholds his hope. Indeed, that cinema works much more openly and insistently not only to repudiate the present, but to deny the possibility of a different future. In films like *Gods of the Plague, The American Soldier* (1970), *Fox and His Friends, Effi Briest*, and *Veronika Voss* (1982), what lies ahead is not only contaminated by the present, but emphatically closed off by death, which Bloch describes as "the hardest counter-utopia."[46] The future literally goes up in smoke in *The Marriage of Maria Braun* (1978), while in *Lili Marlene* (1980) it is denied to the central characters through the agency both of fascism and the family. Moreover, at least three of Fassbinder's texts—*I Only Want You to Love Me* (1976), *Berlin Alexanderplatz*, and *In a Year of Thirteen Moons*—are organized insistently in relation to the past. Not only does the first of these texts assume the structure of a series of flashbacks precipitated by a prison interview, but each of the events which it dramatizes is rigorously determined by what precedes it. Similarly, *Berlin Alexanderplatz* constantly reprises the death of Ida, first as a kind of textual "memory," and then through the violence which is performed upon Mieze's body. The entire "Epilogue" is organized around the repetition of events which have already been shown, and it reconceives figural history as the ruthless subordination of the present and the future to the past.

As Robert Burgoyne has already pointed out, the direction of *In a Year of Thirteen Moons* is also "almost exclusively toward a retrieval of the past."[47] Indeed, the words of the song to which Erwin listens in the video arcade—"There's no tomorrow, no today for us" might well be engraved on the tombstone which the film erects over Armin Meier's grave. Erwin visits the convent in order to recover the childhood memories he has repressed, and in the immediately preceding scene, Soul Frieda speaks about his years in a mental institution, and Erwin about a severe but inexplicable childhood illness. Everyone, from Erwin to Smolik and the man with the evil eye, talks about his or her previous experiences with Anton Saitz, a figure who is also held hostage to the past. A line spoken by Erwin's taped voice-over at the end of the film, "Life is—or was—hope," indicates just how little optimism of the will there is in Fassbinder's world. That line relegates even hope to the past, and since the unrelievedly bleak present tense of the film might be said to be the future in relation to which hope was previously sustained, it further disqualifies the dream of something better.

Fassbinder's cinema also produces representative after representative of psychic stasis. Its prototypical characters cannot muster all of their mental resources on behalf of a better world, not only because self-presence is an impossible goal, and agency extremely limited, but because they carry within themselves a malign past which cannot help but repeat itself. It is consequently not only the social order which seems resistant to change, but subjectivity as well.

Not surprisingly, then, although Fassbinder, like Bloch, projects "wish-landscapes," those landscapes attest less to hope than to its atrophy. Rather than using perspective to locate a second world behind a foreground figure or group of figures, albeit one situated within the same frame and subject to the same material constraints, Fassbinder frequently covers interior walls with blown-up reproductions of advertisements or art works, or hangs religious representations or images of seascapes and countrysides in his characters' apartments. Like Bloch's "wish-landscapes," these wall-coverings invariably attest to their owner's desire for a different world, but either access to that scene is somehow blocked, or it is shown to replicate the world to which it is an ostensible alternative.

We recall that in discussing Leonardo's most famous painting Bloch suggests that the Mona Lisa herself incarnates the principle of a utopian otherness—that under ideal circumstances the background landscape imparts its distant and wish-inducing qualities to the figure in the foreground. Fassbinder's cinema effects a reversal of this strategy, imparting the qualities of the "foreground" or present tense of the film to that which lies spatially "behind" it. In *Katzelmacher*, for instance, a picture of a quaint Bavarian village wrapped in idyllic snow hangs on the wall of the restaurant to which the central characters repeatedly retire. Both in its evocation of winter and its idealized portrait of village life, it stands in marked contrast to *Katzelmacher's* own depreciating account of life in the German provinces. However, the insistently frontal positioning of the camera in relation to this image, as well as the non-perspectival deployment both of the table and of the characters sitting at it, works to flatten out the entire space of the image, and so to deny three-dimensionality not only to the foreground, but to the background.

Petra Von Kant (1972) offers a related example. Barbara Miller has recently shown that the enormous reproduction of Poussin's *Midas and Dionysus* which fills the far wall of the room in which the film takes place is cropped in such a way that its composition is entirely altered. One of the most important consequences of this compositional transformation is that the original vanishing points are lost, and with them the sense of a distant landscape behind the figures in the foreground. The reconfigured Poussin thus works to close space down, rather than to open it up.[48]

As I have already suggested with respect to *Gods of the Plague*, the posters which hang on the walls of Fassbinder's interiors often function as the characters' own ideal images, the mirrors in which they would like to see themselves. This is utopianism with a difference, no longer directed outward, as with Bloch, toward a societal transformation, but rather inward, toward the transformation of the self. The "wish-landscape," in other words, coincides on these occasions with a desired *moi*, for transformation seems imaginable only at the level of the corporeal image. I say "imaginable" rather than "realizable" since Fassbinder's cinema invariably demonstrates the inability of the characters either to step into the idealizing frame, or successfully to internalize the images they hang on their walls.

Despite all of the reservations which Bloch would no doubt have expressed if confronted with Fassbinder's cinema, that cinema is, I would maintain, profoundly utopian. It is utopian, moreover, in precisely the way in which Bloch's own writing might most be said to be—in its unrelenting refusal to affirm any of the psychic, sexual, social, or political "givens" of our symbolic order or our social formation. Fassbinder's refusal to affirm is of course inimical not only to the world we presently inhabit, but to all conventional models of social transformation. His utopianism is further complicated by his double relation to cultural oppression and inequity—by his willingness to enlist suffering as a mechanism for effecting a further deconstruction of masculinity's proud subjectivity, even as he at the same time critiques the agencies responsible for it. Paradoxically, however, it is these very complications which ultimately serve to demarcate a path leading out of masculinity. It consequently seems to me not unreasonable to suggest that the crucial difference between the textual systems represented by the names "Bloch" and "Fassbinder" is not that one generates images of a more perfect world, whereas the other is unable to look beyond the existing social order, but that each makes negativity the starting point for a different set of permutations.

Jameson maintains that Bloch's utopianism assumes the form of a *via negativa* in that within it every negative serves "as a means of access to that positive which it conceals" (133). Consequently, it privileges "horror and the black emotions" as "forms of that elemental ontological astonishment which is our most concrete mode of awareness of the future latent in ourselves and in things" (133, 134), and it knows how to translate the symptoms of anxiety into signifiers of hope. In Bloch's writings, Jameson observes, there is "a kind of prodigious enlargement of the existential horizon, a kind of lifting of the soul by its own bootstraps," which "suffices to transform the most acute anxiety" into "an expectation of the future" (133).

Fassbinder's cinema also, it seems to me, manages at moments to translate negativity into something with which it would seem incommensurable—to change its "valence," as Jameson would say. It too testifies more than once to the exertion of a "soul" lifting itself up so as to look outside the body—if not the world—it inhabits. However, rather than giving way to the expectation of a different future, despair and suffering function at times to "secrete" an intense and simultaneous joy.

In a paragraph from "A Cinema of Vicious Circles" which was in many ways the starting point for this chapter, Thomas Elsaesser speaks both to the circularity and the repetitiveness of Fassbinder's work—to the viewer's sense, when watching that work, of being trapped within an unchanging and unchangeable world, in which past, present, and future fold back upon each other in an endless reprise of the same. At the same time, that cinema searches constantly for a route leading elsewhere, a route which would permit the characters, and hence the viewer, a kind of escape. But because all movement is circumscribed by the "vicious circle," this search necessarily follows the same trajectory as the reality from which it seeks to escape:

> Repetition, reiteration therefore has a particularly important function in [Fassbinder's] work, on the thematic as well as the formal level. The films reproduce human relations "as they are," while constantly retracing the contours of a circularity in the utopian hope of finding a way out at the weakest point. Much of the feel and impact of his films—an almost unbearably self-lacerating pessimism shot through with moments of ecstatic (and in the event gratuitous) optimism—seems to come from the need to discover a linearity or dialectic inside a situation emotionally experienced as inescapable, closed, self-perpetuating.[49]

Although Wilfrid Wiegand varies the metaphor, he, too, suggests that Fassbinder's films are organized around a utopian aspiration.

Indeed, he goes even further than Elsaesser, insisting over and over again not only that those films dramatize the search for an "elsewhere," but that the characters in them find what they are looking for—that utopia somehow comes to reside in what Elsaesser calls the "vicious circle." Wiegand is fascinated by the image of a doll which opens, like a Chinese box, to reveal another doll, and he uses it to describe the structure of Fassbinder's cinema:

> Fassbinder's films are post-revolutionary, and in a very specific sense, "post-revolutionary" means utopian. This is a kind of utopian thinking which no longer steers a course for the naive pre-revolutionary dream of a better world, but which has absorbed the fragments of a negative historical experience. This utopia is not anywhere outside our world, but lies deep within it, like the doll in the doll. Therefore, the dramaturgy in Fassbinder's films maintains a perspective throughout which continually opens up new vistas for us, and yet, in the vanishing point, shows us only ourselves.[50]

Like Elsaesser, Wiegand suggests that the only way out of the darkness of Fassbinder's cinema is to penetrate it more deeply. As he remarks earlier in the same essay, in films like *Katzelmacher*, *The Merchant of Four Seasons* (1971), and *Effi Briest*, "the most terrifying things—war, sickness, pain—assume the highest value" (42). But Wiegand extends the argument even further, suggesting that it is only at the level of the psyche that this escape route is to be found.

In what way might Fassbinder be said to locate utopia either along the trajectory of the vicious circle, or within the world he rejects? And what is the ecstasy which shoots through the "almost unbearably self-lacerating pessimism" of his films? By way of approaching an answer to these questions, let us remember some of the moments in Fassbinder's cinema in which pleasure irradiates the darkness of pain and despair.

After being fatally shot by the police officer at the end of *Gods of the Plague*, Günther (Günther Kaufman) stumbles past a series of brightly lit shops to the apartment of Carla (Carla Aulaulu), the seller of pornography and incriminating information who has betrayed Franz and him to Johanna, and hence to the police. He ties up Carla and interrogates her before shooting her, an act of desperate revenge since he himself is rapidly bleeding to death. As he stands briefly by the door afterwards, immediately before losing consciousness, he says: "Life is very precious, especially right now." This extremely uncharacteristic affirmation of life is somehow made possible only because the character who utters it is on the very threshold of death. It is thus analogous to the party Dr. Katz (Annmarie Duringer) throws for her most famous patient at the end of *Veronika Voss*, a party which is intercut with shots of that patient (Rosel Zech) in her death throes, and which has only been staged as a final concession. As is so often the case in Fassbinder's work, the thrill of that celebratory farewell is communicated as much through the set, lighting, and camera movement as through the performance of the character who ostensibly experiences it most intensely. After showing Veronika singing "Memories Are Made of This" in that brief moment of triumph in which she is adequate to her publicity photos, the camera vertiginously circles the brilliantly illuminated glass house in which the party is taking place, a house which no longer belongs to the UFA star, and which will soon be inhabited by the woman responsible for her death.

Although in both of these textual instances life can be savored only at the moment that death might be said to "bleed" into it, neither moves us radically beyond the accepted poetic trope that it is life's brevity which imparts value to it. *Effi Briest* can also be assimilated to that trope, although—as in *Gods of the Plague*—its instant of exquisite pleasure coincides not only with the approach of death, but with an assault on the body's integrity. The last time Effi (Hanna Schygulla) speaks to her mother (Liselotte Pempeit), she describes the period of her fatal illness as "almost the most beautiful time of my life," and the luminous quality of the immediately preceding shots, in which she and her mother revisit the scenes of her youth, encourages us to delete the qualifying "almost."

However, there are moments of intense excitement in Fassbinder's cinema which cannot be so easily contained within a conventional artistic tradition—moments when pleasure and pain are not only inseparable, but coincident with an exteriorizing identification and a dissolution of identity. Nowhere is this psychic "transport" more intoxicatingly negotiated than in his *In a Year of Thirteen Moons*, a film which stages not only the ruination of masculinity, but the sublation of the male psyche.

6. Masochistic Ecstasy as Utopia

If *In a Year of Thirteen Moons* is the blackest of Fassbinder's films, as his commentators are fond of asserting, it is also the most ecstatic. The first half of that text, from the slaughter-house scene through the visit to Soul Frieda, makes suffering the vehicle of a veritable *Aufhebung*, breaking through despair to a delirium which is not so much its antinomy as its outer limit or extension. *In a Year of Thirteen Moons* suggests that although there may be no escaping the vicious circle of pain and oppression, there is nevertheless a way of functioning within it which permits life to be sustained, at least for a time, and which occasionally yields moments of an intense and self-transcending pleasure.

It will come as no surprise to any reader reasonably familiar with *In a Year of Thirteen Moons* that it is masochism alone which facilitates survival there. I hasten to add that by "survival" I do not mean a comfortable fit within the present symbolic order. That kind of psychic existence is only made possible through the defensive operations of the sort that sustain normative male subjectivity—that subjectivity to which Christoph, for instance, has retreated by the beginning of *In a Year of Thirteen Moons*. I am speaking of life situated at the razor's edge of negativity, predicated upon the absolute refusal of all of those cultural fictions which work both to cover over the abyss at the center of subjectivity, and to disavow the terrible realities of sexual, social and economic oppression.

It is the convent scene which gives fullest expression both to the life-sustaining properties of masochism, and to the extremity of a suffering which will ultimately overwhelm pleasure. As Sister Gudrun (Liselotte Pempeit) recounts her horrific story, Erwin is obliged to re-experience a pain so acute that it once threatened his life, and threatens to do so again—to mentally re-live his childhood abandonment first by his biological mother, and then by his would-be adoptive parents. After the second of these abandonments, Sister Gudrun explains, "young Erwin waited, waited for weeks, without asking for fear of the answer. The child's need was so great that he clung to hope long after there was any reason to hope. So long that it began to make him sick. Erwin became ill with an unexplainable fever which the doctors couldn't cure." Sister Gudrun's narrative once again submerges Erwin in a life-assailing suffering. His immediate response is to drop the curtain on the intolerable past by falling to the ground in a state of unconsciousness, prefigurative of his later suicide. Sister Gudrun continues nevertheless with her story, and it is at this point that we learn what made it possible for the young Erwin to get up from his sick-bed, even though the fever kept burning: "He learned to thoroughly enjoy the horrors of this hell instead of being destroyed by them." Masochism is thus shown to be in hand-to-hand combat with death, to be what alone makes it possible at the same time to eschew positivity, to be beyond hope, and yet to go on living.

In an interview quoted by Douglas Crimp in "Fassbinder, Franz, Fox, Elvira, Erwin, Armin, and All the Others," Fassbinder maintains that after Armin Meier's death he felt "the necessity to do something." Three possibilities opened up before him:

One was to go to Paraguay and become a farmer. I don't know why Paraguay; it just came to me. . . . Another possibility was to stop being interested in what was happening around me. That would have been like a mental illness. The third possibility was to make a film—certainly the easiest for me. It's perfectly logical that that's what I did. What's important for me is that I managed to make a film that doesn't simply translate my emotions about the suicide, my pain and despair about the fact that lots of things went wrong in our relationship. Of course I made a film which takes its impulse from Armin, but—this I wouldn't have been able to do before—it extends far beyond that impulse. It tells much more than I could have told about Armin, and that, for me, was a decision for life. (75)

Fassbinder's extraordinary final pronouncement—his claim that the making of *In a Year of Thirteen Moons* was "a decision for life"—is clearly in part his way of drawing attention to the aesthetic status of his work, a strategy for indicating that although biographical events may have been its starting point, they have been subjected to such a total transmutation in the cinematic telling that Erwin cannot be read as a simple "stand-in" for Meier. However, it also seems to me that Fassbinder is here testifying once again to masochism's capacity for transforming pain and despair (the very feelings which he cites as his starting point) into "life." The stress which Fassbinder places upon his own life in speaking about *In A Year of Thirteen Moons* underscores his imaginary relation to that film's central character.

But I am less concerned here with the pleasure which Erwin, like every cultural subject, is obliged to take in his or her pain[51] than with the rapturous and ultimately political uses to which Fassbinder puts such exquisite suffering in his *In a Year of Thirteen Moons*. Fassbinder's cinema is utopian not only in its attitude of unremitting refusal, but in the access which it yields to a psychic "elsewhere," an access which is synonymous with what I will call "masochistic ecstasy."

The slaughterhouse scene provides perhaps the most striking dramatization of this phenomenon in *In a Year of Thirteen Moons*. As liturgical music plays on the sound track, Erwin and Zora (Ingrid Caven) move almost ceremonially through the large room in which the dying and dead animals disgorge their blood, are stripped of their skin, and are reduced to meat. At the beginning of this scene the camera is separated from the two characters by stalls of still-living animals, and it tracks slightly faster than they walk, so that they can be seen only fragmentarily and intermittently. Later, they are at times lost from sight altogether, as the camera focuses on details of the rendering and dismemberment process (Figure 6–16). Erwin's voice

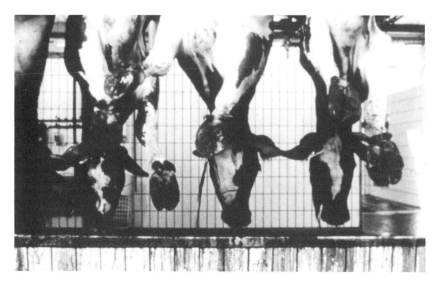

Figure 6–16

is so miked as to draw attention to the fact that although he appears in this scene, his voice does not derive from his body, but proceeds from some other space altogether. If anything, the corporeality which supports that voice is provided by the waiting and dying animals; Erwin's words might be said to be a prolongation of their cries (Figure 6–17).

This is not the only way in which Erwin's suffering is dramatized as situating him psychically "outside" his body. The slaughterhouse scene reaches its emotional crescendo at that moment when it achieves its maximum textual density—when Erwin quotes Christoph quoting a speech assigned to Tasso by Goethe in his play, *Torquato Tasso*:

> "Thus do I see myself in the end, banished, rejected and banished like a beggar here, ha, ha, ha. I was crowned and adorned to be led to the altar as a sacrificial animal. Even on the last day, they mocked my sole possession, stole my poem from me with flattering words, and kept it. My only possession is now in your hands, that which gained me entry to every place, which would yet save me from hunger. Now I see it all, why I must fall; so my song will not be perfected, so my name spreads no further, so my enviers may find a thousand faults, so I am finally, completely forgotten."[52]

Significantly, Erwin's pain is both most powerfully evoked and most pleasurably experienced by the viewer when it is mediated through

Figure 6–17

Christoph's, which also expresses itself most thrillingly and compellingly through another's suffering—this time that attributed by Goethe to a literary character. The slaughterhouse scene suggests that masochism both facilitates identification, and finds a particularly potent form of expression through it—that it fosters and feeds upon an imaginary relay capable of almost infinite extension (here, after all, that relay includes Tasso, Christoph, Erwin, Zora, the viewer, and as I will attempt to demonstrate later, Fassbinder as authorial subject). This peculiar form of identification, which might be said to "ex-corporate" rather than to in-corporate, enables the psyche to take up residence within a different bodily terrain; like Erwin's sex-change operation, it alters the terms of corporeal reference. Significantly, the quotation from *Torquato Tasso* turns upon the erasure of the self, which is precisely what is sacrificed through this "ex-corporation." In a sense, then, masochistic ecstasy can be seen as the logical conclusion of Fassbinder's assault on male subjectivity.

The video arcade scene effects a similar psychic exteriorization. For most of the scene, Erwin sits alone next to a brightly lit slot machine in a corner of the arcade, weeping (Figure 6–18). Bryan Ferry sings "There's no tomorrow, no today for us/Nothing is there for us to share," amid a cacophony of electronic noises. At one point the camera holds for a protracted period upon a screen depicting a car chasing other cars along a highway, and detonating them as soon as it comes close

Figure 6–18

(Figures 6–19a and 6–19b). At another moment, we watch as simulated planes explode and their pilots parachute out.

Upon first glance, this scene would seem to conform to Geoffrey Nowell-Smith's notion of a textual somatic conversion. In "Minnelli and Melodrama," he suggests that music and *mise-en-scène* sometimes function within melodrama as the carriers of what cannot be otherwise expressed, much as the body does within hysteria.[53] However, although the video arcade scene does indeed insist that we read the Ferry song, the burning cars, and the parachuting pilots in relation to Erwin's sufferings, there are two crucial ways in which it exceeds the model of a hysterical conversion.

That model depends, first of all, upon the intervention of repression; the bodily signifier—or in Nowell-Smith's formulation, the textual signifier—exists in a *symptomatic* relation to a censored psychic nucleus. It articulates what the psyche cannot. *In a Year of Thirteen Moons*, on the other hand, does not work to repress Erwin's pain; the camera focuses more than once on his tear-streaked face during the video arcade scene, and the immediately preceding and succeeding scenes expose the past and present reasons for his profound unhappiness. It is not possible, then, to account for the music and *mise-en-scène* as displaced symptoms of a censored "truth."

Somatic compliance also depends upon the notion of the "self-same" body. What the female hysteric represses does not surface at the site

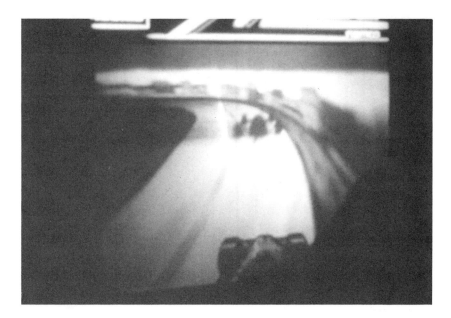

Figure 6–19a

Figure 6–19b

Figure 6–20

of other bodies, but rather at the site of her own.[54] The video arcade scene, however, like the slaughterhouse scene, obliges us to conceptualize a relation between the psyche and the suffering of other bodies. It suggests, that is, that far from functioning as their cause and meaning, Erwin is somehow "in" the exploding cars, the lacerating sorrow of the Ferry song, and the planes that crash to earth—that he resonates to a pain which is no longer his "own."

The visit to Soul Frieda conveys Erwin even farther away from "himself." The idea for the visit is Zora's, who proposes it when she finds Erwin weeping in the corner of the video arcade. "Oh, things aren't so bad," she assures her companion, "Know what I do when I get that way? I go to Soul Frieda's." During a first viewing of the film, these words seem promissory of psychic relief, but Soul Frieda has as profound reasons for sadness as does Erwin. What Zora is actually proposing is an intensification of the latter's masochistic bliss through an externalizing identification.

As is befitting the setting for an ecstasy, the apartment to which Erwin and Zora go is lit by dozens of small candles, and by their twentieth-century equivalent, a flickering television screen (Figure 6–20). Soul Frieda greets his visitors by recounting a melancholy dream:

> Once I dreamed that I went walking in a cemetery, looking at the gravestones. Then something strange occurs to me. The inscriptions

on the gravestones are very different from the other ones I've seen, for instance, born 1918, died 1968, or born 1927, died 1975. But on these gravestones, the dates are, like, 1970 to 1972, '65 to '66, '54 to '57. None of the dead people seem to be older than, at most, two years. Still others died even younger. Some were only a few days old, February 18 to March 11, or May 19 to June 5; others, only a few hours. So I continue along the path and can't make any sense out of this weird cemetery. Suddenly this old, old man is standing in front of me. It's the gardener, and I ask him in amazement how he got to be so old, when all the other people here had to die so young. He smiles, and shakes his head and says, "No, no. The inscriptions on the gravestones don't mean the time a person lived, but the time he was truly happy."

Although Soul Frieda is ostensibly the spectator of other people's pain in this dream, he is clearly not confined to a spectatorial position. The film implies that he is also linked, imaginarily, to the anguish that his dream attributes to other people. Freud would seem to have prepared us for such an eventuality. In *The Interpretation of Dreams* he writes that "every dream deals with the dreamer himself," and that "whenever my own ego does not appear in the context of the dream, but only some extraneous person, I may safely assume that my own ego lies concealed, by identification, behind the other person."[55] However, *In a Year of Thirteen Moons* obstructs the viewer's attempts to trace everything in the dream back to the teller. Soul Frieda subsequently confesses that he may not himself have dreamt this dream—that he may instead have read about it, or heard about it from someone else. He also insists that it makes no difference in his relationship to the dream whether or not he himself dreamt it, as if to underscore further how little the graveyard story hinges upon his ego. Regardless of the origin of the dream, the characters in it are not thinly disguised substitutes for himself; rather, he suffers in and through them. What is this curious form of identification, which seems so intimately allied to masochism, and which precisely conforms to the dictionary definition for ecstasy—an identification which is a "rapture" or "transport," the condition of being "beside oneself"?

Identification, as we learn in *Group Psychology and the Analysis of the Ego*, typically "behaves like a derivative of the first, *oral* phase of the organization of the libido, in which the object that we long for and prize is assimilated by eating and is in that way annihilated as such."[56] Through this imaginary transaction, the subject internalizes the image of the other as "self," and denies the "otherness" of the other. Identificatory incorporation is consequently equivalent, as Mikkel Borch-Jacobsen has recently argued, to "the immediate suppression of the object, to an absence of relation." It is "to put oneself in its place or to place it within oneself, to kill it and live off its death."[57] Since the identificatory system established by *In a Year of Thirteen Moons* turns upon self-loss rather than narcissistic consolidation, however, we need to find some way of theorizing a second form of identification, one which constitutes the antithesis of that described in Chapter 7 of *Group Psychology*.

In "Instincts and their Vicissitudes" Freud maintains that there are times when the sadist derives masochistic pleasure from the pains he inflicts on another through "identification of himself with the suffering object,"[58] but he does not elaborate further upon the nature of this identification. In keeping with Freud's insight, Bersani maintains that the pleasure of the Sadean libertine derives from the "spectacle of the other person's commotion."[59] In another text he and Ulysse Dutoit suggest that the pleasure which the sadist derives from the masochist's pain "disturbs the centeredness of [his or her] self." Bersani and Dutoit go on to elaborate that "disturbance" in terms which are immediately relevant to the present discussion, turning as they do upon the notion of an externalizing identification:

> It is as if we were somewhere "between" ourselves and the suffering victim, somehow ex-centric to ourselves in our identification with the victim's position.[60]

It is to Max Scheler whom we must look for a more fully elaborated account of this "ex-centric" identification. In the second edition of *The Nature of Sympathy* (1922), Scheler distinguishes between an idiopathic or interiorizing variety of identification, which conforms to the Freudian paradigm, and a *heteropathic* or exteriorizing one. He characterizes idiopathic identification as "the total eclipse and absorption of another self by one's own, it being thus, as it were, completely dispossessed and deprived of all rights in its conscious existence and character." Within heteropathic identification, on the other hand, the "I" is "so overwhelmed and hypnotically bound and fettered by the other 'I' " that its "formal status as a subject is usurped by the other person's personality, with all of *its* characteristic aspects." In such a case, Scheler adds, "I live, not in 'myself,' but entirely in the other person."[61] Significantly, on almost every occasion that he refers to heteropathic identification, he characterizes it as a form of "ecstasy."[62]

It cannot have escaped the reader's attention that the will to power or "despotism" (24–25) with which Scheler associates idiopathic identification translates without much difficulty into sadism. Heteropathic identification, on the other hand, would seem to be intimately and complexly allied to masochism. However, since it turns not only

upon the exteriorization of identity, but also upon a pleasurably painful acknowledgment of the "otherness" of all identity—since it represents a refusal, in short, of the imperialism of the "self"—it necessarily
relates to only one of the varieties of masochism enumerated by Freud:
the feminine.[63] Indeed, in my view heteropathic identification is the
end point toward which feminine masochism leads, although it does
not always arrive there. It represents the ultimate divestiture—the
divestiture of "self."

It would seem more than a little appropriate to invoke in this
context the third stage of the female beating fantasy recounted by
Freud, in which the female subject's masochism finds expression
through the pain inflicted on a group of boys.[64] Like *In a Year of
Thirteen Moons*, that stage of the beating fantasy dramatizes the radical implications of heteropathic identification for sexual—and, by
implication, racial and class—difference; it permits the "unwomanly"
women described by Freud to "inhabit" multiple male bodies, just as
it permits Erwin to "occupy" the bodies of the suffering and dying
cattle in the slaughterhouse sequence, or the sado-masochist to "reside" within the body upon which he is inflicting pain. In a sense,
then, heteropathic identification or masochistic ecstasy can be seen
as the logical conclusion of Fassbinder's assault on male subjectivity,
and even as a way out of the vicious circle of masculinity—as the
Fassbinderian counterpart to Bloch's anticipatory illumination.

Heteropathic identification is not only the narcissistic divestiture
toward which feminine masochism ideally leads, but a formation at
the heart of classic female subjectivity, central both to motherhoood
and romantic love, but also to traditional cross-gender cinematic
spectatorship. Laura Mulvey addresses that variety of spectatorship
in terms which are very relevant to the present discussion in her essay
on *Duel in the Sun*. She writes there that the "'grammar' of the [typical
Hollywood] story places the . . . spectator *with* the hero," so that "the
woman spectator in the cinema can make use of an age-old tradition
adapting her to this convention, which eases a transition out of her
own sex into another." Mulvey describes this "trans-sex identification"
as "a *habit* that very easily becomes *second nature*."[65] She accounts for
the facility with which the female subject adopts that habit as a
reactualization of the phallic phase of her sexuality, but her language
points in the direction of another explanation. If Hollywood cinema
works to "place" the female spectator "*with*" male characters, and to
"ease" her "out of her own sex" and "into another," as Mulvey maintains, then it clearly encourages not an *interiorizing* but rather an
exteriorizing identification with masculinity. That cinema does not
conventionally function, in other words, to situate the male character

within her, and thereby to phallicize her, but rather to situate her psychically within his body. However, whereas Hollywood promotes a heteropathic identification between the female spectator and the normative position of "man," it clearly prescribes an idiopathic identification with that of "woman." (I do not, of course, mean to imply that female spectatorship does not at times turn upon quite different imaginary permutations, even within the context of dominant cinema.)

Since I have included the sado-masochist among those susceptible to heteropathic identification, some further clarification of the distinction between sadism and sado-masochism would seem in order. I would like to suggest with Freud and Bersani that the inflicting of pain is indeed incidental to the sado-masochist's pleasure, since that pleasure turns upon an externalizing identification with the masochist. Within this scene, sadism is in effect "nowhere." Sadism proper, on the other hand, concerns itself not at all with the object of its cruelty, with whom it has, as Borch-Jacobsen would say, no "relation"; its goal is the sadist's self-engrossing repudiation of otherness. Fassbinder also insists upon this last point in *Berlin Alexanderplatz*, where he rigorously differentiates sadism both from masochism and from sado-masochism.

Scheler seems at times to propose the idiopath as the perfect partner for the heteropath, with the latter's self-loss contributing lavishly to the former's narcissistic profit. In a strikingly metaphoric passage from Chapter 2, the advantage of this union is shown to depend upon the presumed complementarity of sadist and masochist:

> Schopenhauer recounts the following observation made by an English officer in the Indian jungle: A white squirrel, having met the gaze of a snake, hanging on a tree and showing every sign of a mighty appetite for its prey, is so terrified by this that it gradually moves towards instead of away from the snake, and finally throws itself into the open jaws . . . plainly the squirrel's instinct for self-preservation has succumbed to an ecstatic participation in the object of the snake's own appetitive nisus, namely "swallowing." The squirrel identifies in feeling with the snake, and thereupon spontaneously establishes corporeal "identity" with it, by disappearing down its throat.
>
> *Masochism* . . . resembles its opposite, *sadism*, in being simply a (twofold) manifestation of the erotic craving for power. . . . Even for the masochist, the object of enjoyment is not pure passivity as such, but his self-identifying participation in the dominance of the partner, i.e. a *sympathetic attainment of power*. (21–22)

However, *In a Year of Thirteen Moons*'s ecstatic moments are not those when sadist "swallows" the masochist who jumps down his "throat,"[66] but when a kind of heteropathic chain-reaction is put in place—when, for instance, the viewer inhabits Erwin's suffering, Erwin that of Christoph and the terrified and dying animals, and Christoph that of the protagonist of Goethe's *Torquato Tasso*. In the slaughterhouse scene, as in the scene set in Soul Frieda's apartment, the exteriorization of one psyche never functions to exalt another, and identity is stripped of all "presence." The sadistic figures within *In a Year of Thirteen Moons*—most notably Saitz, and the later Christoph—stand outside its system of identification.

Taken in isolation from the images over which they are superimposed, the chief credits to *In a Year of Thirteen Moons*—"Story, Screenplay, Production, Set Design, Editing, Cinematography, Direction: Rainer Werner Fassbinder"—might seem to give the lie to what I have just said, testifying as they seemingly do to Fassbinder's terrifying ambition to incorporate all enunciatory functions. In his essay on the film, Crimp notes as a typical account of the credits this passage from Wilhelm Roth: "Fassbinder not only wrote the script and directed, but was responsible for the sets and editing, and did the camerawork himself for the first time. Never before had he taken a film so fully into his own hands. . . . " (63). However, these inscriptions of an author "outside" the text are belied by the fact that, as I have argued elsewhere,[67] authorial subjectivity comes into play only in relation either to the "body" of the text, or to a body or series of bodies within the text—that it is, in effect, irreducibly *heteropathic* or exteriorizing in relation to the biographical author, despite the best efforts of readers and viewers to deny the "otherness" of the representations upon which it depends. Fassbinder's sadistic relations with his lovers have been well documented by his sensationalizing biographers,[68] but it is my contention that as an author "inside" the text of *In a Year of Thirteen Moons*, he "inhabits" the suffering body of Erwin/Armin rather than that of Christoph or Saitz. It is indeed that very body which constitutes the focal point of the opening images, and its anguish pulls emphatically away from the self-aggrandizement of the credits. I will go even further, and suggest that the masochistic ecstasy which that film yields is ultimately the thrill of foregoing the mastery inscribed by the credits—the thrill at being lifted up and out of sadism, and at residing within rather than "swallowing" the other.

I base this claim not only upon the unusual system of identification which the film puts so firmly in place—a system which, if we are to place any credence in the argument Freud advances in "Creative Writers and Day-dreaming,"[69] would seem to impinge even more fully upon authorship than upon spectatorship—but upon the dialogical relationship that obtains between *In a Year of Thirteen Moons* and the

Figure 6–21a

twelve months before *In a Year of Thirteen Moons*, Fassbinder's contribution to *Germany in Autumn* also hinges centrally upon his relationship to Armin Meier. However, whereas *In a Year of Thirteen Moons* obliges us to look not only for Meier, but for Fassbinder-as-authorial-subject within the body of Erwin, Meier and Fassbinder play "themselves" in *Germany in Autumn*. Moreover, the most striking feature of the entire film is the insistent corporeality of Fassbinder's "self-presentation"—the bloated body ruthlessly displayed to the camera, sometimes in total nudity, at other times in the throes of alcohol or drug dependency (Figures 6–21a and 6–21b).

Fassbinder's "appearance" in *Germany in Autumn* functions as a powerful acknowledgment that the author-inside-the-text can come into play only in relation either to a body within the text, or to the body of the text, and so as a divestiture of many of the privileges of traditional authorship. However, because the body which sustains authorial subjectivity refers back so emphatically to the body of the historical Fassbinder, it still seems to be his "own." It is thus apparently in the guise of "himself" that he is shown sniffing cocaine, dictating *Berlin Alexanderplatz* into a tape recorder, responding to the current political crisis in Germany, berating his mother, throwing an unwanted guest out of his apartment, and dominating and mistreating his lover.

Figure 6–21b

It is no accident that Fassbinder stages the drama of his relationship with Meier so differently in these two films, for if we read *Germany in Autumn* in relation to *In a Year of Thirteen Moons* we can see that the imperialist behavior which it exposes to our view somehow depends upon the corporeal circumscription of the ego. The earlier text accounts for Fassbinder's appalling sadism precisely through the stubborn persistence of his "self"—through his inability to "occupy" a body other than his own, with all of its exorbitant and lethal demands. It suggests, in a very profound way that we have yet to understand, that the "self-same" body has traditionally functioned as the necessary support for the dream of masculine omnipotence.

Significantly, given its preoccupation with heteropathic identification, *In a Year of Thirteen Moons* makes explicit the relation between the "self-same" body and what Bersani calls "psychic tumescence,"[70] and it does so through another authorial citation. In the scene in which Zora obsessively changes television channels, Fassbinder appears in the guise of the biographical director. In response to questions from an interviewer, he admits that he "fail[s] constantly" in his private relationships. He also gives voice to the desire for subjective change, but then acknowledges that things may very well "go on as [they are]" since "I won't force myself to make [them] different." These interview excerpts are cross-cut with a news report on fascism in Chile, and a terrifyingly brutal exchange between a man and a woman. This montage makes all too evident what it means for Fassbinder to be "himself."

It is important to note, however, that Fassbinder does not appear *in propria persona* in the main narrative of *In a Year of Thirteen Moons*. Instead, he is relegated to a text within the larger text, and to one which is vulnerable to interruption and closure by Zora. This authorial intrusion occurs, moveover, when Erwin is asleep, and hence "absent." The film thus sets up a binary logic equivalent to that set forth in the epigraph to this chapter. In effect, Fassbinder says to Erwin/Armin, "If it's you, I'm not. If it's me, it's you who isn't."[71] In absenting himself from the remainder of the film, and dramatizing over and over again that ex-corporative identification which I have designated "heteropathic," Fassbinder provides no room for the first of these options. He also leaves no other possible site for authorial inscription than that occupied by the character of Erwin, who so clearly memorializes Armin Meier. This commemorative film thus makes it possible for Fassbinder-as-authorial-subject to do something which the historical Fassbinder was presumably unable to effect—to reverse Scheler's parable of the squirrel and the snake by throwing *himself* down the throat of Erwin/Armin. This metaphor permits me to underscore not only the ecstatic, but the erotic aspects of this self-surrendering penetration—to suggest that through it Fassbinder might be said not only to dissolve the identity upon which his masculinity relies, but to "make love" to his dead partner.

7. Sadistic Ecstasy or Psychic Tumescence

I have already spoken at length about the de-idealization and mutilation of the male body in Fassbinder's *Berlin Alexanderplatz*. The text might almost be said to engage in a concerted attempt to return to its corporeal source all of the violence which Franz and Reinhold direct against the female body. However, this aggression also seems expressive of a textual desire for movement outside the vicious circle of endless repetition, and specifically for transformation at the site of male subjectivity.[72] When suffering alone seems inadequate to effect Franz's psychic change, *Berlin Alexanderplatz* goes so far as to stage his crucifixion. The scene to which I refer represents Fassbinder's most extensive exploration of death as a possible avenue of escape from the psychic, sexual, and political givens of classic masculinity. However, it fails to effect the desired metamorphosis—Fassbinder might there be said to negate the possibility of so punctual a negation.

Figure 6–22

Suffering once again emerges as the only antidote, and here it is celebrated less for its transformative than its destructive potential.

Although *Berlin Alexanderplatz* positions Franz as a masochist in relation to Reinhold, there are at least three occasions—the rape of Minna, the murder of Ida, and the beating of Mieze—where he is shown to be capable of an extreme and indeed lethal aggression against women. On the first of these occasions, the aggression is so clearly at the behest of sexual pleasure that it would have to be characterized as sadism, even though it assumes the form which Freud unabashedly claims to be almost a necessary part of "normal" heterosexuality—that of "overpowering the sexual object to the extent necessary for carrying out the sexual act."[73] Like the scenes involving masochistic ecstasy in the earlier *In a Year of Thirteen Moons*, the rape of Minna is shown to lead to a psychic "elsewhere." However, *Berlin Alexanderplatz* goes to great lengths to differentiate sadistic pleasure from its masochistic (or sado-masochistic) counterpart, and it thereafter closes off all access to it. The violation of Minna is thus a crucial scene in determining Fassbinder's authorial relationship to sadism.

Franz's meditation upon the photo of Ida (Figure 6–22) during what is presumably the second day after his release from Tegel prompts

Figure 6–23a

him to head, almost blindly, for the apartment of her sister, Minna. What he says to her as she reluctantly admits him speaks to a profound sense of discursive inadequacy, which he characteristically experiences at the level of the body rather than at that of the psyche. Muttering obscurely about a broken trumpet and a piece of twine on his tongue, Franz grabs Minna's hand and puts it roughly to his mouth, suggesting that it is there that reparation must be made. Significantly, after he has raped Minna he triumphantly exclaims: "The trumpets are blowing, the trumpets are blowing, the hussars ride forth—hallelujah!" The contextualization of the metaphoric trumpet within a military discourse—and specifically, a discourse of military *triumph*—attests to the peculiarly self-aggrandizing form which Franz's pleasure here takes.

As Minna struggles to release herself from Franz's hold, the camera positions itself in front of a large aquarium, which fills the upper half of the frame. Franz knocks her to the floor, straddles her body, and penetrates her, the camera still maintaining its position in front of the aquarium (Figure 6–23a). Meanwhile, Fassbinder's voice-over recounts an anecdote about two men who exchanged a woman, thereby introducing one of the primary themes of the film. The anecdote implies that from a conventional perspective, Franz is merely damaging another man's goods, an action which could presumably be repaired with a small payment. Minna herself simply does not figure in this logic, from which the voice-over ironically dissociates itself:

> What is a woman worth among friends? The London divorce court, in the suit of Captain Bacan, pronounced a dissolution of his marriage on the grounds of his wife's adultery with Captain Furber, a fellow officer, and ruled that he should receive 750 pounds in damages. The captain doesn't seem to place much value on his faithless wife . . .

When Fassbinder finishes speaking, two other disembodied voices speak —first Minna's, and then Franz's. Each of these three voices is detached in a different way from the image track. Whereas the narrator assumes a critical distance from the rape which is being dramatized there, Minna's voice disengages itself from her body both because she is not complicit in what is happening to her, and because she herself is not the object of Franz's desire. Indeed, when it is her turn to speak, Minna comments on the fact that she is not even present in the room as far as Franz is concerned; she is simply the body onto which he has "propped" his memories of Ida. "That's the way he looked at Ida . . . he has Ida in his arms," she murmurs. As Minna utters this terrible truth, the camera cuts to a close-up of her face under Franz's, insisting that we see what he refuses to—the other at whose expense he "renews" himself (Figure 6–23b). This close-up gives way to a similar shot of Franz's face, contorted with pleasure, and his voice-over attests to a corresponding psychic condition, both through its "rapturous" dislocation from the body, and through the words it utters: "There's no more brawls, no more barhopping, no prison. It's the Garden of Eden with beautiful fireworks" (Figure 6–23c).

Lest the viewer attempt to deny the heterocosmic dimensions of Franz's sadistic ecstasy, the camera cuts to an extreme close-up of the aquarium, which now fills the entire frame (Figure 6–23d). The green water and orange fish, irradiated by sunlight, form an aquatic pastoral, a kind of "wish-landscape" deep at the heart of this scene. And when the first male voice-over speaks once again, this time without irony, he articulates what might almost be described as a utopian physics—a physics without laws or constraints: "No house, no gravity, no centrifugal force. It has disappeared, sunk away; extinguished is the red deflection of radiation in the sun's dynamic field. . . ."

However, the film also stubbornly insists upon the material evidence of Franz's violence. As he jubilantly exclaims, "Oh, Minna, I'm so happy," the camera moves in on a close-up of the black eye he has

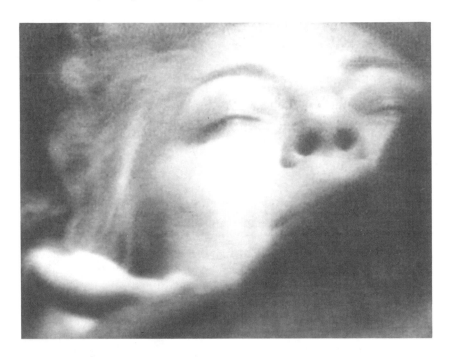

Figure 6–23b

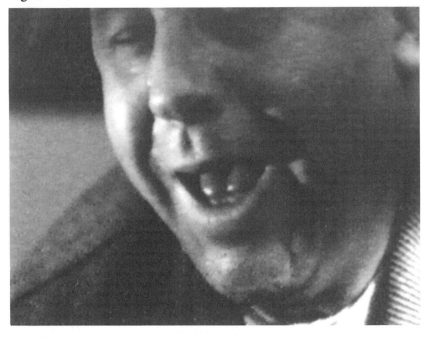

Figure 6–23c

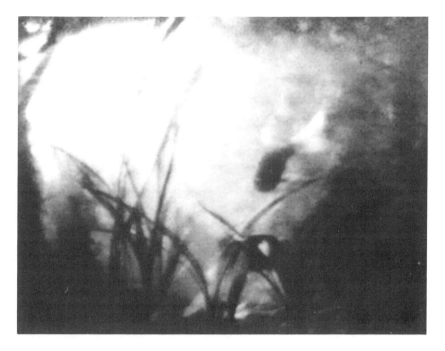

Figure 6–23d

given her (Figure 6–23e). Moreover, *Berlin Alexanderplatz* progresses directly from this scene to the murder of Ida, an event which Franz has attempted to deny by possessing the dead woman once again through her sister. Finally, Fassbinder differentiates the ecstasy of sadism from that provided by masochism by emphasizing the *méconnaissance* it promotes; Franz emerges from his assault upon Minna's body convinced that he is whole and free, in full possession of himself. He cannot repeat his own name enough times, as though to utter it is to affirm the totality which he imagines himself to be: "Franz Biberkopf has been released, he is back!," he exclaims, ". . . everything, everything, Franz, Franz is back. Franz Biberkopf is free again."

But I have not yet sufficiently distinguished sadistic esctasy from its masochistic correlative, nor explained why I have insisted that the former, like the latter, has a utopian dimension. Masochistic ecstasy, as we have seen, implies a sublation of sorts, the lifting of the psyche up and out of the body it ostensibly inhabits into other sites of suffering, and hence a self-estrangement. It turns, in other words, upon a narcissistic deferral, and so works against the consolidation of the isolated ego. Sadistic ecstasy, on the other hand, hinges upon a "swelling" of the self. Freud comments upon the "extraordinarily high degree

Figure 6–23e

of narcissistic enjoyment" which accompanies sadism at its "purest," an enjoyment which derives from the fulfillment of the ego's "old wishes for omnipotence."[74] Since in Freud's account sadism enacts a return to a moment prior to the child's recognition of limits and divisions—since through it the subject is "transported" back to an earlier moment in time, rather than situated within another body— it, too, might be said to project a psychic alternative or "elsewhere" to the present. However, this utopianism is organized insistently in relation to the past, in contradistinction both to the Blochian paradigm and to masochistic ecstasy. It is extremely appropriate, then, albeit more than a little ironic, that *Berlin Alexanderplatz* should evoke that return through a reference to prelapsarian Eden.

The scene where Franz is driven back to Berlin after his automobile accident provides the masochistic counterpart and antidote to this scene. Franz has just been pushed out of a speeding car by Reinhold, and has already effectively lost an arm. All access to pleasure would seem to be completely blocked at this point in the text, yet the macabre car ride becomes the occasion for an extraordinary rapture. What is even more remarkable is that the monologue through which Franz communicates this rapture to the viewer would seem capable of elic-

Figure 6–24

iting only a deeper sense of identificatory gloom. Franz dwells with an exquisite morbidity upon the insignificance of the world and its human inhabitants in relation to the sun, reducing human subjectivity, as he puts it, to a "zero" (Figure 6–24). Once again self-erasure, or—to invert Bersani's metaphor, psychic "detumescence"—generates an extreme excitement. And once again that excitement coincides with an exteriorizing move, whereby the individual ego is lifted up and out of its habitual corporeality, and dispersed across numerous (indeed, here *countless*) bodies. In the process the "I" becomes a "we." "It's important for us to be happy when the sun comes up and the beautiful light comes," Franz dreamily ruminates, from his corner of the front seat,

> The gas lamps have to go out, the electric lights have to go out. But people have to get up when the alarm clock rings, because a new day has begun. The world has continued to turn. The sun has come up. People aren't exactly sure about this sun—it is a subject that occupies many people. It's supposed to be a central body of our planetary system, 'cause our earth is also a small planet. But what are we then? When the sun comes up and we're happy, we should actually be sad, because what are we really? The sun is 30,000 times

as big as the earth, and all the other numbers and zeroes, all they mean is that we're zero and nothing else, absolutely nothing at all. . . . And yet we're happy anyway. You come out onto the street, feel strong, the colors wake up, the faces wake up, and there are shapes, you can touch them with your hands. And it's a lucky thing that we can see . . . these colors and the lines, and we're always happy when we can show what we are. . . . We're happy to have a little warmth, and we're happy that flowers can grow.

As Franz loses consciousness from pain and loss of blood, the text musically amplifies the irrational thrill imparted to the viewer by his soliloquy. Fassbinder's voice-over proclaims, "There is no reason to despair. When I tell this tale further, continuing to its hard, frightful, bitter end, I will use these words often: there is no reason to despair." Since the same voice which tells us that there is no reason to despair also acknowledges that there is in fact every reason to despair, this authorial intrusion must be understood as one of those important occasions in the Fassbinderian textual corpus when dark emotions are somehow made to yield their opposite—when pleasure is extracted from pain, and joy from hopelessness. If that intrusion is to be taken as indicative of more than a Nietzschean affirmation of life (and it seems to me that it is), it must also be read as *Berlin Alexanderplatz's* endorsement of masochistic as against sadistic bliss, its insistence that if the male subject is ever to break out of the vicious circle of masculinity, it will be only through castration and self-cancellation.

However, Franz proves incapable of sustaining this radical subjectivity in relation to any character but Reinhold, and even there it is never fully enacted. Much later, after Mieze has been brutally beaten by Franz in a horrific reprise of Ida's murder, and strangled to death by Reinhold in Freienwalde, a crime in which the text also implicates her lover, *Berlin Alexanderplatz* has recourse to more desperate measures for breaking the vise-like grip of masculinity. After injuring and degrading Franz in a variety of ways, the *Epilogue* embarks upon a sustained interrogation of death as a mechanism for effecting a more permanent rupture with heterosexual sadism.

As Franz digs in the soil of Freienwalde for Mieze's corpse, Death appears to him in the guise of Baumann, who represents himself as the "true force" of change, a force which the central character of *Berlin Alexanderplatz* has steadfastly resisted. "Your whole life you preserved yourself," Death chastises Franz, "Preserve, preserve: that's the terrible desire of man. And so it stays in one place and can't go on." As if to dramatize this principle of changelessness, the *Epilogue* returns over and over again to two scenes depicted earlier in the film, scenes whose complex relationship to each other Franz must somehow be made to grasp—the occasion when he betrays the widow to Luders, thereby setting in motion another of *Berlin Alexanderplatz's* numerous (hetero)sexual exchanges, and leaving the widow vulnerable to Luders's brutal intrusion; and the occasion when he sacrifices his arm to Reinhold. The text offers no evidence suggesting that Franz ever understands the opposition which the second of these memories poses to the first, but he is eventually persuaded that he must somehow "discard" himself, and is led to the slaughterhouse.

But the most complex and conflicted treatment of death is that provided by the crucifixion scene, which represents Fassbinder's final attempt to dispose simultaneously of the male body and masculinity. That scene effects an astonishing condensation both of the Biblical narrative and of twentieth-century European history. It articulates a dense network of figural relationships, but a network which must be read more insistently backward than forward, since each of its tropes functions less to fulfil than to repeat the others.

To begin with, the crucifixion scene makes Calvary simultaneous with Eden and the nativity, thereby collapsing diachrony into synchrony, and effectively foreclosing upon the possibility of transformation. Its central event is of course the death of Franz Biberkopf on the elevated cross to which he has been nailed, but in front of the cross a very different drama unfolds: a naked couple, presumably representative of Adam and Eve, makes love on the ground, scarcely separated from a herd of quietly grazing sheep (Figure 6–25a). To one side of the cross, Frau Kast, dressed as Mary, holds what appears to be a small male child. As if these Biblical citations did not already constitute an inordinately complex textual site, Fassbinder incorporates other references into them. On closer inspection, the male figure held by Frau Kast is revealed to be a doll dressed in a Nazi uniform and swastika armband (Figure 6–25b), and *three* rather than *two* figures can be discerned on the ground in front of the cross. Not only are those three naked figures unassimilable to the sexual economy of Eden, but they are immediately evocative of the libidinal paradigm at the heart of *Berlin Alexanderplatz*.

The crucifixion, moreover, takes place against the backdrop of a large reproduction of *The Garden of Earthly Delights*, the middle panel of Hieronymus Bosch's great triptych, which explicitly designates a period *after* the Fall. (Eden is the topic of the *first* panel in the triptych.) We are thus asked to read Calvary in relation to Naziism, and to imagine Eden as *always already* contaminated by the Fall. Bosch's painting, with its splendidly inventive but deeply ambiguous metamorphoses—metamorphoses which lead inexorably to the third

Figure 6–25a

Figure 6–25b

Figure 6–26

panel, depicting Hell—comments disquietingly upon the topic to which this scene is addressed: the possibility of decisively altering Franz Biberkopf (Figure 6–26). But perhaps the most startling aspect of this astonishing tableau is the way in which it first opens up and then closes down upon the possibility of a utopian reading of its central event.

Berlin Alexanderplatz makes two earlier references to Eden—once during the rape of Minna, and once while Luders violates the widow's trust by helping himself to her cash and valuables. Both of these occasions, as I have already suggested with respect to the first of them, function to consolidate the male ego by fulfilling what Freud would

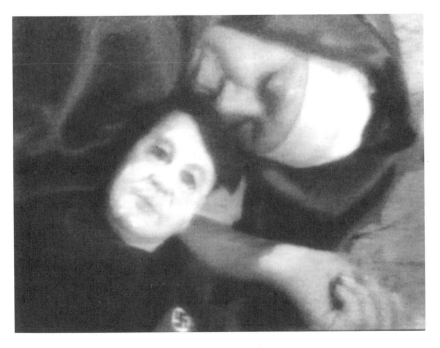

Figure 6–27

describe as an infantile desire for omnipotence. Each time Fassbinder's voice-over invokes Eden not only in order to juxtapose it ironically with the present moment of the film, but so as to suggest that the male character who thus ruthlessly pursues his pleasure has enacted a return to an earlier, solipsistically blissful, condition. These prior events would seem to have little in common with the present scene, but the repetition of the Eden trope encourages us to look for hidden similarities. The Nazi doll provides the basis for such a comparative reading, since it introduces the political discourse which has provided the preeminent twentieth-century context for a proud masculine subjectivity (Figure 6–27). Significantly, fascism is also a discourse with almost infinite resources for recuperating the negativity of death.

When the camera is placed so as to afford the clearest view of the triptych and the naked couple, a statue facing away from the viewer can be partially glimpsed in the left front frame. That statue depicts a virile male body, which, in its evocation of exuberant good health, is more than a little reminiscent of Nazi art. It is thus the antithesis of the pale and emaciated figure so frequently depicted on Catholic crucifixes. It is also ostensibly opposed to the grossly imperfect male body which is put on display a moment later. However, four low-angle shots of Franz's head and shoulders, taken from eye level while the cross holding him is slowly raised, rewrite his corpulance as that monumentalism so dear to both German and Italian fascism (Figures 6–28a thru 6–28d).

As the cross is elevated, the spectators step forward, dressed in costumes whose historical range works further to collapse temporality.[75] At the moment of Franz's apparent death, Fassbinder's voice-over speaks dryly, in words drawn from the Döblin novel, of the new man who "now [lies] in the bed [Franz Biberkopf] has lain in previously." However, it becomes apparent in a number of subsequent scenes that Franz's stay in the mental institution, during which he ostensibly experiences the metaphoric crucifixion, has changed him very little. He demonstrates the same limited understanding of Mieze's murder during Reinhold's trial, and the same blind attachment to her murderer. Nor does his newly acquired determination to keep his wits about him seem all that different from his earlier resolve to remain "decent." *Berlin Alexanderplatz* refuses to constitute death, even allegorically, as a way out of the vicious circle of masculinity. It consequently disassociates itself from the Christian utopianism with which it seems to be consorting in the crucifixion scene, a utopianism within which death, and most specifically death on the cross, has a crucially redemptive function. As Wolfram Schutte remarks, "where the salvation-seeking Döblin cries 'saved, judged, redeemed,' [Fassbinder at the end of his film can be heard] whispering to himself, 'definitely lost, finished.' "[76]

However, there is an important moment prior to Franz's imaginary demise during which Fassbinder's voice-over articulates the fantasy which clearly occupies the center of all of the film's sado-masochistic scenes, a fantasy to whose dramatization the first part of the crucifixion scene also lends itself. Here, it seems to me, it speaks without any of the irony which surfaces in the references to death as an agency of transformation:

> What the pain does to Franz Biberkopf must be celebrated. We must speak of the destruction pain brings about—it breaks off, shakes down, strikes down, dissolves—that's what it does. To everything there is a season, a time to kill, to heal, to break down and build up, to weep and laugh, to wail and dance, to seek and lose, tear apart and close. This is the time to choke, wail, seek, and tear apart.

Once again, then, we find Fassbinder's cinema privileging pain—less in this scene for the pleasure it affords than for the destruction it enacts. And although death is in one sense the logical extension of pain, it also represents the latter's conclusion, and is in this sense its

Figure 6–28a

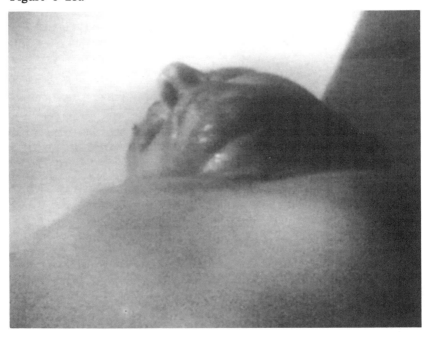

Figure 6–28b

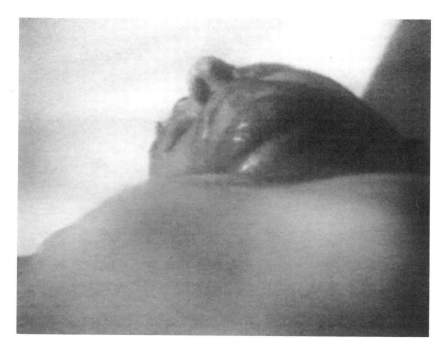

Figure 6–28c

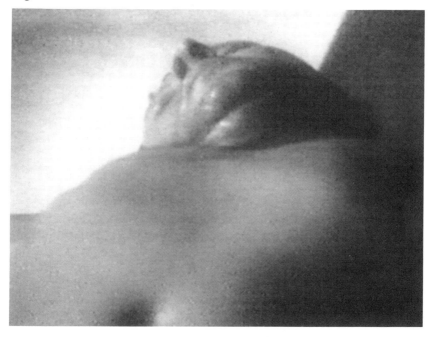

Figure 6–28d

antithesis. The concept of death, in other words, is inadequate to the task of representing the necessary interminability of the struggle which must be waged against the positivities of normative male subjectivity, a struggle which—because it cannot lead to permanent change—can have neither issue nor end-point. Hence, as I suggested earlier, the arrestation at the site of suffering in this and other Fassbinder films.

8. Masculinity and the Self-Same Body

Let us return in closing to the issue with which I introduced my analysis of *Berlin Alexanderplatz*—to the issue, that is, of Fassbinder's psychic connection to the figure of Franz Biberkopf. Ronald Hayman, one of the director's scandal-loving biographers, writes that Fassbinder's identification with Döblin's protagonist was so profound that he was unable to relinquish his desire to play the central role in *Berlin Alexanderplatz* even after he had selected Günther Lamprecht for the part. He adds that Fassbinder's dealings with Lamprecht during the shooting of the film were for this reason extremely strained (88). Hayman does not always seem a very reliable biographer, but I am concerned less with the historical "accuracy" of his story than with its parabolic force. This account of imaginary rivalry serves as a crucial reminder that Lamprecht's image occupies the center not only of Fassbinder's cinematic adaptation of Döblin's novel, but of his own "dream"—that in this staging of the *Berlin Alexanderplatz* fantasmatic, Lamprecht's performance might be said to mediate Fassbinder's access to "himself."

What are we to make of the curious paradox whereby Fassbinder simultaneously proclaimed Döblin's text to be the very basis for his "whole body and soul," and released to German television a cinematic adaptation of that text in which another man performs the part of Franz Biberkopf? I would like to propose that we turn once again in our search for an answer to the distinction drawn by Max Scheler between idiopathic and heteropathic identification.

The reader of "Man's Cities and His Soul," the essay published in *Die Zeit* at the time of *Berlin Alexanderplatz*'s release, can scarcely avoid remarking that Fassbinder's account of his early relationship with Döblin's *Berlin Alexanderplatz* offers a striking instance of the first of these two kinds of identification. All of the verbs he uses to characterize his first encounter with that work—"breathing in," "gulping down," "devouring"—turn upon oral incorporation. Indeed, the assimilation of the "self" with its external object was in this instance so complete that only a second reading of *Berlin Alexanderplatz* was able to put quotation marks once again around that novel's words. The subsequent rediscovery of the alterity of that text induced in Fassbinder initially "astonishment," then "panic," and finally "complete unfaceable anguish" (3), the only emotions commensurate with so radical a denaturalization of identity.

Looked at from the perspective provided by *The Nature of Sympathy*, both Fassbinder's decision to cast Lamprecht as Franz Biberkopf and his publication in 1980 of "Man's Cities and His Soul" can be seen as part of a move to reexteriorize what had been assimilated as the "self" while still maintaining an imaginary connection with it. In effect, each text attempts to substitute *heteropathic* for *idiopathic* identification—to replace incorporation with what I earlier called "ex-corporation." Hayman's anecdote, even if entirely fictive, has the great virtue of underscoring the extraordinary psychic pain which this project must have cost the filmmaker, for what is at issue here is quite simply the annihilation of the ego, sole basis of psychic identity and unity.

Surprisingly, in light of the disclosures made in "Man's Cities and His Soul," Fassbinder not only leaves it to another actor to perform the part of Franz Biberkopf throughout *Berlin Alexanderplatz*, but appears *in propria persona* at a number of points in the "Epilogue." These curious authorial citations occur during the slaughterhouse sequence, and they take the form of a series of virtually identical shots of three closely grouped figures—two angels, Terah (Margit Carstensen) and Sarug (Helmut Griem), in post-punk garb, and Fassbinder, in dark glasses and a slouch hat. These figures are repeatedly positioned as spectators in relation to the spectacle of Franz's pain, through the code of the shot/reverse shot formation. The two angels function as a kind of chorus, commenting on Franz's suffering, but Fassbinder remains entirely absorbed in the act of watching (Figures 6–29a thru 6–29o).

A too hasty reading of these shots would emphasize the divinity of the company which the director there keeps, and subsume them within the authorial system constituted by Fassbinder's voice-over. Such a reading would not only push the voice-over itself in a more emphatically "theological" direction, but would align authorial subjectivity with "enunciation," in the most punctual sense of that word. Fassbinder would emerge from such a reading as the agency which *oversees* and *overspeaks* the text—as a very traditional kind of maker.

However, if Fassbinder's authorial subjectivity is inextricably bound up with the figure of Franz, as he tells us in "Man's Cities and His Soul," and as the title to the "Epilogue" also emphasizes, then it is clearly a mistake to insist upon so punctual a relation of body to psyche. Although Fassbinder is shown standing to one side of the

Figure 6–29a

Figure 6–29b

Figure 6–29c

Figure 6–29d

Figure 6–29e

Figure 6–29f

Figure 6–29g

Figure 6–29h

Figure 6–29i

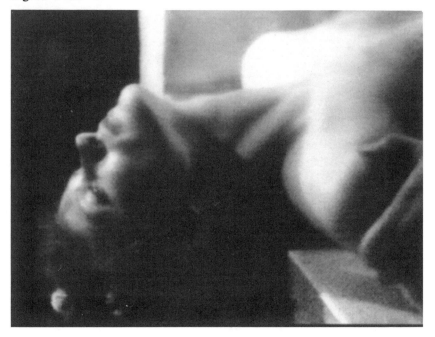

Figure 6–29j

Figure 6–29k

Figure 6–29l

Figure 6–29m

Figure 6–29n

Figure 6–29o

hyperbolically dramatic scene, at which he merely looks on, the film and its accompanying verbal text ask us to understand that he mentally occupies the body of Döblin's protagonist, which provides the central focus of the spectacle. Like the Sadean libertine or the Freudian sado-masochist, he is "ex-centric to [himself] in [his] identification with the victim's position."

Once interpreted along these lines, the cluster of authorial citations is easily assimilable to the sado-masochistic iconography and dynamic of the *Epilogue*. The viewer might legitimately wonder why the director would include his corporeal image in the film at all, however, given the manifold possibilities it opens for misinterpretation. We do not of course know what response Fassbinder would have given to this question, but if we view *Berlin Alexanderplatz* through the conceptual frame provided by "Man's Cities and His Soul" there can ultimately be only one explanation. By appearing *in propria persona* within his cinematic adaptation of Döblin's novel, Fassbinder foregrounds that term which constitutes so palpable a support of identity and sadism within *Berlin Alexanderplatz*, even as he renounces it: the "self-same" body. The series of shots which show Fassbinder looking at Franz's suffering would consequently seem to represent the filmmaker's paradoxical way of saying something like "*I* am *there*," a far more radically alienating declaration even than Rimbaud's "*je est un autre*." And of course since the "*there*" in question is the very scene of masculinity's corporeal ruination, the "self-same" body is doubly erased.

I hope that this analysis of *Berlin Alexanderplatz* has once again conjured forth the image of the squirrel throwing itself down the throat of the snake, and that this image will remain with the reader as a potent signifier not only of psychic detumescence, but of an imaginary expatriation with crucial ramifications for sexual, racial, and class difference. Since in concluding this chapter on such a note I may seem to be granting the psyche an undue importance, I hasten to add that I am not proposing heteropathic identification as a substitute for other forms of political struggle. Nevertheless, films like *In a Year of Thirteen Moons* and *Berlin Alexanderplatz* demonstrate that we can no longer afford to isolate political theory and practice from the issues raised by the constitution of the ego and the formation of the unconscious, nor to imagine that subjectivity sustains no inevitable relation to violence. It may even be that the agendas of feminism, Marxism, post-colonialism, and gay studies need to be opened up to psychic strategies like the ones proposed by Fassbinder's cinema, whatever the resulting disruption. At the very least, we need to begin thinking seriously about the political implications of desire and identification.

The next chapter will refine further upon the concept of a libidinal politics. I will attempt to demonstrate there that T.E. Lawrence's masochism and homosexuality helped to determine the nature of his involvement with the Arab Revolt, and that they played a decisive part in his subsequent decision to serve as an "ordinary" airman in the Royal Air Force. I will also explore some of the ways in which identification and desire can encroach upon race, class, nationality, and the political economy of the group.

Libidinal Politics

7

White Skin, Brown Masks: The Double Mimesis, or With Lawrence in Arabia

> We export two chief kinds of Englishmen, who in foreign parts divide themselves into two opposed classes. Some feel deeply the influence of the native people, and try to adjust themselves to its atmosphere and spirit . . . They imitate the native as far as possible, and so avoid friction in their daily life. However, they cannot avoid the consequences of imitation, a hollow, worthless thing . . . The other class of Englishman is the larger class . . . In reaction against their foreign surroundings they take refuge in the England that was theirs. They assert their aloofness, [and] their immunity . . . They impress the peoples among whom they live by reaction, by giving them an example of the complete Englishman, the foreigner intact.[1]

It is by now a theoretical truism that hegemonic colonialism works by inspiring in the colonized subject the desire to assume the identity of his or her colonizers.[2] As Fanon observes in *Black Skin, White Masks*, "Every colonized people . . . finds itself face to face with the language of the civilizing nation; that is, with the culture of the mother country. The colonized is elevated above his jungle status in proportion to his adoption of the mother country's cultural standards. He becomes whiter as he renounces his blackness . . . "[3] The work to which this chapter is primarily devoted—T.E. Lawrence's *Seven Pillars of Wisdom: A Triumph*—suggests that the colonial relation can also give rise to an inverse desire. That text dramatizes the curious paradox whereby a white man, ostensibly working on behalf of imperial Britain, comes to assume the psychic coloration of the Arabs he seeks to organize.

For Edward Said, Lawrence is one of those benighted Westerners who, not content merely to construct "the Orient," seeks to provide its best representative.[4] Although I will be offering a much fuller elaboration of the same critique, it seems to me that it provides only a partial explanation of Lawrence's Arab "masquerade." Said's formulation forecloses upon Lawrence's homosexuality and masochism, as well as the hyperbolic permeability of his psyche—his propensity for finding himself within the racial and social Other.[5] *Seven*

Pillars of Wisdom foregrounds to a quite unusual degree the subjective conditions enabling its protagonist's military and political participation in a struggle for Arab unification, a struggle that is not at all points subservient to "British interests." Lawrence's second book, *The Mint*, similarly dramatizes the psychic determinants behind his decision to enlist as an ordinary airman in the Royal Air Force rather than to pursue a distinguished governmental career. These two books consequently oblige us to approach history always through the refractions of desire and identification, and to read race and class insistently in relation to sexuality.

Lawrence's sexuality—or, to be more precise, his homosexuality—is enormously complex. Blocked at the site of the genitals, it finds expression primarily through the narrowing down of narcissistic object-choice to erotically resonant identification, and through a masochism which is initially "reflexive," and later "feminine." For most of *Seven Pillars*, to state the case rather differently, Lawrence's masochistic homosexuality assumes forms which are surprisingly compatible with the delusions of leadership, and which underwrite rather than challenge his virility. The flagellation and implicit homosexual rape recounted in Chapter 80 of that text, however, effects the radical desublimation of Lawrence's homosexuality, and reconfigures his masochism, thereby calling into radical question his ambition to lead. In this respect, *Seven Pillars* anticipates Lawrence's second book, *The Mint*, which offers a study in abjection. Together, those two texts make it possible to understand both the conditions under which masochism can sustain an aspiration to mastery, and those under which it can lead elsewhere.

Before embarking upon an extended analysis of these issues, I want to sketch briefly those details of Lawrence's life which provide a necessary background to them. This "contextualization" seems important not only because Lawrence's books are ostensibly autobiographical, but because they presume knowledge of the history in which they are embedded, a history in which Lawrence himself had an important part to play. However, my recourse to "maps" and "chaps" should not be seen as conferring upon *Seven Pillars* and *The Mint* the status of "true books." On the contrary, I hope to suggest through this interplay of textuality and "facticity" that history itself may be both initially penetrable and subsequently recoverable only through fantasy. The astonishingly various accounts of Lawrence's involvement in the Arab Revolt offered by his biographers and critics dramatize the impossibility of knowing what "really" happened during that tumultuous period, but *Seven Pillars* forces us to relativize the present as well as the past—to understand that it, too, can be entered only through the lures of the imaginary, and the promptings of the unconscious.

1. The Biographical Context

Lawrence was born out of wedlock in 1888 to an aristocratic Anglo-Irish father and his daughters' former nursemaid, herself the product of a Scottish upbringing. His birthplace was Tremadoc, Wales, but his family moved shortly thereafter to Kirkcudbright, Scotland, and from there to the Isle of Man, Jersey, and Dinaud, Brittany, before finally settling in Oxford. I mention the mixed nationality of Lawrence's parents, and his peripatetic childhood because they may help to explain the ease with which he later adjusted to a nomad desert life. He was educated at Oxford, where he took First Class Honors in history, and pursued an interest in antiquarianism.[6]

Lawrence's relationship with the Middle East began in 1909, when he undertook a strenuous walking tour of the Middle East, ostensibly to do the research for his thesis on the architecture of Crusader Castles.[7] A year later he departed for Carchemish, Syria, where, under the direction of David Hogarth, Keeper of the Ashmoleon, he worked for four years on an archaeological dig. He raided Carchemish and environs for Hittite artefacts which could be shipped off to the British Museum and the Ashmolean.[8] Under cover of his position as an archaeologist, Lawrence also apparently collected information for British Intelligence about both the declining state of the Ottoman Empire, and the Berlin to Baghdad train, which the Germans, with Turkish approval, were in the process of building.[9]

During this period in Carchemish, Lawrence formed an emotionally resonant relationship with one of his Arab assistants, Dahoum, generally assumed to be the "S.A." addressed in the dedicatory poem to *Seven Pillars*.[10] Lawrence at times traveled with Dahoum, even taking him back to England on a visit. He also produced a nude sculpture of his Arab friend, and on occasion wore his clothing.[11] Lawrence concerned himself with Dahoum's education, but took pains not to Anglicize him.[12] Leonard Woolley, who worked in Carchemish with Lawrence, later wrote that the intimacy between Lawrence and Dahoum generated widespread homosexual rumors, but he denied that there was any basis to the rumors.[13]

In 1914 Lawrence was put to work in Cairo gathering intelligence and working on military maps of the Middle East.[14] Although he was initially preoccupied primarily with Syria, his attention was eventually drawn farther south, to the Hejaz, a strip of Arabia which borders the Red Sea, now subsumed within Saudi Arabia. In 1916 the Hejaz was still part of the Turkish Ottoman Empire, but because it contained Mecca, it was also the Holy Land of Islam, and hence fertile terrain for what was as yet only a nascent Arab nationalism.

The movement on behalf of Arab nationalism was initially led by Grand Sherif Hussein, Emir of Mecca, and his four sons, Ali, Abdulla, Zeid, and Feisal. Although Feisal subsequently emerged as the dominant figure, it was Abdulla who initially approached the British in 1914 with a request for guns to be used in an Arab uprising against the Turks.[15] A lengthy correspondance ensued, culminating in an "apparent promise" in 1915 that the British would recognize Arab independence in those parts of Asiatic Turkey where Arabic predominated, with the exceptions of Lebanon, Alexandretta, and Mersin.[16] This agreement, the McMahon Pledge, substantially recapitulated a plan earlier proposed by Lawrence, which argued on behalf of an Arab Caliphate to consist of interior Syria and its four primary cities, Aleppo, Hama, Homs, and Damascus.[17]

The British clearly did not feel bound by the McMahon Pledge, for in May 1916 they signed a secret document with the French, defining the basis on which they and Russia would divide up the Middle East after the war. According to this notorious document, the Sykes-Picot Agreement, the Arabic provinces of Turkey were to be divided into the following zones: "(a) Palestine from the Jordan to the Mediterranean, to be 'international'; (b) Haifa and Mesopotamia from near Tekrit to the Gulf, to be 'British'; (c) the Syrian coast, from Tyre to Alexandretta, Cilicia, and most of Southern Armenia, from Sivas to Diarbekir, to be 'French'; (d) the interior (mainly the provinces of Aleppo, Damascus, Urfa, Deir, and Mosul) to be 'independent Arab' under two shades of influence," one French and one English.[18]

It is unclear at exactly what point Lawrence became aware of the Sykes-Picot Agreement, since all information about it was withheld for some time not only from the Arabs, but from the British staff in Cairo.[19] However, he clearly knew about it during much of the Arab Revolt. Both *Seven Pillars* and an important wartime message emphasize Lawrence's discomfort with its provisions.[20] He also wrote a letter to Sykes objecting to the terms of the agreement.[21] Jeremy Wilson, Lawrence's most recent biographer, who had access to papers withheld from previous scholars, claims that the latter not only told Feisal about Sykes-Picot shortly after learning about it himself, but urged the Arabs to strengthen their hand *vis-à-vis* the French by capturing Damascus, Homs, Hama, and Aleppo (362–63). It was for this reason, Wilson adds, that Lawrence and Feisal moved the Arab Campaign north as soon as possible, taking Akaba in spite of British desires to the contrary (397–98).

Late in 1916, the Arab Movement laid successful seige to Mecca, and captured the ports of Jidda, Yanbo, and Rambegh. The Arabs were, however, rebuffed at Medina, a city which remained in Turkish hands until late in the war. Ronald Storrs, Britain's Oriental Secretary, made several trips to the Hejaz around this time to establish contact with the Arabs. When he went again to Jidda in October, he took Lawrence with him.[22] For the next two years Lawrence worked closely with the Arab Movement, as it moved triumphantly north to Damascus.

This is the period of which *Seven Pillars of Wisdom* purports to be the historical record. However, although Lawrence's biographers themselves provide conflicting interpretations of the key moments in that text, they agree that it contains factual inaccuracies. They are not alone in their unwillingness to attribute absolute veracity to *Seven Pillars*. Lawrence himself later implied that his first book is better understood as a piece of fiction than as a historical document; in a letter to Sydney Cockerell, he compares it unfavorably not to another account of the Arab Revolt, but to *Ulysses*.[23]

It seems to me fruitless to attempt to establish with absolute accuracy the part Lawrence played in the various battles he recounts in *Seven Pillars*. If, after a brief trip to Athens in 1910, he wondered how much of what he took away with him reflected the city itself, and how much "the coloring of my imagination upon it,"[24] he can scarcely be assumed to have sailed away from Arabia with nothing but objectively verifiable memories of the Arab Campaign. *Seven Pillars* was written under the sign of fantasy, as is clearly indicated by its obsessive lingering over masochistic and homosexual detail. I would even go so far as to suggest that Lawrence *lived* much of the war in the same way. Thus it was that he could write about the bodyguard that he collected around himself late in the Arab Campaign in the following, theatrically inflected terms, which bear the key trademarks of fantasy—an emphasis upon pose and *mise-en-scène*, and a privileging of preliminary arrangement over the moment of ostensible culmination or climax:

> You want apparently some vivid coloring of an Arab costume, or
> of a flying Turk, and we have it all, for that is part of the mise-en-
> scène of the successful raider, and hitherto I am that. My bodyguard
> of fifty Arab tribesmen, picked riders from the young men of the
> deserts, are more splendid than a tulip garden, and we ride like
> lunatics and with our Bedouins pounce on unsuspecting Turks and

> destroy them in heaps: and it is all very gory and nasty after we
> close grips. I love the preparation, and the journey, and loathe the
> physical fighting. Disguises, and prices on one's head, and fancy
> exploits are all part of the pose: how to reconcile it with the Oxford
> pose I know not.[25]

Lawrence also confesses in *Seven Pillars* that the notebooks he kept
during his two years in Arabia were full not of "facts and figures,"
but of "the reveries and self-questioning induced or educed by our
situations, expressed in abstract words to the dotted rhythm of the
camels' marching," and that even at moments of violent action his
"detached self" was always "eying [his] performance from the wings
in criticism" (580). He speaks most eloquently to the mediating role
played by fantasy in his involvement with Arab nationalism when he
describes his own sudden perception of the "unreality" of what had
previously seemed the setting of a tangible historical drama. Significantly, that perception is produced by the intrusion of the "definite-
ness of British troops in uniform" into his beloved Arabian desert:

> I felt guilty at introducing the throbbing car, and its trim crew of
> khaki-clad northerners, into the remoteness of this most hidden
> legendary place: but my anticipation went astray, for it was the
> men who looked real and the background which became scene-
> painting. (576)

To stress the degree to which fantasy structured Lawrence's relationship to the Arab Revolt is not to diminish the historical importance of that episode or its aftermath, nor to bracket the issue of
Lawrence's political responsibility. It is never possible to be "directly"
inside history. The unconscious always intervenes in some determining way, facilitating certain actions, and impeding others, through
the identifications and desires which it sustains. The reader of *Seven
Pillars* should not be surprised, then, to find Lawrence placing less
emphasis, as a reason for involving himself in the Arab Revolt, on his
"pugnacious wish to end the war" than upon the "longing to feel
[himself] the node of a national movement," inspired by a boyhood
reading of *Super Flumina Babylonis* (684). Nor should we be startled
to find Lawrence's Arabs "dreaming" themselves into the "spirit" of
Arab nationalism by sharing stories of "sieges and feasting, raids,
murders, [and] love-singing in the night" (448), since daydreams derive their own force and effectivity from their relation to the "fantasmatic," that variable unconscious *combinatoire* or paradigm governing each subject's libidinal existence, which always assumes a "scenic"
form.[26] If the Lawrence of *Seven Pillars* is able to participate psychically in Arab nationalism, that is in large part because his particular

homosexuality promotes an erotic identification both with its leaders and its servants.

Another aspect of Lawrence's Eastern "adventure" also falls within the purview of fantasy. We know not only from *Seven Pillars* but from numerous photographs and eyewitness accounts that its author wore Arab robes for most of the period he spent in Arabia. This was not an isolated episode. Throughout his life he demonstrated what would seem to have been a predilection for "fancy dress." Earlier, during the Carchemish period, he also at times adopted local Arab dress, which he describes enthusiastically in a letter to V.W. Richards:

> There is a splendid dress called "of the seven kings":—long parallel stripes of the most fiery colours from neck to ankle: it looks glorious: and over that they wear a short blue coat, turned up at the cuffs to show a dull red lining, and they gird themselves with a belt of thirteen vari-colored tassels, and put a black silk & silver weave of Hamath work over their heads under a black goat-hair head-rope. You have then only to add a vest of gold-embroidered silk, and white under-tunics to get the idea of one man's dress . . .[27]

And during the postwar years Lawrence, who was by then an enormously decorated and celebrated figure, changed his name first to Ross, and then to Shaw, and adopted in turn the uniform and position of an ordinary airman, and those of a common soldier.

The two accounts of masquerade that have proven most influential in recent years both stress the dislocation between subjectivity and the role which is thereby assumed.[28] The figure of T.E. Lawrence eludes this paradigm, for there seems to have been no such distance or dislocation between him and certain of his "costumes." An astonishing passage from *The Mint* suggests that dress implied psychic reality for Lawrence—that the garments he wore not only defined the body beneath them, but designated a corresponding subject-position. The passage to which I refer, which provides perhaps the most erotic prose Lawrence ever wrote, describes how it feels to be clad in the dress uniform of an R.A.F. airman. It offers, in other words, an "inside" look at the subjectivity that the regulation blue wool suit produces, a subjectivity organized around an eroticized sense of self, and a powerful sense of belonging to the R.A.F.:

> But first there was a mass trying on and innocent vanity of the new dress, which was to be our best for the next years. . . . These boys, in fancy dress for the first time, went stroking and smoothing their thighs, to make the wings of the breeches stand out richly. The tailors had taken them in at the knees, by our secret request, so tightly that they gripped the flesh and had a riding cut. Dandies put a wire in the outer seams to spread them more tautly sideways. . . .

> These clothes are too tight. At every pace they catch us in a dozen joints of the body, and remind us of it. The harsh friction of the cloth excitingly polishes our skins and signals to our carnality the flexure of each developing muscle or sinew. They provoke lasciviousness . . . Airmen cannot swing along like civvies, unconscious of their envelope of flesh. For them there is a sealed pattern of carriage, of the head, the trunk, the feet, the arms, the hands, the stick.[29]

Obsessed with corporeality as this passage is, it nevertheless derives from an author who elsewhere asserts there to be "no flesh."[30] Significantly, he speaks on that other occasion from the subject-position of someone wearing the garments of a Sherif of the Beni Wejh, garments whose looseness and amplitude serve to obscure rather than to define the male body.

It was this latter costume, consisting of silk Arab robes and head-dress, and a gold circlet, which proved the most historically important of Lawrence's corporeal "envelopes."[31] It identified him with the Arab cause—not so much in the eyes of his comrades, as in his own. To paraphrase the passage I have just quoted, those robes might even be said to have provoked a rarefied kind of "lasciviousness" in him—that desire for the "idea" of Arab nationalism to which he so frequently adverts in his first book. Within *Seven Pillars*, they also bear luminous witness to the extraordinary porousness of Lawrence's subjectivity—to the ease with which he was able to discover himself within the Other.

For two years Lawrence lived and fought with Feisal's army, an entity whose constituency changed with the territories through which it moved. Although he reported regularly to the Cairo office, he also worked to make the Arabs as indispensable as possible to the British war effort, so as to impress upon his native countrymen a sense of obligation to them after the War.[32] Following the liberation of Damascus from the Turks, he assisted in the hasty formation of an Arab government.

I also want to emphasize Lawrence's postwar efforts on behalf of Arab self-determination, since they give strong credence to his claim that, in helping to install Feisal as the ruler of Syria, he hoped to thwart the colonial ambitions of "important elements among the Allies."[33] From 1919 to 1921, Lawrence engaged in a "dog-fight" in the corridors of Downing Street and in the British press on behalf of an equitable Mideast settlement,[34] even functioning as Churchill's advisor on Arab affairs from January 1921 to July 1922. He lobbied energetically against the Sykes-Picot Agreement, and against not only French, but British governance and occupation of the Middle East. He proposed that every British and Indian soldier leave Mesopotamia, for instance, and in the same letter to the *Times* he reminded his readership that the Arabs fought against the Turks during the war "not because the Turk government was notably bad, but because they wanted independence." The Arabs "did not risk their lives in battle to change masters," he added, "to become British subjects or French citizens, but to win a show of their own."[35] He also argued in an official letter to Lord Curzon that Arabia should provide England's "first brown dominion[s]," not its "last brown colon[ies],"[36] i.e. that England should seek to "influence" rather than to occupy or dominate the Middle East. While this proposal left unchallenged Britain's ideological supremacy, it nonetheless revealed Lawrence's discomfort with conventional notions of "Empire."

Lawrence's own plan for a Middle East solution also attested to surprisingly divided loyalties, given his citizenship. It dictated that Britain would continue to play an "advisory" role in some parts of Arabia, but it also seemed to exempt other parts from British supervision, notably those with which Lawrence himself had enjoyed the most intimate relationship. Each Arab state, moreover, was to be under at least nominal self-rule. This plan specified that three Arab states be formed outside Hejaz and its dependencies: Lower Mesopotamia, Upper Mesopotamia and Syria. Lower Mesopotamia was to be placed under Abdullah's rule, and to be subject to effective British control. Upper Mesopotamia was to be under Zeid's governance, and to fall within the British "sphere." Feisal would be the ruler of Syria, and Hussein the King of the Hejaz, to be succeeded by Ali.[37] Unsatisfactory as this plan clearly looks today, and must even in 1919 have appeared to the Arabs who had fought so fiercely for their independence, it occupied a discursive space considerably to the "left," to use a word preferred by Lawrence himself, of any of the more officially sanctioned alternatives.[38]

The Yale Plan was the alternative which Lawrence found least offensive, and which some important Arab leaders agreed to accept. It would have placed Palestine and Northern and Southern Mesopotamia under British "mandate,"[39] and Syria and Mount Lebanon under French "mandate." A number of years later, Lawrence characterized this notion of "mandates" as a "swindle" whereby "England and France got the lot,"[40] but at the time he was presumably reassured by the provisions within the Yale Plan for ostensible Arab self-rule everywhere but Palestine. When the Yale Plan collapsed, Lawrence experienced a period of extreme depression.[41]

In the year and a half during which Lawrence worked with Churchill, another plan was hammered out, and put into effect. France was given a "mandate" over Lebanon and Syria. Feisal was installed in

Iraq under British air supervision. Abdullah was designated the ideal ruler for the Transjordan, which also remained under British "influence." The Balfour Plan, which proposed to transform Palestine into a Jewish homeland, was to hover ambiguously in the background for many years to come. Hussein was "offered" Hejaz in exchange for signing the treaty which formalized this plan. When he refused to accept the arrangement, the British abandoned him to his powerful Arab neighbor, Ibn Saud, the creator of Saudi Arabia, and he lost his throne. Lawrence believed at the time that England emerged from this settlement with clean hands.[42]

In 1918, in an audience with George V, Lawrence declined the Distinguished Service Order, as well as a decoration which would have named him Companion of the Bath for his wartime activities.[43] In 1922, he resigned his position as Churchill's Arab advisor, and enlisted as an ordinary airman in the Royal Air Force under the name John Hume Ross. Four months later Airman Ross was identified in the newspapers as T.E. Lawrence, and he was expelled from the R.A.F. For the next three years he conducted a letter campaign to be readmitted, which finally achieved its aim in July 1925. For much of the interim, Lawrence unhappily served as an ordinary soldier in the Royal Tank Corps, under what was to become a permanent name— T.E. Shaw.[44]

From 1922 until his death in a motorcycle accident in 1935, Lawrence lived a strangely "partitioned life," as one of his biographers has put it.[45] He visited and corresponded with many of the major literary figures of his day, including Hardy, Forster, and G.B. Shaw. He completed and published *Seven Pillars of Wisdom* and *Revolt in the Desert*; wrote *The Mint*, an account of his experiences in the R.A.F.; and translated *The Odyssey* for an American publisher. He also wrote hundreds of letters, almost all of which attest to a wealth of literary knowledge. At the same time Lawrence deliberately sought out obscurity, going into virtual hiding whenever his name resurfaced in the newspapers.[46] He seemed, indeed, to have become a different man under his adopted name; when he was assigned by the R.A.F. to India, from 1927–1929, Lawrence, whose earlier engagement with the East had made him a household name in Britain and America, manifested so little interest in his foreign environment that he never strayed beyond the borders of the military camp.[47] He chose a life of regimentation with little or no privacy, in which most possessions were communally designated, and where he was constantly subject to the often arbitrary authority of others. His meager income placed him below the income tax level for thirteen years, as he confessed in one of his letters, often making it impossible for him to acquire desired books.[48]

However, even this mortification was not enough for Lawrence. In 1922 he formed a sado-masochistic relationship which lasted until 1935 with John Bruce, a young Scotsman, who assumed the periodic responsibility of birching Lawrence severely on the buttocks. Their relationship, like the period spent in Arabia, was saturated with fantasy. Lawrence told Bruce he had been sentenced to be beaten by "The Old Man," who decreed it a necessary punishment for Lawrence's manifold crimes, which supposedly included dragging the family name into the gutter, insulting the King, and ruining the life of a Foreign Minister.[49]

During Lawrence's final years in the R.A.F. he helped to revolutionize the boats used by the R.A.F.[50] Some years before retiring from the Air Force in 1935, he spoke in some of his letters about finding a job as a watchman in a London bank.[51] However, in a conversation with a friend in March 1935, Lawrence said that he might be asked to assume responsibility for the reorganization of Britain's Home Defence,[52] a claim to which Churchill gave credit when, after Lawrence's death, he wrote: "I hoped to see him quit his retirement and take a commanding part in facing the dangers which now threaten the country."[53] It is impossible to know which of these two identities Lawrence would have assumed had he lived, national leader or lowly functionary.

I want to conclude this biographical resume by explaining the perhaps disproportionate attention it gives to the peace settlement. I have dwelt at such length upon Lawrence's role in the postwar disposition of the Middle East so as to demonstrate that by the end of the war he had become more than an agent of British imperialism, whatever his political position may have been prior to the Arab Revolt. His passionate advocacy of Arab self-rule in the surviving letters and documents, however qualified by the desire to maintain a continued British influence, attests to a powerful identification with a racial Other, an identification in frequent conflict with his own position and history as an Anglo-Irishman. Lawrence's R.A.F. experiences aligned him similarly with respect to a class Other. That identification was so intense that Lawrence's English eventually lost its "Oxford" accent, and assumed "that pleasant compound of (perhaps) North London and Birmingham and Sheffield that one associates with men who drive lorries or have to do with mechanical bits and pieces."[54]

Although I will from this point forward scrupulously limit my analysis to the various texts generated by Lawrence, I will be implicitly pursuing the answer to three questions raised not only by *Seven Pillars* and *The Mint*, but by the activities of the biographical author from 1919 to 1935: What were the psychic conditions that sanctioned Lawrence's unorthodox identifications? What form did the identifications themselves take? Finally, what precipitated Lawrence's retreat, around 1922, from the publicity he had previously courted, and his increasing commitment to a life of communality, deprivation, and punishment?

2. The Double Mimesis

Lawrence's writings convey a complex understanding both of "nation," and its biologizing equivalent, "race." The voice of the cultural relativist emerges frequently within his letters, but perhaps most strikingly from one dating from 1912. "It is a very good thing to have a country to grumble over or praise as one wishes—it doesn't matter much which country I fancy," he wrote a female friend.[55] And as if further to deny any notion of a natural connection between the individual and his or her country, Lawrence in the same letter describes wandering about Jerablus for three weeks wearing Arab dress. Later, he also expressed himself in forceful opposition to British assumptions of racial superiority. "I entirely repudiate [the] suggestion that one race is better than another. This is the purest jingoism," he told Edward Garnett in 1927.[56]

Seven Pillars subjects the concepts of nation and race to an even more complete deconstruction through its account of Arab unification. Lawrence describes the Arabs as "a manufactured people" (31), the basis for whose coherence was neither corporeal, spiritual, nor geographical, but only linguistic:

> A first difficulty of the Arab movement was to say who the Arabs were. Being a manufactured people, their name had been changing in sense slowly year by year. Once it meant Arabian. There was a country called Arabia; but this was nothing to the point. There was a language called Arabic; and in it lay the test. (31)

There are many occasions in *Seven Pillars* where Lawrence engages in the most suspect of Orientalizing, but this passage nonetheless remains central to the book's vision of Arab nationalism. Nations, it seems to say, are made, not born.

Lawrence's writings also convey over time an increasing discomfort with British imperialism. In 1912 he was still capable of entering into the point of view which transformed the Parthenon friezes into the Elgin marbles. "I would like to dig in the Persian gulf, and as Bahrein is nominally British, I suppose we might carry off the stuff," he wrote Hogarth from Aleppo.[57] However, by 1927 he was confiding to Dick Knowles, "I . . . wish, hourly, that our great Imperial heritage of the

East would go the way of my private property."[58] His private correspondence also argues more than once against that psychic territorialization which is such a prominent feature of hegemonic colonialism; in one letter he urges a female friend not to "denationalize" her son, and in others he conveys his determination that nothing "Frangi" or European enter into Dahoum's education.[59] Much later, during his stay in Karachi, he referred dismissively to Indians who have been Anglicized.[60]

But although the Lawrence who emerges from his writings is concerned to maintain the specificity of Arabs and East Indians, he himself vividly illustrates psychoanalysis's premise that the "I" always speaks, desires, and enjoys "in the name and place of another"— that the ego's "house is haunted, *its* property inhabited by something entirely 'other.'"[61] A 1910 letter to his mother, for instance, extols the pleasure of self-expropriation through reading:

> . . . if you can get the right book at the right time you taste joys— not only bodily, physical, but spiritual also, which pass one out above and beyond one's miserable self, as it were through a huge air, following the light of another man's thought. And you can never be quite the old self again.[62]

A later letter shows that Lawrence eventually came to understand this self-expropriation less as a form of transcendence than as the very basis for identity itself. In the letter to which I refer, he describes himself as "a sensitized film, turned black or white by the objects projected on me,"[63] thereby locating himself at the site which recent theory has claimed to be that traditionally occupied by woman and/ or the colonized subject.[64] In holding open to himself the possibility of being either "black" or "white," Lawrence defines race in terms of colonial screens[65] rather than biological "essences."

Elsewhere, Lawrence deploys another of the "tropes" of colonial subjectivity in speaking of himself. In the first chapter of *Seven Pillars*, he theorizes his own role in the Arab Revolt as a choice between two options. Confronted with an alien people, Lawrence writes, the Westerner "may stand against them, persuade himself of a mission, batter and twist them into something which they, of their own accord, would not have been." Lawrence quickly dispenses with this first course of action, which would have been familiar even to his contemporary readership under the name of colonialism. To follow it, he warns, is to exploit one's own "environment" in order to "press" others out of theirs. Alternately, the Westerner "may imitate [the residents of another culture] so well that they spuriously imitate him back again." Lawrence maintains that he followed this second course of action during the Arab uprising, but he is equally critical of it: "In neither case does [the Westerner] do a thing of himself, nor a thing so clean as to be his own (without thought of conversion), letting [the native populace] take what action or reaction it please[s] from the silent example" (29–30). But let us look more closely at this double mimesis.

In seeking to imitate the Arabs to the point where they might be prompted to imitate him back, the Lawrence of *Seven Pillars* both inverts and doubles the classic colonial paradigm.[66] Rather than attempting to reproduce himself within the Arabs, he adopts *their* attitudes, customs, and dress. In so far as they emulate him in turn, the Arabs would thus seem to enact a return of the same, to become once again that which they have always been. It might be difficult at first to locate the colonialist impulse in this paradigm, but Lawrence's notorious *Twenty-Seven Articles*, published in the *Arab Bulletin* in 1917, clearly indicates that his Arab masquerade at least initially cloaked a will-to-power.[67] Lawrence suggests in that text that the best way to lead is to constitute oneself as an ideal within the terms of the native culture—to outdo the Arabs in representing "Arabness," becoming in the process a standard to follow. "If you wear Arab things, wear the best," he advises his British colleagues,

> Leave your English friends and customs on the coast, and fall back on Arab habits entirely. It is possible, starting thus to level with them, for the Europeans to beat the Arabs at their own game . . . If you can surpass them, you have taken an immense stride toward complete success. . . . (466)

Lawrence here represents the leader as a model or mold, a definition which is also implicit in the title of his second book—*The Mint*. However, whereas he positions himself as a product of the minting process in that later book, in *The Twenty-Seven Articles* and in *Seven Pillars* he arrogates to himself the status of prototype.

The strategy outlined in the passage I have just quoted is predicated upon the assumption that the Westerner's imitation will remain no more than that, a successful outward "aping" of the Other. Ironically, however, since imitation repeatedly veers over into an identification with the Arab Other, Lawrence's cultural masquerade is ultimately less successful in eliciting Arab conformity to his image than in rewriting his "own" subjectivity.

3. Masochism and Ideality

Throughout *Seven Pillars*, the linguistic markers of Lawrence's subjectivity, otherwise known as his "shifters," place him as frequently in the Arab as in the English camp.[68] Indeed, they often locate him *aggressively* on the side of the Bedouin warriors, in a competitive opposition to his countrymen. In Chapter 34, for instance, he characterizes British demands on the Arab Army as a foreign intrusion upon a political space he shares with the latter: "It was irksome that [Sir Archibald Murray] should come butting into *our* show from Egypt, asking from *us* alien activities. Yet the British were the bigger; and the Arabs lived only by grace of their shadow. *We* were yoked to Sir Archibald Murray, and must work with him, to the point of sacrificing *our* non-essential interests for his. . . . " (203; my emphasis). Elsewhere in the book he reports himself rejoicing to the British that "*we* were half-way to the Wejh: the initiative had passed to the *Arabs*" (149).

However, Lawrence also oscillates in many of these passages between the singular and the plural form of the first-person pronoun. This oscillation, of which the following passage offers a particularly striking example, attests to two very different kinds of Arab identification, one predicated upon a perception of himself as a member of the Bedouin group, and hence subject to its norms, and one predicated upon a perception of himself as the *leader* of that group, and hence *a model to be imitated*:

> All men dream: but not equally. Those who dream by night in the dusty recesses of their minds wake in the day to find that it was vanity: but the dreamers of the day are dangerous men, for they may act their dream with open eyes, to make it possible. This *I* did. *I* meant to make a new nation, to restore a lost influence, to give twenty millions of Semites the foundations on which to build an inspired dream-palace of their national thoughts. So high an aim called out the inherent nobility of their minds, and made them play a generous part in events: but when we won, it was charged against *me* that the British petrol royalties in Mesopotamia were become dubious, and French Colonial policy ruined in the Levant. (23; my emphasis)

The singular pronoun obviously works here at the expense of the plural. Despite Lawrence's commitment to Arab nationalism, and his skepticism about Britain's colonial ambitions, his "I" is the carrier of an imperialist subjectivity.

Lawrence repeatedly characterizes his leadership as the fulfilment of a dream in the passage quoted above, as if to emphasize the importance of fantasy in determining his involvement in the Arab Revolt. The prominence of the first-person singular also attests to the intervention of fantasy, for egoism represents one of the primary features of that textual form.[69] However, whereas Freud associates the "characteristic of invulnerability" with the hero of most daydreams, a more ambivalent libidinal economy is at work in Lawrence's writings. Although he is capable of representing himself at certain moments as the "node" of Arab nationalism,[70] at others he gives voice to the desire for self-mutilation. Thus he confesses in a 1922 letter to feeling a "horrible satisfaction" whenever he is able to "cut a piece out of [himself], and draw the edges neatly together,"[71] a sentiment seemingly at odds with his over-vaunting political ambitions. And throughout *Seven Pillars* the narrator takes a manifest gratification in the "recollection" of his own sufferings. Lawrence's egoism apparently coexists with a profound masochism. Indeed, his heroism often seems to reside primarily in his inordinate capacity for enduring a pain which frequently veers over into pleasure. How are we to account for this curious masochism, which seems more a precondition of than a disqualification for leadership?

There is at least one occasion when Lawrence overtly acknowledges his erotic investment in suffering, and which therefore seems to offer particular insight into his subjectivity. I refer to the climactic chapter 80 of *Seven Pillars*, in which he is flagellated and (apparently) raped, a passage which might plausibly be titled "'A Child Is Being Beaten.'" However, although this section of the book gives most palpable expression to Lawrence's love of pain, it should not be read synecdochically. The masochism addressed by Chapter 80 is of a very different order from that exhibited elsewhere in the book.

One of the things that distinguishes most of *Seven Pillars* not only from the Deraa episode but from Freud's 1919 account of masochism is that in it the agency of pleasurable punishment is curiously abstracted. A passage from early in the book, which functions as a kind of epigraph to what follows, suggests that Lawrence lived the Arab Revolt as the fantasy of subordination to a group *ideal*, rather than to a sadistic Other:

> By day the hot sun fermented us; and we were dizzied by the beating wind. At night we were stained by dew, and shamed into pettiness by the innumerable silences of stars. We were a self-centred army without parade or gesture, devoted to freedom, the second of man's creeds, a purpose so ravenous that it devoured all our strength, a hope so transcendent that our earlier ambitions faded in its glare. (27)

Later in *Seven Pillars*, Lawrence maintains that those who fight in the Arab Revolt wear pain as a badge of commitment to "the ideal, held in common" (476).

I will postpone until later a full analysis of the masochism which underpins Lawrence's leadership—a masochism which, as we will see, is predicated not only upon subservience to the ideal, but upon a partial identification with it. At this point I want merely to note that this ideal exists in a surprisingly intimate relation with the male body. As I have already remarked, the passage just quoted from Chapter 1 offers a strangely de-eroticized account of the pains suffered by Lawrence and his colleagues on behalf of their political struggle. The abstraction for which they are fighting is apparently best represented by the stars in the heavens. The completely de-anthropomorphized and concretely unspecifiable agency of punishment which is conjured forth through the actions of fermenting, dizzying, staining, devouring, and glaring, though, before long assumes a series of much more human forms. It is incarnated in quick succession as a rider, a slave-master, a puppeteer, and a taskmaster:

> As time went by our need to fight for the ideal increased to an unquestioning possession, riding with spur and rein over our doubts . . . We had sold ourselves into its slavery, manacled ourselves together in its chain-gang, bowed ourselves to serve its holiness with all our good and ill content. The mentality of ordinary human slaves is terrible . . . and we had surrendered, not body alone, but soul to the overmastering greed of victory. By our own act we were drained of morality, of volition, of responsibility, like dead leaves in the wind. . . . (27)

It is not surprising, given the scenes of homosexual sado-masochism evoked by these metaphors, that Lawrence should refer a few sentences later to the "gusts of cruelty, perversions, [and] lusts" which "[run] lightly over the surface without troubling us," nor that he should arrive, seemingly without the slightest divagation, at the love that dare not speak its name. Thus we find him invoking male "friends quivering in the yielding sand with intimate hot limbs in hot embrace" as the "sensual co-efficient" of the "mental passion" welding Arab "souls and spirits in one flaming effort" (28). Lawrence's commitment to Arab nationalism clearly depends in some way not only upon masochism, but upon homosexuality. His arrogation to himself of the status of the leader of that movement attests to the same libidinal economy, albeit now in a dramatically sublimated guise. Lawrence's aspiration to provide a model or norm for the Bedouins to follow is predicated, in other words, upon a precariously maintained libidinal "deflection" in the direction of "an aim other than, and remote from, that of sexual satisfaction."[72]

Since the passage under discussion makes heavenly bodies the exemplary representatives of the "transcendent" ideal of Arab nationalism, it provides a very precise working out of Freud's premise that

sublimation involves a displacement "upward."[73] When the body ob-
trudes, it reverses this upward displacement. Lawrence initially describes homosexuality as the "slaking" of human needs in "clean bodies," a characterization which attempts to halt the libidinal "descent,"
but before long he is expatiating upon those men who take "a savage
pride in degrading the body," and who offer themselves "fiercely" in
"any habit which promise[s] physical pain or filth" (28). He later
associates such activities with his own impulse to take his pleasure
"downward" (581).

Sublimation and desublimation are here linked, as they usually are,
to the complementary processes of idealization and de-idealization.
Sublimation, in other words, directs libido toward a culturally vali-
dated goal, whereas desublimation represents an abandonment of
that goal for "baser" pleasures.[74] However, whereas idealization and
de-idealization generally affect the *object*, in the opening chapter of
Seven Pillars the consequences of the de-idealization can be more
clearly perceived in the desiring *subject*, whose "filthy" activities serve
a *self-degrading* function. Although the narrator speaks of those who
engage in these activities in the third person, the subject who is
diminished through the eclipse of the ideal is Lawrence himself, as
can be seen not only in this passage, but in his other writings. For
whereas the Lawrence of *Seven Pillars* suffers primarily at the behest
of an abstraction, both *The Mint* and the service letters bear vivid
testimony to another kind of masochism, one which is constrained by
the force of gravity, and which operates at the expense of the self.
There we find Lawrence attributing his willingness to endure a life of
degradation in the Tank Corps to his desire to burn out "freewill
and self-respect"[75] so as to make himself ineligible for a "responsible
position."[76] A letter to Charlotte Shaw suggests that a similar logic
motivates his commitment to the R.A.F. "Henceforward my life will
lie with these fellows here," he writes,

> degrading myself . . . in the hope that some day I will really feel
> degraded, be degraded to their level. I long for people to look down
> upon me and despise me . . . I want to dirty myself outwardly,
> so that my person may properly reflect the dirtiness which it con-
> ceals . . .[77]

If the desublimation of Lawrence's homosexuality involves the corresponding de-idealization of his ego, then it necessarily follows that
the sublimation of his homosexuality must function to exalt or aggrandize the same psychic entity. The deflection of his libido away from
the male body must somehow work, in other words, to align his ego
with the ideal. Paradoxically, identification provides the vehicle of

this self-aggrandizement; Lawrence emerges within his own thoughts not only as the leader of Arab nationalism, but as its very image, through the incorporation of the movement's indigenous leaders. His self-promoting "I" serves both to avow and to disavow this identification.

4. Identification and the Ideal

As Borch-Jacobsen has recently argued at length, desire cannot be scrupulously differentiated from identification.[78] Freud establishes in *The Ego and the Id* that object-cathexis and identification are initially "indistinguishable," in that oral sexuality internalizes its object much as the ego does. The same text suggests that throughout life the subject is able to relinquish a love-object only by incorporating it—that "identification is the sole condition under which the id can give up its objects." The ego is a "precipitate of abandoned object-cathexes" (29), and as such itself an erotic object. And a little-known Freudian text, *Thomas Woodrow Wilson*, demonstrates repeatedly that identification has the great virtue of making it possible for the ego to transform itself into the desired object, and thereby to promote self-love.[79]

The Ego and the Id encourages us to understand identification not so much as the "resolution" of desire as its perpetuation within another regime, no longer subject to the same moral constraints—as the resituation of the object at the site of the ego, where it can continue to be loved. Significantly, it equates this shift of the object from one psychic modality to another with the process of *sublimation*:

> The transformation [of erotic libido] into ego-libido of course involves an abandonment of sexual aims, a desexualization. In any case this throws light upon an important function of the ego in its relation to Eros. By thus getting hold of the libido from the object-cathexes, setting itself up as sole love-object, and desexualizing or sublimating the libido of the id, the ego is working in opposition to the purposes of Eros . . . (46)

This passage invites us to read identification as the potential occasion for a displacement "upward," an event imaginable only in relation to an ideal. Here that ideal must necessarily coincide with some aspect of the self which has been thereby constituted.

Although ideality is conventionally situated at the site of the ego-ideal, and represents a paradigm in relation to which the ego is always-already deficient, *Seven Pillars* suggests that there may be circumstances under which it is the ego itself which is "elevated" in this way, and in relation to which the subject's libido might be displaced "upward." It proposes, that is, that the ego can exalt itself through identification, for not only does the sublimation of Lawrence's homosexuality require him to love male bodies only through the ideal into which they are translated, but he himself "becomes" that ideal.

This aspect of Lawrence's libidinal economy can only be explained by returning once again to the topic of dress, since through it the narrator of *Three Pillars* might be said to constitute the ego-as-love-object in the image of the Other. I mentioned earlier that during his stay in Syria the historical Lawrence from time to time wore the clothing of his Arab friend, Dahoum, about whom he speaks so fondly in his letters, and in whose likeness he sculpted a nude figure. *Seven Pillars* also makes Arab clothing the site of a number of erotic transactions. The white silk robes which provide the fictional Lawrence's trademark are given to him by Feisal, who is presented through this portrait earlier in the book:

> He looked years older than thirty-one; and his dark, appealing eyes, set a little sloping in his face, were bloodshot, and his hollow cheeks deeply lined and puckered with reflection. His nature grudged thinking, for it crippled his speed in action: the labor of it shrivelled his features into swift lines of pain. In appearance he was tall, graceful and vigorous, with the same beautiful gait, and a royal dignity of head and shoulders. Of course he knew it, and a great part of his public expression was by sign and gesture. (98)

Lawrence adds that Feisal's "personal charm, his imprudence, the pathetic hint of frailty as the sole reserve of this proud character [makes] him the idol of his followers," and he describes the ruler being carried unconscious from the field after victory, annihilated by the force of his own effort. What reader could return to this passage after reading the rest of *Seven Pillars* without recognizing in it the lineaments of the leader Lawrence subsequently becomes: an air of majesty; thought-as-pain; a body determined to out-spend its resources; and a self-consciousness so acute that it transforms every public moment—and many private ones—into performance?[80]

Lawrence-as-leader has clearly been "penetrated" by the discourse and image of the Other, a verb which I hope will communicate a sexual as well as a territorializing significance. It is crucial to remember in this context that the garments which Feisal confers upon Lawrence have been given to the Arab ruler to wear on the occasion of his *wedding*, and that they consequently carry a powerful erotic resonance. To wear them is to be in a position to love that image of the Other's virility which has become the self.

The figure of Ali ibn el Hussein plays an even more central role within Lawrence's psychic economy. It would be difficult to find a human "mirror" in which one could more jubilantly misrecognize oneself than this character, who is so extravagantly heroic as to be completely mythic. Ali, the narrator maintains, is so strong that he can rise from a kneeling position with a man standing on each of his open palms, outstrip a trotting camel for a mile and a half in his bare feet, and leap into the saddle from a running position (397). Lawrence also pays lavish tribute to that figure's physical beauty, noting on one occasion the whiteness of Ali's feet "flash[ing]" in striptease "beneath the tossed folds of his cashmere robes" (424), and on another the "irresistibility" of his face and body:

> The mixed natures in him made of his face and body powerful pleadings, carnal, perhaps, except in so far as they were transfused by character. No one could see him without the desire to see him again; especially when he smiled, as he did rarely, with both mouth and eyes at once. His beauty was a conscious weapon. He dressed spotlessly, all in black or all in white; and he studied gesture. (446)

Needless to say, the immaculate white of Lawrence's own Arab "uniform" is more than a little evocative of this seductive image. Lawrence also has repeated recourse to beauty as a "conscious weapon," often lavishing more verbal attention upon his own clothing and that of his entourage as they ride to battle than upon their arms and artillery. Similarly, he begins his account of his bodyguards' "professionalism" by commenting upon their habiliments, as if therein lies their ferocity ("they dressed like a bed of tulips, in every color but white; for that was my constant wear, and they did not wish to seem to presume" [475]). And lest we overlook these sartorial coincidences, Lawrence later describes a scene where he and Ali literally exchange clothing with each other.

The scene to which I refer, where Lawrence says farewell to Ali, represents perhaps the most complete erotic transaction in *Seven Pillars*, and one where sexuality is almost entirely subsumed within identification. Facing each other for the last time, Ali and Lawrence divide and exchange their clothing. In so doing, each opens himself psychically to the image of the Other:

> He and I took affectionate leave of one another. Ali gave me half his wardrobe: shirts, headcloths, belts, tunics. I gave him an equivalent half of mine, and we kissed like David and Jonathan, each wearing the other's clothes. (458)[81]

The most remarkable feature of this brief passage is its dramatization of a racial transversality. Each man is simultaneously the "sensitized film" about which Lawrence speaks elsewhere, and the point of origin for what the Other becomes; Lawrence thus has "brownness" projected onto him, and Ali "whiteness." Because *Seven Pillars* situates the farewell scene outside the power dynamics that govern most of its other imaginary transactions, while nonetheless articulating a reciprocal identification, that scene indicates the revolutionary potential implicit within Lawrence's homosexuality—a potential which is not fully realized until *The Mint*.

Physical magnificence does not constitute Lawrence's only point of attraction to Ali. A closely adjacent passage makes it possible to draw an even more detailed likeness between Lawrence and Ali, and one which—startlingly—turns precisely upon that tension between the body and the ideal that I noted in Chapter 1:

> Yet, despite this richness, there was a constant depression with him, the unknown longing of simple, restless people for abstract thought. . . . His bodily strength grew day by day, and hatefully fleshed over this humble something which he wanted more. His wild mirth was only one sign of the vain wearing-out of his desire. These besetting strangers underlined his detachment, his unwilling detachment, from his fellows. (447)

In this passage, as throughout *Seven Pillars*, "abstract thought" constitutes a signifier for "leadership." The leader is he who stands aside not only from his own corporeality, but from material gain; unlike his men, he disdains to participate in looting. He relentlessly pursues the "idea" of Arab unification, and his absorption in this political dream makes him auratic, places a distance between himself and his followers. Over the course of *Seven Pillars*, Lawrence can be seen to approximate ever more fully to this subjective paradigm, until he can speak of riding in battle "disbodied, unconscious of flesh or feeling," and of regarding the body when it does obtrude with "hostility," and a "contemptuous sense that [it] reach[es its] highest purpose, not as [a vehicle] of the spirit, but when, dissolved, [its] elements served to manure a field" (477). Simultaneous with this aspiration to weightlessness is an identification with the position of the leader, and a tendency to place himself apart from those he regards as his "followers." The bodyguards with whom he surrounds himself late in the Arab Revolt are clearly intended more to isolate than to protect him. The money he showers on his Arab companions carries much the same distancing value.

It might be useful to pause at this juncture to consider the place of ideality within group formations and the psychic economy of leadership. In *Group Psychology and the Analysis of the Ego*, Freud explains that to be a member of a group is to identify with the other members at the level of the ego, and to put the leader in the place of the ego-ideal.[82] As Borch-Jacobsen points out in his reading of that text, to erect the leader as an ego-ideal means to situate him or her "in that identificatory place where the ego would like to be, *but where it cannot or must not be itself*"—to identify with a model "with which one does not identify completely . . . but from a distance" (213). It means, in short, always to be "elsewhere" in relation both to leadership and ideality.

But what about the leader who enjoys this privileged status? Through what images is his or her *moi* constituted, and what is the relation of that psychic entity to the ego-ideal? Although neither Freud nor Borch-Jacobsen has much to say on this topic, it would seem evidently the case that any subject whose image was incorporated as ego-ideal by a mass of other subjects would be unusually susceptible to an identification with ideality. Such a figure, in other words, might well come to believe him or herself in possession of many of the qualities normally represented by that compound entity which Freud at times designates the super-ego and at other times the ego-ideal, usurping the former's supervisory functions, and the latter's status as model. As Lawrence himself observes at one point, "The mounting together of the devoted hopes of years from near-sighted multitudes, might endow even an unwilling idol with Godhead, and strengthen It whenever men prayed silently to Him" (566).

It is extremely unlikely that the British advisor to the Arab Revolt in fact functioned as that movement's leader, but the Lawrence of *Seven Pillars* clearly arrogates that status to himself. He maintains that the members of his bodyguard "yield" to him "the last service and degree of their flesh and blood," and that they feel disgraced if they "[fall] short of the call." Lawrence glosses this last signifier as "love for a cause—or for a *person*" (475–76; my emphasis), and the slippage between these definitions is more than a little instructive. At another point, the narrator of *Seven Pillars* speaks of its being "a theft of souls to make others die in sincerity for *my graven image*" (567; my emphasis). The phrase "graven image" ostensibly refers to Arab nationalism, but when prefaced by the pronoun "my," it much more forcefully evokes Lawrence himself. In another passage from the same chapter, he first claims to be alone in understanding and serving "the abstract," and then confides to a life-long preoccupation with "self-expression." The two are apparently synonymous for the narrator of *Seven Pillars*:

> Our crowd seeking light in things were like pathetic dogs snuffling round the shank of a lamp-post. It was only myself who *valeted* the abstract, whose duty took him *beyond the shrine* [my emphasis].[83]

> . . . I had had one craving all my life—for the power of self-expression in some imaginative form—but had been too diffuse ever to acquire a technique. At last accident, with perverted humor, in casting me as a man of action had given me place in the Arab Revolt, a theme ready and epic to a direct eye and hand, thus offering me an outlet in literature, the technique-less art. (565)

This passage suggests that Lawrence "sees" Arab nationalism in his own image, or to be more precise, in the image of one side of his fractured or double self. If the narrator of *Seven Pillars* is alone able to go beyond the "shrine" of that ideal, that is because he houses it within, not at the site of the unapproachable ego-ideal, but rather within the ego itself.

5. Reflexive Masochism

Surprisingly, Lawrence identifies not only with the indigenous leaders of the Arab Revolt, but with certain figures who are hyperbolically marked as its "followers," most notably Daud and Farraj, and the members of his own bodyguard. These identifications conform to a masochistic logic, suggesting that for Lawrence the follower is in effect a servant or slave. In his psychic capacity as a member rather than as the leader of the Arab Army, then, Lawrence would seem to occupy the position of the child who is punished/loved by the father.

Daud and Farraj enter the narrative at the moment when the first of them goes to Lawrence's tent to request that the other, his intimate friend, be spared the beating to which he has been sentenced. However, rather than mitigating the punishment, Lawrence offers Daud the possibility of sharing it. Daud, we are told, "[leaps] at the chance," and he and Farraj are so severely beaten that they cannot ride the next day. Lawrence describes the friendship between these two characters as "an instance of the eastern boy and boy affection which the segregation of women [makes] inevitable," often leading to "manly loves of a depth and force beyond our flesh-steeped concept" (244), a description which echoes the libidinally saturated account of homosexuality offered in Chapter 1 of *Seven Pillars*. Although Lawrence subsequently employs Daud and Farraj as servants, and is hence positioned as their master, their masochism and homosexuality clearly reverberate within him. Indeed, the two occasions on which they are whipped anticipate in a very precise way the famous Deraa episode.

A later passage, which is also informed by masochism, situates Lawrence in an identificatory relation with his bodyguard. That passage begins by positing the former as the model to be imitated by the latter, but eventually shows the model itself to be a copy. In Chapter 83, Lawrence claims that the members of his hand-picked entourage mimic not only his "flamboyance" and "professionalism," but his love of pain. All but one of these adolescents, the narrator of *Seven Pillars* maintains, "[seem] to sanctify their risk, to be fascinated by their suffering"; they have "a gladness of abasement, a freedom of consent to yield to their master the last service and degree of their flesh" (475). Yet a few paragraphs later, the paradigm has been inverted. It is no longer Lawrence's followers who are copying him, but he who struggles to equal them. "With quaint justice," he observes, "events forced me to live up to my bodyguard, to become as hard, as sudden, as heedless" (476).

If Lawrence's identification with the position of follower is permeated by a masochistic "thematics," how are we to characterize his identification with leadership? I have already commented upon his identificatory relation to Ali, but I have waited until now to indicate precisely what it means for him to take the latter's image within himself. The scene in which Ali makes his first appearance provides as explicit an evocation of erotic punishment as the first chapter of *Seven Pillars*. It also points forward to the flagellation of Daud and Farraj, and—beyond that—to Deraa. Stopping for water at a well near the bank of the Masturah, where Lawrence and his guide are already resting, Ali and his cousin pretend, for purposes of safety, to be a master and servant from Mecca. When the cousin delays in watering the camels, Ali beats him sharply on the head and shoulders with a riding stick.

Because the little drama which is played out along the edge of the Masturah so obviously functions as a staging of Lawrence's unconscious fantasmatic, it dramatically exposes the libidinal basis of his subsequent identification with Ali. Since Ali there functions not as victim, but as victimizer, it also shows that identification to rest upon sadism. Whereas Lawrence's psychic alignment with Daud and Farraj implies a masochistic positionality at the level of his unconscious desire, then, his psychic alignment with leadership—and, by implication, with the ideal of Arab nationalism—would seem to imply its opposite. Lawrence apparently occupies not only the site of the one who is whipped, but that of the one who whips within the beating fantasy. How are we to account for this curious state of affairs?

The principle of instinctual reversibility set forth in "Instincts and their Vicissitudes"[84] might seem to offer the best psychoanalytic explanation of this psychic duality, but *Seven Pillars* obliges us to imagine Lawrence occupying the sadistic and masochistic positions *simultaneously* rather than *in turn*. Lawrence's sadism is, moreover, primarily directed against himself. Finally, the masochism which *Seven Pillars* showcases does not place its sufferer in a passive position *vis-à-vis* anyone else. Indeed, an important passage from Chapter 81 shows Lawrence actually *dominating* his companions simply by virtue of his greater capacity for enduring pain:

> This night-journey was hard on both men and animals . . . by night everything was blinded, and the march racked with shocks. I had a heavy bout of fever on me, which made me angry, so that I paid no attention to Rahail's appeals for rest. That young man had maddened all of us for months by his abundant vigor, and by laughing at our weaknesses; so this time I was determined to ride him out, showing no mercy. Before dawn he was blubbering with self-pity. . . . (460)

Another concept from the same essay would seem better calculated to explain Lawrence's libidinal economy. Freud speaks briefly in "Instincts and their Vicissitudes" about "reflexive masochism," a pathology which operates independently of an external object, and which is situated between sadism and masochism "proper":

> In the case of the pair of opposites sadism-masochism, the process may be represented as follows:
>
> (a) Sadism consists in the exercise of violence or power upon some other person as object.
>
> (b) This object is given up and replaced by the subject's self. With the turning round upon the self the change from an active to a passive aim is also effected.
>
> (c) An extraneous person, is once more sought as object; this person . . . has to take over the role of the subject.
>
> Case (c) is what is commonly termed masochism . . . That it is not superfluous to assume the existence of stage (b) is to be seen from the behavior of the sadistic instinct in obsessional neurosis. There is a turning round upon the subject's self *without* an attitude of passivity towards another person . . . The desire to torture has turned into self-torture and self-punishment, not into masochism [as it is generally understood]. The active voice is changed, not into the passive, but into the reflexive, middle voice. (127–28)

The crucial point here, and the one which connects this passage to *Seven Pillars*, is that the reflexive masochist suffers/enjoys pain without renouncing activity. The reflexive masochist might indeed as appropriately be designated a "reflexive sadist," for he or she incorporates both functions. A closely adjacent passage from "Instincts and their Vicissitudes," in which Freud describes the masochist as someone who not only derives gratification from his or her suffering, but "shares in the enjoyment" of the "assault" (127), would consequently seem primarily relevant to reflexive masochism. Like the woman of whom Freud speaks in "Hysterical Phantasies and their Relation to Bisexuality," who, under the influence of an unconscious fantasy, "pressed her dress up against her body with one hand . . . while she tried to tear it off with the other,"[85] the reflexive masochist occupies at the same time both an active and a passive position.

Although reflexive masochism also involves a "turning back" of sadism against the self, it must be distinguished from that form of masochism which Freud characterizes as "moral" in "The Economic Problem of Masochism." In the latter, as we recall, the ego has become masochistic under the rigors of the super-ego's discipline, while sadism remains the prerogative of the super-ego.[86] I say "prerogative" because the super-ego in its imaginary guise—i.e. in its guise as ego-ideal—represents that which the ego aspires to be but can never become, the super-ego in its symbolic guise working always to maintain the gap between the two. However, in my view, the super-ego stands to one side of reflexive masochism, although it may further complicate the psychic picture. As the passage from "Instincts and their Vicissitudes" indicates, reflexive masochism not only maps out two very different desiring positions at the level of the unconscious, but fosters the production of two contrary images of self—the image of the one who pleasurably inflicts pain on behalf of the exalted standard which it purports to be, and that of the one who pleasurably suffers that pain. Consequently, within that libidinal economy the ego itself assumes the partial status of a tyrannical ideal.

Lawrence comments more than once upon his divided desires, and his conflicted *moi*. At one point he describes himself as "a standing court martial on myself" (583), and at another he complains of not liking "the 'myself' I could see and hear" (584). But whereas these observations might be subsumed within moral masochism, Chapter 81 articulates Lawrence's self-division in terms which connect directly with the present discussion. That chapter describes a particularly grueling camel ride, during which the narrator of *Seven Pillars* breaks into "parts":

> There was one [part of my self] which went on riding wisely, sparing or helping every pace of the wearied camel. Another hovering above and to the right bent down curiously, and asked what the flesh was doing. The flesh gave no answer, for, indeed, it was conscious only

of a ruling impulse to keep on and on; but a third garrulous one talked and wondered, critical of the body's self-inflicted labor, and contemptuous of the reason for effort. (461)

This passage clearly indicates that Lawrence's ego has appropriated the functions and values of the super-ego, without at the same time completely eliminating that agency. The super-ego manifests itself in the guise of the curious questioner; it is recognizable not only through its apparent spatial elevation, its position "above" the ego, but through its characteristic preoccupation with the "flesh." However, it seems unusually benign; it demonstrates none of the usual imperiousness or cruelty. At the same time, the "flesh," which is the persona through which Lawrence's masochistic *moi* invariably presents itself, attests to a harsh governance—to the "ruling impulse to keep on and on." The super-ego has apparently been relieved of its duties by another psychic faculty—by the garrulous voice, which manages to compound the suffering of the masochistic ego by voicing criticism and contempt. Here is the sadistic ego, which speaks on behalf of unconscious desire.

Elsewhere, Lawrence complains of his "*eagerness* to overhear and oversee myself," actions which he describes as "my assault upon my own inviolate citadel" (580). Freud repeatedly associates the functions of overhearing and overseeing the ego with the super-ego. However, the sentence as a whole is marked by an intense reflexivity which cannot be explained through simple reference to the ego/super-ego relationship. The fact that the same possessive pronoun, "my," is used to designate both the agency which performs the assault, and that which suffers it—a coincidence which is underscored by the repetition of the signifier "own"—suggests that aggression has been launched from within rather than from without the ego. Lawrence's "eagerness" to overhear and oversee himself also indicates that he is speaking here not about the super-ego's practiced invigilation, but about the disciplinary efforts of a psychic agency which seeks to replicate or assimilate the super-ego. "Eagerness," after all, implies an impatient anticipation of a condition which has not yet been fully realized.[87]

Because reflexive masochism does not demand the renunciation of activity, it is ideally suited for negotiating the contradictions inherent in masculinity. The male subject can indulge his appetite for pain without at the same time calling into question either his virility, or his paternal lineage. Indeed, since reflexive masochism manages without "real" others, it promotes the illusion of a contained and autonomous self. (Significantly, Lawrence at one point remarks that his "craving for solitude seem[s] part of the delusion of self-sufficiency" [161].)

Judging by the authorial subjectivity articulated in *Seven Pillars*, feminine and reflexive masochism would seem to share the same structuring fantasy. The flagellation scenario which plays such a pivotal part in Lawrence's reflexive masochism also represents the most classic erotic tableau of the feminine masochist, as exemplified not only by the case histories in "'A Child Is Being Beaten,'" but by the novels of Sacher-Masoch. However, these two forms of masochism could not be more antithetical. Whereas the reflexive masochist sustains a dual identificatory relation to the beating fantasy, whether it remains purely ideational or is literally played out, the feminine masochist manifests a single-minded determination to inhabit the passive role. Indeed, *Seven Pillars* suggests that reflexive masochism, in its maintenance of the active, masculine position, can best be seen as a defense against the castrating consequences of feminine masochism. As a number of important passages suggest, it is compatible with—indeed, perhaps a prerequisite for—extreme virility.

In one such erotically charged passage, in which ice mixes with blood to produce tropical fruit, Lawrence describes using his bare hands and feet to carve out a "beautiful little road" for his camel out of a snowbank: "The snow was so frozen on the surface that it took all my weight, first to break it down, and then to scoop it out. The crust was sharp, and cut my wrists and ankles till they bled freely, and the roadside became lined with pink crystals, looking like pale, very pale, water-melon flesh" (509). Elsewhere in *Seven Pillars*, he writes of walking across a plain onto which artillery shells are falling, with "harsh stalks of wormwood stabbing into [his] wounded"—and deliberately bare—feet (487). In Chapter 53 he describes his skin being torn away in "ragged sheets" by the burning rocks onto which he and his Arab colleagues fling themselves while shooting their rifles (308).

However, the reader must turn to Chapter 100 to find a *theoretical* account of the apparent paradox whereby a man can be virilized, and even constituted as the leader of a group, through what is ostensibly self-sacrifice, a juxtaposition which is unthinkable within feminine masochism.[88] There we learn that there is "nothing loftier than a cross, from which to contemplate the world," and that to place oneself in the position of winning "redemption, perhaps for all a race" by assuming "another's pain or experience"—i.e. by multiplying and deepening one's own suffering—is always to aggrandize the self. Such martyrdom effects a primarily personal "triumph," and produces in the ostensible sufferer a "mood of enlargement." Finally, Lawrence points out that such a subjective expansion always occurs at the expense of everyone else in the group; that the one who heaps the greatest pain upon himself diminishes those around him. To demonstrate true generosity of spirit would be to leave this privilege to someone else:

To each opportunity there could be only one vicar, and the snatching of it robbed the fellows of their due *hurt*. The vicar rejoiced, while his brethren were wounded in their manhood . . . His purer part, for the mediator, might have been to stand among the crowd, to watch another win the cleanness of a redeemer's name. By the one road lay self-perfection, by the other self-immolation, and a making perfect of the neighbor. Hauptmann told us to take as generously as we gave: but rather we seemed like the cells of a bee-comb, of which one might change, or swell itself, only at the cost of all. (568; my emphasis)

This passage establishes perhaps more forcefully than any other that the masochism which Lawrence exhibits throughout most of *Seven Pillars* exists in a binary relation to feminine masochism. Far from functioning as a form of phallic divestiture, it operates at the behest of a terrifying psychic imperialism, one which is as troubling in its own way as the French and British colonization of the Middle East, against which the historical Lawrence struggled.

6. Deraa

I have attempted to demonstrate that throughout most of *Seven Pillars* Lawrence is psychically positioned as a reflexive masochist— that he himself represents the agency whereby he pleasurably suffers, and that he performs this function not at the level of the super-ego, but at that of a fractured ego. I have also tried to show that reflexive masochism poses no threat to masculinity, and that it may even represent a necessary component of virility. At least in Lawrence's case, it promotes as well a powerful identification with leadership. However, I have not yet looked closely at Chapter 80, the most famous passage in *Seven Pillars*, and the one in which Lawrence's masochism is startlingly reconfigured. I refer, of course, to the passage in which he is abducted, beaten, and (apparently) raped.

Here is the story of that infamous night as it is recounted in *Seven Pillars*: In residence at Azrak, Lawrence decides to go on a spying mission to the nearby town of Deraa accompanied by an "insignificant" old peasant. Inside the town, he is arrested by a Turkish sergeant, and taken to a military compound, where he is stripped of his belt and knife, and made to wash "carefully." He is then led to the bedroom of the Turkish Bey, who awaits him in bed. The Bey admires Lawrence's "whiteness" and "freshness," and makes sexual overtures to him. When Lawrence resists, the Bey summons some sentries, who tear off his clothing, and "pinion" him while their commanding officer "paws" him "over." At a certain point, Lawrence kicks the Bey in the groin. In retaliation, the latter beats him with a slipper, bites him in the neck, and sticks a bayonet through the skin covering his ribs. After Lawrence declines a second sexual invitation, the Bey orders that he be punished. He is taken to another room and stretched over a guardbench, with two men kneeling on his ankles, and two more holding his wrists. Taking turns, the soldiers "unspeakably" play with and severely beat him. Afterwards, they return him to the Bey, but the latter is no longer interested. Lawrence is subsequently dragged to another building, where his wounds are washed and dressed. After the soldiers leave him, he finds a "suit of shoddy clothes," and makes his escape.

It is impossible to know how much of this story has its basis in history,[89] but in a way that is irrelevant. Fantasy has clearly intervened forcefully here, giving the "memory" of what happened a different psychic effectivity than the event itself could have had. Stewart has already noted some of the "impossibilities" of the story as it appears in *Seven Pillars*. He points out how unlikely it would be that a man who had been living in such grim conditions as Lawrence would have appeared "fresh" to the Turkish Bey, himself accustomed to relative luxury, or that the latter, a Circassian, and hence fair-skinned, would have been particularly captivated by the pallor of Lawrence's complexion. It seems even less probable, Stewart continues, that Lawrence, who was lying with his face down, would have been able to see the "white mark like a railway, darkening slowly into crimson" left by each stroke of the whip. However, it is positively inconceivable that Lawrence would have been able to attend to the Circassian riding whip with sufficient leisure to know that its thong was "of supple black hide, rounded, and tapering from the thickness of a thumb at the grip (which was wrapped in silver) down to a hard point finer than a pencil" (241–42). Knightley and Simpson maintain that Hacim Muhittin Bey, the Governor of Deraa during the period in question, "was known in Turkey as an aggressive heterosexual." They also describe him as a "clever and patriotic official," who would never have allowed Lawrence to escape (248).

Stewart has a novel explanation for these lapses in verisimilitude: he maintains that during Lawrence's stay with Ali in Azrak, the two men engaged in sado-masochistic activities which *Seven Pillars* displaces onto Deraa (188–89). By relocating the whipping elsewhere, Stewart manages both to salvage it as an historical event, and to add new excitement to the relationship between Lawrence and Ali. It seems to me preferable to abandon all attempts to establish what "really" happened, and to read Chapter 80 of *Seven Pillars* as another staging of Lawrence's unconscious fantasmatic.

Before doing so, however, I want to stress that I do not mean to minimize the gravity of homosexual rape, nor to understate its emotional consequences. The point I am trying to make is that the Deraa incident so closely replicates certain other crucial scenes in the book, and so explicitly addresses Lawrence's masochism, that it obviously has enormous libidinal significance. It may be largely fabricated, or organized around a factual nucleus, but its importance resides in its status as fantasy. Lawrence may even have been painfully and traumatically raped, and then have reconceived that event as the beating he recounts in *Seven Pillars*. This would not make him complicit with the violence performed upon his body, nor in any way extenuate it.

Nothing points so inexorably to the intervention of fantasy in *Seven Pillars*'s account of Deraa than the extravagant attention it lavishes upon Lawrence's body. It is washed, scrutinized, admired, stripped, molested, beaten, stabbed, and kicked. We thus see the same "demonstrative feature" at work here as in the fantasies recounted by Reik in *Masochism in Sex and Society*.[90] Lawrence's body is also at all points the locus of everyone's attention, most notably that of its owner. Lawrence maintains that at a certain moment during his ordeal he ceases to feel himself a participant and becomes its imaginary spectator (454). Every fantasizing subject is of course both; he or she "sees" him or herself being seen within that tableau which constitutes the *mise-en-scène* of desire. It is thus Lawrence's own mental "eyes" rather than the Bey's physical ones which round "at the half-healed places where the bullets [have] flicked through [his] skin" (452). The same interiorized "look" permits him to "see" the details of the riding whip, and the welts it leaves behind on his back.

It is also extremely significant that the passage describing Lawrence's approach to Deraa should dwell so insistently on the topic of his sufferings, sufferings which at one point veer over into pleasure. He confides that "scarcely one day in Arabia [has] passed without a physical ache to increase the corroding sense of my accessory deceitfulness towards the Arabs, and the legitimate fatigue of responsible command" (450). Lawrence cites his journey along the slippery railroad tracks outside Deraa as a case in point; afflicted with a broken foot which complicates walking under the best of circumstances, his progress is here made torturous by the necessity of spreading out his toes "widely" in order to "[take] hold of the ground" (450). However, the ambiguity of the phrase with which he characterizes his progress—"exquisitely painful"—suggests that it may not be without its compensatory gratification.

Elsewhere in the chapter, Lawrence twice refers to pain as his life's innermost preoccupation. "I [have] strung myself to learn all pain until I [die]," he says at one point, by way of explaining how it is that he is capable of "[snuggling] down, dazed, panting, but vaguely comfortable" after being savagely beaten (454). A few paragraphs later he confesses that "pain of the slightest [has] been my obsession and secret terror, from a boy" (455). "[Have] I now been drugged with it, to bewilderment?.," he wonders. Here, as elsewhere, pain translates into pleasure. When one of the guards kicks Lawrence savagely with a nailed boot in order to rouse him from the floor where he has fallen after his beating, the injured man smiles "idly" in return, overcome by the "delicious warmth, probably sexual," which is "swelling" through him. It is no violation of the terms of the fantasy that the soldier should then strike him at the site of his genitals with "the full length of his whip" (454).

By contextualizing the flagellation scene in this way, Lawrence makes it impossible to avoid seeing the continuity between it and the rest of his psychic life. Not surprisingly, he feels impelled a moment later to acknowledge the dream-like properties of the scene, not the least of which is its uncanny similarity to an event "five years ago" (455). That he tells us nothing more about this earlier event does nothing to diminish the *prévisibilité* of Deraa, which so many earlier passages seem to anticipate.

Thus far I have stressed only those features of the Deraa episode which link it to the many other passages in *Seven Pillars* which are also dominated by a masochistic "thematics." However, Lawrence attributes to that "event" consequences which set it apart from those other passages. He writes that his beating at the hands of the Turkish soldiers results in "a gradual cracking apart of my whole being by some too-great force whose waves rolled up my spine till they were pent within my brain, to clash terribly together" (453), and he later claims that "in Deraa that night the citadel of my integrity [was] irrevocably lost" (456). What is it about Deraa which sets it apart from the scene at the Masturah well where Ali beats his ostensible servant, the stabbing of wormwood into Lawrence's bare feet, or the tearing of flesh from his arms by scorching rocks?

Although "citadel" figures importantly here as a signifier for the "stronghold" which was Lawrence's psyche prior to Deraa, it seems to me that "integrity" represents an even more crucial term. The *OED* glosses that word as "the condition of having no part or element wanting," which provides a startlingly precise definition of reflexive masochism. The reflexive masochist incorporates activity as well as passivity, and represents his own sadistic complement. As I have attempted to indicate through the figure of Lawrence, he is seemingly self-sufficient, and hyperbolically virile. Deraa, however, changes all of this by rupturing Lawrence's identification with ideality. He no longer fills all roles within the beating fantasy, but is confined exclusively to the masochistic one. The sadistic position, moreover, remains irreducibly exterior, as a consequence of which it can no longer be said that Lawrence's masochism involves "a turning round upon the subject's self *without* an attitude of passivity toward another person." Because those who torture Lawrence are Turks rather than Arabs, they stand not only outside the national entity with which the narrator of *Seven Pillars* consistently identifies himself, but in binary opposition to it. The figures occupying the sadistic position in this structuring fantasy are, in other words, *unassimilable*. Lawrence cannot "become" them, and thereby recover a sadistic positionality.

In the Oxford text of *Seven Pillars*, which contains material not included in any printed version, Chapter 80 concludes with the suggestion that Lawrence's experiences at Deraa effectively destroyed one part of his *moi*. "I was feeling very ill," the narrator observes there,

> as though some part of me had gone dead that night in Deraa, leaving me maimed, imperfect, *only half myself* for ever after. It could not have been the defilement, for no one ever held the body in less honor than I did myself. Probably it had been the breaking of the spirit by that frenzied nerve-shattering pain which had degraded me to the beast level when it made me grovel to it, like a dog before its master, and which had journeyed with me since, a fascination and terror and morbid desire, lascivious and vicious, perhaps, but like the striving of a moth towards its flame. [my emphasis][91]

Significantly, the part of Lawrence which is "broken" or "shattered" by Deraa is his "spirit" rather than his masochistic "flesh"—it is that psychic component whose earlier inclusion made him "perfect." What "[goes] dead," in other words, is his ideal or sadistic ego. Lacking the representational resources necessary to stage the fantasmatic as a scene in which the self occupies all places, and stimulated by the pleasure of a purely passive masochism, unconscious desire henceforth concentrates itself at the site marked "pain" and "degradation." Lawrence has been transformed from a reflexive to a feminine masochist.

It is crucial that we understand all of these dramatic changes to turn upon the *desublimation* of Lawrence's *homosexuality*. As we have already seen, identification earlier provides the mechanism of sublimation by situating the erotic object within the ego, and thereby deflecting libido away from a directly sexual aim. Not only does Deraa place the erotic object emphatically outside the ego, but—as Lawrence's emphasis upon his engorged genitals clearly indicates—it permits sexuality to reassert itself.

Chapter 80 also provides a vivid enactment of what it might mean to take one's pleasure "downward," focusing as it obsessively does upon the defilement of Lawrence's body. The ostensibly admiring words which the narrator attributes to the Turkish Bey actually function less to glorify Lawrence's physical beauty than to demarcate the pristine surface which is to be sullied, for by the end of the whipping he is covered not only by blood and lacerations, but by dirt and vomit, and no longer constitutes a possible object of desire:

> [The Turkish soldiers] splashed water in my face, wiped off some of the filth, and lifted me between them retching and sobbing for mercy, to where [the Bey] lay: but he now rejected me in haste, as a thing too torn and bloody for his bed, blaming their excess of zeal which had spoilt me . . . (454)

The desublimation of Lawrence's homosexuality thus results in a radical de-idealization, but one affecting less the object of desire than the ego previously exalted through an identification with mastery.

Not surprisingly, this de-idealization proves inimical to Lawrence's political ambitions, since he can no longer see Arab nationalism in his own image. It is, for instance, *after* the Deraa episode, and as its logical sequel, that Lawrence condemns leadership as a swelling of the individual "at the cost" of all others. In another subsequent passage, he complains about being "tired to death of free-will" (514), and wishes for a chief who would exercise relentless control over him, and to whom he could be a slave (582). Allenby, he adds, "[comes] nearest to my longings for a master, but I [have] to avoid him, not daring to bow down for fear lest he show feet of clay with that friendly word which must shatter my allegiance" (582).

Of course, in emphasizing passages after Deraa which eroticize servitude to an external agency, I do not mean to locate that scene as a historically locatable moment at which Lawrence's subjectivity abruptly changes. Fantasy does not "happen" in this way, once and for all; it is rather a matter of a gradual reworking of memories into a pattern which is either consistent with, or transformative of, existing desire. Nor does *Seven Pillars* itself regularly sustain the fiction that after whatever happens at Deraa, Lawrence's "will" is forever "gone" (514). It is only later, after all, that he surrounds himself with a bodyguard, that he participates in the massacre of Turks in the village of Tafas, and that he helps the Arabs put together their own government in Damascus. Indeed, Lawrence's identification with leadership often seems most secure in the last book of *Seven Pillars*. However, the consequences of Deraa can be traced not only in certain key passages from that work, but in his subsequent biography, his later letters, and *The Mint,* all of which enact a dramatic repudiation of power.

7. "One of Them"

Whenever the dream of leadership falters in Lawrence's writings, as it does decisively in the early twenties and thereafter, something radically different takes its place, something for which the Deraa incident provides the fantasmatic underpinnings. In a 1925 letter, Lawrence characterizes his longing to be in the R.A.F. as "a homesickness which attacks me at the most casual sight of [the names of the airmen] in the papers, or their uniform in the street."[92] Although he was at this point barred from entering the ranks of the R.A.F., he might have served either as an officer or an official historian of that branch of the military. However, Lawrence declined both offers lest he debar himself from becoming, as he puts it, "one of them," i.e. one of the ordinary airmen.

This curious ambition to become an undistinguished member of a collectivity, which inverts the phrase with which Marlow incorporates Jim into the class of English gentlemen in Conrad's *Lord Jim*—"one of us"—represents the very antithesis of the aspiration to lead. It attests to Lawrence's determination "not to be [individually] big anymore," but rather to "belong to a big thing, which will exist for ever and ever in unnumbered generations of standard airmen, like ourselves."[93] As Keith N. Hull remarks, the Lawrence of *The Mint* and many of the post 1922 letters seeks a "corporate" or group identity.[94]

"One of them" also effects a reversal of the Conrad phrase at the level of class. Whereas Marlow's "us" indicates the site of privilege, Lawrence's "them" refers instead to those excluded from privilege—to the working class. It designates in addition the desire implicit in the first half of the double mimesis: the desire to imitate to the point of actually becoming the racial or class Other. Here, however, there is no colonizing sequel, no "I" to triumph over the "we." In a 1929 missive to Ernest Thurtle, Lawrence implores his correspondent: "Please don't get the public feeling that I'm different from the crowd. By experience in many camps I've assured myself (so certainly that all the print in the world won't shake my conviction) that I'm a very normal sort of Anglo-Irishman."[95] And in a 1934 communication with Lincoln Kirstein, he explicitly indicates that his aspiration to be "average" implies as well a rejection of his inherited class status:

> Your letter of last December has been troubling me, for you made it hard to answer, and yet I have to answer it. See now, there are . . .

no men very different from ourselves. I walk the streets of an evening, or work in the R.A.F. camps all day, and by measuring myself against the airmen or passers-by I know that I am just an average chap. You write as though there were degrees, or distinctions. I see likenesses, instead.[96]

However, it is to *The Mint* that the reader must turn in order to grasp the full political import of the words "one of them"—the challenge they pose both to a virile masculinity, and to all ideologies predicated upon the priority and autonomy of the individual:

Service life . . . teaches a man to live largely on little . . . As we gain attachment, so we strip ourselves of personality. (248)

This learning to be sterile, to bring forth nothing of our own, has been the greater half of our training and the more painful half . . . Fellows want to forestall orders out of self-respect. Self-respect is one of the things troops have to jettison, as a tacit rebelliousness of spirit, a subjective standard. We must have no standard of our own. (190)

As Lawrence makes clear elsewhere in *The Mint*, the R.A.F. not only erases social and economic distinction ("of class-difference there isn't a suspicion" [90]), but it virtually abolishes private property ("none of us has any property we love" [158]). It also requires its members to live without privacy—to sleep in barracks, and use doorless toilets. All of this works, in Lawrence's view, to diminish the *moi*, and thereby to prevent that psychic swelling which occurs only at the expense of others.

These are familiar utopian stipulations, but Lawrence's beloved R.A.F. community is also predicated upon another, less orthodox requirement, and one which connects it intimately to Deraa. This requirement is the *servitude* of each enlisted man to his superior officers. More than once in *The Mint*, Lawrence links the "equality" of the men who sleep together in the barracks to their collective enslavement. Thus in Chapter 21 he confides that "we are bound and equal" (90), and in Chapter 17 he compares himself and his colleagues to "ridden beasts," in a reprise of the metaphor employed at the beginning of *Seven Pillars*. He pushes this logic even further elsewhere in *The Mint*, insisting that the sympathy which links one enlisted man to another is inspired by their "common defenselessness against authority," and that "except under compulsion there is no equality in the world" (32). As in Chapter 80 of *Seven Pillars*, feminine masochism provides the psychic agency whereby Lawrence effects a retreat from a heroic masculinity. It also functions as the libidinal support for an egalitarian social unity, albeit one strictly subordinate to a higher authority.

Given that the military system described by Lawrence eliminates power from one domain only by leaving it apparently unchallenged in another, it seems important to add that the narrator of *The Mint* is quick to protest when he sees authority abused. "If the Powers blunder and ask that a drill be done well, for its own sake: or for a decoration, to smarten our bearing:—why then the body politic festers," he writes at one point, and he goes on to describe approvingly some of the ploys adopted by angry airmen to obstruct work supervised by unjust officers (232–33). More surprisingly, given his willingness to conceive of himself as a slave, prisoner, or beast of burden, Lawrence speaks out angrily against officer sadism:

> While my mouth is yet hot with it I want to record that some of those who day by day exercise their authority upon us, do it in the lust of cruelty. There is a glitter in their faces when we sob for breath; and evident through their clothes is that taughtening of the muscles (and once the actual rise of sexual excitement) which betrays that we are being hurt not for our own good, but to gratify a passion. (124)

As in the Deraa fantasy, this passage closes down all identificatory access to sadism. It also plays havoc with the notion that sadism and masochism always imply each other—that each necessarily represents the other's complement. Finally, it suggests that masochism need not imply quietism with respect to power and its abuses.

Lawrence's shift from reflexive to feminine masochism can also be charted through his changing attitudes toward both the Arab and British Armies in *Seven Pillars*. Early in the book, he frequently celebrates the mobility and flexibility of the guerrilla warfare deployed by the Arabs. In a crucial passage in Chapter 39, he compares it favorably to the massive deployment of troops by the British, arguing that whereas the latter "[plays] down [the ninety-nine] to the level of the weakest man on parade," seeks "to render the unit a unity, the man a type," and deliberately sacrifices "capacity in order to reduce the uncertain element," the former is predicated upon the strengths of each individual soldier. Indeed, Lawrence even goes so far as to argue that the Arab war "should . . . be simple and individual," and that each of its soldiers should be as self-sufficient as the leader ostensibly is. "Our ideal should be to make our battle a series of single combats," Lawrence writes, "our ranks a happy alliance of agile commanders-in-chief" (348).

Late in *Seven Pillars*, however, the British Army becomes the site of an intense libidinal investment, and a sado-masochistic fantasmatization reminiscent of Deraa. Using language which in many ways anticipates Pauline Réage's characterization of Roissy in *Histoire d'O*, Lawrence describes the uniform of the ordinary soldier as a "death's livery" which "[walls] its bearers from ordinary life," and which signals that they have "contracted themselves into a service not the less abject for that its beginning was voluntary." "The soldier," Lawrence adds, "[assigns] his owner the twenty-four hours' use of his body," and "sole conduct of his mind and passions"; his affections "must be hired pieces on the chess-board of the king" (662–63). Also at issue here is that desire, upon which I have already commented, no longer to stand "apart," as individual or leader, but rather to be submerged in the group. In the same passage, Lawrence writes that the ordinary British soldiers "[cling] two and two, in a celibate friendliness which express[es] the level of the ranks: the commonness of their Army clothes. 'Holding together,' they called it . . . "

8. The Politics of Identification

In this chapter, I have attempted to demonstrate that symbolic and imaginary identification have concrete political consequences—that although at the most profound level we are all both "nothing" and "nowhere,"[97] the specific positions from which we live our desire have important extra-psychic ramifications, as do the images through which we acquire our fictive selves. I have also tried to show that the *moi* is not the simple product of the gaze passing through the screen, but that it is also determined in part by the fantasmatic.[98] A subject's imaginary identifications are coerced to a significant degree, in other words, by the position which that subject occupies within the *mise-en-scène* of desire. Conversely, since imaginary identification always carries meanings in excess of its fantasmatic use value, it is in turn capable of transforming the ideological import of unconscious desire, or even of pushing the latter in new directions.

Seven Pillars provides a vivid dramatization not only of the political implications of fantasy and the *moi*, but of their mutual determination. Lawrence's imaginary alignment with a series of Arab figures is facilitated not only by the intimacy of his working relationship with them, with its implicitly colonial logic, but by the fact that each of those figures is at some point displayed for him within a literal or metaphoric tableau which conforms to his fantasmatic. Feisal, Ali, Daud, Farraj, and the members of Lawrence's bodyguard are all shown to occupy either the position of the victim or that of the victimizer within a scene which is in some way assimilable to the homosexual and masochistic fantasy anatomized by Freud in "'A Child Is Being Beaten.'"

Lawrence's assumption of "Arabness," however, implies more than "homosexuality" or "masochism"; it also includes a preference for desert landscapes, transportation by camel, asceticism, white flowing robes, and golden daggers. Much more importantly, it prompts him to dynamite Turkish trains, and to subvert France's—and at times, Britain's—colonial designs. Because of Lawrence's imaginary alignment with a group of Bedouin men, the Arab Revolt supplants the British war effort as the primary site for the staging of his unconscious desire, and so leads him to struggle passionately over a period of six years on behalf of Arab self-determination.

Finally, Lawrence's incorporation of "Arabness" helps to reconfigure his fantasmatic during the psychic working-over of history that he calls "Deraa." As we have seen, the sadistic position within that fateful articulation of the beating fantasy is occupied by the Turkish Bey and his soldiers, rather than by Arabs, which renders it enemy territory. Because of the intensity of Lawrence's Arab identification, he cannot occupy the same symbolic space as his Turkish tormentors, nor see himself in their image. The sadistic position is consequently foreclosed to him, and—with it—the role of leader.

Lawrence's identification with the collectivity of R.A.F. airmen has political reverberations which are as profound, if not as globally dramatic, as his earlier incorporation of "Arabness." It isolates him psychically from the privileges and values which would otherwise be his by virtue of his class and achievements, and integrates him into a group structure. It also motivates him to lobby on behalf of substantial changes in the rules governing the R.A.F. rank and file.[99]

Because they articulate identity and desire so insistently in relation to history, race, class, nationality, and power, *Seven Pillars* and *The Mint* make unusually evident the dangers of effecting a theoretical cleavage between the "public" and the "private." Although the next chapter will ostensibly be more concerned with the second than with the first of those categories, it, too, will pursue the social implications of the psychic structures it addresses. However, Chapter 8 will focus more on sexual than on racial, class, or national politics. It will consequently mark a return to a number of the more explicitly feminist issues addressed earlier in this book.

8

A Woman's Soul Enclosed in a Man's Body: Femininity in Male Homosexuality

> There are some who, should we intrude upon them in the morning, still in bed, will present to our gaze an admirable female head, so generalized and typical of the entire sex is the expression of the face; the hair itself affirms it, so feminine is its ripple; unbrushed, it falls so naturally in long curls over the cheek that one marvels how the young woman, the girl, the Galatea barely awakened to life in the unconscious mass of this male body in which she is imprisoned has contrived so ingeniously, by herself, without instruction from anyone else, to take advantage of the narrowest apertures in her prison wall to find what was necessary to her existence.[1]

Although the audacity of my epigraph might suggest otherwise, I have hesitated for a long time before beginning this chapter. The question which provokes it is of crucial importance to the analysis of sexual difference, yet it seems politically impossible to ask at this moment in the history of representation—impossible not only because I am both heterosexual and a woman, but because the question itself appears to solicit a cultural stereotype which many homosexual men have struggled to put behind them. My query, which I dare to pose only because a few gay writers have recently begun to do so, is this: What is the place of femininity within male homosexuality?

Despite the familiarity of the question, I will not be looking for conventional answers. Indeed, in this chapter I will be attempting to break with a number of orthodoxies. It is frequently assumed, not only within dominant representation, but within certain kinds of psychoanalytic discourse, that there are only two possible subject-positions—that occupied on the one hand by heterosexual men and homosexual women, and that occupied on the other by heterosexual women and homosexual men. Not only does this formulation afford a preposterously monolithic reading of male homosexuality,[2] but it depends upon a radically insufficient theory of subjectivity. The pages that follow will work to complicate certain accepted formulations both of homosexuality and of sexual difference, and in so doing to effect a theoretical expansion of the erotic and identificatory possibilities open to gay men.

My search for femininity within male homosexuality will lead me to texts by Félix Guattari, D.A. Miller, Leo Bersani, and Daniel Schreber. However, it will take me as well to some seemingly less likely or even *discreditable* theorists of same-sex desire—to Freud and Proust, whose accounts of homosexuality are far more complex and interesting than may at first appear. Under the pressure of a feminist reading, a group of Freudian texts will be induced to yield three different homosexual variants, all of which accommodate femininity in some guise. I will then attempt to demonstrate that the third of these erotic paradigms subtends *A la recherche du temps perdu*. As we will see, the homosexuality which structures authorial subjectivity within that text defines itself so insistently in relation to femininity that it finds most palpable expression within a scene of lesbian love-making.

1.   Two Kinds of Drag

The title of this chapter derives from the writings of Karl Heinrich Ulrichs, a German lawyer and sexologist, who wrote numerous books and pamphlets between 1862 and 1895 defending and explaining same-sex desire. For Ulrichs, the man-loving man is "*anima muliebris in corpore virili inclusa*"—a female soul enclosed in a male body.[3] In the first volume of *The History of Sexuality*, Foucault argues that it was precisely with this model of "interior androgyny" or "hermaphroditism of the soul" that, in the ninteenth century, the male homosexual became a species, acquiring "a type of life" and a "morphology." Before the advent of nineteenth-century psychiatry, psychology, medicine, and jurisprudence, he insists, engaging in man-to-man sodomy did not imply having a distinct identity.[4] However, in Volume 2 of *The History of Sexuality*, Foucault acknowledges that the association of masculine sexual receptivity with femininity can be traced all the way back to Plato:

> In nineteenth-century texts there is a stereotypical portrait of the homosexual or invert: not only his mannerisms, his bearing, the way he gets dolled up, his coquetry, but also his facial expressions, his anatomy, the feminine morphology of his whole body, are regularly included in this disparaging description . . . Now this image, with the repulsive aura that surrounds it, has come down through the centuries. It was already clearly delineated in the Greco-Roman literature of the imperial age . . . But in its essential traits, the portrait is more ancient still. Socrates' first speech in the *Phaedrus* alludes to it, when he voices disapproval of the love that is given to

soft boys, too delicate to be exposed to the sun as they are growing up, and all made up with rouge and decked out in ornaments.[5]

David Halperin also maintains that ancient Mediterranean cultures "tended to construe sexual desire as normative or deviant according to whether it impelled social actors to conform to or to violate their conventionally defined gender roles."[6] Classical Greece, he argues later in the same text, organized sexuality around phallic penetration, which provided the erotic correlative of social superiority. The practitioners of this ideal sexuality were adult free men. Women and boys, on the other hand, are repeatedly cited in Greek sources as penile receptacles, and hence as "hetero" or other (34f.). Like the sexual "activity" of Greek citizens, the sexual "passivity" of women and boys carried an unambiguous social significance:

> Not only is sex in classical Athens not intrinsically relational or collaborative in character . . . it effectively divides, classifies, and distributes its participants into distinct and radically opposed categories. Sex possesses this valence, apparently, because it is conceived to center essentially on . . . the penetration of the body of one person by the body—and specifically by the phallus—of another. Sex is not only polarizing, however; it is also hierarchical. For the insertive partner is construed as a sexual agent . . . whereas the receptive partner is construed as a sexual patient, whose submission to phallic penetration expresses sexual "passivity." Sexual "activity," moreover, is thematized as domination: the relation between the "active" and the "passive" sexual partner is thought of as the same kind of relation as that obtaining between social superior and social inferior. (30)

Halperin suggests that the structural affinities between women and boys in classical Greek society encouraged their conceptual alignment. Consequently, any male subject who voluntarily embraced the "passive" sexual position was likely to be characterized precisely as "a woman's soul confined by a man's body" (23). More surprisingly, Halperin also locates a prestigious instance of Greek man-to-man love in which femininity defines the "*active*" position. He persuasively demonstrates that Socrates' account of true love in *The Symposium* relies heavily upon metaphors of female procreativity to describe the role of the man who culturally reproduces himself in the desired youth (146–51).[7]

David F. Greenberg's recent sociological history of homosexuality also suggests that even before Western Europe gave rise to the concept of "the homosexual," a wide range of cultures accounted for at least one aspect of "same-sex" sodomy in terms of gender inversion. He argues that a number of early civilizations, including not only Greece, but Egypt and Rome, as well as many kinship-structured societies, coded the receptive position within that sexual practice as "feminine."[8] And of course Ulrichs's definition of male homosexuality extends well into the twentieth century within many Western societies, not only dictating the precise terms through which Proust describes the inhabitants of Sodom in the passage with which I began this chapter, but fueling a good deal of homophobia within the present North American "scene."

In thus extending the trope of the female soul in a man's body both backward in time and across diverse social boundaries, I in no way mean to essentialize it as a definition of male homosexuality, or to foreclose upon other libidinal paradigms. I have been attempting, rather, to suggest that the notion of inversion is probably as old as the hierarchical binarizing of "man" and "woman," and that human culture has to date shown itself to be stubbornly resistant to conceptualizing sexual positionality—and, more recently, object-choice—apart from the binary logic of gender. Since the category of masculinity has traditionally been a very restrictive one, those defying its conditions generally find themselves relegated to the more accommodating category of femininity.

It is perhaps not very surprising, given the wide currency and naturalization of a feminizing account of male homosexuality, that it also found expression within early homosexual subcultures, just as it has within some of their contemporary counterparts. According to Jeffrey Weeks, a male transvestite subculture appeared as early as the fourteenth century in Italy, and the fifteenth century in France.[9] Greenberg claims that there were also transvestite balls in Lisbon in the seventeenth century, and instances of homosexual transvestism in the eighteenth century in the Dutch Republic (334). Stephen Orgel has recently advanced a similar argument with respect to Renaissance England, proposing that there may have been a homosexual subtext to the theatrical practice of assigning female parts to male actors.[10] And of course frequenters of the "molly houses" which sprang up in London in the eighteenth and nineteenth centuries also mimicked the verbal and behavioral mannerisms of contemporary women, and called each other by female names.[11] When a distinct homosexual subculture finally began to emerge in the United States in the late nineteenth century, it, too, gave a central place to signifiers of femininity.[12]

Although these homosexual self-definitions cannot be read in isolation from the dominant representations which coerced them—and continue to coerce them—it seems to me that we must nevertheless grant them some significant oppositional value. Let us consider for a moment only those subcultural irruptions of femininity which post-date the writings of Ulrichs and his contemporaries. Foucault maintains that the discursive construction of "the homosexual" in the nineteenth century "made possible the formation of a 'reverse' discourse" in that "homosexuality began to speak in its own behalf," albeit "often in the same vocabulary, using the same categories by which it was medically disqualified."[13] In thus borrowing its terms from the dominant discourse, this homosexual representational practice would seem not only to have abrogated all claim to "autonomy" or "authenticity," but to have consorted with the cultural enemy. However, Foucault emphasizes that "there is not, on one side, a discourse of power, and opposite it, another discourse that runs counter to it," but that it is rather "strategy" or "tactical productivity"—or, to state the case somewhat differently, how a discourse is deployed—that makes the crucial difference between dominance and opposition:

> . . . there can exist different and even contradictory discourses within the same strategy; they can, on the contrary, circulate without changing their form from one strategy to another, opposing strategy. We must not expect the discourses on sex to tell us . . . what ideology—dominant or dominated—they represent; rather we must question them on the two levels of their tactical productivity (what reciprocal effects of power and knowledge they ensure) and their strategical integration (what conjunction and what force relationship make their utilization necessary in a given episode of the various confrontations that occur). (101–2)

Foucault argues here for the theoretical priority of the "field of force relations" over the seemingly more immediate question of what might constitute a "correct" or "non-prejudicial" representation of male homosexuality. He also suggests that dominance can sometimes be better contested *within* than *without* the discourses upon which it relies, through the counter-deployment of the terms of the familiar rather than through an attempted production of the "new."[14] This seems to me an important reconceptualization of resistance; I agree with Foucault that there are no authentic sexualities, and that the issue of effectivity should always be given precedence over that of "correctness." However, *The History of Sexuality* cannot by itself adequately account for why so many gay men have subversively aligned themselves with femininity.

Our definition of the field of force relations must be enlarged to the point where it is capable of including something which has no place within the Foucauldian paradigm—to the point where it encompasses not only discursivity, but the human psyche, grasped in its necessary psychoanalytic complexity. In other words, we must be prepared to entertain the possibility that a gay man might deploy signifiers of femininity not only because to do so is to generate a counter-discourse, but because an identification with "woman" constitutes the very basis of his identity, and/or the position from which he desires.

Greenberg offers a glibly voluntarist account of the oppositional value which may come to inhere in femininity, one that fails to attribute any subjective value to its insignia. "To those willing to brave the stigma," he writes in *The Construction of Homosexuality*, "overstepping gender boundaries was a way to express defiance of restrictive conventions, as well as to identify oneself as homosexual to potential partners" (395). The only instances of effeminacy and/or cross-dressing which can be so easily explained are those which exercise no psychic hold—those which cast femininity effortlessly aside once the masquerade is over. In limiting his analysis to these instances, Greenberg safely cordons off the whole question of subjectivity, declining to consider in any way those homosexual men who might be said to "find" themselves or their partners within "the feminine," and, in doing so, to pose a libidinal and identificatory challenge to conventional notions of masculinity.

Greenberg is not the only recent commentator on homosexuality to rule out of order the notion that a gay man might be a "woman" at the level of his unconscious identifications. Mario Mieli suggests in *Homosexuality and Liberation: Elements of a Gay Critique* that it is only from the vantage point of heterosexual masculinity that anal intercourse appears to be a feminization,[15] while other writers have critiqued Ulrichs's definition of the gay man as "a woman's soul enclosed in a man's body" for its heterosexist bias—for its conception of homosexuality as a "misplaced heterosexuality."[16] And C.A. Tripp, a popularizing advocate of homosexuality, who is quoted approvingly both by Dennis Altman and J.E. Rivers, is so phobic about femininity that he actually goes so far as to propose that "transvestism and transsexuality seldom involve either homosexual or effeminate men."[17] Gay men, within his account, only mimic women as a result of a slavish relationship to dominant representation, and they generally do so before rather than after coming out (161).

One gay response to the unpleasure generated by the association of femininity with homosexuality has been to deflect attention away from the issue of homosexual identity to that of sexual selection, where masculinity is at least anatomically secure. As Weeks explains, "increasingly sexual variants have been defined and have defined themselves less as gender deviants and more as variants in terms of object choice."[18] Another, perhaps more significant response has been to shift the symbolic terms of reference. Recent gay representational practice has worked to combat the notion of inversion by fore-grounding the place of *masculinity* within homosexuality. In an essay published in the collective volume *Homosexuality: Power and Politics*, Altman maintains that over the course of the seventies, homosexuality was increasingly "signified by theatrically 'macho' clothing (denim, leather, and the ubiquitous key rings) rather than by feminine style drag."[19] In *The Homosexualization of America*, he suggests that mascu-line self-presentation had become the norm by the beginning of the eighties:

> By the beginning of the eighties a new type of homosexual man had become visible in most large American cities and could also be found, to a somewhat lesser extent, in most other Western urban centers. No longer characterized by an effeminate style, the new homosexual displayed his sexuality by a theatrically masculine ap-pearance: denim, leather, and the ubiquitous key rings dangling from the belt. The long-haired androgynous look of the early seven-ties was now found among straights, and the super-macho image of the Village People disco group seemed to typify the new style per-fectly . . . (1)

Richard Dyer attributes to this hyperbolic masculinity much of the transgressive value that some gay men have identified with cross-dressing and other homosexual incursions into the domain of feminin-ity. In a frequently cited passage, he writes that "by taking the signs of masculinity and eroticising them in a blatantly homosexual context, much mischief is done to the security with which 'men' are defined in society, and by which their power is secured. If that bearded, muscular beer-drinker turns out to be a pansy, how ever are you going to know the 'real' men any more?"[20]

Others, however, find less to celebrate about this new self-definition. Altman laments that the masculine-identified homosexual is "likely to be non-apologetic about his sexuality, self-assertive, highly con-sumerist and not at all revolutionary, though prepared to demonstrate for gay rights," and that he generally has "little contact with women, either gay or straight."[21] And in an important essay in the AIDS issue of *October*, Leo Bersani offers an even more chilling critique. Far from functioning as a subversive parody of traditional masculinity, he argues, the gay macho style works to idealize the very representa-tional standard which oppresses the homosexual man. Moreover, since homosexuality turns upon "same-sex" desire, or what Freud calls "narcissistic object-choice," the gay macho style encourages not only an *erotic investment* in traditional masculinity, but an *identification* with it.[22]

It is by no means clear, anyway, that even the most committed practitioner of macho homosexuality can ever succeed in entirely extirpating the "woman" within. As Lacan remarks in "The Signification of the Phallus," "virile display" always seems feminine.[23] This is less the case because the female subject seeks "refuge" in a "phallic mask," as he suggests, than because exhibitionism is so fully associated with women in our culture. Don Mager echoes Lacan's point in his description of the "Castro Street clone" look, a look which includes such masculine signifiers as leather, denim, work boots and military clothes, but gives them an unwonted emphasis:

> Jeans are worn snugly . . . to emphasize and tease, hiding yet revealing the genital/buns/thigh areas. This is traditional to female clothes usage. Materials may be rugged and weathered, speaking to masculine tradition, but they are worn in rigidly precise, almost tailored ways—thus speaking to feminine traditions of dressing one's self up in clothes as a presentation, as opposed to throwing clothes on oneself as a practical necessity. Need one even comment on the feminine base to ear-piercing and ear rings, even if those rings are worn only in one ear?[24]

Ironically, then, even this hyperbolically masculine uniform serves to "unman" its wearer; as Jamie Gough points out, the latter seems to be masquerading as a man.[25] Yet, worn without the feminine "accent," there is no longer anything to distinguish the clothing of the homosexual man from his heterosexual counterpart. Simon Watney makes the poignant observation that when feminized, the homosexual body faces contempt; yet untheatrically masculinized, it simply disappears.[26]

It is perhaps as much because of this impasse as out of a commitment to gender politics that both Weeks and Altman conclude their essays in *Homosexuality: Power and Politics* with the call for an end to all sexual categories, including that of homosexuality itself.[27] However, it should be evident by now, almost two decades into the history of feminism, that sexual difference, through whose binarisms both homosexuality and heterosexuality are conceptualized, cannot be wished or even written away. It is also becoming increasingly apparent to me that we have barely begun to understand the full complexity of the concept of "femininity," whether we locate that signifier at the site of woman, or at that of the homosexual man. I suspect that a theoretical undertaking in that direction would do much to dissipate the hostility that greets any resurrection of the Ulrichsian formula. Once divested of its global pretensions, the formula might even seem to have a certain epigrammatic force with respect to certain kinds of male homosexuality.

2. Four Variations on the Feminine Man

Apart from the models of homosexuality put forward in Freud's writings, our own century has given rise to at least four implicitly poststructuralist accounts of what Havelock Ellis would call the male "invert"—those articulated recently by Félix Guattari, D.A. Miller, and Leo Bersani, as well as that advanced by a much earlier text, Paul Daniel Schreber's *Memoirs of My Nervous Illness*. Three of these accounts make clear that homosexuality cannot be analyzed in isolation from sexual difference, and that gay studies and psychoanalytic feminism consequently need to be in constant dialogue with each other. The fourth—Guattari's "Becoming a Woman"—posits femininity as a way station along the road leading toward a radical deanthropomorphism. As a group, these four accounts of same-sex desire attest eloquently to the importance of femininity for male homosexuality, whether they define the former as the latter's very *raison d'être*, or as the condition whereby it transcends its aspiration to the phallic norm.

Let us begin with Guattari's text, which, in its refusal of psychoanalysis, serves less as a positive than a negative model for theorizing femininity within male homosexuality.[28] In "Becoming a Woman," Guattari maintains that both because of its secrecy and its perception of itself as a perversion, male homosexuality is still tied to the heterosexual norm.[29] He acknowledges that a number of gay liberation movements have begun to move beyond the logic of that norm, but objects that these movements still cling to the binary oppositions separating one category of sexuality from another. Guattari argues for the "molecularization" of male homosexuality—for its break with all molar oppositions. He presents "feminine becoming" as an important vehicle for achieving such a break.

This "feminine becoming" must be sharply distinguished both from female subjectivity, and from "the category of woman as considered in marriage, the family, and so on" (234). It represents not only "an escape route from the repressive social structure," but a process leading beyond the symbolic order altogether. In an interview published elsewhere, Guattari makes clear that what "femininity" ultimately signifies for him is a deterritorialized corporeality. "Woman has preserved the surfaces of the body," he asserts, "a bodily *jouissance* and pleasure much greater than that of [the heterosexual] man," who concentrates his libido on domination and the penis. Femininity consequently implies a condition closer to "desire," which—according to Guattari's unorthodox usage of that word—describes a way of existing beyond the opposition between "persons, organs, material flows, and semiotic flows,"[30] i.e. outside subjectivity as psychoanalysis defines it. However, because femininity still retains some connection to the phallus, and also represents a category through which homosexuality is normalized by dominant representation, it should be seen by the gay man only as a temporary stop on the path toward "becoming animal, cosmos, words, color, music."[31]

This account of homosexuality-as-feminine-corporeality "pastoralizes" homosexuality, as Bersani would say, projecting it into a space beyond conflict, power, and sexual difference.[32] It also entirely brackets the troubling question of psychic identity. Entirely missing from these two texts by Guattari is any acknowledgment of the fact that the human subject cannot survive or even articulate his or her desires without a fantasmatic and a *moi*, which are necessarily constructed in some organizing relation to dominant representation and its definitions of gender.

D.A. Miller effects a very different variation upon the theme of the feminine man, and one which is fully responsive to subjectivity's theoretical dictates. His stunning analysis of *The Woman in White* proceeds from the assumption that the Ulrichsian formulation functions as a traumatic kernel at the heart of that novel, determining not only its "thematics," but its relation to the reader—a relation predicated initially upon certain sensational effects, and later upon a "carceral problematic."

As its title suggests, "*Cage aux folles*: Sensation and Gender in Wilkie Collins's *The Woman in White*" provides an analysis of how sensation is sexually conceptualized and differentiated in an important Victorian novel. The most exemplary feature of this text is its insistence upon the mutual determination of homophobia and misogyny within the discourses upon which that novel draws. Miller maintains that in the wake of Ulrichs, who for him represents nineteenth-century sexology, homosexuality functioned as a signifier of the terrifying permeability of masculinity to femininity—as proof positive of man's vulnerability to the "contagion" of woman. Because *The Woman in White* situates itself within the purview of the sensation novel, he argues, it is ideally positioned first to dramatize, and then to resolve this crisis. It dramatizes the psychic plague of femininity by designating sensation itself as the female soul or "breath" capable of being transmitted from woman to man, and—even more horrifyingly—man to man. Thus it is that "nervousness touches and enters" Walter Hartwright when the

Woman in White touches him "from behind,"[33] and that the body of the (implicitly male) reader "resonate[s]" with hers, so that "his rib cage, arithmetically Adam's, houses a woman's quickened respiration," and "his pallor . . . is mirrored back to him only as hers" (153–54). *The Woman in White* resolves the crisis it sets into narrative motion through a double incarceration—through the sequestration of Laura and the Woman in White within marriage and the asylum; and through a "homophobic monitoring" of the "woman" who might be said to have entered certain male bodies (155–56).

"*Cage aux folles*" entertains an ambivalent relation to the Ulrichsian formulation. It relies upon that formulation to provide a gay reading of *The Woman in White*, yet at the same time it complains that the notion of "*anima muliebris in corpore virili inclusa*" functions to "channel into the homosexual's 'ontology' the social and legal sanctions that might otherwise be imposed upon him"—to hold the homosexual man rather than the larger culture responsible for the sequestration of "the feminine." However, Miller directs his criticism not at the notion that femininity might somehow reside within male homosexuality, but rather at the implied terms of that indwelling. In the passage from which I quoted a moment ago, where he takes strongest exception to the Ulrichsian definition, he translates "*inclusa*" as "incarcerated or shut up," with an abridgment of freedom (155), thereby making clear that what he resents is the characterization of the homosexual man as a kind of prison guard. "*Cage aux folles*" advances a very different argument: the argument that it is the heterosexual rather than the homosexual man who keeps femininity under psychic lock and key. To be a gay man, on the other hand, would seem to mean letting one's female "soul" out of the closet.

Leo Bersani is more concerned with "shattering" the male *moi* than with that which it might be said to "incarcerate." However, he, too, argues for the feminization of homosexuality in "Is the Rectum a Grave?," an essay which explores the psychic consequences for the male subject of being anally penetrated by another man. Here, however, that feminization is synonymous less with homosexuality than with homosexual self-immolation. The ultimately suicidal extremity of Bersani's argument can perhaps best be apprehended by briefly juxtaposing "Is the Rectum a Grave?" with a more fashionably "French" account of male homosexuality. In an essay dedicated to Roland Barthes, Harold Beaver proposes not only that the homosexual "transgresses morphology, grammar, discourse," but that he "is charged with castrating creative play, with literally castrating society's generative forces."[34] Bersani advances a strikingly different claim, and one that turns the knife-blade against the self—the claim that in occupying a female subject-position the gay man himself submits to a kind of castration.

Bersani's argument proceeds from the assumption that sexuality necessarily turns upon the power dynamic which feminists like Catherine A. MacKinnon and Andrea Dworkin have condemned within traditional heterosexuality—that it *inevitably* polarizes its participants into "relations of mastery and subordination" (216).[35] The thrusting penis marks the site of mastery, and its receptacle the locus of subordination. "*To be penetrated is to abdicate power,*" asserts Bersani (212). Now, while this formulation hinges upon a disturbing naturalization of the connection between penis and mastery, which is not entirely put to rest by Bersani's insistence that he is speaking less about that organ itself than about the male fantasies which surround it (216), the point of reception is feminized regardless of whether it is situated on the male or the female body. In other words, Bersani conflates anus and vagina, much as Freud does in "On Transformations of Instinct as Exemplified in Anal Erotism."[36] Having effected this collapse, he then proposes using the posterior side of the male body to cancel out the masculinity which stubbornly asserts itself on the anterior side. Thus, although leaving unchallenged the equation between power and the penis, and lack and the vagina/anus, Bersani privileges the latter rather than the former. Indeed, he goes so far as to affirm the "*value* of powerlessness in both men and women," which he defines as a "radical disintegration and humiliation of the self" (217). He also valorizes the pleasure of the orifice over that of the solid organ, a pleasure which is bodied forth through the "seductive" and "intolerable image of a grown man, legs high in the air, unable to refuse the suicidal ecstasy of being a woman" (212).

As I have already indicated, femininity does not for Bersani represent the "truth" of male homosexuality. Rather, the defining feature of the gay man is that he narcissistically loves the phallic attributes of other male bodies. Unfortunately, those are precisely the attributes through which traditional masculinity is consolidated. The gay man consequently faces a double danger—the danger not only of desiring, but of *becoming* that which is both most virulent about the existing social order, and most profoundly antagonistic to his own existence:

> . . . a gay man doesn't run the risk of loving his oppressor *only* in the ways in which blacks or Jews might more or less secretly collaborate with their oppressors—that is, as a consequence . . . of that subtle corruption by which a slave can come to idolize power . . . blacks and Jews don't *become* blacks and Jews as a result of that internalization of an oppressive mentality, whereas that internalization is in

> part constitutive of male homosexual desire. . . .An authentic gay male political identity therefore implies a struggle not only against definitions of maleness and homosexuality as they are reiterated and imposed in a heterosexist social discourse, but also against those very same definitions so seductively and so faithfully reflected by those (in large part culturally invented and elaborated) male bodies that we carry within us as permanently renewable sources of excitement. (209)

A symbolic alignment with femininity emerges within Bersani's argument as the vital political corrective to this intolerable situation. Through anal receptivity the homosexual man can "violate" and even demolish his "perhaps otherwise uncontrollable identification" (222) with that which oppresses both him and the female subject.

Interestingly, this feminization of the male homosexual is effected more at the level of the body than at that of the psyche, which seems to remain irreducibly masculine until the point at which it is "shattered." Indeed, it is through a penile image—slackness—that Bersani encourages us to imagine the effects of the "self-annihilation" he advocates, since psychic tumescence is his preferred metaphor for the consolidation of the male ego (218). "Is the Rectum a Grave?" might thus be said to reverse the terms of the Ulrichsian inversion. It calls for the redefinition of the male homosexual as "a man's soul in a woman's body," or—to state the case slightly differently—for a male psyche put at risk by its pleasurable relation to the vagina/anus.

Daniel Schreber's *Memoirs of My Nervous Illness*, upon which Freud bases his "Psycho-Analytic Notes on an Autobiographical Account of a Case of Paranoia," not only anticipates the terms of Bersani's argument, but it pushes the deconstruction of masculinity even further.[37] As within "Is the Rectum a Grave?," a male homosexual identification with femininity is counterposed to phallic masculinity, here evoked by the position of *Senatspräsident* in the *Oberlandesgericht* in Dresden to which Schreber accedes at the moment of the beginning of the "nervous illness" recorded in the *Memoirs*. ("Fancy a person who was a Senatspräsident allowing himself to be f----d,"[38] taunt his inner voices at one point, foregrounding the opposition between his sexuality and his professional position.) Once again, moreover, the identification with woman is effected at the level of the body. Here, however, that identification goes far beyond the conflation of anus and vagina; it takes both the negative form of a radical "unmanning," and the positive form of a sexual reterritorialization.

The first of these processes is literalized at the level of Schreber's imaginary by the retraction of his penis, and the gradual disappearance of his moustache and beard (132). At the same time, he experi-

ences a diminution in his corporeal stature. The complementary process of feminization is signaled primarily through the dispersal of
voluptuous sensation over the entire surface of his body, in defiance
of masculinity's strictly phallic *jouissance* (204). Schreber also claims
more than once to have female breasts, buttocks, legs, and genitalia
(148 and 181), which he offers to exhibit to the medically trained eye
(207). He further purports to have skin of feminine softness (94), and
to have once felt "quickening" in his body "the first signs of life of a
human embryo" (43f.).

Schreber's identification with the female body has as its result not
so much the "shattering" of his conventionally masculine ego as the
formation of a classically female *moi*. He gives voice near the end of
the *Memoirs* to the desire to be seen standing in front of the mirror
with his chest exposed, while wearing some of the accoutrements of
a woman. This confession attests to the narcissism and exhibitionism
culturally decreed to be feminine, as does the wish for a medical
examination. Almost unimaginably, Schreber would seem to become,
during the duration of his "illness," a woman's soul in a woman's
body. This double transformation is apparently the consequence not
only of a redefinition of the corporeal image so complete that it extends even to the genital region, but of the direction of Schreber's
desire toward a disembodied "object," which cannot function like
the male bodies of which Bersani speaks to foster both desire and
identification. For although Schreber imagines himself being penetrated by God, and uses the masculine pronoun when referring to that
entity, he is penetrated not by a penis, but by "rays," the "radiant
picture" of which "[becomes] visible to [his] inner eye" when he lies
awake in bed (124). There is thus a curious foreclosure of the male
body from this homosexual economy; that body is to be found neither
on the side of the subject, nor on that of the object.

The Schreberian paradigm further differs from Bersani's in its heterocosmic tendencies, for Schreber feels himself to be entrusted with
the production of a different world. His emasculation, as Freud observes in "Psycho-Analytic Notes on an Autobiographical Account of
a Case of Paranoia," "[takes] its place in a great cosmic chain of events,
and [will be] instrumental in the re-creation of humanity after its
extinction;"[39] in submitting himself to God's rays, Schreber believes
himself to be making possible a new variety of men. This aspect of the
Senatspräsident's delusionary system may perhaps best be understood
as a displaced recognition that there is apparently no place within
the world as it is presently constructed for a homosexuality such as
his—for a homosexuality, that is, without any relation to the penis.
However, as I will attempt to demonstrate later in this chapter,

Schreber's *Memoirs* is not the only homosexual text to exclude the male genitals in this way. *A la recherche du temps perdu* also at times gives so much primacy to femininity as seemingly to exclude the penis altogether.

3. Femininity as Fantasy

It would seem crucial at this point to acknowledge that there may be forms of male homosexuality within which the feminine does not have an important part to play, although I will not attempt to address them in this chapter. I also want to concede before proceeding any further that in his essay on *The Woman in White*, D.A. Miller speaks not so much about a feminine "soul" or psyche as about "what is fantasized as the 'woman inside,'" and that the other texts I have just briefly discussed also hinge upon a fantasmatic femininity. However, to recognize this rhetorical qualification is to strengthen rather than to diminish the subjective value of femininity within male homosexuality, since the category of fantasy encompasses not only sexuality, but the subject's very self. As I have emphasized more than once over the course of this book, identity is not "real," although it has a powerful hold on belief. The ego or *moi* is put in place through the subject's constantly repeated identification with images which have, at the level of the psyche, only a "virtual" existence, and which are profoundly marked by alterity. The concept of fantasy also accommodates the various agencies which determine and sustain identity—the gaze, the screen, the fantasmatic, and that matrix of familial imagoes within which the subject's founding identifications occur.

As I attempted to demonstrate in Chapter 3 of this volume, we are all dependent for our identity upon the "clicking" of an imaginary camera. This metaphoric apparatus is what Lacan calls the "gaze." The gaze does not "photo-graph" the subject directly, but only through the mediation of the screen, i.e. through the repertoire of culturally intelligible images. Unfortunately, all such images are ideologically marked in some way; at the very least, they are carriers of sexual and racial difference, but they also project values of class, age, and nationality onto those who are seen through them. Because their object-choice defies the libidinal logic of conventional masculinity, gay men are frequently viewed through the alternative screen of femininity. This means not only that others see them as feminine, but that they themselves feel the pressure of that definition at the site of the *moi*.

Since the gaze is unlocalizable, and radically exceeds any individual human look, it, too, must be apprehended through visual and discursive fictions. Traditionally, those fictions have insisted not only upon the masculinity, but upon the heterosexuality of the "camera" that "pictures" us for ourselves and others, thereby situating gay men, with women, decisively on the side of the spectacle. Once again, then, the homosexual subject finds himself situated in an apparently feminine position. It is hardly surprising that so many gay men have attempted to renegotiate their gender identity precisely at the level of spectacle.

However, the homosexual subject may also recognize himself within representations of women for two other compelling reasons. The self is not the simple product of the gaze passing through the screen, but depends as well upon the subject's structuring identifications with other family members. Those identifications are normatively masculine in the case of the adult male subject, but there are clearly many instances in which they are feminine. This is hardly surprising, since for most subjects the mother provides the first image of self. Much has been made of the difficult erotic itinerary of the little girl, who is asked at an early age to surrender her first object of love for another, and not enough of the tortuous identificatory itinerary of the little boy, who is expected at an equally tender age to relinquish one identity for another.

Finally, a gay man may identify more fully with women than with men because he sometimes or even always occupies a feminine position at the level of his unconscious fantasmatic. The fantasmatic, a category which I have consistently foregrounded throughout my various discussions of male sexuality in this book, provides the "blueprint" for each subject's desire, the *combinatoire* which each successful amorous experience assembles. Proust represents perhaps the greatest theorist of the fantasmatic, although he lacks the signifier with which to designate it. He suggests that in the final analysis a subject's erotic history might be said to repeat the same four notes upon which all of the seemingly very different parts of a septet are based (3, 408), or to resemble a song which is played over and over until the listener knows it so well that he or she can enter it at any point ("Since we know its song, which is engraved on our hearts in its entirety, there is no need for a woman to repeat the opening strains . . . for us to remember what follows. And if she begins in the middle . . . we are well enough attuned to the music to be able to take it up and follow our partner without hesitation at the appropriate passage" [1, 214]). Proust speaks elsewhere in the same text about the "pattern, if not of all of our loves, [then] at least of certain of our loves which alternate with the others" (3, 694–95).

Like the images through which the *moi* is formed, the fantasmatic is incorporated into the subject from outside. As Laplanche and Pontalis advise with respect to fantasy in general, it is "an intrusion from without into an interior which perhaps did not exist before this intrusion," a "new *language*, that of passion, which is introduced by the adult into the infantile 'language' of tenderness."[40] This libidinal paradigm is generally drawn, within Western cultures, from what might be called the "Oedipal scene," whose potential cast of characters includes not only the mother and father, brother and sister, nanny, governess and tutor, but—as we will see—the desiring subject "itself," now in the guise of the desired object.

The fantasmatic not only regulates erotic investment, but it maps out a symbolic position for the subject, the position from which it lives its desire. Within some of the male homosexualities theorized by Freud, and narrativized by Proust, the mother's position is especially favored. For a subject to occupy the maternal site at the level of unconscious desire may imply a variety of different things, most of which have little to do with the "personality" or "psychology" of the actual mother. It may signify, for instance, lack; receptivity; specularity, with the related tropes of narcissism and/or exhibitionism; passivity; masochism; or maternity, with all that such a concept may imply. (Astonishingly, as we will see, an identification with maternity may turn not only upon activity, but upon penile penetration).

Laplanche and Pontalis maintain that all kinds of "permutations of roles and attributions are possible" within fantasy.[41] It increasingly seems to me that this claim applies more to certain fantasmatics than to others. For some subjects there may be a kind of arrestation at the site of suffering, for instance, while others as easily assume a sadistic position. Reversibility of subject and object would seem to come into play with particular facility within those fantasmatics which are predicated upon a predominently narcissistic object-choice. Since desire there hinges upon the subject's relation to a lost or desired "self," the position of the object is one to which it easily gravitates.

Because of the premium which homosexuality places upon the anatomical similitude of desiring subject and erotic object, it represents a fertile terrain for narcissistic object-choice. Not surprisingly, then, there would seem to be particular forms of male homosexuality which accommodate reversibility at the level of the fantasmatic. If the position conventionally occupied by the subject is structurally feminine, then one important consequence of this reversibility is the potential feminization of the erotic object. "Woman" would thus seem to function at times not only as the locus of gay identification, but as the pivot of gay desire.

It should be evident by now that I am committed to a radically de-essentializing account both of femininity and of male homosexuality.

What is the place of the sexed body within such an account? I will attempt to address this issue later in the chapter. Before doing so, however, I want to effect a more precise psychoanalytic specification of the place of femininity within male homosexuality.

4. Rethinking Freud

Any search for a theoretical paradigm capable of explaining in greater detail how femininity can function to define both the subject and the object of male homosexuality would lead before long to Freud. However, I have waited until well into this chapter to examine what that writer has to say about homosexuality, not only because it was crucial to listen first to what some recent gay critics have written on the subject, but because I hoped to create a context that would make it possible to read him differently. Let us look first at that writer's general contribution to a theory of homosexuality, and then at the three paradigms of male homosexuality which can be extracted from *The Standard Edition.*

Surprisingly, given his historical moment, Freud breaks decisively with the view that homosexuality is congenital, and hence with the notion of a "third sex." Indeed, he even goes so far as to maintain that "inversion and somatic hermaphroditism are on the whole independent of each other."[42] There is also no basis for distinguishing homosexuals from heterosexuals at a strictly *psychic* level, we learn in *Three Essays on the Theory of Sexuality*, since not only are "all human beings . . . capable of making a homosexual object-choice," but they have "in fact made one in their unconscious" (145f.).[43] In "The Psychogenesis of a Case of Homosexuality in a Woman," Freud advances the equally important proposition that it may be possible to be *consciously homosexual,*[44] and *unconsciously heterosexual*, a proposition which once again challenges any hard and fast distinction between heterosexuality and homosexuality. And *PsychoAnalytic Notes on an Autobiographical Account of a Case of Paranoia* suggests that sexuality may remain in a constant state of flux with respect to the question of object, since "generally speaking, every human being oscillates all through his life between heterosexual and homosexual feelings."[45] Consequently, an erotic decision on behalf of heterosexuality demands as full an explanation as one on behalf of homosexuality.[46]

While Freud is not unwilling to use the word "inversion," he insists in a 1910 footnote to *Three Essays* that it can apply either to the subject or to the object (145). Ferenczi, who elaborates this distinction much more fully in an essay delivered at the Third Congress of the International Psycho-Analytical Association a year later, explains that the male subject invert "feels himself to be a woman, and this not only in genital intercourse, but in all relations of life." The object invert, on the other hand, is "as a rule very energetic and active."[47] Freud, too, acknowledges that male homosexuality can exhibit "the most complete mental masculinity."[48] Consequently, the homosexual man cannot always be defined through reference to Ulrichs's formulation; as *Three Essays* suggests, he is not necessarily "a woman in search of a man," but may instead be looking for a male object with "feminine mental traits" (144).

This frequently revised text fails to break with the notion that homosexuality, like heterosexuality, always pairs masculinity with femininity, even though it denaturalizes those categories. However, a later essay calls that assumption into question. In "Psychogenesis of a Case of Homosexuality in a Woman," Freud concedes that identification and object-choice do not necessarily reverse each other. On the contrary, a masculine identification can coexist with the desire for a masculine love-object, and a feminine identification with the desire for a feminine love-object:

> . . . a man with predominantly male characteristics and also masculine in his erotic life may still be inverted in respect to his object, loving only men instead of women. A man in whose character feminine attributes obviously predominate, who may, indeed, behave in love like a woman, might be expected , from this feminine attitude, to choose a man for his love-object; but he may nevertheless be heterosexual, and show no more inversion in respect to his object than an average normal man. The same is true of women; here also mental sexual character and object-choice do not necessarily coincide. The mystery of homosexuality is therefore by no means so simple as it is commonly depicted . . . " "a feminine mind, bound therefore to love a man, but unhappily attached to a masculine body; a masculine mind, irresistibly attracted by women, but alas! imprisoned in a feminine body" (170).

In breaking down the binarism which heterosexuality is assumed to maintain, and homosexuality to invert, this passage further erodes the distinction between the two.

Freud accounts for the possible copresence of homosexual and heterosexual impulses within the same individual in two ways—by stressing the multiple possibilities for pleasure implicit within the human organism, and by showing the nuclear family to be a structure which makes available to each subject more than one kind of identification and one axis of desire. Freud speaks in *Three Essays* about the potential "polymorphous perversity" of the newborn child—about its capacity for experiencing sexual gratification at sites other than those designated culturally appropriate (191). It is only through a sexual territorialization of the body that pleasure subsequently comes to be localized at certain sites.

Conventionally, three erotogenic zones are privileged within Western childcare—the mouth, the anus, and the genitals. Although Freud maintains that the first two of these zones properly yield over time to the primacy of the third, he nevertheless accords to oral and anal sexuality a status fully equivalent to their genital counterpart. Indeed, he remarks at one point in *Three Essays* that "what is true of one [erotogenic zone] is true of all" (210), and he describes oral sexuality as the anticipatory mirror image of genital sexuality:

> No one who has seen a baby sinking back satiated from the breast and falling asleep with flushed cheeks and a blissful smile can escape the reflection that this picture persists as a prototype of the expression of sexual satisfaction in later life. (182)

If oral and anal eroticism are able to prefigure their genital counterpart, that is because all three are, in Freud's account, equally divorced from the instinctual. Genitality, in other words, is no more "natural" than its oral and anal counterparts. Laplanche's close reading of *Three Essays* in *Life and Death in Psychoanalysis* draws out the radical implications of Freud's text, the most significant of which is that sexuality bears no relation to the actual implementation of the vital functions upon which it leans; whereas the aim of the nutritive instinct, for instance, is the appeasement of hunger, oral sexuality seeks the pleasure of the organ in place, i.e. of the mouth. Moreover, not only is its object—the breast rather than the milk—marginal in relation to nutrition, but it is potentially and perhaps even definitionally fantasmatic. This, Laplanche argues, is what is implied by Freud's emphasis upon the initial auto-eroticism or object-lessness of sexuality, which forecloses upon the material world. The sexual drive turns back upon the subject's own body, and upon an internal, fantasized object.[49] Freud's characterization of oral sexuality as "incorporation" also points to the centrality of fantasy within the erotic, since that characterization overlays the concept of ingestion with connotations indicative of a complex psychic working-over:

> With incorporation, the aim [of the oral drive] has become the scenario of a fantasy, a scenario borrowing from the function its register and its language, but adding to ingestion the various implications grouped under the term "cannibalism," with such meanings as: preserving within oneself, destroying, assimilating. Incorporation, moreover, extends ingestion to an entire series of possible

relations . . . reference is thus made in psychoanalysis to incorporation at the level of other bodily orifices, of the skin or even . . . the
eyes.[50]

Thus although the child is born with an all-engrossing potentiality
for corporeal pleasure, before any erotogenic zone can be constituted
there must be a psychic intervention.

Freud's attempt late in *Three Essays* to elevate the conjunction of
penis and vagina to the position of an "end-pleasure" different in
kind from the pleasures of the mouth or anus—to insist that such a
conjuncture offers gratification of the "highest . . . intensity" because it
"brings about the discharge of the sexual substances" (210)—depends
upon a belated recourse to the biological. It is of course only by
invoking an implicitly procreative norm that other erotic pleasures
can be relegated to the category of potentially dangerous foreplay—
dangerous because capable of preempting heterosexual genitality,
and so of leading to "perversion." Since, according to the ramifications
of Freud's own argument, sexuality always "lies in a *movement which
deflects the instinct, metaphorizes its aim, displaces and internalizes its
object, and concentrates its source on what is ultimately a minimal
zone,*"[51] it always perverts the biological.

I have dwelt at such length upon what Freud has to say about
orality, anality, and genitality because male homosexuality articulates the latter term in relation to the former two. It, too, like heterosexual coitus, generally involves "the discharge of the sexual substances," but within orifices which ostensibly belong to an earlier
stage both within infantile sexuality, and within the normative micro-
narrative of the adult sexual transaction. The temporality of male
homosexuality is thus quite different from that of prototypical heterosexuality. Not only does it conflate "moments" which Freud would
like to maintain in relative isolation from each other, but, as I will
attempt to demonstrate later, it might be said to mix the "generations."

Male homosexuality, like lesbianism, also collapses the distinction
between "fore-pleasure" and "end-pleasure," at least at the site of the
mouth. That erotogenic zone is thus in a sense the most quintessentially "gay," even though cultural representations of homosexuality
more prominently feature the anus. I emphasize this point because
oral sexuality also enjoys a curiously privileged status both within
Three Essays, and within Laplanche's seminal analysis of that text.
Even though it stands for that which must be rigorously subordinated
to heterosexual coitus, the picture sketched by Freud of the child at
the mother's breast not only *prefigures* adult sexuality, but represents

somehow its "truth." Similarly, Laplanche dramatizes the transition from the instinct to the drive, and the emergence of sexuality as such, as the psychic incorporation of an image of the child's lips at the mother's breast, and the experience of erotic pleasure at the mouth (17–20). It may be that the oral drive is constitutive not merely of certain forms of homosexuality, but of sexuality *tout court*, despite Freud's effort to relegate its pleasures to the category of *anticipation*.

Freud also accounts for the presence of homosexual elements even within the most seemingly heterosexual of persons through reference to the negative Oedipus complex. As several previous chapters have already indicated, he outlines his theory of a double Oedipus complex in an important passage from *The Ego and the Id*, from which I will quote at length:

> ... one gets an impression that the simple Oedipus complex is by no means its commonest form. . . . Closer study usually discloses the more complete Oedipus complex, which is twofold, positive and negative ... that is to say, a boy has not merely an ambivalent attitude towards his father and an affectionate object-choice towards his mother, but at the same time he also behaves like a girl and displays an affectionate feminine attitude to his father and a corresponding jealousy and hostility towards his mother. . . .
>
> In my opinion it is advisable in general . . . to assume the existence of the complete Oedipus complex. Analytic experience then shows that in a number of cases one or the other constituent disappears, except for barely distinguishable traces; so that the result is a series with the normal positive Oedipus complex at one end and the inverted negative one at the other, while its intermediate members exhibit the complete form with one or other of its two components preponderating. At the dissolution of the Oedipus complex the four trends of which it consists will group themselves in such a way as to produce a father-identification and a mother-identification. The father-identification will preserve the object-relation to the mother which belonged to the positive complex and will at the same time replace the object relation to the father which belonged to the inverted complex: and the same will be true, *mutatis mutandis*, of the mother-identification. The relative intensity of the two identifications in any individual will reflect the preponderance in him of one or other of the two sexual dispositions.[52]

This passage suggests that every subject goes through both a heterosexual and a homosexual version of the Oedipus complex—that at an early point in its history the subject desires the father as well as the mother, and identifies with the mother as well as the father.[53] It is presumably for this reason that each of us can be said to have made a homosexual object-choice at the level of the unconscious.[54] However, the negative Oedipus complex is not necessarily only a relic of infantile sexuality; there are also adults whose libidinal economy seems to be structured almost exclusively by that complex, just as there are others who seem constantly to enact the positive Oedipus complex in their identifications and object-choices. Yet others are psychically situated somewhere between the two Oedipal variants, drawing elements from each, or moving back and forth between them, as is implied by the feminine but heterosexual, or masculine but homosexual men of whom Freud speaks in "Psychogenesis of a Case of Homosexuality in a Woman."

Let us return for a moment to an earlier point in the history of male subjectivity. At the end of the complete Oedipus complex, at least in its directly familial form (I make this qualification because it should be clear by now that structural elements of the complex persist long beyond childhood), the boy will enter into two different identifications, one with the father and one with the mother. Identification, as Freud repeats more than once in *The Ego and the Id*, represents the primary mechanism for escaping desire,[55] and our hypothetical male subject must resolve his erotic relation both to the mother and the father. The result is an imaginary connection with each parent. However, since the positive Oedipus complex already implies an identification with the father, and the negative Oedipus complex one with the mother, there remains a certain irreducible ambiguity about these and future identifications. An imaginary alignment with one parent or the subsequent figures who replace him or her may attest *both* to the positive and the negative Oedipus complex. Identification with the father, in other words, may be read *either* as "resolved" love for him or as a concomitant of love for the mother, and identification with the mother *either* as "resolved" love for her or as a concomitant of love for the father. It is consequently with a certain unjustified confidence that Freud concludes that "the relative intensity of the two identifications in any individual will reflect the preponderance in him of one or other of the two sexual dispositions." In fact, while a male subject may indeed enact at the level of his sexual practice a startlingly explicit performance of a (displaced) negative Oedipus complex, his identification with femininity may also attest in part to an earlier desire for the mother, just as love for the father might be found to underpin the most seemingly heterosexual of masculine identifications.

I cannot proceed any further in my discussion of Freud's account of male homosexuality without introducing the three models which are the primary concern of this chapter. First, though, I want to emphasize that the systematicity of what follows is largely the product of my own secondary revision of Freud's texts. As Kenneth Lewes notes in *The Psy-*

choanalytic Theory of Male Homosexuality,[56] the various theories Freud
proposes to account for the etiology of homosexuality are far from consistent, and it is often difficult to determine whether one is supposed to
extend, supplement, or supersede those that came before.

5. Three Models of Male Homosexuality

Given Freud's assertion that there are men whose adult lives are
largely organized by the negative Oedipus complex, that complex
would seem to represent not only a psychic paradigm for universalizing infantile homosexuality,[57] but one possible form of adult male
homosexuality. Strachey, indeed, invokes it as a way of accounting
for the libidinal economy of the the Wolfman, even though Freud's
case history of that figure predates *The Ego and the Id* by nine years.[58]
Because it involves desire for the father, and identification with the
mother, the negative Oedipus complex clearly gives a privileged place
to femininity. It consequently represents the first of the three models
of male homosexuality towards which this chapter has been moving.

Since the negative Oedipus complex may seem to conform with
an unpleasing exactitude to the dominant cultural stereotype of the
homosexual man, I would like to begin my analysis of it with a few
remarks about the adjective by means of which we are asked to designate both that psychic structure and its more culturally exemplary
counterpart. The signifiers "positive" and "negative" might seem necessarily to imply a judgment as to the relative moral value of the two
versions of the Oedipus complex. However, as I have argued at length
with respect to female subjectivity,[59] the designation of the homosexual Oedipus complex as "negative" can also be deployed as a rhetorical
device for foregrounding its important oppositional status with respect to the dominant fiction—its capacity for challenging and subverting the heterosexual imperative, and for scrambling the socially
acceptable temporality and narrative sequencing of normative human
sexuality. More importantly, it might be said to negate the most
fundamental premise of male subjectivity—an identification with
masculinity—and in so doing to obstruct paternal lineality. As Jonathan Dollimore remarks in his recent study of perversion, a gay man's
imaginary alignment with the mother doubles the transgressive value
of his "deviant" object-choice.[60] In effecting such an alignment, he
turns away from the phallic legacy.

What, precisely, does identification with the mother imply in the case
of the negative Oedipus complex? Because this homosexual variant
conforms more fully to the notion of an inverted heterosexuality than
do the other models I will be discussing here, its prototypical desiring

subject would seem destined to occupy a classically feminine position. Such is certainly the case both with Schreber and the Wolfman, both of whom manifestly inhabit the negative Oedipus complex. A maternal identification apparently translates in the case of paradigm 1 not only into sexual receptivity, but narcissism and exhibitionism. The last of those "tropes" works to hyperbolize the male subject as spectacle, and hence represents an implicit acknowledgment of the "Otherness" of the gaze. The first functions not only to eroticize the anus and/or mouth, but to release the male body from its phallic stranglehold, and so to open up the possibility for that more diffuse sense of voluptuousness that Schreber associates with women.[61] The resident of paradigm 1 would also seem a likely candidate for feminine masochism, which hinges upon theatricality and a non-phallic corporeal paradigm.

However, even as I emphasize the "femininity" of the homosexual whose desires are organized by the negative Oedipus complex, I want to reiterate once again that receptivity, specularity, and narcissism represent constitutive features of *all* subjectivity, even though masculinity is predicated upon their denial. Only the narrowest of borders, moreover, separates normative male subjectivity from masochism. Insofar as gay sexuality foregrounds receptivity, specularity, narcissism and masochism, it might be said not so much to embrace "the feminine" as to refuse the defensive maneuvers through which sexual difference is constituted.

The male version of the negative Oedipus complex, which I will designate "paradigm 1," can be schematized according to the following diagram:

Paradigm 1 (The Negative Oedipus Complex)

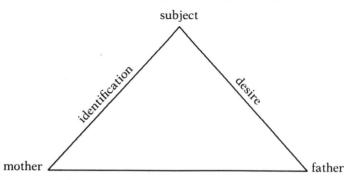

Although my reasons for including this diagram will become evident later, I want to provide a brief explanation now. Since all three of the homosexualities outlined by Freud can be articulated according to a similar triangle, it will presumably be easier to conceptualize the differences between them by providing a comparable "visualization" of each. Such a schematization will also help to dramatize the challenge which these homosexualities pose with respect to psychoanalytic orthodoxy. Within a classically Freudian context, the triangle inevitably evokes the Oedipus complex. However, the other homosexualities I will be articulating involve only two players. Each is made to "fit" the triangular structure through the doubling of one of its players. These two forms of homosexuality thus mimic the Oedipal structure while subverting it from within.

Although a careful reading of Freud clearly indicates that the negative Oedipus complex represents one possible variant of male homosexuality, it nevertheless seems to me that we should stop thinking of the Oedipus complex, positive or negative, as a structure which *necessarily* survives in its totality rather than through some component or set of components around which adult sexuality has congealed. The fantasmatic, in other words, may *derive* in some ultimate sense from the Oedipal scenario, but does not necessarily reproduce in its entirety either the latter's negative or its positive version. It may, indeed, quite dramatically reconfigure the Oedipal paradigm.

We should consequently not be surprised to discover that neither of the other two variants of male homosexuality isolated by Freud conforms either to the negative or to the positive Oedipus complex, although each entertains some relation to one or the other, or even both. Paradigm 2, for instance, turns upon the male subject's imaginary alignment with the father, while paradigm 3 entails the psychic incorporation of the mother. As we have seen, both of these identifications have a part to play within the double version of the Oedipus complex. However, although both homosexual variants retain two of the Oedipal players, each excludes the third. Both also challenge certain of the normative functions of the positive Oedipus complex.

Freud does not have much to say about the second variant of male homosexuality. He devotes only one long paragraph of *Three Essays* to it, a paragraph which provides a strangely garbled account:

> It is clear that in Greece, where the most masculine men were numbered among the inverts, what excited a man's love was not the *masculine* character of a boy, but his physical resemblance to a woman as well as his feminine mental qualities—his shyness, his modesty and his need for instruction and assistance. As soon as the boy became a man he ceased to be a sexual object for men and himself, perhaps, became a lover of boys. In this instance, therefore, as in many others, the sexual object is not someone of the same sex but someone who combines the characters of both sexes; there is, as it were, a compromise between an impulse that seeks for a man and one that seeks for

a woman, while it remains a paramount condition that the object's body (i.e. genitals) shall be masculine. Thus the sexual object is a kind of reflection of the subject's own bisexual nature. (144)

At first glance, the model of homosexuality described in this passage seems to be nothing more than a reversal of paradigm 1, or, to state the case rather differently, to be paradigm 1 looked at from the point of view of the subject occupying the paternal rather than the maternal position. Freud begins, after all, by stressing the feminine attributes of the desired object. However, as he continues his explanation it appears that this kind of homosexuality hinges less upon an inverted negative Oedipus complex than upon *narcissistic object-choice.*

Freud tells us elsewhere that narcissistic object-choice has four possible modalities; it can involve self-love, love for what one once was, love for what one would like to be, and love for "someone who was once part of [oneself]."[62] The operative modality here would seem to be the subject's desire for what he once was, perhaps even for that which he once was to another figure who occupies in relation to him the position which he himself presently occupies in relation to the young man. Freud implies as much in imagining a future in which the latter will have "ceased to be a sexual object of men and . . . [will have become] a lover of boys"—in which the figure who occupies the lower right point of the triangle will have moved to the apex. Presumably, then, the desiring subject of paradigm 2 has functioned in an earlier incarnation as the object of desire. This libidinal model would thus seem to turn upon the subject's wish to bring himself into erotic contact with his earlier self, while at the same time identifying with the "father" or structural predecessor. It is, in other words, articulated across three generations, rather than the usual two. This curious splitting of the self into desiring subject and desired object forces a different resolution to the Oedipal drama than any Freud ever imagined. I would like to suggest that the resulting erotic triangle be diagrammed in this way:

Paradigm 2 (The "Greek" Model)

Although the mother is deleted from the erotic cast of characters, she nonetheless plays an indirect role even within this paradigm. The youthful love object has a "bisexual nature," i.e. one structured at the level of the unconscious by an identification both with the father *and* with the mother. So, Freud maintains, does the desiring subject. Given the sharp bifurcation of the lovers' respective roles, and the importance of generational difference within their homosexuality, it would seem as though this imaginary duality seeks to express itself serially rather than simultaneously or through alternation; in youth one plays out one's feminine identification, and in maturity one's masculine identification. The adult subject might thus be said, in loving the youth, to love a femininity which was once his own, but which has become "encrypted" or sealed up, to borrow a metaphor from Nicolas Abraham and Marie Torok.[63] Identification with the mother would here seem to imply primarily receptivity and specularity, possibly overlaid with narcissism.

Freud is adamant about one point at which the "Greek" model of homosexuality converges with all others, a point which the present discussion has not sufficiently stressed. It is obligatory within paradigm 2 that the youth be genitally masculine, despite his "physical resemblance to a woman" and "his feminine mental qualities." In this respect, he functions as a more immediate mirror of the desiring subject. The latter can consequently be seen to love narcissistically in a second way as well; he not only looks to the boy for the image of what he once was, but for the image of what he presently is. He also loves the boy, in other words, for the masculinity to which the latter will eventually accede, a masculinity of which his penis is the proleptic signifier.

I have bracketed the word "Greek" with quotation marks when designating this model of male homosexuality as a way of calling its referential value seriously into question. As I indicated at the outset of this chapter, both Foucault and Halperin have argued for the interchangeability of women and boys as erotic objects in classical Greek society, and both have also corroborated Freud's claim that at a certain age the free male member of that society would conventionally graduate from the position of erotic object to that of desiring subject, and henceforth love others as he himself was earlier loved. However, the reference to bisexuality in the passage under discussion, along with its implicit invocation of the double Oedipus complex, suggests that Freud is speaking as much about contemporary as about classical Greek homosexuality.

Freud is considerably more verbose about the third paradigm of male homosexuality, although it finds its way into *Three Essays* only in the guise of a 1910 footnote. His study of Leonardo, written in the same year, conducts an extended analysis of this variant of homosexuality, an analysis to which "Some Neurotic Mechanisms in Jealousy, Paranoia and Homosexuality" offers some important additions. However, since the footnote from *Three Essays* provides the most compressed account, it is with it that I propose we begin our examination of the "Leonardo" model of homosexuality:[64]

> In all the cases we have examined we have established the fact that the future inverts, in the earliest years of their childhood, pass through a phase of very intense but short-lived fixation to a woman (usually their mother), and that, after leaving this behind, they identify themselves with a woman and take *themselves* as their sexual object. That is to say, they proceed from a narcissistic basis, and look for a young man who resembles themselves and whom *they* may love as their mother loved *them*. Moreover, we have frequently found that alleged inverts have been by no means insensible to the charms of women, but have continually transposed the excitation aroused by women on to a male object. They have thus repeated all through their lives the mechanism by which their inversion arose. Their compulsive longing for men has turned out to be determined by their ceaseless flight from women.
>
> It must, however, be borne in mind that hitherto only a single type of invert has been submitted to psycho-analysis—persons whose sexual activity is stunted and the residue of which is manifested as inversion. (145f.)[65]

It can scarcely have escaped the reader's attention that this passage is characterized by a homophobia which is absent from the accounts offered in *Three Essays* of the other two homosexual variants. The resident of paradigm 3, we are told, is initially "fixated" to the mother, and later flees ceaselessly from her. In both cases the relationship is marked by excess and abnormality. "Fixation," however, seems an inappropriate adjective with which to characterize a "short-lived" psychic condition. And although Freud contradicts himself upon this detail in "Some Neurotic Mechanisms," where the relationship to the mother is assumed to last until "a few years after the termination of puberty" (230), "fixation" still seems a severe characterization, particularly given that an attachment of such duration is not incompatible with conventional Oedipal structuration.

Freud's assertion that this kind of homosexuality results in "stunted" sexual activity suggests that his homophobia is actually displaced misogyny. That diminishing adjective implies that the author of *Three Essays* is responding to the prototypical occupant of that libidinal configuration as though he were a female subject, and hence both pathological and lacking. For whereas Freud's essays on sexual difference always describe the penis as "strikingly visible and of large proportions," they invariable envisage the clitoris as a "small and inconspicuous organ"[66]—in other words, as underdeveloped or stunted. The fact that homophobia here doubles as misogyny suggests that femininity may play an even more central role within this variant of homosexuality than it does within the negative Oedipus complex, which escapes a pejorative characterization.

Freud also elaborates this erotic paradigm in extremely inconsistent ways. He is most inconsistent in his characterization of the relationship that ostensibly obtains between the male subject and his mother. He claims, for instance, that this relationship begins as a "fixation," but is transformed over time into a phobia. In "Some Neurotic Mechanisms," Freud explains that desire gives way to aversion with the discovery of woman's anatomical difference,[67] which makes her an impossible erotic object. However, the footnote from *Three Essays* challenges the notion that the castration crisis marks an absolute divide. Even as an adult, the resident of paradigm 3 is "by no means insensible to the charms of women." Indeed, according to Freud, his attraction to men is constantly fueled by the "excitation" aroused in him by women.

This is not the only feature of the footnote from *Three Essays* which contradicts the notion of phobic avoidance. Freud claims earlier in the same passage that the "short-lived fixation" on the mother gives way at a certain point to identification with her. Since identification classically operates on the model of *incorporation*, it represents the very antithesis of retreat; it entails ostensibly closing the gap between subject and object, taking the latter within the psyche as the basis of the self. Moreover, as is frequently the case, identification here incorporates a loved other—an other whose attributes continue, by Freud's own admission, to elicit admiration and excitement. Far from being in flight from the mother, the occupant of the "Leonardo" paradigm establishes himself in the closest possible intimacy with her.

Identification with the mother is not a negligible feature of this homosexuality. On the contrary, it provides a centrally structuring term, dictating the conditions not only of self but of object-choice. Having "become" the mother, the subject can only love others as she loved him, which means that he is attracted to those particular others who occupy in relation to him the position he himself earlier occupied in relation to her. "Some Neurotic Mechanisms" indicates that paradigm 3 can be extremely punctilious upon this last point, demanding that "the male object . . . be of the same age as [the homosexual lover] was when the change took place," i.e. when he translated his desire for the mother into identification with her (230).

Like the second paradigm, then, the third paradigm articulates itself across three generations. It does not, however, seem to presuppose that the youth will at some future moment accede to the position of lover, and himself love youths as he was once loved. Instead, this homosexual variant seems to admit of a potential reversibility of roles at all times, including that of the present tense. This reversibility would seem to be particularly marked when only a year or two separates the ages of the partners, as would initially be the case if the subject indeed makes his first homosexual object-choices at puberty. However, a text like *A la recherche du temps perdu*, which brilliantly showcases this variant of narcissistic homosexuality, suggests that even beyond the pubertal moment it may be possible both for the desiring subject and the love-object to represent either "giver" or "receiver." Since this reversibility would seem to be at odds with the stipulation that the erotic object be younger than the desiring subject, I will attempt to clarify the terms of its functioning.

In Part III of "Leonardo da Vinci and a Memory of His Childhood," Freud reiterates in relation to the eponymous artist the libidinal paradigm also articulated in the 1910 footnote to *Three Essays*, thereby indicating once again that within this paradigm the desiring subject identifies with the mother, and desires an object that represents what he himself once was. The Leonardo homosexual experiences

> a very intense erotic attachment to . . . [his] mother, during the first period of childhood . . .
> After this preliminary stage a transformation sets in whose mechanism is known to us but whose motive force we do not understand . . . The boy represses his love for his mother: he puts himself in her place, identifies himself with her, and takes his own person as a model in whose likeness he chooses the new objects of his love . . . the boys whom he now loves as he grows up are . . . only substitutive figures and revivals of himself in childhood—boys whom he loves in the way in which his mother loved *him* when he was a child. He finds the objects of his love along the path of *narcissism* . . . (99–100)

Elsewhere in the same essay, however, Freud speaks at length about a passage from Leonardo's scientific notebooks. In that passage, the latter cites as one of his earliest and most formative memories the experience of being visited in his cradle by a bird who opened his mouth, and struck him repeatedly on the mouth with its tail. Freud argues persuasively both that this memory was a fantasy dating from a later moment, subsequently transposed onto infancy, and that it played a determining role within the sexuality and textual practice of the adult artist. He offers this interpretation of what would seem to have been Leonardo's fantasmatic:

> A tail, "*coda,*" is one of the most familiar symbols and substitutive expressions for the male organ, in Italian no less than in other languages; the situation in the phantasy, of a vulture opening the child's mouth and beating about inside it vigorously with its tail, corresponds to the idea of an act of *fellatio,* a sexual act in which the penis is put into the mouth of the person involved. (85–86)

The irreducible precondition for a smooth alignment of this passage with the one I quoted a moment ago is that the desiring subject of the Leonardo fantasmatic be understood to occupy the position of the vulture or kite, i.e. of the *active* mother.[68] However, Freud insists upon a contrary reading, and one whose peculiarity he himself notes: he maintains, that is, that it is a *passive* fantasy, and hence that its erotic center coincides with the position of the child: "It is strange that this phantasy is so completely passive in character . . . it resembles certain dreams and phantasies found in women or passive homosexuals" (86).

Although these two passages dramatically reverse each other, neither cites reversibility as one of the constitutive features of Leonardo's libidinal economy. However, a third passage, later in the same text, suggests that the desiring subject of the third model of homosexuality is indeed capable of traveling between an active and a passive position. After quoting a sentence from Vasari's biography of Leonardo ("In his youth he made some heads of laughing women out of clay, which were reproduced in plaster, and some children's heads which were as beautiful as if they had been modelled by the hand of a master"), Freud observes that Leonardo's fantasmatic made available to him not one, but two possible love-objects:

> Thus we learn that he began his artistic career by portraying two kinds of objects; and these cannot fail to remind us of the two kinds of sexual objects that we have inferred from the analysis of the vulture-phantasy. If the beautiful children's heads were reproductions of his own person as it was in his childhood, then the smiling women are nothing other than repetitions of his mother Caterina, and we begin to suspect the possibility that it was his mother who possessed the mysterious smile—the smile that he had lost and that fascinated him so much when he found it again in the Florentine lady. (111)

Since there are only two possible positions in the "vulture" fantasmatic, in order for each of them to emerge as the site of the love object it must have been possible for Leonardo as subject to occupy at least temporarily the position of the other, and hence to move back and forth between an identification with the mother, and an identification with his own youth. Paradigm 3 would consequently seem to require two diagrams, one illustrating the first (and presumably the more stable) of those identifications, and the other schematizing the second:

Paradigm 3 (The Leonardo Model)

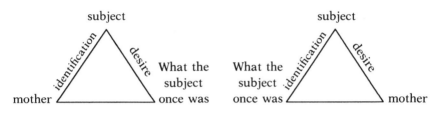

The reversibility of paradigm 3 can perhaps best be explained through the pivotal role played by the mother within it. As Freud emphasizes once again in "Leonardo da Vinci and a Memory of His Childhood," identification with the mother here works to cover over love for her. "A man who has become homosexual in this way," he writes, "remains unconsciously fixated to the mnemic image of his mother. By repressing his love for his mother he preserves it in his unconscious and from now on remains faithful to her" (100). The Leonardo model is not merely a palimpsest, in which identification with the mother is inscribed over the more archaic text of desire for her, but a constant oscillation between those two modalities. Its resident subject continues throughout life to be attracted to women, but "on each occasion he hastens to transfer the excitation he has received from women on to a male object, and in this manner he repeats over and over again the mechanism by which he acquired his homosexuality" (100). Since desire for the (phallic) mother[69] implies occupying the passive or receptive position of the child in the Leonardo fantasmatic, whereas identification with her necessitates occupying instead the active or insertive position of the vulture or kite, and since both are perpetually operative, it is easy to see why things are much more volatile within this libidinal paradigm than in the other two. The age differential between subject and object presumably functions as a stabilizing mechanism, as a device for consolidating identification with the mother over desire for her. However, both Freud's study of Leonardo and Proust's *A la recherche* show that it can be superseded.

Judging by the "vulture" fantasmatic, the third homosexual variant would seem to mark out the mouth as the ideal locus for the penis. This detail attests once again to the centrality of the mother, for the mouth represents a privileged site of maternal care. The principle of reversibility upon which I have already commented enables the desiring subject both to commemorate his earlier love for the mother by experiencing pleasure at the site of that erotogenic zone, as he did when he was a child, and to dramatize his subsequent identification with her by inserting his penis between the lips of the love-object.

It should be evident by now that this variant of homosexuality dramatically reconceives identification with the mother. Maternal identification within paradigm 3 depends upon none of the usual tropes of femininity, with the single exception of those that hinge directly on motherhood. In other words, it signifies neither receptivity, exhibitionism, passivity, nor masochism, but rather *activity* and *penetration*. Indeed, I will go further: it is only from the maternal position that one wields the penis. How are we to account for this radically revisionary inscription of femininity?

I indicated earlier that Freud isolates the castration crisis as the moment at which desire for the mother yields to "ceaseless flight" from her. Although it seems to me that this homosexual subject does not so much flee from the mother as relocate her within himself, I agree with Freud that the relinquishment of the mother as an overtly sexual object cannot be explained apart from the castration crisis. However, although the revelation of anatomical difference can be theoretically located at the point of transition from one psychic modality to another, identification with the mother functions as a mechanism for disavowing it, i.e. for refusing to acknowledge her penile "lack." By incorporating the mother, the homosexual subject is able to make good her anatomical "deficiency"; in effect, he provides the missing organ through his own body.

This peculiar fetishism, which covers over the absence of a penis with the penis itself rather than with fur or a shoe, admits of two quite diverse political readings. On the one hand, it can be explained as the inability of the homosexual subject to assimilate the anatomical particularity of the mother—as a stubborn refusal of alterity. On the other hand, it can be understood as a resistance to the whole process of devaluation which is made to follow from woman's "difference"— as a refusal to accede to the equation of the mother with insufficiency. Although the first of these readings has a whole psychoanalytic tradition behind it, the second cannot be entirely ruled out of order. It may, indeed, be the more compelling, given the dramatic exclusion of the father from the Leonardo model of homosexuality. As the diagrams introduced a moment ago make clear, the mother occupies one point of this libidinal structure, and the homosexual subject the other two, thereby eliminating the necessity for a paternal third term.[70]

Because of the privileged position which it gives to the mother/child axis, the "Leonardo" model of homosexuality works even more definitively against Oedipal normalization than does the negative Oedipus complex. It not only defies the rule of paternal succession, but it situates the father altogether outside the fields of desire and identification. At the same time, this erotic paradigm is fully triangular, and capable of articulating a complexly functioning subjectivity. I also want to stress that although the subject of the Leonardo model of homosexuality is unable to relinquish his demand for the penis, and incapable of either loving or identifying with the mother except through relation to it, that organ functions not as a marker of symbolic privilege and the Law, but rather as an erotically resonant organ. And because it remains unauthorized by the Name-of-the-Father, the penis is able to circulate freely between desiring subject and desired object, and even to function as an imaginary appendage to the mother.

Paradigm 3 not only poses a series of important challenges to sexual difference, but it obliges us to rethink many of the accepted premises of subjectivity. Nevertheless, like the other two models of homosexuality I have "discovered" within Freud's texts, it affords the male genitals a privileged position. From all three of the variants discussed here, the penis represents the irreducible condition of gay sexuality, that which it cannot relinquish without becoming something altogether other.[71]

But despite the premium which male homosexuality conventionally places on the male sexual organ, Western literature has given us at least two texts which are willing to put that term at risk. One of them—Schreber's *Memoirs of My Nervous Illness*—is easily discounted as "pathological." However, the other—Proust's *A la recherche du temps perdu*—represents one of the defining monuments not only of modernism, but of a quintessentially gay sensibility. I would like to end my investigation of male homosexuality with that text.

6. In Search of a Kissing Organ

Although *A la recherche* is less an autobiography than the fiction of one, its insistent extra-textual referentiality encourages the conflation of narrator and author, as does their shared first name. However, Proust's critics have found it difficult to know where to locate his homosexuality in the story of a man who is presented as loving only women. The classic hermeneutic solution has been to posit a concealed subtext to the novel. Thus J.E. Rivers, for instance, suggests that Albertine is modeled on Alfred Agostinelli, Proust's chauffeur-mechanic in Cabourg, and live-in secretary in Paris.[72] Justin O'Brian pushes this logic further, arguing that Albertine is in fact a disguised boy.[73]

There is clearly a certain urgency at this moment in history about the production of gay readings of canonical works, particularly when the sexuality of their authors seems to encourage doing so. The recourse to Proust's biography provides one strategy for effecting such a reading of *A la recherche*, but Eve Kosofsky Sedgwick suggests that to assume Albertine to be a disguised representation of a male lover is to beg a number of unanswerable questions:

> . . . if Albertine and the narrator are of the same gender, should the supposed outside loves of Albertine, which the narrator obsessively imagines as imaginatively inaccessible to himself, then, maintaining the female gender of their love object, be transposed in orientation into heterosexual desires? Or, maintaining the transgressive same-sex orientation, would they have to change the gender of their love object and be transposed into male homosexual desires? Or, in a homosexual framework, would the heterosexual orientation after all be more transgressive?[74]

The biographical strategy also fails to distinguish, as I have been arguing we must, between the author "inside" the text and the author "outside" the text—between authorial subjectivity and the historical author. Finally, it assumes that gay writers will always generate texts which are at least indirectly expressive of their "true" sexuality. However, as we have seen, erotic consistency cannot be assumed even at the level of the psyche, which may be divided between contradictory desires. Rather than attempting to bring *A la recherche* into conformity with Proust's biography by reading Albertine as the transposed representative of one of his lovers, let us instead focus our attention upon the constellation of identifications and object-choices which accrete around the name "Marcel."

As has frequently been noted by critics of *A la recherche*, the mother occupies a central place within the narrator's subjectivity.[75] Not only does the drama surrounding her good-night kiss dominate Marcel's childhood memories, but it casts a long shadow over his adult sexuality. "This terrible need of a person was something I had learned to know at Combray in the case of my mother, to the point of wanting to die if she sent word to me by Francoise that she could not come upstairs," he observes in *Sodome et Gomorrhe*, by way of explaining his insistence upon Albertine's presence (2, 759). The comparisons he establishes between his mother and his mistress at times assume even more detailed forms, as when he laments that the "unknown world" in which Albertine delights, a world constituted of "her memories, her friendships, her childhood loves," exhales the same "hostile, inexplicable atmosphere . . . that used to float up to my bedroom at Combray, from the dining-room in which I could hear, talking and laughing with strangers amid the clatter of knives and forks, Mama, who would not be coming upstairs to say good-night" (2, 1158), or when he compares touching his lips to Albertine's "bronzed" and "strongly built" neck to the kisses he gave to his mother as a child in order "to calm a childish grief which I did not believe that I would ever be able to eradicate from my heart" (2, 1162). This insistent analogizing of mother and mistress would be easily contained within the structure and temporality of the positive Oedipus complex were it not for two things—a tendency for libidinal investment in the mother to give way to identification with her, and a certain exorbitance with respect to pleasures of the mouth, with a corresponding short-circuiting of genitality.

In *Le temps retrouvé*, the narrator suggests that over time people become less and less like "themselves," and more and more like their parents. Encountering his old friends again after many years, the narrator of that volume cannot help but marvel that

> . . . many of these people could be identified immediately, but only as rather bad portraits of themselves hanging side by side in an exhibition . . . Comparing these effigies with those that the eyes of my memory could show me, I preferred the latter . . . to each of these people, presented with the new image which they showed me of themselves, I should have liked to say: "No, not this one, it is not so good of you. . ." I would not have dared to add: "Instead of your own straight and handsome nose, it has given you your father's crooked nose. . ." And yet this was what had happened: the nose was new, but it was a family nose. (3, 978)

As Serge Doubrovsky emphasizes in *Writing and Fantasy in Proust*, Marcel also discovers himself increasingly over the course of the novel within his familial antecedents, most particularly his mother and her surrogates, the grandmother and Aunt Léonie.[76] However, it is less their physical appearance than their subject-position that he assumes. In *La prisonnière* he ruefully confesses that he has become a man "full of common sense, of severity towards the morbid sensibility of others, a man resembling what my parents had been to me" (3, 103). Elsewhere in the same volume he maintains that "little by little" he is "beginning to resemble all [his] relations" (72), but it is primarily about Aunt Léonie, who is represented as having "transmigrated" into him, that he then speaks. And as Leo Bersani has already remarked, the narrator gives expression to a powerful identification with his mother when, at the conclusion of *A la recherche*, he characterizes himself as "pregnant" with the novel he is about to write.[77]

Even when the adult Marcel visualizes himself as a young man, he sees himself from the maternal point of view. On these occasions he effects an imaginary identification with the image of the boy he once was, and a symbolic identification with his mother. A particularly striking example of this fractured identification occurs late in *Le temps retrouvé*, at the moment when an aging Gilberte de Saint-Loup invites Marcel to dine with her in a restaurant. Marcel responds "Yes, if you don't find it compromising to dine alone with a young man," and then adds parenthetically:

> As I said this, I heard everyone round me laugh, and I hastily added: "or rather, with an old man." I felt that the phrase which had made people laugh was one of those which my mother might have used in speaking of me, my mother for whom I was still a child. And I realized that I judged myself from the same point of view as she did. If in the end I had registered, as she had, certain changes which had taken place since my early childhood . . . I had not advanced beyond the particular one which, long ago . . . had made people say: "He's almost a grown-up man now." (3, 973)

Although this passage occurs near the conclusion of *A la recherche*, indicating that even late in life the narrator of that novel is able from time to time to align himself imaginarily with his adolescent self, it is more typical for the adult Marcel to install others in the structural position of the "child," and to love them as his mother loved him. Since that which he seeks to recover is not a lost object, but "himself," he searches not for "the girls whom [he] had known in the past, but those who now possessed the youthfulness which the others had then had" (3, 1037). It is of course Mlle de Saint-Loup, miraculous point of convergence for the Méséglise and Guermantes Ways, who is consigned to that place at the conclusion of *A la recherche*. "I thought her very beautiful," confides the narrator, "still rich in hopes, full of laughter, formed from those very years which I myself had lost, she was like my own youth" (3, 1088). However, although the novel ends with the image of Mlle de Saint-Loup, it is Albertine who occupies this position earlier in the novel, and who is most extravagantly loved according to the modality of paradigm 3. It is she, above all, who exudes the "aura of adolescence" with which all the girls in the "band" glow, and from which the narrator, young as he still is during his first stay at Balbec, has "already emerged" (1, 966). His love for her consequently represents "but a transitory form of [his] devotion to youth" (3, 659).

Despite the identificatory centrality of the mother throughout the last four volumes of *A la recherche*, Marcel's relationship with Albertine dramatizes the reversibility implicit in narcissistic desire, the possibility of moving back and forth between the maternal position and that of the adolescent or child. The narrator desires that character not only as if *he* were the mother, but as if *she* were the mother. Thus in *La prisonnière*, he describes himself talking to Albertine "at one moment as the child that I had been at Combray used to talk to my mother, [and] at another as my grandmother used to talk to me," and he characterizes his love for her as both "filial and maternal" (3, 73). Elsewhere, Marcel suggests that he keeps Albertine by his bedside not only as a daughter, but as a mistress, a sister, and a mother (3, 107).

Doubrovsky, whose theoretical agenda differs from mine, nevertheless makes the crucial observation that the father is excluded from the system of authorial production out of which *A la recherche* is given as emerging: "...as a *writer*, the Narrator *has no father. His name cannot be Proust.* As a writer ... all his primary identifications are with the maternal imago (Mamma, grandmother, Aunt Léonie). The only name the Narrator of the *Recherche* can bear is his first name...." (90). It seems to me that the argument can be made even more sweepingly and forcefully: the father has no part to play within the authorial subjectivity which structures *A la recherche*, a subjectivity which comes into play around the voice of the narrator. He is foreclosed both as image and name from Marcel's psychic economy, but without any of the catastrophic consequences Lacan imputes to such a foreclosure, since triangulation is nevertheless maintained. The mother occupies the place which the positive Oedipus complex assigns to the father, and the negative Oedipus complex to the mother, while the position of erotic object is filled instead by Albertine in the guise of "Marcel's youth." The Leonardo model of homosexuality is thus clearly, indeed dramatically, at work in *A la recherche*. However, one very large question persists: How are we to account for Albertine's presence within an erotic structure which seems to require precisely that "Albert" whom certain of Proust's critics have wanted to procure from his biography?

Before attempting to answer this question, I want to deepen the reader's puzzlement by looking at the famous passage in which Marcel celebrates Albertine's naked body, a celebration which would seem incompatible with the homosexuality I have located within the pages of *A la recherche*:

> Her two little uplifted breasts were so round that they seemed not
> so much to be an integral part of her body as to have ripened there
> like fruit; and her belly (concealing the place where a man's is
> disfigured as though by an iron clamp left sticking in a statue that

has been taken down from its niche) was closed, at the junction of her thighs, by two valves with a curve as languid, as reposeful, as cloistral as that of the horizon after the sun has set. (3, 74)

The critic hot in pursuit of a disguised male body hidden beneath a feminine disguise might well alight triumphantly, as Rivers does (212), upon the seemingly revealing detail that the breasts imputed to Albertine do not seem an integral part of her anatomy. However, such a reading would have necessarily to minimize another salient feature of these apparent addenda, which is their appeal to the mouth—an appeal which the narrator makes more explicit when he later compares the act of awakening Albertine to cutting open a fruit, and "releas[ing] the gushing juice which quenches thirst" (3, 394).

The mouth represents the privileged site of all of the narrator's erotic transactions with his mother, just as it does within Freud's account of Leonardo.[78] It retains this function even after desire for the mother has yielded to identification with her, for reasons that will become clear later in this analysis. Whenever the narrator speaks of his sexual interactions with Albertine, he always presents himself as one of those "epicures in kissing" of whom *Three Essays* speaks (182). So enamored of oral pleasure is the narrator of *A la recherche* that he at one point confesses his willingness to pay more than one hundred francs a day in order to have Albertine's breath "between my lips which I laid half-open upon hers, through which her life flowed against my tongue" (3, 68). Elsewhere in the text he speaks of the tranquility conferred upon him by the "kisses of peace" which Albertine slips "into my mouth, in making me the [reciprocal] gift of *her* tongue [my emphasis]" (3, 72). Marcel is so completely absorbed within an oral erotics that the mere sound of Albertine's laugh is sufficient to conjure forth the moist interior of her mouth and throat as a lush pleasure-zone. That sound "at once evoke[s] the flesh-pink, fragrant surfaces with which it seem[s] to have just been in contact and of which it seem[s] to carry with it, pungent, sensual and revealing as the scent of geraniums, a few almost tangible and mysteriously revealing particles" (2, 823).[79] Female cheeks also represent a privileged site for voluptuous grazing, whether real or fantasmatic.

(This is perhaps the moment to suggest that because of the importance which it gives to the mouth, even the larger project of *A la recherche* can be read as a textual extension of the Leonardo model of homosexuality. Not only is the novel organized around Marcel's reconstitution of his earlier "selves," but it is through the oral pleasure of a madeleine dipped in tea that he first communicates with or "makes love" to what he once was.)

The narrator's treatment of the male and the female genitals in the passage under discussion is rather more puzzling. Rivers maintains that "when the narrator looks at the curve of Albertine's belly, the first thing he notices is that there is no penis in the place where, in the body of a man, we would normally expect to find one" (212), an observation which should encourage us to take the rest of the passage, with its apparent erotic enshrinement of the female body, with a large grain of salt (213). Doubrovsky, on the other hand, maintains that this description of Albertine's body attests to Marcel's desire to rid himself of the penis, and thereby to become "like his Mother" (104). Both of these readings import into the Proustian text something which is, at this juncture, quite remarkably absent from it—a thematics of castration. The dominant trope of sexual differentiation here is not "lack," but "superfluity," or "term in excess."

What would seem to emerge with absolute clarity from any careful reading of this little "essay" on anatomical distinction is that the female genitals are *not*, in and of themselves, a locus of excitement for the narrator of *A la recherche*. Far from expressing a desire to open up what has been closed off by the "valves" of the thighs, he sanctions the isolation of the "belly" from the genitals, and characterizes the former in terms more evocative of a convent than a boudoir. Again, the too-hasty reader might explain the narrator's failure to include the female genitals in his erotic blazon as the careful delimitation of that part of Albertine's body which would be intolerable to a homosexual spectator—as the cordoning off of what would otherwise precipitate a "flight" from woman. However, such a reading would be predicated upon the equation of the labial region with penile lack, and such an equation is emphatically inoperative here. This passage marks the *male* rather than the *female* body negatively, and precisely at that site whose conventional valorization facilitates a masculine identification with the phallus. Rather than dwelling upon woman's "wound," the narrator of *A la recherche* focuses instead upon the male genitals, which he characterizes in terms suggestive not merely of superfluity but foreignness. How are we to reconcile Marcel's depiction of the penis as a cumbersome and aesthetically displeasing "clamp left sticking in a statue that has been taken down from its niche" with the premium normally placed upon that organ by all forms of male homosexuality?

Before attempting to answer this question, I would like to suggest that this curious reconceptualization of the elements of sexual difference results neither from Proust's attempt to conceal the narrator's homosexuality—and, by implication, his own—nor from some implicitly feminist agenda, but rather from the preference given to oral over genital sexuality. Kissing repeatedly emerges as the preeminent synecdoche not only for sexual pleasure, but for desire and carnal "knowledge." The temporal interval during which male lips move slowly toward female lips or cheeks provides a favored figure for the intoxication of anticipation (it is during one such gradual approach that Marcel fantasizes that in kissing Albertine he will be "kissing the whole of Balbec beach" (2, 376). Similarly, the moment at which lips reach lips or cheeks is made to dramatize the disappointment which always follows immediately upon possession, along with the radical diminution of the beloved object. Kissing also provides a privileged signifier both for the will to epistemological mastery and for the frustration of that imperative; the narrator always imagines as he embarks upon his amorous journey that oral contact with the object will generate knowledge of it—that in touching Albertine's cheeks he will come to "know the taste of this fleshly rose" (2, 377). However, he is obliged to halt at the surface of the skin, prevented from delving more deeply.

Significantly, despite his stated desire to descend beneath the body's surface, the narrator does not substitute penis and vagina for lips and cheeks, "end-pleasure" for "fore-pleasure." He meditates instead upon his desire for a new organ, an organ for kissing. And whereas the rhetoric of lack in no way informs the passage anatomizing Albertine's body, it does permeate the narrator's account of the actual kissing "equipment" which he would like to exchange for this imaginary appendage:

> . . . man, a creature obviously less rudimentary than the sea-urchin or even the whale, nevertheless lacks a certain number of essential organs, and notably possesses none that will serve for kissing. For this absent organ he substitutes his lips, and thereby arrives perhaps at a slightly more satisfying result than if he were reduced to caressing the beloved with a horny tusk. But a pair of lips, designed to convey to the palate the taste of whatever whets their appetite, must be content, without understanding their mistake or admitting their disappointment, with roaming over the surface and with coming to a halt at the barrier of the impenetrable but irresistible cheek. (2, 377–78)

The narrator goes on to enumerate as features missing from the lips, but presumably incorporated into the fantasmatic kissing organ, the senses both of smell, and of a multivalent sight, capable of taking in simultaneously all the "changes of perspective and . . . coloring which a person presents to us in the course of our various encounters" (378–79). Kissing as we presently know it, on the other hand, blinds the eyes and crushes the nose.

Within this context, then, the fantasmatic kissing organ can best be understood not only as a vehicle for achieving knowledge through penetration, but as a device for making the moment of realization equal to the moment of anticipation. This important passage resituates the insufficiency which all too often seems to reside in the object at the site of the subject's perceptual machinery. It also refuses to specify lack according to a logic of sexual differentiation, preferring instead to conceptualize it in terms of an organ which is absent to every subject, but the possession of which would make erotic conjunction commensurate with desire. And it locates this utopian sexuality precisely where it consistently situates its more quotidian counterpart—at the site of the mouth. That orifice consequently functions not only as the preferred site for erotic reception, but as the imaginary locus for an organ capable of penetrating other bodies. It represents the narrator's erotogenic zone of choice, in other words, both when he identifies with the youth he once was, and when he identifies with the mother.

Marcel's orality would align him as smoothly with the Leonardo paradigm of homosexuality as do the other elements of his libidinal economy were it not for its apparent indifference to the penis, and its designation of Albertine as a privileged love-object. Once again I will ask: What are we to make of these anomalies? The answer, it seems to me, resides within the pages of *Sodome et Gomorrhe*. Part One of that volume informs us that there are two broad categories of homosexuals—those who can love only men, and those who can love lesbian women as well as men. Those who restrict themselves to men place few limitations on sexual activity, but those who are more accommodating in their object-choice demand very specific kinds of sexual pleasure. What this would seem to imply is that although the first kind of homosexual is capable of entering into a variety of sexual practices, he can do so only in some direct or indirect relation to his partner's penis. What is at issue for the second kind of homosexual is less the partner's genitals than a particular kind of sexual conjunction. It is a prerequisite that this conjunction occur on a "same-sex" basis, but sexual identity need not be established along narrowly anatomical lines. "Same-sex" can consequently mean two morphological men; a gay man and a lesbian woman, both of whom occupy a masculine psychic position; or a lesbian woman and a gay man, both of whom occupy a feminine psychic position. *A la recherche* consequently invites us to conceptualize a male homosexuality within which the penis does not play the usually requisite role at the site of the erotic object—a male homosexuality which is not in flight from female "lack" because its definition of sexual identity is not exclusively anatomical:

> Some . . . are not greatly concerned with the kind of physical pleasure they receive, provided that they can associate it with a mascu-

line face. Whereas others, whose sensuality is doubtless more violent, feel an imperious need to localize their physical pleasure. These latter, perhaps, would shock the average person with their avowals. They live perhaps less exclusively beneath the sway of Saturn's outrider, since for them women are not excluded as they are for the former sort . . . But the second sort seek out those women who love other women, who can procure for them a young man . . . better still, they can, in the same fashion, enjoy with such women the same pleasure as with a man . . . in their relations with women, they play, for the woman who loves her own sex, the part of another woman, and she offers them at the same time more or less what they find in other men, so that the jealous friend suffers from the feeling that the man he loves is riveted to the woman who is to him almost a man, and at the same time feels his beloved almost escape him because, to these women, he is something which the lover himself cannot conceive, a sort of woman. (2, 645–46)

If the avowals of the second type of man "would shock the average person" more than the first would, it is because he poses a formidable challenge not only to the heterosexual norm, but to our usual ways of thinking about homosexuality. Let us pause for a moment to consider just how extreme that challenge can be, since it is only by doing so that we will be able to account for Marcel's sexuality. What is it that a woman and a man would be typically perceived as having in common sexually with respect to a second man? Anus, mouth, and epidermis. What actions might the second man take in relation to these shared erotogenic zones? Apart from simply looking, he might bring his hand, body, or mouth in contact with any of them, or penetrate mouth or anus with his penis. Bondage and flagellation encompass a range of other possible forms of sexual practice involving these same erotogenic zones. The point I am trying to make with this far from exhaustive list is that we ought not to assume that homosexuality necessarily implies only penises and anuses, or penises and mouths. Although each of the homosexuals designated by Proust's second category has repeated recourse to a specific erotic event, either with a second man or a lesbian woman, those events are far more varied than conventionally assumed. *A la recherche* encourages us to understand that even epicurean kissing between a man and a woman aligned along same-sex lines is encompassable within the second category of homosexuality. Much more startlingly, it obliges us to conceive of a male homosexuality which not only takes as one of its objects a lesbian woman, but which dispenses with the possibility of "using" her as a man.

Marcel and Albertine are not lovers "in the full sense of the word" 3, 91), an acknowledgment which would seem to imply the foreclosure from their sexual activity of vaginal penetration. As Sedgwick has recently pointed out, Albertine also refers to anality at one point in the text as a pleasure which is excluded from their erotic interactions, although not from her thoughts.[80] Nor does there seem to be a place for the penis within their pursuit of *oral* gratification. It is consequently difficult to conceptualize their relationship as one involving two "men," however de-essentialized the definition of masculinity. Disquieting as the thought may be to many readers of *A la recherche*, however, Proust *does* encourage us to conceive of Marcel's affair with Albertine as one between two "women." It is thus only through lesbianism that we are finally able to locate the homosexuality which so clearly structures authorial subjectivity in *A la recherche*. And although a homosexual relationship which expresses itself through lesbianism would seem to have jubilantly triumphed over anatomical destiny, we will here discover the same-sex imperative assuming surprisingly literal forms.

The narrator of *A la recherche* never explicitly associates himself with the second group of homosexuals he describes in *Sodome et Gomorrhe*. Nevertheless, he does come perilously close at one point to acknowledging that Albertine's lesbianism is not so much a difficulty within their relationship as its precondition. However, at the last minute he obliges Saint-Loup to stand in for himself as a representative of the kind of homosexual man who does not demand anatomical masculinity in his love-object:

> Now I understood what Robert had meant when he said to me at the Princesse de Guermantes's: "It's a pity your Balbec girl friend hasn't the fortune that my mother insists upon. I believe that she and I would have got on very well together." He had meant that she belonged to Gomorrah as he belonged to Sodom. . . . And on the whole it was the same thing that had given both Robert and myself a desire to marry Albertine—to wit, the knowledge that she was a lover of women. But the causes of our desire . . . were the reverse of each other. In my case, it was the despair in which I had been plunged by the discovery [of her sexual predilections] . . . (3, 697)

Confession would not so readily ooze out of this passage were it not for the fact that Marcel's desire for Albertine never assumes more feverish intensity than when she has given him new reason to suspect her of lesbian inclinations, whether in relation to Andrée, Mlle Vinteuil and her friend, Léa, or laundry-girls. It is also worth noting in this context that his interest in Albertine is initially piqued by her proximity to the other girls in the Balbec "band," particularly given that early in *A la recherche* the narrator hints at Charlus's homosexuality by observing of his voice that it "seemed to embody choirs of betrothed maidens," or, alternately, a "bevy of young girls" (1, 820). The grouping together of young women would seem to function as an all-purpose inscription of same-sex eros.

Marcel's erotic investment in lesbianism is most tellingly signaled by the particular kinds of anxieties that are evoked in him by the thought of Albertine's amorous adventures, and the fantasies with which he dispels those anxieties. Interestingly, given the closed valves of Albertine's thighs in the passage celebrating her nudity, the female genitals do have a role to play here. They figure, predictably, as a potential signifier of alterity. However, that alterity is less a term to be suppressed than a condition to which Marcel aspires. It is his own body rather than Albertine's which represents a possible obstacle in the way of their homosexual union. We find Marcel worrying that Albertine's lesbian affairs may feature pleasures different in kind from those he gives her, pleasures based upon anatomical difference. "What else can a woman represent to Albertine?" he wonders at one point (3, 311). At another juncture he laments that the person he loves "is finding pleasure with beings who are different from [himself], who give her sensations which [he is] not capable of giving her, or who at least by their configuration, their aspect, their ways, represent to her something quite different from [himself]" (3, 556).

In order for the narrator to establish a same-sex relationship with Albertine, the threat posed by his own anatomical otherness must somehow be neutralized. That is precisely what happens in Marcel's most fully-articulated fantasy about lesbianism. That fantasy occurs after Albertine's death, which has intensified rather than diminished his anxiety about female sexuality, and in immediate response to new information about her lesbian infidelities. The discovery that Albertine was fond of making love with a laundry-girl and her friends on the bank of the Loire when staying at Châtellerault elicits from Marcel the recollection of two paintings by Elstir of naked women in wooded landscapes. One of these remembered images provides the starting point for a singular reverie:

> In one of [the paintings], a girl is raising her foot as Albertine must have raised hers when she offered it to the laundress. With her other foot she is pushing into the water another girl who gaily resists, her thigh raised, her foot barely dipping into the blue water. I remembered now that the raised thigh made the same swan's-neck curve with the angle of the knee as was made by the droop of Albertine's thigh when she was lying by my side . . . Remembering Albertine as she lay on my bed, I seemed to see the curve of her thigh, I saw it as a swan's neck, seeking the other girl's mouth. Then

> I no longer even saw a thigh, but simply the bold neck of a swan, like the one that can be seen in a voluptuous sketch seeking the mouth of a Leda who is rapt in the palpitating specificity of feminine pleasure, because there is no one with her but a swan . . . In this sketch, the pleasure, instead of reaching out to the woman who inspires it and who is absent . . . is concentrated in her who feels it. (3, 538)

This fantasy enacts an astonishing series of transformations and displacements, by means of which the narrator is able to insert himself into a scene from which he would seem, by definition, to be excluded. Over the course of the passage I have just quoted, Albertine is evoked first as a thigh joined to a knee, then as the curve of a thigh, later as the "bold neck of a swan," and finally as "no one . . . but a swan." In the process the female genitals[82] are both de-anthropomorphized, and moved from the focal point of the fantasy to its margins. Albertine's partner, on the other hand, is metamorphosed from "another girl," to "a Leda," to the fantasy's center of consciousness. Concomitantly, the "palpitating specificity of feminine pleasure" is shifted from the composite erotogenic zone where it is usually assumed to reside to a site which is not particular to woman—from Albertine's genitals to her sexual partner's mouth. This relocation makes it possible for the narrator to occupy the position of Albertine's imagined lover through identification with her, and in so doing to accede to the place marked out as the locus of female *jouissance*. In effect, then, his lips have transferred to them the pleasure which is initially localized at Albertine's genital "lips."

It should be evident by now that the narrator's homosexuality is able to find expression not only through the strictly oral gratification which he derives from Albertine, but through fantasized scenes of lesbian love-making in which the mouth is given priority over the genitals, while at the same time existing in a metaphoric relation to them. It also seems obvious that some version of this lesbian fantasy, so reminiscent of Leonardo's own ornithological "memory," underwrites Marcel's relationship with Albertine. I might almost be tempted to invoke Irigaray's "two lips kissing two lips" by way of ending this chapter were it not for that organ which threatens to obtrude precisely at the location of the mouth—Marcel's fantasmatic kissing organ. What, given the Châtellerault fantasy, are we to make of this fantasmatic feature? Does it mark the return of the repressed penis?

As I have already suggested, the mythical kissing organ is possessed of qualities which distinguish it from the male sexual member, most notably the faculties of vision and smell. Moreover, since everyone lacks this organ it cannot presumably function, like the phallus, as a signifier of privilege. However, the imaginary appendage does possess one notable penile attribute—the capacity to penetrate. We are thus obliged, in attempting to account for the kissing organ, both to compare it to, and to differentiate it from, the male sexual organ.

Engaging for the moment only in the second half of this double reading, I will suggest that Marcel's prosthetic fantasy can perhaps best be understood as a dramatization of his desire both to complicate and improve upon the erotic properties of the mouth, and to enjoy the pleasure of penetration without that pleasure being in any way marked by masculinity. Given Marcel's insistent psychic factoring out of his own genitals, and equally obsessive "recognition" of himself within his female relatives, this fantasy may even stage the desire to penetrate the surface of a loved body while remaining at the same time a "woman."

It may seem surprising, in light of the reading I have just suggested, that I have accommodated Proust's narrator and authorial representative within this discussion of male homosexuality. Why not think of Marcel simply as a lesbian? I have incorporated *A la recherche* here in part because its central character is established as being psychically female, but corporeally male, and hence "a woman's soul enclosed in a man's body." I have also made *A la recherche* the "last stop" in my analysis of male homosexuality because Marcel's love for Albertine is predicated not upon her anatomical femininity, but rather upon the combined possibility of deriving oral gratification from her, and of entertaining a same-sex relationship with her. If, as I have been arguing, the second category of male homosexuality defined in *Sodome et Gomorrhe* includes Marcel, woman represents less his *preferred* love-object than a *possible* love-object. Proust claims, after all, not that this kind of man seeks out women, but that women are not "entirely excluded" for him—that he lives "perhaps less exclusively beneath the sway of Saturn's outrider" than do some of his compatriots. Finally, I have included *A la recherche* in this discussion of male homosexuality because its narrator's fantasy about a kissing organ is predicated upon his desire to penetrate the body of a "same-sex" object with an erotically sensitized corporeal appendage. Given the hyperbolic reversibility of Marcel's libidinal economy, that fantasy necessarily includes as well the desire to be so penetrated, which returns us, once again, to the Leonardo model of male homosexuality.

In describing the kissing organ as the "trace" of that which is anatomically specific to male homosexuality, I am performing the other half of the reading for which I called above. Despite their incompatibility, both of these formulations must be advanced, just as it was imperative earlier in this chapter to propose two contrary accounts of the fetishism I found at the center of the Leonardo model of homosexuality—to claim, that is, that in covering the mother's lack with his own penis, the prototypical resident of paradigm 3 attests both to an inability to accept woman's alterity, and to a rejection of sexual difference as it has been culturally codified.

In refusing to give one of these conflicting interpretations priority over the other, I am attempting to foreground the subjective contradiction which structures that variant of male homosexuality which, for the reasons I have already outlined, may finally have the most resonance for feminism—the contradiction of sustaining at least a partial identification with femininity while occupying a masculine body, and of looking for femininity within the loved object while at the same time placing a premium on the penis. By articulating the same-sex imperative through lesbianism rather than male homosexuality, and by giving himself identificatory access to that alien eroticism by concentrating all sexual gratification at the site of the mouth, Marcel attempts to resolve the contradiction in the Châtellerault fantasy. The passage in which he makes this attempt represents a transcendent and utopian moment within the history of gay representation, for it abolishes anatomical difference by conforming the male body to the female rather than the female body to the male. But this moment cannot be endlessly sustained.

It may seem that the last few pages have launched an assault upon the male sex organ—that I have attempted, indeed, to write that organ out of male homosexuality, or to discredit the part it plays there. This is not my wish. The very different project of this chapter has been to demonstrate that femininity inhabits male homosexuality in all kinds of interesting, enabling, and politically productive ways—to show that the subject-positions and psychic conditions which are conventionally designated by that signifier may ultimately be as central to gay identity and erotic practice as are the male genitalia. However, I have ultimately privileged the Châtellerault fantasy over the fantasy of the kissing organ because it showcases something which the third model of homosexuality classically occludes, something which Leonardo, indeed, was unable to draw:[82] the female body. By acknowledging what is particular to that body without immediately subsuming it within what we have come to call "sexual difference," Proust forces an important resolution to the crisis precipitated by what Freud would call the "anatomical distinctions between the sexes," a resolution whose uses exceed a strictly homosexual deployment. It effects an imaginary relay between the male mouth and the female genitals, a relay which it makes conducive not of trauma and revulsion, but of ecstasy.

I would like to conclude not only this chapter but the book of which it is a part with the image of the curved thigh approaching the throbbing mouth, since it provides such a vivid demonstration of the gains implicit for the female subject in the "denormalization" of male subjectivity—gains which extend beyond the bedroom to the far reaches of our "world." For what is finally at issue here is not just an erotic economy which defies the procreative imperative, and blurs the distinction between fore-pleasure and end-pleasure, but one which decenters the male sexual organ, delineates a continuity of pleasure extending from male lips to female genitals, and refuses to write "lack" at the site of the female body. What the Châtellerault fantasy dramatizes, in other words, is a particularly emphatic suspension of masculine belief in the dominant fiction and its injurious binarisms— the refusal to project castration onto the corporeality of the sexual Other, and thereby to secure the phallus as the unquestioned signifier of power, privilege, and wholeness.

But the Châtellerault fantasy attests to more than the advantages to be derived by the female subject from the relaxation of the "masculine protest." It also bodies forth a few of the unexpected pleasures and possibilities that await the male subject when he renegotiates his relation to the Law of Language—when he accedes to his castration, his specularity, and the profound "otherness" of his "self" by embracing desires and identifications which are in excess of the positive Oedipus complex. After even a partial glimpse of those pleasures and psychic possibilities, who would still opt for the straight and narrow path of conventional masculinity?

Afterword

In the preceding pages, I have attempted to show that our desires and identifications have such important extra-psychic ramifications that it is no exaggeration to speak of a "libidinal politics." I have also tried to complicate the notion of "the feminine"—to show that it designates a number of conditions that are constitutive of all subjectivity, although they are antipathetic to conventional masculinity. Finally, I have struggled to expose the murderous logic of traditional male subjectivity, and to articulate some alternative ways of inhabiting a morphologically masculine body. The marginal male subjectivities that I have most fully valorized are those which absent themselves from the line of paternal succession, and which in one way or another occupy the domain of femininity.

What is my own connection to these "deviant" masculinities? It will perhaps come as no surprise to the reader to learn that while writing this book I often felt myself to be somehow "outside" my corporeal "envelope," and "inside" the subjectivities I was exploring. Since the psychic space into which I thereby stepped was generally one which was familiar to me, I might not seem to have traveled very far away from myself through these exteriorizing identifications. However, for a female subject to re-encounter femininity from within a male body is clearly to experience it under different terms—to live it no longer as disenfranchisement and subordination, but rather as phallic divestiture, as a way of saying "no" to power. It is thus, as I discovered, to alter forever her own relationship to femininity's defining tropes.

Notes

Introduction

1. Michel Foucault, *The History of Sexuality, Volume 1: An Introduction*, trans. Robert Hurley (New York: Vintage Books, 1980), 105–6.

2. Elsewhere in the same paragraph, however, Foucault does impute to sexuality an oppositional force, albeit not under that name. He speaks of countering "the grips of power with the claims of bodies, pleasures, and knowledges, in their multiplicity and their possibility of resistance."

3. I draw loosely here upon Jacques Lacan, "The Mirror Stage," in *Ecrits: A Selection*, trans. Alan Sheridan (New York: Norton, 1977), 1–7. For Freud, the ego is also a "precipitate" of external images—or, to be more precise, of "abandoned object-cathexes" (see *The Ego and the Id*, in *The Standard Edition of the Complete Psychological Works*, trans. James Strachey [London: Hogarth Press, 1961], vol. 19, 29).

4. Jean Laplanche and J.-B. Pontalis, *The Language of Psycho-Analysis*, trans. Donald Nicholson-Smith (New York: Norton, 1973), 317.

5. See Jacques Lacan, *Four Fundamental Concepts of Psycho-Analysis*, trans. Alan Sheridan (New York: Norton, 1978), 203–29 for a discussion of the incompatibility of being and meaning.

6. Jacques Lacan, *The Seminar of Jacques Lacan, Book II: The Ego in Freud's Theory and in the Technique of Psychoanalysis, 1954–1955*, trans. Sylvana Tomaselli (Cambridge: Cambridge University Press, 1988), 167 and 175.

7. Jacques Lacan, *The Seminar of Jacques Lacan, Book I: Freud's Papers on Technique, 1953–1954*, trans. John Forrester (Cambridge: Cambridge University Press, 1988), 141.

8. "Pound of flesh" is how Lacan metaphorizes being in "Desire and the Interpretation of Desire in *Hamlet*," trans. James Hulbert, *Yale French Studies*, nos.55 & 56 (1977): 28.

9. Lacan, *The Seminar I*, 142.

10. The primary process, which has an important part to play in the formation of dreams and fantasies, privileges similitude over difference, and sensory and affective intensity over logic. It is likelier to collapse two related terms into each other than to distinguish between them. For a discussion of the primary process, see Sigmund Freud, *The Interpretation of Dreams, Standard Edition*, vol. 5, 588–609. I provide a commentary on this section of *The Interpretation of Dreams* in *The Subject of Semiotics* (New York: Oxford University Press, 1983), 54–86.

11. Jean Laplanche and J.-B. Pontalis, "Fantasy and the Origins of Sexuality," *The International Journal of Psycho-Analysis*, vol. 49, no. 1 (1968):13 and 16.

12. As Laplanche and Pontalis explain in "Fantasy and the Origins of Sexuality," "the indication here of the primary process is not the absence of organization, as is sometimes suggested, but the peculiar character of the structure, in that it is a scenario with multiple entries, in which nothing shows whether the subject will be immediately located as *daughter*; it can be fixed as *father*, or even in the term *seduces*" (14).

13. Laplanche and Pontalis, *The Language of Psycho-Analysis*, 318. I am drawing here not only upon this text, but upon Freud's "'A Child Is Being Beaten,'" *Standard Edition*, vol. 17, 179–204, and "Leonardo da Vinci and a Memory of His Childhood," *Standard Edition*, vol. 11, 63–137, each of which hinges upon the articulation of a particular unconscious fantasmatic. In both of these fantasmatics, the ego is central. Freud also stresses the centrality of the ego within fantasy in "Creative Writers and Day-Dreaming," *Standard Edition*, vol. 9, 141–53.

14. Lacan, *The Seminar II*, 214.

15. Lacan, *The Seminar I*, 79.

16. Lacan, *The Seminar II*, 167.

17. Laplanche and Pontalis, *The Language of Psycho-Analysis*, 318.

18. For the text which relies most fully upon Laplanche and Pontalis to authorize an insistence upon the mobility of the subject within fantasy, see Elizabeth Cowie, "Fantasia," *m/f*, no. 9 (1984): 71–105.

19. Jean Laplanche, *Life and Death in Psychoanalysis*, trans. Jeffrey Mehlman (Baltimore: The Johns Hopkins University Press, 1976), 125–26. Freud associates the secondary process with the anchoring of linguistic signifiers to perceptual memories, with the diminution of affect, and with the articulation of difference. It also has an important part to play in the formation and maintenance of the Freudian ego. For a fuller explanation of the secondary process in Freud, see *The Interpretation of Dreams*, 588–609, and Silverman, *The Subject of Semiotics*, 54–86.

20. Slavoj Žižek, *The Sublime Object of Ideology* (London: Verso, 1989), 118.

21. What I am calling "imaginary identification" corresponds to what Žižek describes under the same name. His definition of symbolic identification,

however, differs from mine. For him, symbolic identification is "identification with the very place *from where* we are being observed" (*The Sublime Object of Ideology*, 104–105).

1. The Dominant Fiction

1. The term with which Foucault effects this "epistemological break" is of course "discourse," which has since the publication of *The Archaeology of Knowledge and the Discourse on Language*, trans. A.M. Sheridan Smith (New York: Pantheon, 1972), largely displaced "ideology" as a category of social analysis in Britain and North America.

2. This is a phrase used by Siegfried Kracauer in "Those Movies With a Message," *Harper's Magazine*, vol. 196, no. 1177 (June 1948): 572.

3. See Louis Althusser, "Ideology and Ideological State Apparatuses," in *Lenin and Philosophy and Other Essays*, trans. Ben Brewster (London: Monthly Review Press, 1971), 177–83 for a discussion of Christianity as an ideological system.

4. Althusser, "Ideology and Ideological State Apparatuses," 169.

5. Slavoj Žižek, *The Sublime Object of Ideology* (London: Verso, 1989), 34.

6. Althusser, "Ideology and Ideological State Apparatuses," 168.

7. Michel Foucault, *Discipline and Punish: The Birth of the Prison*, trans. Alan Sheridan (New York: Vintage-Random House, 1979), 138.

8. Louis Althusser, "Theory, Theoretical Practice and Theoretical Formation: Ideology and Ideological Struggle," in *Philosophy and the Spontaneous Philosophy of the Scientists and Other Essays*, trans. Ben Brewster, James H. Kavanagh, Thomas E. Lewis, Grahame Lock, and Warren Montag (London: Verso, 1990), 26.

9. Sigmund Freud, *The Project for a Scientific Psychology*, in *The Standard Edition of the Complete Psychological Works*, trans. James Strachey (London: Hogarth Press, 1966), vol. 1, 333.

10. See Sigmund Freud, *The Interpretation of Dreams, Standard Edition*, vol. 5, 509–621 for an elaboration of this theoretical model.

11. *The Complete Letters of Sigmund Freud to Wilhelm Fliess, 1887–1904*, trans. and ed. Jeffrey Moussaieff Masson (Cambridge, Mass.: Harvard University Press, 1985), 264.

12. Sigmund Freud, "Formulation on the Two Principles of Mental Functioning," *Standard Edition*, vol. 12, 225.

13. J. Laplanche and J.-B. Pontalis, *The Language of Psycho-Analysis*, trans. Donald Nicholson-Smith (New York: Norton, 1973), 363.

14. Laplanche and Pontalis attribute these two functions to fantasy in *The Language of Psycho-Analysis*, 317–18.

15. Sigmund Freud, "The Uncanny," *Standard Edition*, vol. 17, 249.

16. *The Complete Letters of Sigmund Freud to Wilhelm Fliess*, 272. This letter demands to be read in relation to the one cited earlier, dating from September 21, 1897.

17. Jacques Lacan, *The Seminar of Jacques Lacan, Book II: The Ego in Freud's Theory and in the Technique of Psychoanalysis, 1954–1955*, trans. Sylvana Tomaselli (Cambridge: Cambridge University Press, 1988), 28.

18. Marcel Proust, *Remembrance of Things Past*, trans. C.K. Scott Moncrieff and Terence Kilmartin (New York: Vintage Books, 1982), vol. 1, 201.

19. Lacan, *The Seminar II*, 211. For a discussion of the fundamental objectlessness of desire, see the "Introduction" to the present volume.

20. In "Kant avec Sade," *Ecrits*, vol. 2 (Paris: Editions du Seuil, 1971), 129, Lacan explains that in the formula for fantasy, "*le poinçon < > se lit «désir de»*."

21. Jacques Lacan, *Four Fundamental Concepts of Psycho-Analysis*, trans. Alan Sheridan (New York: Norton, 1978), 103.

22. Laplanche and Pontalis, *The Language of Psycho-Analysis*, 363.

23. Lacan stresses the centrality of the ego to psychic reality in *The Seminar II*: "The image of [the subject's] body is the principle of every unity he perceives in objects. Now, he only perceives the unity of this specific image from the outside, and in an anticipated manner. Because of this double relation which he has with himself, all the objects of his world are always structured around the wandering shadow of his own ego" (166).

24. Jacques Lacan, "The Mirror Stage," in *Ecrits: A Selection*, trans. Alan Sheridan (New York: Norton, 1977), 2.

25. Jane Gallop, *Reading Lacan* (Ithaca: Cornell University Press, 1985), 74–92.

26. We might even schematize the subject's relation to the ego in much the way that Lacan schematizes fantasy—as $ < > a'$, a formula which would maximize the mirroring relation of ego (a) and object (a') emphasized in an important diagram from *Seminar II*:

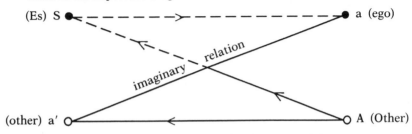

The Imaginary function of the ego and the discourse of the unconscious

I have modified this diagram slightly so as to bring the notations "*a*" and "*a'*" into closer conformity with the similar diagram provided in "D'une question préliminaire à tout traitement possible de la psychose," in *Ecrits*, vol. 2 (Paris: Editions du Seuil, 1971), 63.

27. Jean Laplanche, *Life and Death in Psychoanalysis*, trans. Jeffrey Mehlman (Baltimore: The Johns Hopkins University Press, 1976), 80.

28. Louis Althusser, "Marxism and Humanism," in *For Marx*, trans. Ben Brewster (London: New Left Books, 1977), 234.

29. See Stephen Heath, "The Turn of the Subject," *Ciné-Tracts*, vol. 2, nos.3 & 4 (1979): 32–48.

30. Althusser, "Ideology and Ideological State Apparatuses," 171.

31. Louis Althusser, "'The Piccolo Teatro': Bertolazzi and Brecht," in *For Marx*, 144.

32. This aspect of the Althusserian paradigm has been much criticized. Jacques Rancière, for instance, maintains that Althusser suppresses the class struggle in insisting upon the unifying function of the ideology of the ascendent class ("On the Theory of Ideology [The Politics of Althusser]," *Radical Philosophy*, vol. 7, no.19 [1974]: 2–15). For a fuller account of Rancière's relationship to Althusser's work, see the text from which this essay derives, *La leçon d'Althusser* (Paris: Gallimard, 1974). Paul Hirst, Colin Sumner, and Ted Benton object not only to Althusser's equation of hegemony with the ideology of the dominant class, but to what they describe as his "functionalism"—to his representation of ideology as a vehicle and effect of the economic structure. Hirst writes that ideology as Althusser conceives it is "a means to the fulfilment of a functional end." Moreover, "this means has no determinant effect on the form for which it is functional," but "merely performs the function of maintenance or reproduction" ("Althusser and the Theory of Ideology," in *On Law and Ideology* [London: Macmillan, 1979], 43). Sumner maintains that at least up through "Ideology and Ideological State Apparatuses," Althusser presents ideology as "a reflection of the economic structure which travels via the state into the workers' brains" (*Reading Ideology: An Investigation into the Marxist Theory of Ideology and Law* [London: Academic Press, 1979], 38). Benton complains that Althusser's "functional perspective on the ISA's, that they reproduce the relations of production, has more than a ring of 'economism' about it: the economy sets up requirements which are 'met' by the superstructures" (*The Rise and Fall of Structural Marxism: Althusser and His Influence* [London: Macmillan, 1984], 104).

33. Louis Althusser, "The Transformation of Philosophy," in *Philosophy and the Spontaneous Philosophy of the Scientists and Other Essays*, 258.

34. Chantal Mouffe, "Hegemony and Ideology in Gramsci," in *Gramsci and Marxist Theory*, ed. Chantal Mouffe (London: Routledge & Kegan Paul, 1979), 195.

35. In "The Agency of the Letter in the Unconscious," Lacan suggests that for the male and female subjects, the lavatory signs "Ladies" and "Gentle-

men" represent "two countries towards which each of their souls will strive on divergent wings" (*Ecrits: A Selection*, 152).

36. Jean Laplanche and J.-B. Pontalis, "Fantasy and the Origins of Sexuality," *The International Journal of Psycho-Analysis*, vol. 49, no.1 (1968): 11.

37. Laplanche, *Life and Death in Psychoanalysis*, 24, and 44–47.

38. In "Fantasy and the Origins of Sexuality," 9, Laplanche and Pontalis equate this discourse with the symbolic order. It will become clearer later in this chapter why I have attributed it instead to the dominant fiction.

39. Ernesto Laclau, "Fascism and Ideology," in *Politics and Ideology in Marxist Theory: Capitalism-Fascism-Populism* (London: Verso, 1977), 108.

40. Jacques Rancière, "Interview: The Image of Brotherhood," trans. Kari Hanet, *Edinburgh Magazine*, no. 2 (1977): 28.

41. Not surprisingly, there is some confusion in the passage under discussion about the status of this "structure" or "configuration." At moments, Althusser distinguishes it from ideology, but at other times he collapses the two.

42. Quoted in "Publisher's Note to 'Freud and Lacan,'" in Louis Althusser, *Lenin and Philosophy*, 190.

43. Louis Althusser, "Freud and Lacan," *Lenin and Philosophy*, 198–99.

44. Althusser, "Marxism and Humanism," 233.

45. I would like to join Michèle Barrett in suggesting that relations of production include not only class divisions, but "the divisions of gender, of race, definitions of different forms of labor (mental, manual and so on), of who should work and at what." See her *Women's Oppression Today: Problems in Marxist Feminist Analysis* (London: Verso, 1980), 99.

46. For a discussion of the "fading" of the subject's being upon the entry into language, see Lacan, *Four Fundamental Concepts*, 203–29.

47. Claude Lévi-Strauss, *The Elementary Structures of Kinship*, trans. James Harle Bell and John Richard von Sturmer (Boston: Beacon, 1969), 30.

48. Claude Lévi-Strauss, "Language and the Analysis of Social Laws," in *Structural Anthropology*, trans. Claire Jacobsen and Brooke Grundfest Schoepf (Garden City, N.Y.: Anchor-Doubleday, 1967), 60.

49. Claude Lévi-Strauss, "Structural Analysis in Linguistics and in Anthropology," in *Structural Anthropology*, 45.

50. Gayle Rubin, "The Traffic in Women: Notes on the 'Political Economy' of Sex," in *Toward an Anthropology of Women*, ed. Rayna Raiter (New York: Monthly Review Press, 1975), 174.

51. Sigmund Freud, *Totem and Taboo, Standard Edition*, vol. 13, 141–43.

52. Quoted by Anthony Wilden in "Lacan and the Discourse of the Other," in Jacques Lacan, *The Language of the Self: The Function of Language in Psychoanalysis*, ed. Anthony Wilden (New York: Dell, 1968), 271.

53. Jacques Lacan, "The Function and Field of Speech and Language in Psychoanalysis," in *Ecrits: A Selection*, 67.

54. Juliet Mitchell, *Psychoanalysis and Feminism: Freud, Reich, Laing and Women* (New York: Vintage-Random House, 1975), 372.

55. Jacques Lacan, "Desire and the Interpretation of Desire in *Hamlet*," trans. James Hulbert, *Yale French Studies*, nos. 55 & 56 (1977): 28.

56. Claude Lévi-Strauss, "The Family," in *The View From Afar*, trans. Joachim Neugroschel and Phoebe Hoss (New York: Basic Books, 1985), 44.

57. Serge Leclaire, "Sexuality: A Fact of Discourse, An Interview by Hélène Klibbe," trans. Hélène Klibbe, in *Homosexualities and French Literature: Cultural Contexts/Critical Texts*, ed. George Stambolian and Elaine Marks (Ithaca: Cornell University Press, 1979), 46.

58. Through projection, Freud writes in "The Unconscious," "the ego behaves as if the danger of a development of anxiety threatened it not from the direction of an instinctual impulse but from the direction of a perception, and it is thus enabled to react against this external danger with the attempts at flight represented by phobic avoidances" (*Standard Edition*, vol. 14, 184).

59. See "Some Psychical Consequences of the Anatomical Distinction Between the Sexes," *Standard Edition*, vol. 19, 248–58; "Fetishism," *Standard Edition*, vol. 21, 152–57; and *An Outline of Psycho-Analysis, Standard Edition*, vol. 23, 202–3.

60. For a fuller elaboration of this reading, see Kaja Silverman, *The Acoustic Mirror: The Female Voice in Psychoanalysis and Cinema* (Bloomington: Indiana University Press, 1988), 13–22.

61. Annette Kuhn, "Structures of Patriarchy and Capital in the Family," in *Feminism and Materialism: Women and Modes of Production*, ed. Annette Kuhn and AnnMarie Wolpe (London: Routledge & Kegan Paul, 1978), 57–58.

62. Roisin McDonough and Rachel Harrison, "Patriarchy and Relations of Production," in *Feminism and Materialism: Women and Modes of Production*, 28.

63. Julia Kristeva, "Women's Time," in *The Kristeva Reader*, ed. Toril Moi (New York: Columbia University Press, 1986), 210.

2. Historical Trauma and Male Subjectivity

1. Barbara Deming, *Running Away from Myself: A Dream Portrait of America Drawn from the Films of the Forties* (New York: Grossman, 1969), 39–40. The first version of this book was finished in 1950, although it was not published in its entirety until nineteen years later.

2. As I will attempt to demonstrate, the "obviousness" of the film's ideological project does not necessarily function to dismantle it.

3. Siegfried Kracauer, "Those Movies With a Message," *Harper's Magazine*, vol. 196, no. 1177 (June 1948): 572.

4. I will provide an extended discussion of these deviations only in the case of *The Best Years of Our Lives* and *The Guilt of Janet Ames*.

5. This is how Ernesto Laclau describes ideology in "The Impossibility of Society," *Canadian Journal of Political and Social Theory*, vol. 7, nos. 1 & 2 (1983): 24.

6. Fredric Jameson, *The Political Unconscious: Narrative as a Socially Symbolic Act* (Ithaca: Cornell University Press, 1981), 102.

7. Sigmund Freud, *Beyond the Pleasure Principle*, in *The Standard Edition of the Complete Psychological Works*, trans. James Strachey (London: Hogarth Press, 1955), vol. 18, 24–33.

8. See in particular Freud, *Beyond the Pleasure Principle*, 29–30.

9. Sigmund Freud, "Introduction to *Psycho-Analysis and the War Neuroses*," *Standard Edition*, vol. 17, 208.

10. In "Rivers and Sassoon: The Inscription of Male Gender Anxieties," included in *Behind the Lines: Gender and the Two World Wars*, ed. Margaret Randolph Higonnet et al. (New Haven: Yale University Press, 1987), 61–69, Elaine Showalter maintains that war trauma is in fact a form of hysteria, and as such, a protest against masculinity.

11. For a further elaboration of this model, see *The Project for a Scientific Psychology*, in *Standard Edition*, vol. 1, 352–57, and *Studies on Hysteria*, in *Standard Edition*, vol. 2, 125–34, where Freud elaborates his theory of deferred action. That theory permits him to define trauma as an internal breach resulting from the interaction between a memory or a fantasy, and an external event.

12. For a discussion of trauma as that which attacks the subject "from within," see Jean Laplanche, *Life and Death in Psychoanalysis*, trans. Jeffrey Mehlman (Baltimore: The Johns Hopkins University Press, 1976), 41–43.

13. Freud also accounts for the game as an act of revenge, which would constitute another form of mastery (see *Beyond the Pleasure Principle*).

14. Freud also attributes the compulsion to repeat to "instinctual impulses" in "The Uncanny," in *Standard Edition*, vol. 17, 238.

15. See Chapters 5 and 7 for a discussion of the ways in which the death drive can complicate desire.

16. The concept of the "fantasmatic," which will figure prominently in subsequent chapters, derives from Jean Laplanche and J.-B. Pontalis, *The Language of Psycho-Analysis*, trans. Donald Nicholson-Smith (New York: Norton, 1973), 317. I borrow the notion of the "stereotype plate" from Freud, "The Dynamics of Transference," *Standard Edition*, vol. 12, 99–100.

17. Freud claims in *An Outline of Psycho-Analysis* that the aim of the death drive is "to undo connections and to destroy things" (*Standard Edition*,

vol. 23, 148). Laplanche also associates the death drive with a radical unbinding, and opposes it forcefully to the ego in *Life and Death in Psychoanalysis*, 124–26.

18. Samuel Weber, *The Legend of Freud* (Minneapolis: University of Minnesota Press, 1982), 122. Weber offers this account of repetition in *Beyond the Pleasure Principle* in the course of summarizing the argument advanced by Gilles Deleuze in *Masochism: An Interpretation of Coldness and Cruelty*, trans. Jean McNeil (New York: George Braziller, 1971).

19. In *Beyond the Pleasure Principle*, Freud characterizes death as "an initial state from which the living entity has at one time or other departed and to which it is striving to return by the circuitous paths along which its development leads." Consequently, "everything living dies for *internal* reasons," and "'*the aim of all life is death*'" (38).

20. Sigmund Freud, *The Ego and the Id, Standard Edition*, trans. vol. 19, 54.

21. Sigmund Freud, "Why War?," *Standard Edition*, vol. 22, 211.

22. Freud, *Beyond the Pleasure Principle*, 12.

23. Freud, *Beyond the Pleasure Principle*, 55.

24. I am indebted to Leo Bersani for the notion of "shattering," which will occupy a privileged place in the pages which follow. Bersani, who introduces that word in the context of a discussion of *Beyond the Pleasure Principle*, also associates it with an increase in psychic excitation (see *The Freudian Body: Psychoanalysis and Art* [New York: Columbia University Press, 1986], 55–67). However, he relates that increase less to the death drive than to a necessarily masochistic sexuality. Although I do not maintain the same one-to-one relation between masochism and sexuality, I will in Chapter 5 indicate my agreement with Bersani that when sexuality assumes a masochistic form it is indeed characterized by an increase in excitation. I will attribute the "shattering" effects of "feminine" masochism to the convergence within it of the erotic and the death drives.

25. Laplanche, *Life and Death in Psychoanalysis*, 118 and 122.

26. Deleuze, *Masochism: An Interpretation of Coldness and Cruelty*, 100.

27. Jacques Lacan, *Four Fundamental Concepts of Psycho-Analysis*, trans. Alan Sheridan (New York: Norton, 1978), 239. Bersani also calls into question the notion that the *fort/da* game involves simple mastery. In *The Freudian Body*, he writes that the game involves the "satisfying representation of a separation painful to both the mother and the child. In other words, mastery is simultaneous with self-punishment; a fantasy of omnipotence and autonomy . . . is inseparable from a repetition of pain" (58–59).

28. See Klaus Theweleit, *Male Fantasies, Volume I: Women, Floods, Bodies, History*, trans. Stephen Conway (Minneapolis: University of Minnesota Press, 1987), and *Male Fantasies, Volume II: Male Bodies—Psychoanalyz-*

ing the White Terror, trans. Erica Carter and Chris Turner (Minneapolis: University of Minnesota Press, 1989); Susan Jeffords, *The Remasculinization of America: Gender and the Vietnam War* (Bloomington: Indiana University Press, 1989); and Susan Gubar, "This Is My Rifle, This Is My Gun: World War II and the Blitz on Women," in *Behind the Lines: Gender and the Two World Wars*, ed. Margaret Randolph Higonnet et al., 227–59. Dana Polan also notes the ideological coincidence of "the world of war" and "the world of the family" in *Power and Paranoia: History, Narrative, and the American Cinema, 1940–1950* (New York: Columbia University Press, 1986), 88. For a discussion of the imbrication of sexual difference and the discourse of World War I, see James Longenbach, "The Women and Men of 1914," in *Arms and the Woman: War, Gender, and Literary Representation*, ed. Helen M. Cooper et al. (Chapel Hill: University of North Carolina Press, 1989), 97–123.

29. Quoted by Paul Fussell, *The Great War and Modern Memory* (New York: Oxford University Press, 1975), 271.

30. Jean Bethke Elshtain, *Women and War* (New York: Basic Books, 1987), 207.

31. See Sandra Gilbert, "Soldier's Heart: Literary Men, Literary Women, and the Great War," in *Behind the Lines: Gender and the Two World Wars*, ed. Margaret Randolph Higonnet et al., 197–226; and Showalter, "Rivers and Sassoon," 62.

32. In his insistence upon the interiority of the danger which threatened the men of the Freicorps, Theweleit's argument converges with mine. However, he accounts for that danger in very different terms than those I deploy here; he traces the soldier's fear of dissolution back to his pre-Oedipal fusion with the mother.

33. In "The Double Helix," Margaret Randolph Higonnet and Patrice L.-R. Higonnet suggest that the demobilization of a country's fighting force threatens to "feminize the male population" (*Behind the Lines: Gender and the Two World Wars*, ed. Margaret Randolph Higonnet et al.), 38.

34. Slavoj Žižek warrants mention in this context, since he has recently described Lacan's *das Ding* in terms which may seem very similar to the ones I have just suggested. He defines that entity as "the real-traumatic kernel in the midst of [the] symbolic order," and he says of it that it "enables us to conceive the possibility of a total, global annihilation of the signifier's network" (*The Sublime Object of Ideology* [London: Verso, 1989], 135). But whereas Žižek conceives of *das Ding* as an undigestible "nut" at the heart of the symbolic, and insists that it is radically *nonhistorical*, the agency of disruption that I am attempting to theorize assumes more dynamic forms. Indeed, it has emerged here precisely as a "historical" agency, not only because the catastrophes through which it expresses itself are often experienced as our directest encounters with history, but because it works to expose the constructedness and impermanence of what a given socius has long assumed to be "actuality."

The Sublime Object of Ideology connects *das Ding* so intimately with the death drive that it emerges as "the exact theoretical concept for [the] Sadeian notion of 'the second death'—the possibility of the total 'wipeout' of historical tradition opened up by the very process of symbolization/historicization as its radical, self-destructive limit" (135–36). Although the death drive also figures centrally within what I am calling "historical trauma," it does so less as the "brute, pre-symbolic reality" from which language alienates us than as the psychic basis of an aggression which is in the first instance directed by the subject against itself. Like Laplanche in *Life and Death in Psychoanalysis*, it is above all the *unbinding* principle of Freud's death drive which I am attempting to isolate here—its antagonism to any coherence, most particularly that of the ego. Historical trauma designates the massive release of that psychic force most capable of revealing the contingency and fictiveness of the "self," and thereby of reducing the subject to a "zero."

Like the Law of Language, historical trauma is thus the carrier of castration rather than of the "enjoyment" about which Žižek writes. Whereas the Law of Language introduces the subject to lack by alienating it from "being," however, historical trauma does so by leveling the compensatory structures which take the place of the excluded real. Within the context of the present discussion, it is consequently an agency of the purest negativity, which has no more allegiance to "being" than it does to the dominant fiction.

35. This is not to say that the female subject in fact supplanted the male subject in the World War II workforce, merely that she was at times represented and perceived as having done so. In the "Introduction" to *Behind the Lines: Gender and the Two World Wars*, the editors argue that "when the homefront is mobilized, women may be allowed to move 'forward' in terms of employment or social policy, yet the battlefront— preeminently a male domain—takes economic and cultural priority" (6).

36. For a discussion of binding, see Sigmund Freud, *Project for a Scientific Psychology*, 295–387; *Beyond the Pleasure Principle*, 7–33 and 62–64; and Laplanche, *Life and Death in Psychoanalysis*, 103–26.

37. André Bazin, *What Is Cinema?*, trans. Hugo Gray (Berkeley: University of California Press, 1971), vol. 2, 60.

38. André Bazin, "William Wyler ou le janséniste de la mise-en-scène," *Qu'est-ce que le cinéma?* (Paris: Editions du cerf, 1958), vol. 1, 156. English translation by Christopher Williams, in *Realism and the Cinema: A Reader*, ed. Christopher Williams (London: Routledge & Kegan Paul, 1980), 40–41.

39. Bazin, "William Wyler ou le janséniste de la mise-en-scène," 155; Williams, *Realism and the Cinema*, 40.

40. William Wyler, "No Magic Wand," in *Hollywood Directors 1941–1976*, ed. Richard Koszarski (New York: Oxford University Press, 1977), 104.

41. It is perhaps not entirely superfluous to add that I do not mean to privilege the long take and deep focus as capable of delivering "more" than classical editing and the close-up. Their historical value resides only in their deviation from an established norm.

42. Jameson associates this demystification with "realism" (*The Political Unconscious*, 152).

43. "A Long Way From Home" was the original title of Deming's *Running Away From Myself* (see foreward, xii).

44. Charles Affron suggests that Millie is the very embodiment of the "home" from which Al is estranged (*Cinema and Sentiment* [Chicago: University of Chicago Press, 1982], 90).

45. This is how Althusser describes ideological interpellation in "Ideology and Ideological State Apparatuses," *Lenin and Philosophy and Other Essays*, trans. Ben Brewster (New York: Monthly Review Press, 1971), 172.

46. Freud claims in "Some Psychical Consequences of the Anatomical Distinction Between the Sexes," *Standard Edition*, vol. 19, that after the "discovery" of woman's anatomical otherness, the male subject responds to the "mutilated creature" either with "horror" or "triumphant contempt" (252).

47. Robert Warshow, "The Anatomy of Falsehood," in *The Immediate Experience: Movies, Comics, Theatre and Other Aspects of Popular Culture* (Garden City, N.Y.: Doubleday-Anchor, 1962), 112.

48. Wyler, "No Magic Wand," 107.

49. Jean-Louis Comolli discusses cinema's "impression of reality" and the disavowal which it encourages in "Machines of the Visible," in *The Cinematic Apparatus*, ed. Teresa de Lauretis and Stephen Heath (New York: St. Martin's Press, 1980), 121–42. For a discussion of the relation between the impression of reality and the lack which haunts all subjectivity, see my *The Acoustic Mirror: The Female Voice in Psychoanalysis and Cinema* (Bloomington: Indiana University Press, 1988), 1–41.

50. This is how Christian Metz accounts for the cinematic signifier in *The Imaginary Signifier: Psychoanalysis and the Cinema*, trans. Celia Britton, Annwyl Williams, Ben Brewster, and Alfred Guzzetti (Bloomington: Indiana University Press, 1982), 43. As he writes later in the same paragraph, "it is the [cinematic] signifier itself, and as a whole, that is recorded, that is absence: a little rolled up perforated strip which 'contains' vast landscapes, fixed battles, the melting of the ice on the River Neva, and whole life-times, and yet can be enclosed in the familiar round metal tin, of modest dimensions, clear proof that it does not 'really' contain all that" (43–44).

51. In "Machines of the Visible," Comolli observes: "The succession of technical advances cannot be read, in the manner of Bazin, as the progress towards a 'realism plus' other than in that they accumulate realistic

supplements which all aim at reproducing . . . the impression of reality; which aim, that is, to reduce as much as possible, to minimize the gap which the 'yes-I-know/but-all-the-same' has to fill" (133). See also Metz, *The Imaginary Signifier*, 69–78.

52. For an articulation of the ideological opposition between "power" and "the people," see Ernesto Laclau, *Politics and Ideology in Marxist Theory* (London: Verso, 1977), 81–142.

53. For a discussion of Hugo Friedhofer's score, see Samuel L. Chell, "Music and Emotion in the Classic Hollywood Film: The Case of *The Best Years of Our Lives*," *Film Criticism*, vol. 8, no.2 (1984): 27–38.

54. In *Powers of Horror: An Essay on Abjection*, trans. Leon S. Roudiez (New York: Columbia University Press, 1982), Julia Kristeva speaks of "excrement and its equivalents (decay, infection, disease, corpse, etc.)" as "the danger to identity that comes from without: the ego threatened by the non-ego, society threatened by its outside, life by death" (71).

55. Roger Manvell, *Films and the Second World War* (New York: Dell-Delta, 1976), 248.

56. Michael Wood, *America in the Movies, or Santa Maria, It Had Slipped My Mind* (New York: Basic Books, 1975), 119.

57. Richard Glatzer, "A Conversation with Frank Capra," in *Frank Capra: The Man and His Films*, ed. Richard Glatzer and John Raeburn (Ann Arbor: University of Michigan Press, 1975), 37.

58. Quoted by Jeanine Basinger in *The "It's a Wonderful Life" Book* (New York: Alfred A. Knopf, 1986), 18, from a Los Angeles *Times* interview conducted by drama critic Edwin Schallert. I have relied while writing this chapter upon the shooting script for *It's a Wonderful Life* included in this volume.

59. Leland A. Poague, *The Cinema of Frank Capra: An Approach to Film Comedy* (New York: A.S. Barnes and Co., 1975), 217.

60. Peter Roffman and Jim Purdy, *The Hollywood Social Problem Film: Madness, Despair and Politics from the Depression to the Fifties* (Bloomington: Indiana University Press, 1981), 273.

61. Charles J. Maland, *Frank Capra* (Boston: Twayne, 1980), 150.

62. "One important function of good art or entertainment is to unite and illuminate the heart and the mind, to cause each to learn from, and to enhance, the experience of the other," writes James Agee in *"It's a Wonderful Life."* "Bad art and entertainment misinform and disunite them. Much too often this movie appeals to the heart at the expense of the mind; at other times it urgently demands of the heart that it treat with contempt the mind's efforts to keep its integrity; at still other times the heart is simply used, on the mind, as a truncheon" (in *Frank Capra: The Man and His Films*, ed. Richard Glatzer and John Raeburn), 157. In an essay published in the same volume, Richard Griffith observes that

"the shifts of mood between the naturalistic and the fantastic are too abrupt" in *It's a Wonderful Life*, and "there are too many of them; you can't make the required adjustments, and the picture leaves you with a tear in the eye and an unresolved dissatisfaction in your mind" (*"It's a Wonderful Life* and Post-War Realism," 162).

63. Robert B. Ray, *A Certain Tendency of the Hollywood Cinema, 1930–1980* (Princeton: Princeton University Press, 1985), 212.

64. The youthful Mary is played by Jean Gale, and her adult counterpart by Donna Reed.

65. Raymond Carney also comments upon the normative aspects of Mary's desires. He enlists her maiden name, Hatch, in his analysis of those desires: "The mildness, biological rootedness, and natural attainability of Mary Hatch's dreams—in contrast to the dangerous exorbitance and exhilarating unnaturalness of George's—are emphasized by her last name, which Capra makes sure is recalled to our attention by having George pun on it in the stork scene, when he asks her if she is "on the nest" (*American Vision: The Films of Frank Capra* [Cambridge: Cambridge University Press, 1986], 410).

66 Brenda Wineapple reads this sign as a signifier of the "social and ideological matrix" into which the film inserts its protagonist ("The Production of Character in *It's a Wonderful Life*," *Film Criticism*, vol. 5, no. 2 [1981]: 10).

67. In the scene following the school dance, George and Mary sing "Buffalo Gal" outside the house in which they will later live, and George offers to lasso the moon for Mary.

68. As Carney suggests, George's dream is converted first "into the stuff of Mary's needlepoint and then into an announcement of her pregnancy" (*American Vision*, 408).

69. This is not the only detail in *It's a Wonderful Life* which literalizes the "hailing" metaphor. The partial deafness from which George suffers concretizes what might be called his ideological "hearing impairment."

70. As other critics have noted, the nightmare sequence breaks with the representational codes governing the Bedford Falls scenes, offering a kind of *film noir* fantasy (see, for instance, Ray, *A Certain Tendency of the Hollywood Cinema*, 203–4, and Carney, *American Vision*, 416–17). It is important to note, however, that the heavenly "frame" story works to denaturalize the Bedford Falls scenes as well—to define the narrative of George Bailey as a kind of film within the film. Like *The Best Years of Our Lives* and *The Guilt of Janet Ames*, then, *It's a Wonderful Life* attests to a crisis of belief in the "realism" of Hollywood cinema, which is itself closely interdependent with the dominant fiction.

71. Again, Deming seems to grasp better than most other commentators what is most fundamentally at issue in the nightmare sequence. For her,

"the real drama of this sequence is the drama of George's anguish as he tries to get one person after another to recognize him" (115).

72. For a discussion of the place of masochism within masculinity, see Chapters 5, 6, and 7 of this volume, and my "Masochism and Subjectivity," *Framework*, no. 12 (1980): 2–9.

73. Serge Leclaire, "Sexuality: A Fact of Discourse, An Interview by Hélène Klibbe," trans. Hélène Klibbe, in *Homosexualities and French Literature: Cultural Contexts/Critical Texts*, ed. George Stambolian and Elaine Marks (Ithaca: Cornell University Press, 1979), 46. For an analysis of this passage, see Chapter 1.

74. Michael Renov, *Hollywood's Wartime Women: Representation and Ideology* (Ann Arbor: UMI Research Press, 1988), 79. This would seem the moment to indicate that whereas I have stressed the temporary crisis in ideological belief during the immediate postwar period, Renov emphasizes instead the "consensus" or "community of interest" which in his view prevailed during the war period (77).

75. For a discussion of soldier resentment over the assumption of male jobs by civilian women, see Gilbert, "Soldier's Heart," 207–9.

76. There is by now too extensive a body of feminist literature on the topic of femininity and specularity for me to encompass within this footnote, so I will content myself with reminding the reader that the pioneering essay on this topic is Laura Mulvey's "Visual Pleasure and Narrative Cinema," *Screen*, vol. 16, no. 3 (1975): 8–18, recently reprinted in her *Visual and Other Pleasures* (Bloomington: Indiana University Press, 1989), 14–26. For a more Lacanian reading of woman-as-spectacle, see Stephen Heath, "Difference," *Screen*, vol. 19, no. 3 (1978): 3–92.

77. Metz, *The Imaginary Signifier*, 45.

78. *The Guilt of Janet Ames* makes no overt reference to the 1935 Henry Hathaway film, *Peter Ibbetson*.

79. Confession here conforms to the paradigm articulated by Foucault in *The History of Sexuality, Volume 1: An Introduction*, trans. Robert Hurley (New York: Vintage Books, 1980), in that it clearly produces what it claims to disclose.

80. Sigmund Freud, "Fetishism," in *Standard Edition*, vol. 21, 152–57.

81. Mary Ann Doane, "Film and the Masquerade—Theorizing the Female Spectator," *Screen*, vol. 23, nos. 3 & 4 (1982): 80.

82. Jacques Lacan, "The Signification of the Phallus," in *Ecrits: A Selection*, trans. Alan Sheridan (New York: Norton, 1977), 290.

83. Sarah Kofman, *The Enigma of Woman: Woman in Freud's Writings*, trans. Catherine Porter (Ithaca: Cornell University Press, 1985), 88–89.

84. Elizabeth L. Berg, "The Third Woman," *Diacritics*, vol. 12, no. 2 (1982): 12.

85. Naomi Schor, "Female Fetishism: The Case of George Sand," in *The Female Body in Western Culture: Contemporary Perspectives*, ed. Susan Rubin Suleiman (Cambridge, Mass.: Harvard University Press, 1986), 363–72.

86. Octave Mannoni, *Clefs pour l'imaginaire de l'autre scène* (Paris: Editions du Seuil, 1969).

87. Stephen Heath, "Lessons from Brecht," *Screen*, vol. 15, no. 2 (1974): 107.

3. Fassbinder and Lacan: A Reconsideration of Gaze, Look, and Image

1. The phrase "field of vision" derives from the title of Jacqueline Rose's book, *Sexuality in the Field of Vision* (London: Verso, 1986).

2. Christian Braad Thomsen, "Five Interviews with Fassbinder," in *Fassbinder*, ed. Tony Rayns (London: B.F.I., 1980), 86.

3. Tony Pipolo, "Bewitched by the Holy Whore," *October*, no. 21 (1982): 112, 92.

4. Richard Dyer, "Reading Fassbinder's Sexual Politics," in *Fassbinder*, ed. Rayns, 55, 60.

5. Wilfred Wiegand, "The Doll in the Doll: Observations on Fassbinder's Films," in *Fassbinder*, ed. Ruth McCormick (New York: Tanam Press, 1981), 52.

6. Thomas Elsaesser, "Primary Identification and the Historical Subject: Fassbinder and Germany," in *Narrative, Apparatus, Ideology*, ed. Philip Rosen (New York: Columbia University Press, 1986), 540.

7. Ruth McCormick, "Review [of *The Marriage of Maria Braun*]," in *The Marriage of Maria Braun*, ed. Joyce Rheuban (New Brunswick: Rutgers University Press, 1986), 222.

8. Peter W. Jansen, "*Die Zeit*," in *The Marriage of Maria Braun*, 221.

9. See Luce Irigaray, "Women on the Market," in *This Sex Which Is Not One*, trans. Catherine Porter (Ithaca: Cornell University Press, 1985), 170–91.

10. Sigmund Freud, *The Ego and the Id*, in *The Standard Edition of the Complete Psychological Works*, trans. James Strachey (London: Hogarth Press, 1961), vol. 19, 27.

11. Freud, *The Ego and the Id*, 34–37. See also Otto Isakower, "On the Exceptional Position of the Auditory Sphere," *International Journal of Psycho-Analysis*, vol. 20, nos. 3–4 (1939): 340–48, for a discussion of the super-ego as the internalization of external voices.

12. Jacques Lacan, "The Mirror Stage as Formative of the Function of the I," *Ecrits: A Selection*, trans. Alan Sheridan (New York: Norton, 1977), 1–7.

13. In *The Four Fundamental Concepts of Psycho-Analysis*, trans. Alan Sheridan (New York: Norton, 1978), 80, Lacan remarks: "*I saw myself seeing myself*, young Parque says somewhere. . . . We are dealing with the philosopher, who apprehends something that is one of the essential correlates of consciousness in its relation to representation, and which is designated as *I see myself seeing myself*. . . . [this formula] remains . . . correlative with that fundamental mode to which we referred in the Cartesian *cogito*. . . . "

14. Judith Mayne, "Fassbinder and Spectatorship," *New German Critique*, no. 12 (1977): 61–74.

15. Kaja Silverman, *The Acoustic Mirror: The Female Voice in Psychoanalysis and Cinema* (Bloomington: Indiana University Press, 1988), 161–62.

16. Lacan, *Four Fundamental Concepts*, 106. Joan Copjec has recently taken issue with the assumption that implicit in the notion of the gaze is the visibility of the subject. She maintains that the hyphenated form of "photo-graph" in the passage I have just quoted refers to Lacan's graph of desire rather than, as I will argue, with the diagrams included in *Four Fundamental Concepts* (see "The Orthopsychic Subject: Film Theory and the Reception of Lacan," *October*, no. 49 [1989]: 53–71). Indeed, Copjec goes so far as to claim that *Seminar XI* is about semiotics rather than vision, and that the gaze refers to the effects of language. While I am in fundamental agreement with her claim that the thrust of *Four Fundamental Concepts* is to show that sense does not found the subject, I see the gaze as a signifier for that which constitutes the subject as lacking *within the field of vision*. As Lacan says in the passage quoted above, the gaze "determines me, at the most profound level, *in the visible*" (my emphasis).

17. Lacan, *Four Fundamental Concepts*, 84.

18. Lacan, *Four Fundamental Concepts*, 72 and 103.

19. Lacan, *Four Fundamental Concepts*, 83.

20. See Laura Mulvey, "Visual Pleasure and Narrative Cinema," in *Visual and Other Pleasures* (Bloomington: Indiana University Press, 1989), 14–26.

21. In his account of the voyeur surprised at the keyhole, Lacan draws on Jean-Paul Sartre, *Being and Nothingness: An Essay on Phenomenological Ontology*, trans. Hazel B. Barnes (London: Methuen, 1957), 277, which relies upon a similar example. Sartre is less concerned with the voyeur's desire, however, than with the shame induced in him by the gaze.

22. Judith Mayne suggests that this self-embrace "might be situated in relation to another narcissistic gesture," that in which Fassbinder "literally exhibits himself" in *Germany In Autumn* (1978). See "The Feminist Analogy," *Discourse*, no. 7 (1985): 39.

23. See Sigmund Freud, "On Narcissism: An Introduction," *Standard Edition*, vol. 14, 89.

24. Leon Battista Alberti writes that painters "should only seek to present the form of things seen on [the picture] plane as if it were of transparent glass. Thus the visual pyramid could pass through it, placed at a definite distance with definite lights and a definite position of center in space and in a definite place in respect to the observer" (see *On Painting*, trans. John R. Spencer [London: Routledge & Kegan Paul, 1956], 51). For a discussion of Alberti within a cinematic context, see Michael Silverman, "Rossellini and Alberti: The Centering Power of Perspective," *Yale Italian Studies*, vol. 1, no.1 (1977): 128–42, and Stephen Heath, *Questions of Cinema* (Bloomington: Indiana University Press, 1981), 19–75.

25. Roger Caillois, "Mimicry and Legendary Psychasthenia," trans. John Shepley, *October*, no. 31 (1984): 28.

26. These two forms of Lacanian mimicry are not unlike those presented by Irigaray in *This Sex Which Is Not One*. The first kind of mimicry discussed there follows from the unquestioning acting out of an assigned role. Irigaray calls it "masquerade," and she associates it with traditional femininity. *This Sex* places a much higher premium upon a second form of mimicry, which involves the travesty of woman's assigned role. About it, Irigaray has this to say: "One must assume the feminine role deliberately. Which means already to convert a form of subordination into an affirmation, and thus to begin to thwart it. . . . To play with mimesis is thus, for a woman, to try to recover the place of her exploitation by discourse, without allowing herself to be simply reduced to it. It means to resubmit herself . . . to 'ideas,' in particular to ideas about herself, that are elaborated in/by a masculine logic, but so as to make 'visible,' by an effect of playful repetition, what was supposed to remain invisible: the cover-up of a possible operation of the feminine in language" (76).

27. Sheridan's translation is here less than felicitous, suggesting that the mask or the double may somehow have its derivation in the self. The French text reads rather differently because its grammatical construction is more rigorously parallel; although the subject has no identity without an alienating image, that image may be put in place either *by the subject* or *by the other* ("*l'être donne de lui, ou il reçoit de l'autre*"). (See *Les Quatre concepts de la psychanalyse* [Paris: Editions du Seuil, 1973], 98.) The next sentence emphasizes that the screen is no more integral to the subject in the former instance than in the latter; in either case it is through a "separated form of himself" that the subject is constituted.

28. Maurice Merleau-Ponty clearly exercised an important influence upon Lacan's thinking about the gaze. In *The Visible and the Invisible*, trans. Claude Lefort (Evanston: Northwestern University Press, 1968), the text to which *Four Fundamental Concepts* refers, Merleau-Ponty insists upon the reciprocity of subject and object (hence Lacan's paradoxical description of the gaze as the "spectacle of the world"): " . . . the vision [which the seer] exercises, he also undergoes from the things, such that, as many painters have said, I feel myself looked at by the things, my activity is

equally passivity ... so that the seer and the visible reciprocate one another and we no longer know which sees and which is seen" (139).

29. See in particular Michel Foucault, *Discipline and Punish: The Birth of the Prison*, trans. Alan Sheridan (New York: Pantheon, 1978), and *The Birth of the Clinic: An Archaeology of Medical Perception*, trans. Alan Sheridan (New York: Random House, 1975).

30. Although Mulvey's "Visual Pleasure and Narrative Cinema" initiated this interrogation, a number of other texts have also contributed to it in important ways. See, for example, Teresa de Lauretis, *Alice Doesn't: Feminism, Semiotics, Cinema* (Bloomington: Indiana University Press, 1984), 12–36; Stephen Heath, "Difference," *Screen*, vol. 19, no. 3 (1978): 51–112; Linda Williams, "Film Body: An Implantation of Perversions," *Ciné-Tracts* vol. 3, no. 4 (1981): 19–35; Jacqueline Rose, *Sexuality and the Field of Vision*, 199–233; Leslie Stern, "Point of View: The Blind Spot," *Film Reader*, no. 4 (Evanston: Northwestern University Press, 1979), 214–36; Sandy Flitterman, "Woman, Desire and the Look: Feminism and the Enunciative Apparatus in Cinema," *Ciné-Tracts*, vol. 2, no. 1 (1978): 63–68; Janet Bergstrom, "Enunciation and Sexual Difference," in *Feminism and Film Theory*, ed. Constance Penley (New York: Routledge, 1988), 159–85; Mary Ann Doane, *The Desire to Desire: The Woman's Film of the 1940s* (Bloomington: Indiana University Press, 1987), 38–69; and Lucy Fischer, "The Image of Woman as Image: The Optical Politics of *Dames*," in *Genre: The Musical*, ed. Rick Altman (London: Boston & Henley, 1981), 70–84.

31. Slavoj Žižek accounts for the gaze almost exclusively in terms of the real in his very interesting essay, "Looking Awry," *October*, no. 50 (1989): 31–55.

32. J.C. Flugel, *The Psychology of Clothes* (London: Hogarth Press, 1930), 117–19. For a feminist discussion of fashion in general, and of this text in particular, see my "Fragments of a Fashionable Discourse," in *Studies in Entertainment: Critical Approaches to Mass Culture*, ed. Tania Modleski (Bloomington: Indiana University Press, 1986), 139–52.

33. Lacan, *Ecrits*, 319.

34. Wiegand, "The Doll in the Doll," 50.

35. Again, I refer the reader to Dyer's essay, "Reading Fassbinder's Sexual Politics."

36. Sigmund Freud, "Fetishism," *Standard Edition*, vol. 21, 152–53.

37. In a published conversation with Margit Carstensen, Fassbinder makes the outrageous claim that "Women who let themselves be oppressed often are more beautiful than women who fight back." See "Talking About Oppression with Margit Carstensen," in *West German Filmmakers on Film: Visions and Voices, 1967–1986*, ed. Eric Rentschler (New York: Holmes and Meier, 1988), 168–71.

4. Too Early/Too Late: Male Subjectivity and the Primal Scene

1. David Carroll, *The Subject in Question: The Languages of Theory and the Strategies of Fiction* (Chicago: University of Chicago Press, 1982), 56. Carroll goes on to say that "the fictional-subject as center and origin is not solid enough ground for the [Jamesian] novel, not sufficiently substantial or autonomous. The author-subject will provide the definitive origin and center of the novel outside or *behind* [my emphasis] the novel . . . " (56). Carroll is of course referring here to the terms through which the Jamesian fictional system presents itself, not to a theoretical model which he himself endorses. For a further discussion of the central consciousness within James's novels as a "metonym" for the author, see John Carlos Rowe, *The Theoretical Dimensions of Henry James* (Madison: University of Wisconsin Press, 1984), 240.

2. Peter Brooks, *The Melodramatic Imagination: Balzac, Henry James, Melodrama, and the Mode of Excess* (New York: Columbia University Press, 1985), 171.

3. For James's account of the house of fiction, see *The Art of the Novel*, ed. R.P. Blackmur (London: Scribner's, 1962), 46–47.

4. James, *The Art of the Novel*, 201.

5. See Rowe, *Theoretical Dimensions*, 241.

6. Sigmund Freud, "Creative Writers and Day-Dreaming," in *The Standard Edition of the Complete Psychological Works*, trans. James Strachey (London: Hogarth Press, 1959), vol. 9, 149–50.

7. Henry James, *The Ambassadors*, ed. S.P. Rosenbaum (New York: Norton, 1964), 344. All future quotations will be from this edition.

8. Sigmund Freud, "The Economic Problem of Masochism," in *Standard Edition*, vol. 19, 159–70.

9. Sigmund Freud, "'A Child Is Being Beaten,'" *Standard Edition*, vol. 17, 179–204.

10. Sigmund Freud, "Leonardo da Vinci and a Memory of His Childhood," in *Standard Edition*, vol. 11, 82.

11. See Chapter 8 for an extended discussion of this form of male homosexuality.

12. For an analysis of this drawing, see Jacqueline Rose, *Sexuality in the Field of Vision* (London: Verso, 1986), 225–26.

13. Sigmund Freud, "The Dynamics of Transference," *Standard Edition*, vol. 12, 100.

14. J. Laplanche and J.-B. Pontalis, *The Language of Psycho-Analysis*, trans. Donald Nicholson-Smith (New York: Norton, 1973), 317.

15. For a further discussion of the author "inside" the text, see Kaja Silverman, "The Female Authorial Voice," in *The Acoustic Mirror: The Fe-*

male Voice in Psychoanalysis and Cinema (Bloomington: Indiana University Press, 1988), 187–234. In insisting upon the distinction between these two authors, I am attempting to avoid two common fallacies within narratological theory: the "intentional fallacy," which unproblematically conflates the biographical author with the voice of the narrator; and the "implied author," who is so distanced from the biographical author that there is no relation between the two. For a critique of both fallacies, see Mieke Bal, *Femmes imaginaires* (Paris: Nizet, 1986), 65–70.

16. I quote here from "Alternation, Segmentation, Hypnosis," an interview with Raymond Bellour conducted by Janet Bergstrom (*Camera Obscura*, nos. 3 & 4 [1979]: 98).

17. Maxwell Geismar, *Henry James and the Jacobites* (New York: Hill and Wang, 1962), 207.

18. Indeed, a collection of Foucault's interviews and essays has been published under the title *Power/Knowledge: Selected Interviews and Other Writings, 1972–1977*, trans. Colin Gordon, Leo Marshall, John Mepham, and Kate Soper (New York: Pantheon, 1980).

19. For a Foucauldian reading of James which is in no way intractable, see Mark Seltzer, *Henry James and the Art of Power* (Ithaca: Cornell University Press, 1984).

20. This *Nachträglichkeit* is dramatized in *The Ambassadors*, 310–13.

21. Henry James, *The Notebooks of Henry James*, eds. F.O. Matthiessen and Kenneth B. Murdock (New York: Oxford University Press, 1961), 226–28.

22. Sigmund Freud, "Some Psychical Consequences of the Anatomical Distinction Between the Sexes," *Standard Edition*, vol. 19, 250.

23. See Sigmund Freud, *From the History of an Infantile Neurosis, Standard Edition*, vol. 17, 48–60, for an extended discussion of the status of the Wolfman's primal scene. Building on this case history, Ned Lukacher has defined the primal scene as "an ontologically undecidable intertextual event that is situated in the differential space between historical memory and imaginative construction, between archival verification and interpretive free play" (*Primal Scenes: Literature, Philosophy, Psychoanalysis* [Ithaca: Cornell University Press, 1986], 24).

24. Christian Metz, *The Imaginary Signifier: Psychoanalysis and the Cinema*, trans. Celia Britton, Annwyl Williams, Ben Brewster, and Alfred Guzzetti (Bloomington: Indiana University Press, 1982), 59.

25. Jean Laplanche, *Life and Death in Psychoanalysis*, trans. Jeffrey Mehlman (Baltimore: The Johns Hopkins University Press, 1976), 102.

26. Freud, "Some Psychical Consequences of the Anatomical Distinction Between the Sexes," 250.

27. Sigmund Freud, *Fragment of an Analysis of a Case of Hysteria, Standard Edition*, vol. 7, 47.

28. James, *The Art of the Novel*, 90.

29. Henry James, *The Portrait of a Lady* (New York: Modern Library, 1966), 407.

30. Henry James, *The Princess Casamassima* (New York: Harper and Row, 1964), 445. Future quotations will be taken from this edition.

31. Henry James, *The Golden Bowl* (New York: Grove, 1962), 318. Leo Bersani has commented on the "scenic" quality of this and several of the other passages I have cited here, and in terms which very much anticipate the present discussion: "Each of these scenes is interpreted as a betrayal, and the betrayal takes the form of an intimacy which excludes its witness. The violent, traumatic nature of these sights is not always immediately explicit . . . but they haunt the consciousness of the Jamesian hero as images of a hidden and threatening truth from which, for what usually turn out to be sinister reasons, he has been excluded" (*A Future for Astyanax: Character and Desire in Literature* [Boston: Little, Brown and Company, 1976], 133–34).

32. Ned Lukacher also relates *The Turn of the Screw* to the primal scene in *Primal Scenes*, 115–32, although his project is very different from mine. He is primarily concerned with establishing what, with respect to the events related within that story, might be said to be "real." For a different kind of psychoanalytic reading, one more concerned with the transferential relation of author and reader, see Shoshana Felman, "Turning the Screw of Interpretation," *Yale French Studies*, nos. 55 & 56 (1977), 94–207.

33. "The Beast in the Jungle," in *Henry James: Selected Fiction*, ed. Leon Edel (New York: Dutton, 1964), 500. All future quotations will be from this edition.

34. Eve Kosofsky Sedgwick, *Epistemology of the Closet* (Berkeley: University of California Press, 1990), 182–212. For other readings of homosexuality in James, see Michael Moon, "A Small Boy and Others: Sexual Disorientation in Henry James, Kenneth Anger, and David Lynch," in *Comparative American Identities: Selected Essays from the 1989 English Institute*, ed. Hortense J. Spillers (New York: Routledge, 1991); and Michael A. Cooper, "Discipl(in)ing the Master, Mastering the Discipl(in)e: Erotonomies in James' Tales of Literary Life," in *Engendering Men: The Question of Male Feminist Criticism*, ed. Joseph A. Boone and Michael Cadden (New York: Routledge, 1990), 66–83.

35. See, for instance, Metz, *The Imaginary Signifier*; Laura Mulvey, "Visual Pleasure and Narrative Cinema," *Screen*, vol. 16, no. 3 (1975): 6–18; Stephen Heath, "Difference," *Screen*, vol. 19, no. 3 (1978): 51–112; and Teresa de Lauretis, *Alice Doesn't: Feminism, Semiotics, Cinema* (Bloomington: Indiana University Press, 1984), 12–36. For a critique of the Metzian and Mulveyan scopic paradigm, and the elaboration of a "reactive" gaze, see Carol Clover, *Men, Women, and Chainsaws: Gender in the Modern American Horror Film* (Princeton University Press, 1992).

36. Interpellation is a concept theorized by Louis Althusser in "Ideology and Ideological State Apparatuses," in *Lenin and Philosophy*, trans. Ben Brewster (London: Monthly Review Press, 1971), 127–86. For a discussion of normative Oedipal interpellation, see Chapter 1 of this volume.

    This would seem the most appropriate moment to emphasize how many of James's protagonists are women or girls, and with what facility his narrators adopt a female point of view.

37. Henry James, *The Awkward Age* (New York: Norton, 1969), 212. All future quotations will be taken from this edition.

38. Mieke Bal discusses a story which provides an interesting Biblical analogue to this scene in *Death and Dissymmetry: The Politics of Coherence in the Book of Judges* (Chicago: University of Chicago Press, 1988), 84–86, and 90–92, and "Tricky Thematics," *Semeia*, no. 42 (1988): 117–32. In that story, told in Genesis 31:34–35, Rachel steals the household gods from her father's household, and takes them to her husband's household. When her father comes looking for the gods, Rachel hides them by sitting on them. Bal argues that this theft transfers authority from Rachel's father to her husband, thereby symbolizing the end of the patrilocal kinship structure, and the beginning of the virilocal clan, predecessor of the nuclear family.

39. James, *The Art of the Novel*, 111.

40. For a reproduction of that photograph, see Ralph F. Bogardus, *Pictures and Texts: Henry James, A.L. Coburn, and New Ways of Seeing in Literary Culture* (Ann Arbor: UMI Research Press, 1984), 33.

41. See, for instance, Sigmund Freud, *Three Essays on the Theory of Sexuality*, in *Standard Edition*, vol. 7, 144 and 144f.; "Leonardo da Vinci and a Memory of His Childhood," 99–102; and "On Narcissism: An Introduction," *Standard Edition*, vol. 14, 88, 96, 101–2. Freud remarks in the last of those texts that all libidinal investment is inflected to some degree by narcissism, an observation which depathologizes narcissistic object-choice (88). For a discussion of the place of the latter within male homosexuality, and of the reversibility which it affords at the level of the fantasmatic, see Chapter 8 of this volume.

42. Freud enumerates these narcissistic variants in "On Narcissism," 90.

43. Nancy Blake also comments on the limited erotic means of the Jamesian hero in *Henry James: Ecriture et absence* (Petit-Roeulx, Belgium: Cistre, 1985): "Object of desire, he does not have anything with which to satisfy the demand which is addressed to him" (115; my translation).

44. James, *The Art of the Novel*, 85.

5. Masochism and Male Subjectivity

1. Sigmund Freud, *Three Essays on the Theory of Sexuality*, in *The Standard Edition of the Complete Psychological Works*, trans. James Strachey (London: Hogarth Press, 1953), vol. 7, 150.

2. Freud, *Three Essays on the Theory of Sexuality*, 149.

3. Jean Laplanche, *Life and Death in Psychoanalysis*, trans. Jeffrey Melhman (Baltimore: The Johns Hopkins University Press, 1976), 28, 30.

4. Michel Foucault, *The History of Sexuality, Volume I: An Introduction*, trans. Robert Hurley (New York: Vintage Books, 1980), 47–48.

5. *Semiotext(e)*, vol. 4, no. 1 (1981).

6. Janine Chasseguet-Smirgel, *Creativity and Perversion* (New York: Norton, 1984), 12.

7. Sigmund Freud, *The Ego and the Id, Standard Edition*, vol. 19, 41.

8. Gilles Deleuze, *Masochism: An Interpretation of Coldness and Cruelty*, trans. Jean McNeil (New York: George Braziller, 1971).

9. See George Bataille, "The Use Value of D.A.F. de Sade," in *Visions of Excess: Selected Writings, 1927–1939*, trans. Allan Stoekl (Minneapolis: University of Minnesota Press, 1985), 91–102, and *Literature and Evil*, trans. Alastair Hamilton (New York: Urizen Books, 1973), 83–107.

10. Roland Barthes, *Sade, Fourier, Loyola*, trans. Richard Miller (New York: Hill and Wang, 1976), 15–37, and 123–71.

11. Jane Gallop, *Intersections: A Reading of Sade with Bataille, Blanchot, and Klossowski* (Lincoln: University of Nebraska Press, 1981).

12. *Obliques*, nos. 12 & 13 (1977).

13. I have returned frequently to this topic over the past eight years, but always through a literary or cinematic intermediary. See, for instance, "*Histoire d'O*: The Story of a Disciplined and Punished Body," *Enclitic*, vol. 7, no. 2 (1983): 63–81; "Changing the Fantasmatic Scene," *Framework*, no. 20 (1983): 27–36; "Male Subjectivity and the Celestial Suture: *It's a Wonderful Life*," *Framework*, no. 14 (1981): 16–21, part of which is contained in Chapter 2 of the present volume; and "Masochism and Subjectivity," *Framework*, no. 12 (1980): 2–9. This time the approach will be more insistently theoretical and speculative.

14. Sigmund Freud, "The Economic Problem of Masochism," in *Standard Edition*, vol. 19, 159.

15. See Freud, "The Economic Problem of Masochism," 166, and "Dostoevsky and Parricide," *Standard Edition*, vol. 21, 179.

16. Freud, "The Economic Problem of Masochism," 161.

17. Freud, "The Economic Problem of Masochism," 162.

18. Freud, *The Ego and the Id*, 26.

19. Freud, *The Ego and the Id*, 26f.

20. Freud, "The Economic Problem of Masochism," 16l.

21. Freud, "The Economic Problem of Masochism," 162.

22. Sigmund Freud, "'A Child Is Being Beaten,'" *Standard Edition*, vol. 17, 175–204.

23. The most crucial of Freud's qualifications on this point is of course central to the present discussion—the qualification that whereas "femininity" may indeed imply passivity, and in many cases masochism, there is no necessary connection between "woman" and "femininity." See *Civilization and its Discontents, Standard Edition*, vol. 21, 105f. for an extremely interesting discussion of the slippage between these last two categories.

24. Richard von Krafft-Ebing, *Psychopathia Sexualis: A Medico-Forensic Study*, trans. Franklin S. Klaf (New York: Stein and Day, 1965), 86–143.

25. Theodor Reik, *Masochism in Sex and Society*, trans. Margaret H. Beigel and Gertrud M. Kurth (New York: Grove Press, 1962), 243.

26. Freud, "'A Child Is Being Beaten,'" 194–98.

27. I borrow the concept of "shattering" from Leo Bersani, who develops it at length in his important book, *The Freudian Body: Psychoanalysis and Art* (New York: Columbia University Press, 1986).

28. Freud, "The Economic Problem of Masochism," 169.

29. Freud, "The Economic Problem of Masochism," 169.

30. In *The Language of Psycho-Analysis*, trans. Donald Nicholson-Smith (New York: Norton, 1973), Jean Laplanche and J.-B. Pontalis suggest that "the subject's life as a whole . . . is seen to be shaped and ordered by what might be called, in order to stress this structuring action, a 'phantasmatic.' This should not be conceived of merely as a thematic— not even as one characterized by distinctly specific traits for each subject—for it has its own dynamic, in that the phantasy structures seek to express themselves, to find a way out into consciousness and action, and they are constantly drawing in new material" (317). For a fuller discussion of the fantasmatic, see Chapters 4, 7, and 8.

31. Freud, "The Economic Problem of Masochism," 169.

32. Sigmund Freud, *New Introductory Lectures on Psycho-Analysis, Standard Edition*, vol. 22, 60–68.

33. Freud, *The Ego and the Id*, 31–34.

34. For an extended discussion of the female version of the negative Oedipus complex, and its relation to feminism, see Chapters 4 and 5 of my *The Acoustic Mirror: The Female Voice in Psychoanalysis and Cinema* (Bloomington: Indiana University Press, 1988). For a further analysis of the male version, see Bersani, *The Freudian Body*, 49, and Chapter 8 of this volume.

35. There are striking similarities between the degradations Reik associates with Christian masochism, and those Krafft-Ebing links with the sexual perversion of masochism. See, for instance, Cases 80, 81, 82, and 83 in *Psychopathia Sexualis*.

36. Of course, Christian masochism rarely exists in the form I have described here. It is more often deployed as the vehicle for worldly or heavenly

advancement, i.e. put to extrinsic uses. Observing the expedient uses to which such suffering can be put, Reik mistakenly assumes self-advancement to be an inherent part of Christian masochism.

37. Here, too, there is an implied familial prototype, that provided by the relation of God to Christ. The Christian models himself on the latter, and directs against himself what is in effect a "divine" punishment.

38. Freud, *Beyond the Pleasure Principle, Standard Edition*, vol. 18, 9.

39. Freud, *The Ego and the Id*, 54.

40. Freud constructs phase 2 of the girl's beating fantasy by inverting phase 3 of the boy's fantasy, a discursive action that points to the asymmetrical symmetry of the two sequences.

41. For a different account of "'A Child Is Being Beaten'" in general, and phase 3 of the girl's fantasy in particular, see D.N. Rodowick, *The Difficulty of Difference: Psychoanalysis, Sexual Difference, and Film Theory* (New York: Routledge, 1991), 1–17.

42. I discuss the primal scene and its implications for male subjectivity in Chapter 4 of this volume.

43. The concepts of idiopathic and heteropathic identification derive from Max Scheler, *The Nature of Sympathy*, trans. Peter Heath (Hamden: Conn.: Archon, 1970).

44. See Stephen Heath, "Difference," *Screen*, vol. 19, no. 3 (1978): 51–112 for an insightful discussion of this scopic regime.

45. Jacques Lacan metaphorizes that which is lost to the subject with the entry into language as a "pound of flesh." See Chapter 1, p. 58.

46. Leopold von Sacher-Masoch, *Venus in Furs*, in Deleuze, *Masochism*, 80–130; Deleuze, *Masochism*, 96.

47. Mary Russo has some very thoughtful things to say about the social and political implications of masquerade in "Female Grotesques: Carnival and Theory," in *Feminist Studies/Critical Studies*, ed. Teresa de Lauretis (Bloomington: Indiana University Press, 1986), 213–29.

48. In "'A Child Is Being Beaten,'" Freud writes that "it seems to be only with the girl that the masculine protest is attended with complete success.... With the boy the result is not entirely satisfactory; the feminine line is not given up, and the boy is certainly not 'on top' in his conscious masochistic phantasy" (203). In an essay critiquing the article from which this chapter derives, Paul Smith argues that masochism is never more than a passing moment within male subjectivity ("Action Movie Hysteria, or Eastwood Bound," *Differences*, vol. 1, no. 3 [1989]: 106). While I am clearly in disagreement with this formulation, I do concur with his claim that masochism is generally narratively contained within Hollywood cinema. This, however, tells us less about the place of masochism within male subjectivity than about the normalizing operations of the dominant fiction.

49. Gayle Rubin provides another utopian reading of masochism in "The Leather Menace: Comments on Politics and S/M," in *Coming to Power*, ed. Samois (Boston: Alyson Publications, 1981), 192–335.

50. Gaylyn Studlar conflates Deleuze's oral mother with the pre-Oedipal mother of object relations psychoanalysis, and extrapolates from that conflation a highly dubious argument about the origin of masochism. According to Studlar, that perversion has its basis in the (male) child's relationship with the actual mother prior to the advent of the father, a relationship predicated upon his helpless subordination to her, and the insatiability of his desire for her. Masochistic suffering consequently derives from the pain of separation from the mother, and the impossible desire to fuse with her again, rather than from the categorical imperatives of the Oedipus complex and symbolic law. This is a determinedly apolitical reading of masochism, which comes close to grounding that perversion in biology. (See "Masochism and the Perverse Pleasures of the Cinema," in *Movies and Methods*, vol. 2, ed. Bill Nichols [Berkeley: University of California Press, 1985], 602–21.)

6. Masochistic Fantasy and the Ruination of Masculinity in Fassbinder's Cinema

1. Jacques Lacan, *The Seminar of Jacques Lacan, Book II: The Ego in Freud's Theory and in the Technique of Psychoanalysis, 1954–1955*, trans. Sylvana Tomaselli (Cambridge: Cambridge University Press, 1988), 169.

2. For a reading of the film which deploys biography in extremely interesting and unconventional ways, see Douglas Crimp's essay, "Fassbinder, Franz, Fox, Elvira, Erwin, Armin, and All the Others," *October*, no. 21 (1982): 63–81.

3. "Die Städte des Menschen und seine Seele. Alfred Döblins Roman *Berlin Alexanderplatz*," *Die Zeit*, March 14, 1980. I have relied upon the English translation of the essay, "Man's Cities and His Soul," included as part of the press packet which circulated with prints of the film.

4. Mary Ann Doane proposes this formulation in "Woman's Stake: Filming the Female Body," recently anthologized in *Feminism and Film Theory*, ed. Constance Penley (New York: Routledge, 1988), 223.

5. For an elaboration of the concept of the "body-schema," see Wallon, "Kinesthesia and the Visual Body Image in the Child," in *The World of Henri Wallon*, ed. Gilbert Voyat (New York: Jason Aronson, 1984), 115–31. It falls outside the scope of this chapter to discuss the implications of Wallon's work for the theory of the mirror stage, and for the notion of a bodily ego. However, I hope to explore both of these issues in *Destination Unknown*, an extended study of female subjectivity.

6. Leo Bersani, "Is the Rectum a Grave?," *October*, no. 43 (1987): 222.

7. The reader will recall that Freud defines sublimation as "something that

has to do with the [drive]," and idealization as "something to do with the object" ("On Narcissism: An Introduction," in *The Standard Edition of the Complete Psychological Works*, trans. James Strachey [London: Hogarth Press, 1957], vol. 14, 94).

8. In *Three Essays on the Theory of Sexuality, Standard Edition*, vol. 7, 149f., Freud writes: "The most striking distinction between the erotic life of antiquity and our own no doubt lies in the fact that the ancients laid the stress upon the [drive] itself, whereas we emphasize its object. The ancients glorified the instinct and were prepared on its account to honor even an inferior object; while we despise the instinctual activity in itself, and find excuses for it only in the merits of the object." However, Freud offers a rather different account of Greek homosexuality in another footnote from the same text (see 144). For a discussion of this later footnote, see Chapter 8.

9. Because of the rhetorical awkwardness of referring to this character through a double name or pronoun, I will for the remainder of this chapter substitute only the male name or pronoun. I have chosen "Erwin" over "Elvira" because, as I suggested above, the film insists that we grasp his sex-change operation as a loss and/or transformation experienced at the site of male subjectivity.

10. Guy Hocquenghem, *Homosexual Desire*, trans. Daniella Dangoor (London: Allison and Busby, 1978), 87.

11. For a discussion of two male homosexual texts which relinquish the penis, see Chapter 8.

12. In "Notes on Camp," in *Against Interpretation* (New York: Dell, 1969), Sontag writes: " . . . when a person or a thing is a 'camp,' a duplicity is involved" (283). For an incisive critique of Sontag's "phobic de-homosexualization of Camp," see D.A. Miller, "Sontag's Urbanity," *October*, no. 49 (1989): 93.

13. David Harris, "Effeminacy," *The Michigan Quarterly Review*, vol. 30, no. 1 (1991), 78.

14. For a very different reading of camp, one concerned more with its historical vicissitudes, see Andrew Ross, "Uses of Camp," in *No Respect: Intellectuals and Popular Culture* (New York: Routledge, 1989), 135–70.

15. Jean Laplanche, *Life and Death in Psychoanalysis*, trans. Jeffrey Mehlman (Baltimore: The Johns Hopkins University Press, 1976), 73.

16. In *The Ego and the Id*, Freud suggests that the ego and the object "compete" for the same libido, and that each is impoverished through the enrichment of the other (*Standard Edition*, vol. 19, 46). See also "On Narcissism," where Freud writes: "We . . . see, broadly speaking, an antithesis between ego-libido and object-libido. The more the one is deployed, the more the other becomes depleted" (76).

17. See Jacques Lacan, "The Mirror Stage As Formative of the Function of

the I as Revealed in Psychoanalytic Experience," *Ecrits: A Selection,* trans. Alan Sheridan (New York: Norton, 1977), 1–2.

18. Robert Burgoyne also comments upon the "evacuation and self-erasure" effected by the film in general, and this scene in particular, in "Narrative and Sexual Excess," *October,* no. 21 (1982): 55.

19. Freud introduces the notion that the ego is a reservoir of libido in a section added to the third edition of *Three Essays* (*Standard Edition,* vol. 7, 218).

20. Eric Rentschler, "Terms of Dismemberment: The Body in/and/of Fassbinder's *Berlin Alexanderplatz* (1980)," in *German Film and Literature: Adaptations and Transformations,* ed. Rentschler (New York: Methuen, 1986), 306.

21. In *Civilization and its Discontents, Standard Edition,* vol. 21, Freud writes: "The fateful process of civilization would thus have set in with man's adoption of an erect posture. From that point the chain of events would have proceeded through the devaluation of olfactory stimuli . . . [to] the founding of the family and so to the threshold of human civilization" (99f.).

22. For a discussion of the sexually differentiating uses to which Hollywood cinema puts the medical discourse, see Mary Ann Doane, *The Desire to Desire: The Woman's Film of the 1940s* (Bloomington: Indiana University Press, 1987), 38–69.

23. For a discussion of the disembodied male voice-over, see my *The Acoustic Mirror: The Female Voice in Psychoanalysis and Cinema* (Bloomington: Indiana University Press, 1988), 48–52.

24. In "Instincts and their Vicissitudes," *Standard Edition,* vol. 14, 138, Freud says of infantile orality that it involves "a type of love which is consistent with abolishing the object's separate existence."

25. Mikhail Bakhtin, *Rabelais and His World,* trans. Helene Iswolsky (Cambridge, Mass.: M.I.T. Press, 1968), 317.

26. *Berlin Alexanderplatz* accounts for heterosexuality in much the same terms as those proposed by Luce Irigaray in *This Sex Which Is Not One,* trans. Catherine Porter (Ithaca: Cornell University Press, 1985), i.e. as displaced homosexuality. See in particular Chapter 8 of that text, where she writes: "The use of and traffic in women subtend and uphold the reign of masculine hom(m)o-sexuality, even while they maintain that hom(m)o-sexuality in speculations, mirror games, identifications, and more or less rivalrous appropriations, which defer its real practice. Reigning everywhere, although prohibited in practice, hom(m)o-sexuality is played out through the bodies of women, matter, or sign, and heterosexuality has been up to now just an alibi for the smooth workings of man's relations with himself, of relations among men" (172). For a related account of male "homosocial desire," but one less inclined to read heterosexuality as a *simple* stand-in for homosexuality, see Eve

Kosofsky Sedgwick's important book, *Between Men: English Literature and Male Homosocial Desire* (New York: Columbia University Press, 1985).

27. See Rentschler, "Terms of Dismemberment," 316.

28. Sigmund Freud, "Some Psychical Consequences of the Anatomical Distinction Between the Sexes," *Standard Edition*, vol. 19, 252.

29. For a discussion of imaginary rivalry, see Lacan's "Aggressivity in Psychoanalysis," in *Ecrits: A Selection*, 8–29.

30. Freud, "On Narcissism," 88.

31. Alfred Döblin, *Berlin Alexanderplatz: The Story of Franz Biberkopf*, trans. Eugene Jolas (New York: Ungar, 1983), 408.

32. Wildred Wiegand, "Interview with Rainer Werner Fassbinder," in *Fassbinder*, ed. Ruth McCormick (New York: Tanam Press, 1981), 78. See also Michael Töteberg, ed., *Rainer Werner Fassbinder: l'Anarchie de l'imagination (entretiens et interviews)*, trans. Jean-François Poirier (Paris: L'Arche, 1987), 77–79.

33. Christian Braad Thomsen, "Five Interviews with Fassbinder," in *Fassbinder*, ed. Tony Rayns (London: B.F.I., 1980), 93.

34. Thomsen, "Five Interviews with Fassbinder," 97.

35. Bion Steinborn and Rudiger V. Maso, "An Interview with Rainer Werner Fassbinder," *Wedge*, no. 2 (1982): 23. In "Fassbinder's Reality: An Imitation of Life," Ruth McCormick remarks that for Fassbinder love is "the utopian moment in the process of change, both political and personal, the impossible which must be made possible by a radical upheaval in human attitudes" (*Fassbinder*, ed. McCormick, 85).

36. "Something's Missing: A Discussion Between Ernst Bloch and Theodor W. Adorno on the Contradictions of Utopian Longing," in Ernst Bloch, *The Utopian Function of Art and Literature: Selected Essays*, trans. Jack Zipes and Frank Mecklenburg (Cambridge, Mass.: M.I.T. Press, 1988), 16.

37. Fredric Jameson, *Marxism and Form: Twentieth-Century Dialectical Theories of Literature* (Princeton: Princeton University Press, 1971), 129.

38. Ernst Bloch, "Art and Utopia," in *The Utopian Function of Art and Literature*, 108.

39. Bloch, "Art and Utopia," 105.

40. Bloch, "Art and Utopia," 108.

41. Ernst Bloch, "Art and Society," in *The Utopian Function of Art and Literature*, 73.

42. Ernst Bloch, "The Representation of Wish-Landscapes in Painting, Opera, and Poetry," in *The Utopian Function of Art and Literature*, 283–87.

43. In that section of "Art and Utopia," Bloch writes: "The course of the world is still undecided, unended, and so is the depth in all aesthetic

information. . . . For the world itself . . . lies in incompleteness . . . The figures that this process generates, the ciphers, the allegories, and the symbols, in which the process is so rich, are *altogether fragments, real-fragments themselves through which the process flows unevenly and through which the process proceeds dialectically toward further forms of fragments*" (153).

44. Jameson, *Marxism and Form*, 137.

45. Bloch, "Art and Utopia," 107.

46. Bloch, "Something's Missing," 9.

47. Burgoyne, "Narrative and Sexual Excess," 56.

48. Barbara Miller, "'Un'-framing *Petra Von Kant*," in *Subjects/Objects* no. 6 (1988): 44–55.

49. Thomas Elsaesser "A Cinema of Vicious Circles (and Afterward)," in *Fassbinder*, ed. Rayns, 25.

50. Wilfried Wiegand, "The Doll in the Doll: Observations on Fassbinder's Films," in *Fassbinder*, ed. McCormick, 52. In an essay published since the writing of this chapter, Peter Ruppert provides an extended analysis of the utopian impulse in Fassbinder's cinema. Ruppert, who also invokes Bloch at one point in his essay, argues that in Fassbinder's films "the desire for utopian alternatives arises where they seem most powerfully negated—precisely in those conditions of 'entrapment, imprisonment, double-binds' that Fassbinder portrays so forcefully—and their 'production' depends on our readiness as viewers to 'fill in' the gaps and absences with possible alternatives dialectically evoked by the film. Put another way, Fassbinder's films plant the seeds of utopia negatively: they arouse utopian desire by making manifest the need to displace images of human misery and exploitation with more desirable alternatives, the need to imagine a world without negativity" ("Fassbinder, Spectatorship, and Utopian Desire," *Cinema Journal*, vol. 28, no. 2 [1989]: 34). Ruppert thus finds a more conventional utopianism within Fassbinder's cinema than the one I have presented here, a utopianism within which masochism seemingly has no part to play. However, although Ruppert's argument differs in most respects from the one advanced in this chapter, he suggests on p. 33 that the viewer who conjures forth an alternative world to the one portrayed in Fassbinder's films might be said to effect a "negation of [their] negation," a rhetorical formula virtually identical to that I have used to characterize the deconstruction of masculinity in *Berlin Alexanderplatz*.

51. For a discussion of the masochism at the heart of all subjectivity, albeit generally disavowed at the site of masculinity, see my "Masochism and Subjectivity," *Framework*, no. 12 (1980): 2–9.

52. Here and elsewhere in this chapter, I have relied upon the script of *In a Year of Thirteen Moons* published in *October*, no. 21 (1982): 5–50.

53. Geoffrey Nowell-Smith, "Minnelli and Melodrama," *Screen*, vol. 18, no. 2 (1977): 117–18. Burgoyne also invokes this essay in his "Narrative and Sexual Excess."

54. Hysteria does, however, accommodate *identification* with other people's physical symptoms, and this identification can play a part in somatic conversion. See, for instance, Sigmund Freud and Joseph Breuer, *Studies on Hysteria, Standard Edition*, vol. 2, 135–81.

55. Sigmund Freud, *The Interpretation of Dreams, Standard Edition*, vol. 4, 322–33.

56. Sigmund Freud, *Group Psychology and the Analysis of the Ego, Standard Edition*, vol. 18, 105.

57. Mikkel Borch-Jacobsen, *The Freudian Subject*, trans. Catherine Porter (Stanford: Stanford University Press, 1988), 181.

58. Sigmund Freud, "Instincts and their Vicissitudes," in *Standard Edition*, vol. 14, 129.

59. Leo Bersani, *The Freudian Body: Psychoanalysis and Art* (New York: Columbia University Press, 1986), 42.

60. Leo Bersani and Ulysse Dutoit, *The Forms of Violence: Narrative in Assyrian Art and Modern Culture* (New York: Schocken, 1985), 37.

61. Max Scheler, *The Nature of Sympathy*, trans. Peter Heath (Hamden, Conn.: Archon, 1970), 18–19.

62. See, for instance, Scheler, *The Nature of Sympathy*, 20, 21–22, and 27.

63. Freud distinguishes between "erotogenic," "moral," and "feminine" masochism in "The Economic Problem of Masochism," *Standard Edition*, vol. 19, 159–70.

64. Sigmund Freud, "'A Child Is Being Beaten,'" *Standard Edition*, vol. 17, 185–86, and 190–91.

65. Laura Mulvey, "Afterthoughts on 'Visual Pleasure and Narrative Cinema' Inspired by King Vidor's *Duel in the Sun*," in *Visual and Other Pleasures* (Bloomington: Indiana University Press, 1989), 32–33.

66. Astonishingly, Zora at one point reads Erwin to sleep with a fairy tale which closely parallels Scheler's parable about the snake and the squirrel. In this story, a witch transforms a small girl and her brother into a snail and a mushroom. As night progresses, the girl complains of hunger to her brother. He identifies so fully with her need for food that he invites her to take a bite out of him.

67. See my *The Acoustic Mirror*, 187–234.

68. Detailing these relations often seems to constitute the primary concern of Fassbinder's biographers. See, for instance, Ronald Hayman, *Fassbinder: Film Maker* (London: Weidenfeld and Nicolson, 1984), and Robert Katz, *Love Is Colder Than Death: The Life and Times of Rainer Werner Fassbinder* (New York: Random House, 1987).

69. In "Creative Writers and Day-Dreaming," Freud maintains that in works of fiction the hero functions as a representative for the author, and that the two are linked through identification (*Standard Edition*, vol. 9, 143–58).

70. Bersani, "Is the Rectum a Grave?," 218.

71. At one point during the television montage, Zora turns away from the television set to look instead at a photograph of a younger Erwin, thereby further emphasizing this binary logic.

72. Thomas Elsaesser has also recently suggested that *Berlin Alexanderplatz* addresses "the illusory, mis-taken and murderous nature of identity when posited as 'male' and pursued in an affirmative, phallic mode" ("*Berlin Alexanderplatz*: Franz Biberkopf/S/Exchanges," *Wide Angle*, vol. 12, no. 1 [1990]: 31–32).

73. Sigmund Freud, *Beyond the Pleasure Principle, Standard Edition*, vol. 18, 54.

74. Freud, *Civilization and its Discontents*, 121.

75. The historical references extend beyond fascism to our own moment, and potentially even farther. When Franz utters a great cry and slumps forward lifelessly, artificial flames leap up noisily behind him, a parodic inversion of the darkness which, within the Biblical account, is said to have descended over the land during Christ's crucifixion. But almost immediately there is the sound of a second explosion; a white light fills the background of the image, slowly resolving itself into an atomic cloud, and Franz's death becomes a proleptic signifier of the mass destruction which lies only a few brief years ahead of the year (1929) in which that fantasmatic event occurs. One by one the spectators fall to the ground beneath the cross as Glenn Miller's "In the Mood" plays jauntily on the sound track, an obvious reference, along with the atomic cloud and the Nazi doll held by Frau Kast, to the mid-to-late–1940s. *Berlin Alexanderplatz* cuts to a close-up of what seems to be a container for nuclear materials or waste, an equally obvious reference to our own period, before returning to the room full of corpses. The film's signifying network thus expands to include the apocalypse which may well lie in the viewer's future.

The referential network encompasses the nineteenth century as well. As the angels move the dead around, to the accompaniment of "Silent Night, Holy Night," they deliver an ironic celebration of Death, beginning with an encomium on the "goodness" of the new life into which Franz has just been ushered, and ending with a call to arms on behalf of Naziism. In their enthusiasm for slaughter the angels fold not only the Russian Revolution but the Napoleonic campaigns into their panegyric: "Death begins his drum roll . . . 'I've got Franz Biberkopf here, I've smashed him to pieces. But because he's strong and good, he'll have a new life.' Then Death moved, and his gigantic grey cloak fluttered. Shouts, shots, noise, triumph and rejoicing around Death. The river and the marching legions, the legions marched in icy cold and icy wind, they came over from France, great Napoleon leads them. The wind blows, the snow flurries, the bullets fly. . . . The trains come rolling, the cannons roar, the hand grenades explode, a barrage. Rest easy, dear Fatherland of mine. The soldiers have fallen, buried in their trenches. Death rolls up his cloak and sings: 'March, march.' We're off to war, marching true, a hundred drummers are with us, too. Morning sky, evening sky, light the way for us to die."

76. Wolfram Schutte, "Franz, Mieze, Reinhold, Death and the Devil: Rainer Werner Fassbinder's *Berlin Alexanderplatz*," *Fassbinder*, ed. McCormick, 109.

7. White Skin, Brown Masks: The Double Mimesis, or With Lawrence in Arabia

1. My epigraph is taken from Lawrence's introduction to Charles Doughty's *Arabia Deserta*, which he arranged to have republished. It is quoted by Stephen Ely Tabachnick, in *T.E. Lawrence* (Boston: Twayne, 1978), 87.

2. Renajit Guha has recently reminded us that not all forms of colonialism are hegemonic—that colonialism can also assume the guise of simple economic exploitation ("Dominance Without Hegemony," *Subaltern Studies 6: Writings on South Asian History and Society*, ed. Renajit Guha [Oxford: Oxford University Press, 1981], 210–309). However, the colonial model which *Seven Pillars* inverts does in fact conform to a hegemonic logic.

3. Frantz Fanon, *Black Skin, White Masks*, trans. Charles Lamm Markmann (London: Pluto, 1986), 18.

4. Edward Said, *Orientalism* (New York: Random House, 1979), 242–43.

5. The words "race" and "racial" will be bracketed in implicit quotation marks throughout this chapter.

6. For a discussion of Lawrence's childhood and education, see Desmond Stewart, *T.E. Lawrence* (London: Hamish Hamilton, 1977), 3–65; John E. Mack, *A Prince of Our Disorder: The Life of T.E. Lawrence* (Boston: Little, Brown & Co., 1976), 18–67; and Jeremy Wilson, *Lawrence of Arabia: The Authorized Biography* (New York: Atheneum, 1990), 21–55.

7. Stewart, *T.E. Lawrence*, 38–59; Mack, *A Prince*, 48–75; and Wilson, *Lawrence of Arabia*, 57–75.

8. Stewart, *T.E. Lawrence*, 69–119; Mack, *A Prince*, 76–98; and Wilson, *Lawrence of Arabia*, 76–134.

9. Stewart, *T.E.Lawrence*, 84–89; Phillip Knightley and Colin Simpson, *The Secret Lives of Lawrence of Arabia* (London: C. Nicholls & Co., 1971), 35–40, and 51–57; and Gideon Gera, "T.E. Lawrence: Intelligence Officer,"

in *The T.E. Lawrence Puzzle,* ed. Stephen Ely Tabachnick (Athens: University of Georgia Press, 1984), 204–7.

10. Mack, *A Prince,* 97; Wilson, *Lawrence of Arabia,* 544–45. Stewart, however, believes S.A. to have been Ali ibn el Hussein (248–55).

11. Stewart, *T.E. Lawrence,* 99–105; Mack, *A Prince,* 96–98; and Wilson, *Lawrence of Arabia,* 127–28.

12. T.E. Lawrence, *The Letters,* ed. David Garnett (London: Spring Books, 1984), 148.

13. Mack, *A Prince,* 7; and Wilson, *Lawrence of Arabia,* 127–28.

14. Stewart, *T.E. Lawrence,* 129–36; Mack, *A Prince,* 130–46; and Wilson, *Lawrence Arabia,* of 167–94.

15. Stewart, *T.E. Lawrence,* 137–41; and Mack, *A Prince,* 119–29. Wilson claims that the meeting was rather about "what the British attitude would be if the Turks attempted to depose [Abdulla's] father," and that it was the British who chose to push the relationship further (165).

16. Stewart, *T.E. Lawrence,* 141; Mack, *A Prince,* 124–25; and Jeffrey Meyers, *The Wounded Spirit: A Study of Seven Pillars of Wisdom* (London: Martin Brian & O'Keefe, 1973), 23.

17. Wilson, *Lawrence of Arabia,* 184–86, and 212–13.

18. Lawrence, *Letters,* 281. See Wilson, *Lawrence of Arabia,* 236–41, for a fuller discussion of this document.

19. Wilson, *Lawrence of Arabia,* 250.

20. A message written by Lawrence to Brigadier-General Clayton, but never sent, has recently been deciphered. It speaks eloquently to his discomfort with Britain's double-dealing during the Arab Revolt: "Clayton. I've decided to go off alone to Damascus, hoping to get killed on the way: for all sakes try and clear up this show before it goes further. We are calling them to fight for us on a lie, and I can't stand it" (T.E. Lawrence, *Selected Letters,* ed. Malcolm Brown [New York: Norton, 1989], 111).

21. Wilson, *Lawrence of Arabia,* 442–45. The letter was never conveyed to Sykes by Clayton.

22. Stewart, *T.E. Lawrence,* 146–50; Mack, *A Prince,* 147.

23. Lawrence, *Letters,* 488.

24. Lawrence, *Letters,* 89.

25. Lawrence, *Letters,* 246.

26. In *The Language of Psycho-Analysis,* trans. Donald Nicholson-Smith (New York: Norton, 1973), 317, Jean Laplanche and J.-B. Pontalis define the fantasmatic as a "structuring action" which shapes and orders "the subject's life as a whole," and which "constantly [draws] in new material." For a fuller discussion of the fantasmatic, see the "Introduction" and Chapters 4, 5, and 8 of this volume.

27. Lawrence, *Letters,* 147.

28. See Joan Riviere, "Womanliness as a Masquerade," in *Formations of Fantasy*, ed. Victor Burgin, James Donald, and Cora Kaplan (London: Methuen, 1986), 35–44, and Mary Ann Doane, "Film and the Masquerade: Theorizing the Female Spectator," *Screen*, vol. 23, nos. 3 & 4 (1982): 74–87.

29. T.E. Lawrence, *The Mint* (New York: Doubleday, 1955), 56–57.

30. T.E. Lawrence, *Seven Pillars of Wisdom: A Triumph* (New York: Penguin, 1962), 581.

31. Although the concept of a corporeal envelope derives from Jean Laplanche, *Life and Death in Psychoanalysis*, trans. Jeffrey Mehlman (Baltimore: The Johns Hopkins University Press, 1976), 80–81, it was Freud who first stressed the importance of bodily definition for the ego. In *The Ego and the Id*, he defines the ego as "first and foremost a bodily ego" (*The Standard Edition of the Complete Psychological Works*, trans. James Strachey [London: Hogarth Press, 1961], vol. 19, 27). For a further analysis of the role played by clothing in the definition of the body and the psyche, see my "Fragments of a Fashionable Discourse," in *Studies in Entertainment: Critical Approaches to Mass Culture*, ed. Tania Modleski (Bloomington: Indiana University Press, 1986), 139–52.

32. See, for instance, Wilson, *Lawrence of Arabia*, 399.

33. Lawrence, *Seven Pillars*, 673.

34. See Mack, *A Prince*, 245–316, and Wilson, *Lawrence of Arabia*, 586–663, for a forceful and persuasive defense of Lawrence's postwar efforts on behalf of the Arabs. Aaron Klieman offers a more measured account in "Lawrence as Bureaucrat," in *The T.E. Lawrence Puzzle*, 243–68.

35. Lawrence, *Letters*, 307. I will use Lawrence's letters in two different ways in this chapter—as biographical documents, and as "texts," analogous to his two books. When deploying them in the first of these capacities, I will generally use the past tense, but when deploying them in the second, I will for the most part utilize the present. Since I will also speak about Lawrence both as an historical figure and as a fictional construction, my references to him will betray a similar grammatical inconsistency.

36. Lawrence, *Letters*, 291.

37. Lawrence, *Letters*, 270.

38. In a 1919 letter to Lord Curzon, Lawrence advised that "with regard to the French coastal area of Syria, they have accepted the formula 'French in Syria as British in Mesopotamia.' Therefore so long as we are the more liberal ('left' in the Parliamentary sense) we call the tune" (*Letters*, 293).

39. Lawrence, *Letters*, 286.

40. Lawrence, *Letters*, 671.

41. In an editor's note in Lawrence, *Letters*, Garnett writes: "Lawrence had . . . returned to Oxford after his defeat, and lived partly at Polstead Road,

sometimes at All Souls. His mother has described to me how at this period of extreme depression and nervous exhaustion Lawrence would sometimes sit the entire morning between breakfast and lunch in the same position, without moving, and with the same expression on his face" (294).

42. Mack, *A Prince*, 297–316; Wilson, *Lawrence of Arabia*, 643–63.

43. Stewart, *T.E. Lawrence*, 215; Mack, *A Prince*, 257; Knightley and Simpson, *Secret Lives*, 161–62; and Wilson, *Lawrence of Arabia*, 577–78.

44. Mack, *A Prince*, 319–54; Wilson, *Lawrence of Arabia*, 683–729.

45. Stewart titles the last chapter of his volume "The Partitioned Soul."

46. Lawrence even went to India to escape the publicity surrounding the publication of *Revolt in the Desert*, a condensed version of *Seven Pillars* (Mack, *A Prince*, 359). I do not mean, however, to suggest that he was not prey to strong counter-impulses. He repeatedly attended Lowell Thomas's famous lectures on his role in the Arab Revolt (Mack, *A Prince*, 276).

47. Mack, *A Prince*, 367; Wilson, *Lawrence of Arabia*, 791–81, and 828–44.

48. Lawrence, *Letters*, 800.

49. Mack, *A Prince*, 428–41; Knightley and Simpson, *Secret Lives*,195–205; and Wilson, *Lawrence of Arabia*, 750–51.

50. Mack, *A Prince*, 388–405; Knightley and Simpson, *Secret Lives*, 278–83; and Wilson, *Lawrence of Arabia*, 879–925.

51. In a 1927 letter to Garnett, for example, Lawrence asked: "Didn't I tell you what I hope for, when I come out of the R.A.F.? Robin Buxton, my banker, and now Trustee, is going to try and get me a night job in the city, either as watchman in a Bank, or caretaker in a group of offices" (*Letters*, 526; see also 323 and 387).

52. Garnett communicates this piece of information in an editorial note in Lawrence, *Letters*, 844–45.

53. Quoted by Garnett in Lawrence, *Letters*, 845.

54. This description by Robert Graves is cited by Wilson, *Lawrence of Arabia*, 870.

55. Lawrence *Letters*, 148.

56. Lawrence, *Letters*, 550.

57. Lawrence, *Letters*, 136–37.

58. Lawrence, *Letters*, 506.

59. Lawrence, *Letters*, 119; Lawrence, *Selected Letters*, 39.

60. Lawrence, *Letters*, 531.

61. Mikkel Borch-Jacobsen, *The Freudian Subject*, trans. Catherine Porter (Stanford: Stanford University Press, 1988), 22, 6. Homi Bhabha advances a similar formulation in his "Foreword" to Fanon's *Black Skin*,

White Masks, although in terms more specific to the debates around colonialism: "This ambivalent identification of the racist world . . . turns on the idea of Man as alienated image, not Self and Other but the 'Otherness' of the Self inscribed in the perverse palimpsest of colonial identity" (xiv–xv).

62. Lawrence, *Letters*, 85.

63. Lawrence, *Letters*, 245.

64. For an analysis of projection as a vehicle of colonialism, see Octave Mannoni, *Prospero and Caliban: The Psychology of Colonialization*, trans Pamela Powesland (London: Methuen, 1956); Patrick Brantlinger, "Victorians and Africans: The Geneology of the Myth of the Dark Continent," in *Race, Writing, and Difference*, ed. Henry Louis Gates, Jr. (Chicago: University of Chicago Press, 1986), 215–17; and Abdul R. JanMohamed, "The Economy of Manichean Allegory: The Function of Racial Difference in Colonialist Literature," in *Race, Writing, and Difference*, 86. For a discussion of its place within the construction of sexual difference, see Jacqueline Rose, *Sexuality and the Field of Vision* (London: Verso, 1986), 199–223; Tania Modleski, "Film Theory's Detour," *Screen*, vol. 23 no. 5 (1982); and Kaja Silverman, *The Acoustic Mirror: The Female Voice in Psychoanalysis and Cinema* (Bloomington: Indiana University Press), 1–41.

65. See Chapter 3 for an exploration of Lacan's notion of the "screen."

66. For Fanon, one of the primary ways in which colonialism works is through instilling in the colonized subject the desire to imitate his colonizer. Bhabha has complicated this theoretical paradigm considerably by focusing upon what he calls "mimicry," a category which includes a whole range of parodic strategies whereby mimesis is subverted, and its power relations redefined. The relevant texts here are "Signs Taken for Wonders: Questions of Ambivalence and Authority Under a Tree Outside Delhi, May 1817," in *Race, Writing, and Difference*, 163–84; and "Of Mimicry and Man: The Ambivalence of Colonial Discourse," *October*, no. 28 (1984): 125–33.

67. This document is included as an appendix in Mack, *A Prince*, 463–67.

68. Stephen Ely Tabachnick also notes Lawrence's shifting use of the first-person plural pronoun in *T.E. Lawrence*, 100.

69. See Sigmund Freud, "Creative Writers and Day-Dreaming," *Standard Edition*, vol. 9, 143–53 for an account of the role of egoism within the formation of fantasy.

70. Lawrence, *Seven Pillars*, 684.

71. Lawrence, *Letters*, 379–80.

72. Freud defines sublimation in this way in "On Narcissism: An Introduction," *Standard Edition*, vol. 14, 94.

73. This is how Freud speaks of sublimation at one point in *Fragment of An Analysis of a Case of Hysteria, Standard Edition*, vol. 7, 50.

74. In "On Narcissism," Freud writes: "Sublimation is a process that concerns object-libido and consists in the [drive] directing itself towards an aim other than, and remote from, that of sexual satisfaction; in this process the accent falls upon deflection from sexuality" (94).

75. Lawrence, *Selected Letters*, 241.

76. Lawrence, *Selected Letters*, 227.

77. Lawrence, *Selected Letters*, 290.

78. Borch-Jacobsen, *The Freudian Subject*, provides an extended discussion of the interpenetration of desire and identification within Freud's account of subjectivity.

79. In *Thomas Woodrow Wilson: A Psychological Study* (Cambridge, Mass.:Houghton Mifflin, 1966), Freud and William C. Bullitt write: "Identification seeks to satisfy the instinctive desire by transforming the Ego itself into the desired object, so that the self represents both the desiring subject and the desired object" (43).

80. Meyers, *The Wounded Spirit*, also comments on Lawrence's identification with Feisal (57).

81. This Biblical reference is very meaningful; Mieke Bal tells me that the story of David and Jonathan represents not only one of the few references to male homosexuality in the Hebrew Bible, but the only one which is not negatively coded. Significantly, the erotic relationship between those two men permits them to transcend the power hierarchy which would otherwise separate them.

82. Sigmund Freud, *Group Psychology and the Analysis of the Ego, Standard Edition*, vol. 18, 116.

83. As Mieke Bal pointed out to me when reading this chapter, the phrase "graven image" also links the Arabs with paganism and false worship. Insofar as Lawrence serves the abstract, he is a true worshipper. However, in his guise as the graven image he resembles the Golden Calf; he functions, that is, as a forbidden and necessarily false representation of what is fundamentally unrepresentable.

84. In "Instincts and their Vicissitudes," *Standard Edition*, vol. 14, Freud claims that a drive can undergo "reversal into its opposite." This reversal can involve the transformation of love into hate, or vice versa. However, more classically it entails "a change from activity to passivity"—from scopophilia to exhibitionism, or sadism to masochism (126–27).

85. Sigmund Freud, "Hysterical Phantasies and their Relation to Bisexuality," *Standard Edition*, vol. 9, 166.

86. Sigmund Freud, "The Economic Problem of Masochism," *Standard Edition*, vol. 19, 165–67.

87. It is no doubt evident to the reader that the past few pages have not at all points sustained the necessary distinction between Lawrence's ego, and the position from which he desires. The notion of a sadistic or masochistic ego imputes to that psychic entity a libidinal agency which more properly belongs to the subject of desire. Paradoxically, however, the fantasmatic features a "someone" only through the intervention of those images of self which are synonymous with the ego. Conversely, the ego is defined by the uses to which it is put—here sadism and masochism. Finally, the constitution of the ego as an ideal is, as we have seen, absolutely central to reflexive masochism. It is for these reasons that I have been unable to avoid a certain elision of the distinction between the ego and the positions from which Lawrence desires.

88. It is also unimaginable within an uncorrupted version of Christian masochism, as I attempted to demonstrate in Chapter 5. The defining instance of this masochism is the Crucifixion of Christ, which contains at least one moment at which suffering, abjection, and loss are embraced without any confidence of a triumphant sequel—the moment at which Christ cries out "My God, my God, why hast thou forsaken me?" (Matthew 27.46). However, because of the redemptive temporality which the resurrection of Christ makes available to his followers, Christian masochism can easily become the vehicle for an imperialism of the self.

89. In a letter to Charlotte Shaw, Lawrence offers a different account of the Deraa incident: "About that night. I shouldn't tell you, because decent men don't talk about such things. I wanted to put it plain in the book, and wrestled for days with my self-respect . . . which wouldn't, hasn't, let me. For fear of being hurt, or rather to earn five minutes respite from a pain which drove me mad, I gave away the only possession we are born into the world with—our bodily integrity. It's an unforgiveable matter, an irrecoverable position: and it's that which has made me forswear decent living, and the exercise of my not-contemptible wits and talents" (*Selected Letters*, 261–62).

90. In *Masochism in Sex and Society*, trans. Margaret H. Beigel and Gertrude M. Kurth (New York: Grove, 1962), Theodor Reik maintains that "in no case of masochism can the fact be overlooked that the suffering, discomfort, humiliation, and disgrace are being shown and so to speak put on display . . . In the practices of masochists, denudation and parading with all their psychic concomitant phenomena play such a major part that one feels induced to assume a constant connection between masochism and exhibitionism" (72). For a further discussion of masochism's demonstrative feature, see Chapter 5.

91. This passage is quoted in Meyers, *The Wounded Spirit*, 63.

92. Lawrence, *Letters*, 476.

93. Lawrence, *The Mint*, 248.

94. Keith N. Hull, "Lawrence of *The Mint*, Ross of the R.A.F.," *South Atlantic Quarterly*, vol. 74, no. 3 (1975): 341.

95. Lawrence, *Letters*, 649.

96. Lawrence, *Letters*, 796.

97. For a discussion of the subject who is both "nothing" and "nowhere"— i.e. of what Lacan calls the acephalic subject, who is in the most profound sense the subject of desire—see the "Introduction" to this volume. I there define "imaginary identification" as identification with an external image, and "symbolic identification" as identification with a structural position.

98. It is only when a subject's identification with a particular image is reinforced both by the gaze and by unconscious desire that it can be entirely naturalized as the self. Because Britain never ceased to project onto Lawrence the screen of a British agent, and because the color of his skin and the sound of his voice made it difficult for his desert companions to see and hear him through the screen of "Arabness," his imaginary identification with Bedouin masculinity was vulnerable to contradiction and interruption. Similar difficulties attended his imaginary alignment with the R.A.F. rank and file. Not surprisingly, then, Lawrence was not always able to believe himself to be "one of them." For a discussion of the sense of alterity that at times afflicted him during the service years, see Mack, *A Prince*, 324, and Thomas J. O'Donnell, "The Assertion and Denial of the Romantic Will in *Seven Pillars of Wisdom* and *The Mint*," in *The T.E. Lawrence Puzzle*, 84–88.

99. Lawrence was an active reformer during his final years in the R.A.F. For an account of the improvements for which he agitated, see Mack, *A Prince*, 326.

8. A Woman's Soul Enclosed in a Man's Body: Femininity in Male Homosexuality

1. Marcel Proust, *Remembrance of Things Past*, trans. C.K. Scott Moncrieff and Terence Kilmartin (New York: Vintage Books, 1982), vol. 2, 643–44. All future citations from Proust will be taken from this edition, although I will preserve the French titles both of this work and of the individual novels within it throughout the body of the text.

2. Needless to say, it affords an equally preposterous account both of lesbianism and of male and female heterosexuality.

3. For a summary of Ulrichs's theory of male homosexuality, see Appendix B in Havelock Ellis, *Studies in the Psychology of Sex: Sexual Inversion* (Philadelphia: F.A. Davis Company, 1901), 225–39.

4. Michel Foucault, *The History of Sexuality, Volume I: An Introduction*, trans. Robert Hurley (New York: Vintage Books, 1980), 43. Jeffrey Weeks also maintains that there was no real sense of "the homosexual" until the nineteenth century (see "Capitalism and the Organization of Sex," in *Homosexuality: Power and Politics*, ed. Gay Left Collective [London:

Allison and Busby, 1980], 16–17, and *Sexuality and its Discontents: Meanings, Myths and Modern Sexualities* [London: Routledge & Kegan Paul, 1985], 92).

5. Michel Foucault, *The Uses of Pleasure*, trans. Robert Hurley (New York: Pantheon, 1985), 18–19.

6. David Halperin, *One Hundred Years of Homosexuality and Other Essays on Greek Love* (New York: Routledge, 1990), 25.

7. Halperin notes, however, that in this particular instance it was crucial that femininity be lightly worn: " . . . for the cultural construction of masculinity to succeed it is necessary that the process intended to turn boys into men be genuinely efficacious, no less 'generative' than female procreativity itself, but it is also necessary that the men who do the initiating retain their identity as men—something they can do only if their assumption of 'feminine' capacities and powers is understood to be an impersonation, a cultural fiction . . . " (146).

8. See David F. Greenberg, *The Construction of Homosexuality* (Chicago: University of Chicago Press, 1988), 127, 130–32, 145, 147–51, 158, 167, and 176.

9. Jeffrey Weeks, *Coming Out: Homosexual Politics in Britain, from the Nineteenth Century to the Present* (London: Quartet Books, 1977), 35.

10. Stephen Orgel, "Nobody's Perfect: Or Why Did the English Stage Take Boys for Women?," *South Atlantic Quarterly*, vol. 88, no. 1 (1989): 7–29.

11. See Greenberg, *Construction of Homosexuality*, 332–33; and Weeks, *Coming Out*, 35–37.

12. Greenberg, *Construction of Homosexuality*, 383–84.

13. Foucault, *The History of Sexuality*, 101.

14. Jonathan Dollimore defines the "perverse," of which homosexuality constitutes an especially privileged instance, as "what not only departs from, but actively contradicts the dominant in the act of deviating from it, and does so within, and in terms of inversion, distortion, reversal, [and] subversion" (*Sexual Dissidence: Augustine to Wilde, Freud to Foucault* [forthcoming]).

15. Mario Mieli, *Homosexuality and Liberation: Elements of a Gay Critique*, trans. David Fernbach (London: Gay Men's Press, 1980), 140.

16. See Christopher Craft, "Kiss Me With Those Red Lips," in *Speaking of Gender*, ed. Elaine Showalter (New York: Routledge, 1989), 223–24; and Eve Kosofsky Sedgwick, *Epistemology of the Closet* (Berkeley: University of California Press, 1990), 87.

17. C.A. Tripp, *The Homosexual Matrix* (New York: New American Library, 1987), 30. Dennis Altman cites Tripp in support of his own notion that bisexuality is more common among women than men in *The Homosexualization of America* (Boston: Beacon Press, 1982), 46. J.E. Rivers invokes Tripp repeatedly in *Proust and the Art of Love: The Aesthetics of Sexuality*

in the Life, Times, and Art of Marcel Proust (New York: Columbia University Press, 1980).

18. Weeks, *Sexuality and its Discontents*, 191.

19. Dennis Altman, "What Changed in the Seventies?," in *Homosexuality: Power and Politics*, 52.

20. Richard Dyer, "Getting Over the Rainbow: Identity and Pleasure in Gay Cultural Politics," in *Silver Linings: Some Strategies for the Eighties* (London: Lawrence and Wishart, 1981), 60–61.

21. Altman, "What Changed in the Seventies?," 52.

22. Leo Bersani, "Is the Rectum a Grave?," *October*, no. 43 (1987): 208–9.

23. Jacques Lacan, *Ecrits: A Selection*, trans. Alan Sheridan (New York: Norton, 1977), 291.

24. Don Mager, "Gay Theories of Gender Role Deviance," *SubStance*, no. 46 (1985): 44.

25. Jamie Gough, "Theories of Sexual Identity and the Masculinization of the Gay Man," *Coming On Strong: Gay Politics and Culture*, ed. Simon Shepherd and Mick Wallis (London: Unwin, 1989), 121.

26. Simon Watney, "The Spectacle of Aids," *October*, no. 43 (1987): 78–79.

27. See Weeks, "Capitalism and the Organization of Sex," 20, and Altman, "What Changed in the Seventies?," 61–62.

28. This essay is problematic in other respects as well. For a feminist critique of the ways in which Félix Guattari and Gilles Deleuze displace woman in their theorization of "the feminine," see Alice Jardine, *Gynesis: Configurations of Woman and Modernity* (Ithaca: Cornell University Press, 1985), 208–17.

29. Félix Guattari, "Becoming a Woman," in *Molecular Revolution: Psychiatry and Politics*, trans. Rosemary Sheed and David Cooper (New York: Penguin Books, 1984), 233.

30. Félix Guattari, "A Liberation of Desire: An Interview by George Stambolian," in *Homo-Sexualities and French Literature: Cultural Contexts/Critical Texts*, ed. George Stambolian and Elaine Marks (Ithaca: Cornell University Press, 1979), 57–58.

31. Guattari, "Becoming a Woman," 234.

32. In "Is the Rectum a Grave?," Bersani takes exception to the "pastoralizing" and "redemptive" impulses implicit in some contemporary discourses about gay sexuality. See especially 205–7, and 218–20.

33. David Miller, "*Cage aux folles*: Sensation and Gender in Wilkie Collins's *The Woman in White*," in *The Novel and the Police* (Berkeley: University of California Press, 1988), 152. For Miller, to be taken "from behind" means primarily to be taken by surprise. However, his reading of Collins's novel also encourages us to activate the homosexual implications

of that phrase. For a discussion of those implications, see Chapter 4 of this volume.

34. Harold Beaver, "Homosexual Signs (In Memory of Roland Barthes)," *Critical Inquiry*, vol. 8, no. 1 (1981): 117.

35. The texts he discusses in this context are Catherine MacKinnon, *Feminism Unmodified: Discourses on Life and Law* (Cambridge, Mass.: Harvard University Press, 1987), and Andrea Dworkin, *Intercourse* (New York: The Free Press, 1987).

36. Sigmund Freud, "On Transformations of Instinct as Exemplified in Anal Erotism," in *The Standard Edition of the Complete Psychological Works*, trans. James Strachey (London: Hogarth Press, 1955), vol. 17, 127–33.

37. I do not mean to suggest that this text represents a *conscious* deconstruction of masculinity, nor that it belongs in the same category as Guattari's "Becoming a Woman," Miller's "Cage aux folles," or Bersani's "Is the Rectum a Grave?." Schreber's *Memoirs of My Nervous Illness* can make no claim to being a metacritical or theoretical text. I have nevertheless included it here because it takes so seriously the equation between homosexuality (i.e. the desire to be penetrated by God-the-Father) and femininity, and because its author is prepared to sacrifice even the corporeal signifiers of masculinity in order to achieve that latter condition.

38. Daniel Schreber, *Memoirs of My Nervous Illness*, trans. and ed. Ida Macalpine and Richard A. Hunter (London: Wm. Dawson & Sons, 1955), 148.

39. Sigmund Freud, "Psycho-Analytic Notes on an Autobiographical Account of a Case of Paranoia," *Standard Edition*, vol. 12, 48.

40. Jean Laplanche and J.-B. Pontalis, "Fantasy and the Origins of Sexuality," *The International Journal of Psycho-Analysis*, vol. 49, no. 1 (1968): 5.

41. J. Laplanche and J.-B. Pontalis, *The Language of Psycho-Analysis*, trans. Donald Nicholson-Smith (New York: Norton, 1973), 318.

42. Sigmund Freud, *Three Essays on the Theory of Sexuality*, *Standard Edition*, vol. 7, 142.

43. In "Leonardo da Vinci and a Memory of His Childhood," Freud writes: "everyone, even the most normal person, is capable of making a homosexual object-choice, and has done so at some time in his life, and either still adheres to it in his unconscious or else protects himself against it by vigorous counter-attitudes" (*Standard Edition*, vol. 11, 99f.).

44. Sigmund Freud, "The Psychogenesis of a Case of Homosexuality in a Woman," *Standard Edition*, vol. 18, 168–69.

45. Freud, "Psycho-Analytic Notes on an Autobiographical Account of a Case of Paranoia," 46.

46. Freud, *Three Essays*, 146n.

47. Sandor Ferenczi, "The Nosology of Male Homosexuality," in *First Contributions to Psycho-Analysis*, trans. Ernest Jones (London: Hogarth Press, 1980), 300.

48. Freud, *Three Essays*, 142.

49. Jean Laplanche, *Life and Death in Psychoanalysis*, trans. Jeffrey Mehlman (Baltimore: The Johns Hopkins University Press, 1976), 8–47.

50. Laplanche, *Life and Death*, 20.

51. Laplanche, *Life and Death*, 23.

52. Sigmund Freud, *The Ego and the Id, Standard Edition*, vol. 19, 33–34.

53. In Chapters 4 and 5 of *The Acoustic Mirror: The Female Voice in Psychoanalysis and Cinema* (Bloomington: Indiana University Press, 1988), I argue that the female version of the negative Oedipus complex does not reverse the boy's, but involves rather both identification with and desire for the mother.

54. Francis Pasche also argues in "Symposium on Homosexuality" that the complete Oedipus complex constitutes "the best justification for the Freudian theory of bisexuality" (*International Journal of Psycho-Analysis*, vol. 45 [1964]: 210).

55. Freud makes this assertion most forcefully in *The Ego and the Id*, 29, where he writes: "Identification is the sole condition under which the id can give up its objects."

56. Kenneth Lewes, *The Psychoanalytic Theory of Male Homosexuality* (New York: New American Library, 1988), 35–36. Lewes identifies four models of homosexuality in Freud. The first of these grows out of a heterosexual attachment to the mother which is brought to an end by the castration crisis. At that point, the male subject transfers his desire to "a woman with a penis," i.e. a feminine boy, and identifies with the mother. He also regresses to the anal stage of sexuality, and a primitive object-relationship. The love-object is chosen according to a narcissistic model (36–38). Within Lewes's second model of male homosexuality, the mother is once again loved for a long period of time before becoming the object of identification, and masculine love-objects are sought who resemble the subject's self. The mother continues to be loved at the level of the unconscious. Lewes claims that this second model of homosexuality is "distinct from, but not incompatible with the first" (38–39). The third variant of homosexuality Lewes finds in Freud is the negative Oedipus complex. It begins with love for the mother, but subsequently yields to a passive, anal identification with her, and the desire to be loved like a woman by the father (39–41). The fourth variant of homosexuality converts rivalry with the father to a libidinal investment in him, but does not involve identification with the mother, or horror of her genitals. Heterosexuality is not foreclosed upon (42–3). As the reader will see, although there are important points of convergence between Lewes's account of homosexuality in Freud and my own, his third category is the

only one upon which we entirely agree. The reading which he gives of his four categories is also very different from that proposed in the present chapter. Lewes's theoretical framework derives from clinical psychology, whereas mine comes from psychoanalytic feminism and cultural studies.

57. Otto Fenichel also suggests the negative Oedipus complex as the basis for one variety of male homosexuality. However, he associates this libidinal paradigm less with phallic divestiture than with apprentice-love, and he claims that it may be governed by a latent hostility to the father (see *The Psychoanalytic Theory of Neurosis* [New York: Norton, 1945], 333–34). For Pasche, the negative Oedipus complex underpins *all* male homosexuality. He writes that the latter is "the sum total of behavioral attitudes which express a feminine relationship towards the father" ("Symposium on Homosexuality," 210).

58. In his "Editor's Note" to *From the History of an Infantile Neurosis*, Strachey suggests that there is an implicit continuity between that text and the passage in *The Ego and the Id* where Freud puts forward the negative Oedipus complex (*Standard Edition*, vol. 12, 6).

59. See Silverman, *The Acoustic Mirror*, 101–86.

60. Dollimore, *Sexual Dissidence*.

61. As John Fletcher suggests in a different context, this "'perverse' eroticism can release the male body from its subjection to the phallic function and enable a re-symbolization and re-investment of maleness . . . " ("Freud and His Uses: Psychoanalysis and Gay Theory," in *Coming On Strong: Gay Politics and Culture*, 115). Although he does not distinguish between different kinds of male homosexuality, Fletcher provides a reading of male same-sex desire which is ideologically congruent with mine. Drawing upon Fenichel's distinction between the "subject-homoerotic" and the "object-homoerotic," he reads both as "a ground or potential in the psychical structure of homosexual men for a *possible* opposition at the level of social and political practice to the dominant forms of gender and the patriarchal fantasies of castration and possession/submission that fuel them." For him, male homosexuality also at times enacts a refusal of the Oedipal injunction: "You cannot *be* what you desire, you cannot *desire* what you wish to be" (114).

62. Sigmund Freud, "On Narcissism," *Standard Edition*, vol. 14, 90

63. See their *The Wolf Man's Magic Word: A Cryptonomy*, trans Nicholas Rand (Minneapolis: University of Minnesota Press, 1986), for a discussion of psychic encrypting.

64. There is a certain ambiguity about the phrase "in all the cases we have examined" which demands explanation. It is not clear whether we are to read that phrase as encompassing all homosexuals, or as referring only to the third variant. However, the 1910 edition of *Three Essays* supplements this footnote with an addendum suggesting that there is

more than one type of male homosexuality. I have included the first sentence of that addendum at the conclusion of the passage quoted above. The rest of it reads as follows: "The problem of inversion is a highly complex one and includes very various types of sexual activity and development. A strict conceptual distinction should be drawn between different cases of inversion according to whether the sexual character of the *object* or that of the *subject* has been inverted" (145).

65. Fenichel also isolates a form of male homosexuality which hinges upon identification with the mother and love for an object resembling the self: "The type of individual who is more narcissistic than 'feminine' endeavors first of all to secure a substitute for his Oedipal strivings. Having identified himself with his mother, he behaves as he previously had wished his mother to behave toward him. He chooses as love objects young men or boys who, for him, are similar to himself, and he loves them and treats them with the tenderness he had desired from his mother. While he acts as if he were his mother, emotionally he is centered in his love object, and thus enjoys being loved by himself" (332). The last sentence of this passage anticipates a feature of the Leonardo model of homosexuality which I will address later—the propensity of its subject to move back and forth between an identification with the mother, and an identification with his own youth. In Fenichel's formulation, that subject even seems capable of effecting both of these imaginary alignments simultaneously.

66. Sigmund Freud, "Some Psychical Consequences of the Distinction Between the Sexes," *Standard Edition*, vol. 19, 252.

67. Sigmund Freud, "Some Neurotic Mechanisms in Jealousy, Paranoia and Homosexuality," *Standard Edition*, vol. 18, 230–31.

68. In his "Editor's Note" to "Leonardo da Vinci and a Memory of His Childhood," Strachey maintains that Freud translated the Italian word "*nibio*" as "*Geier*" ("vulture"), whereas it in fact means "kite" (61).

69. Lewes insists that when discussing maternal identification within male homosexuality it is necessary to distinguish between the castrated mother and the phallic mother. The mother, he writes, "can serve as the model for identification in her 'phallic' preoedipal guise, in which she is thought to be equipped with a penis, and in her 'castrated' postoedipal guise, in which she is understood as not having a penis" (84). Paradigm 1 would seem at least in certain instances to feature her in the second of these guises, and paradigm 3 in the first.

70. Fletcher describes a gay man's identification with the mother in terms that are very relevant to the present discussion. He characterizes it as "a stubborn refusal to leave the side of the mother, to change sides.... The retention of the loving mother-son relation as the scenario of desire is an attempt to preserve the lost phallic ego-ideal in one's object, while bearing the burden of maternal castration oneself" (112).

71. Freud also emphasizes that male homosexuality revolves in a fundamental way around the penis. In "Analysis of a Phobia in a Five-Year-Old Boy" he writes that "it is the high esteem felt by the homosexual for the male organ which decides his [sexual] fate" (*Standard Edition*, vol. 10, 109).

72. Rivers, *Proust and the Art of Love*, 82–106. The parallels between Proust's relationship with Agostinelli and Marcel's with Albertine do not, however, lead Rivers to argue that the reader of *A la recherche* should mentally substitute the name "Albert" or "Alfred" for Albertine. Rather, he insists upon the androgynous qualities of Marcel's mistress, and upon the links Proust establishes between androgyny and homosexuality (207–54).

73. See Justin O'Brian, "Albertine the Ambiguous: Notes on Proust's Transposition of Sexes," *PMLA*, no. 64 (1949): 933–52.

74. Eve Kosofsky Sedgwick, "The Epistemology of the Closet (II)," *Raritan*, vol. 8, no. 1 (1988): 112.

75. This is a central premise, for instance, of Serge Doubrovsky, *Writing and Fantasy in Proust: La Place de la madeleine*, trans. Carol Mastrangelo Bové and Paul A. Bové (Lincoln: University of Nebraska Press, 1986); Lisa Appignanesi, *Femininity and the Creative Imagination: A Study of Henry James, Robert Musil, and Marcel Proust* (New York: Harper, Barnes and Noble, 1973), 157–215; and Milton L. Miller, *Nostalgia: A Psychoanalytic Study of Marcel Proust* (Cambridge, Mass.: Houghton Mifflin, 1956). Miller, who tends to read *A la recherche* as a transparent window onto Proust's psychic life, accounts for the latter in terms of a very schematic version of the Leonardo model of male homosexuality: "Playing the maternal role himself, [Proust] formed attachments to handsome adolescent boys, who came to inhabit his apartment like prisoners" (15).

76. See especially Doubrovsky, *Writing and Fantasy in Proust*, 19–96.

77. Leo Bersani, *Marcel Proust: The Fictions of Life and Art* (New York: Oxford University Press, 1965), 54–55.

78. Doubrovsky also comments upon Marcel's orality, but he subsumes it within the larger system of ingestion and excretion which for him governs both the novel and its economy of authorial production. He argues that Marcel devours the mother "in order to appropriate her substance," and thereby produce text. For him, to "shit Mama" is equivalent to "mak[ing] Combray" (*Writing and Fantasy in Proust*, 23–24).

79. In the course of commenting upon Albertine's orality, Sedgwick suggests that "a grainy blowup of [her] sexuality might begin with a vista of tonsils," an observation which is certainly congruent with this passage ("The Epistemology of the Closet [II]," 115).

80. Sedgwick, "The Epistemology of the Closet (II)," 117.

81. This invocation of the female genitals may come as something of a surprise to the reader who carries away from this passage primarily its

initial image, that of a girl lifting her foot to the laundress. That image, like the swan simile, seems to suggest that erotic contact here takes place between one woman's foot, and another woman's mouth, as in the story about Albertine and the laundry-girl told by Aimé to Marcel. However, the second sentence of the passage directs attention away from the foot of one of the girl's legs, to the raised thigh and lowered foot of the other. The next sentence forecloses upon the foot, focusing instead upon the "droop" of Albertine's second thigh, and the angle of her knee. Finally, as we approach the erotic center of the passage, the curve of Albertine's thigh is isolated from the rest of her anatomy. There is no further reference to her knee. It is thus Albertine's curved thigh ("*sa cuisse recourbée*"), rather than her foot, which seeks "the mouth of a Leda who is rapt in the palpitating specificity of feminine pleasure." Significantly, the earlier passage in which Marcel contemplates Albertine's naked body also contains a reference to a curve in her thighs, and there it functions as an explicit signifier for her genital region: "Her belly (concealing the place where a man's is disfigured as though by an iron clamp left sticking in a statue that has been taken down from its niche) was closed, at the junction of her thighs, by two valves with a curve ["*d'une courbe*"] as languid, as reposeful, as cloistral as that of the horizon after the sun has set."

82. In a 1919 footnote to "Leonardo da Vinci and a Memory of His Childhood," Freud comments upon the "remarkable errors" in the rendition of the female breasts and vagina in a sketch drawn by Leonardo of the sexual act" (70–71). For a feminist discussion of this sketch, see Jacqueline Rose, *Sexuality in the Field of Vision* (London: Verso, 1986), 225–26.

Index